MODERN IRISH WRITERS
AND THE WARS

ULSTER EDITIONS AND MONOGRAPHS
General Editors
Robert Welch
Joseph McMinn

ULSTER EDITIONS & MONOGRAPHS SERIES
ISSN 0954-3392

MODERN IRISH WRITERS AND THE WARS

Edited by
Kathleen Devine

Ulster Editions and Monographs: 7

Copyright © 1999 by Elmer Andrews, Terry Boyle, Terence Brown,
Kathleen Devine, John Fletcher, Jacqueline Genet, John Goodby,
A. Norman Jeffares, Keith Jeffery, Declan Kiberd, Josette Leray,
Christopher Murray, Alan J. Peacock, Patrick Walsh

First published in 1999 by Colin Smythe Limited
Gerrards Cross, Buckinghamshire SL9 8XA

British Library Cataloguing in Publication Data
A catalogue record of this book is available from the British Library

ISBN 0-86140-353-3

Distributed in North America by Oxford University Press,
198 Madison Avenue, New York 10016

Printed in Great Britain
by T. J. International Ltd., Cornwall

CONTENTS

ACKNOWLEDGEMENTS

The editor would like to thank the Research Committee and the Dean and Faculty of Humanities of the University of Ulster for financial support towards the present volume, the Arts Council of Northern Ireland and the Community Relations Council for grants towards the 1992 session of the Ulster Symposium on which it is based, and the sub-Librarian (Humanities) and staff of the Inter-Library Loans Service of the University Library for practical assistance. Particular thanks are due to Professor Robert Welch, the General Editor of the Series, for his unfailingly generous advice and support.

INTRODUCTION

KATHLEEN DEVINE

This book derives from a symposium held at the University of Ulster at Coleraine in 1992.[1] As the title indicates, the intention was to gain, through the examination of the work of a number of representative writers from different periods, a broad picture of the course and achievement of Irish writing in response to twentieth-century wars. The recent Troubles have of course provoked a rich vein of creative achievement in various genres and a correspondingly extensive critical response. What seemed valuable therefore was to place the emphasis of the Symposium and the volume not so much upon these recent developments as upon the more general corpus of writing on themes of war of which they can be seen as a part, though the literature of the Troubles is not strictly war literature by conventional definition.

The line of development or succession is inevitably complicated by such questions of definition and boundary. The Symposium for instance itself began with a reading by Michael Longley to which he gave the title, 'Carrying Flowers out of the Smoke', adding the subtitle, 'War Poems', in the booklet which he prepared for the occasion. The use of the term 'war poems' immediately and inevitably invokes a tradition going back to World War One (just as 'Second Sight', the poem from which 'carrying flowers out of the smoke' is taken, makes thematic links, through familial experience, with that conflict). This brings into consideration the fact that in English literature 'war poetry', the term used to describe the realistic, protest poetry of the soldier poets of the 1914–18 war, has long acquired the status of a distinct genre in a way that has tended to set the critical agenda for consideration of war literature. Such was the impact of that period and group that Robert Graves (one of its number), in 1941, could posit the terms 'war poet' and 'war poetry' as 'terms first used in World War I and perhaps peculiar to it'.[2] The young soldier-poets of 1939–45 in Britain were of course to prove his exclusivist definition inadequate – as has the history of Irish war literature.

The protest poetry of, specifically, 1916–18 established the attitudes against which the literature of later wars would tend to be judged. So much was this the case that in another narrowly limiting definition Philip Larkin could claim that only a poet who 'reacts against having a war thrust upon him'[3] could be termed a 'war' poet. Obviously this in many ways arbitrary definition relates to a particular tradition and a particular historical experience. This concept of war poetry is however extremely durable and is still an instinctive focus of reference for 'war' poetry of different times and places. As will be seen it is only partially relevant to the writing surveyed in this volume.

Crucially, the work of World War I poets in England was that of combatants and it was the combatants' experience, so different from what was conventionally envisaged in the work of, e.g., Henry Newbolt, that informed their verse and generated a new language appropriate to the brutality of day-to-day battlefront existence. Hence a writer like Sassoon would alter his shocked view of what war poetry should *not* be ('War ought not to be written about in such a realistic way') to the extent that he would later express some pride at having been the first to introduce the word 'syphilitic' into English poetry. What effected this change was the personal experience of what in books had sounded so glorious. ('Dulce et decorum est pro patria mori', Owen would write with satiric force when men died agonizingly from gas poisoning, having earlier written to his mother of the attractions of joining the Italian cavalry because of its aesthetically pleasing uniform.) Recognition of the real nature of modern war and of at least part of the sacrifice it demanded (civilian suffering remained largely outside the soldier-poets' concern) was to underlie the poetry of 1916–18 which has tended to usurp to itself the title of 'war poetry'. The influence of this paradigm has to be appreciated in any survey of modern 'war' literature. However, such received definitions are tested by the Irish experience.

Francis Ledwidge, for instance, at the very beginning of the period covered in the present survey, provides an illustration of the complexities of outlook and allegiance which might complicate an Irish writer's response to war and lead even a poet with his extensive First World War trench experience in quite different directions from those of his English contemporaries. Ledwidge saw a longer period of front-line service than Owen. A member of the Irish Volunteers, he had rejected Redmond's recruitment call in September, 1914 – yet, paradoxically, he enlisted shortly afterwards, impelled by a mixture of motives. There seems no doubt about one thing however – primarily Ledwidge saw himself as an Irish patriot. As such, he was still mentally fighting Ireland's war at Gallipoli or Flanders. And before Sassoon and Owen were to produce their strong body of protest poetry the Easter Rebellion of 1916 and the deaths of his friend, Thomas MacDonagh, and the other rebel leaders, made Ledwidge's position, serving in the British army, extremely problematic. And so, while Owen and Sassoon were identifying with their immediate combatant situation to the point where they were moved to the questioning of war aims and profiteering (and hence Sassoon's 1917 protest), Ledwidge had to come to terms with a more intractable dilemma. Identifying as he did with Pearse and MacDonagh, it would have rendered meaningless his own enlistment for him to admit to himself that the path he had followed had done no more than supply the 'gold-filled tusk' of Owen's profiteering 'food-hog'. And so his poetry shows no direct response to battlefield experience such as defines the accepted notion of the war poet. War agony is displaced to mythic Irish wars of Maeve and Conor; laments for war dead are for Thomas MacDonagh, for Joseph Plunkett and Pearse in Dublin. All this is the complete reversal of precisely what characterized the new-found allegiance of the English war poets to their immediate experience and comrades. Yet his moving elegy for Thomas MacDonagh can nevertheless be fairly described as a war poem in that its emotional charge derives from the circumstances in which he found himself – but a war poem that demands a wider definition of the term than that offered by Graves.

The complexity of the socio-political dispensation in Ireland of course also provides the contrasted example of Ledwidge's patron, Lord Dunsany, who writes entirely from an English standpoint in his two wartime collections of prose tales. Yet his unwillingness to engage at any serious level with the actual experience of the war means that he cannot bear comparison with the English combatant poets. His remark in the Preface to his 1918 *Unhappy Far-Off Things* indicates his distance from them: 'I have chosen a title that shall show that I make no claim for this book to be up to date'. It seems that for Dunsany in 1918, as for the early Sassoon, war still ought not to be written about in a realistic way. As an illustration of a further complication of possible attitudes, however, there is the case of Patrick MacGill, an Irishman who writes as one – but one who is perfectly content to be a part of the British war effort; and his work in many ways seems to be a part of, or have cogent affinities with, the emerging English tradition. If Ledwidge's troubled mind was with the friends executed by men wearing the uniform in which he himself was serving, MacGill's thoughts seem to have been primarily in the day-to-day experience of the Great War. In his *The Red Horizon* and *The Great Push*, both of which were produced well before the popular spate of prose works in England which appeared a decade after the end of the conflict, there is none of the cynicism that characterizes the later prose of, e.g., Robert Graves. As a serving soldier writing while the war was in progress MacGill of course would have had to be aware of possible repercussions but, that said, the tenor of his work, as Keith Jeffery notes in his essay here, is not subversive. In these books MacGill seems happy to conform to the world he has joined. Like Sassoon and Graves, he relies on realism to convey the truth of war and *The Great Push* in fact chronicles incidents that are, if anything, more horrific in their detail than anything in Sassoon's wartime poetry. Monk Gibbon, in his autobiography, *Inglorious Soldier*, describes *The Red Horizon* and *The Great Push* as 'perhaps the first books to delineate the protagonists on the western front as they actually were'. Yet interestingly, it is not MacGill's work that seems to have caught the attention of Owen and Sassoon, despite its realism and early appearance during the war, but that of Barbusse, whose *Le Feu* they both acknowledge. Such is the fluidity of interrelations between writers of different provenance during this period. In all this First World War material, however, it becomes clear that there is no body of Irish war writing to compare with the combined achievement of, say, Graves, Sassoon, Owen and Rosenberg.

Even if we include non-combatant writing, and with due allowance to an experimental work such as O'Casey's *The Silver Tassie* (see Christopher Murray's essay), the picture is not much altered. The main factor here of course is that Yeats remained essentially aloof. His well-known letter to Henry James in reply to a request for a poem about the war contrasts markedly with his characteristically very deep involvement with wars on Irish soil. The hint of the aesthete's pose implicit in his term 'bloody frivolity', applied to what was happening in Europe, seems determinedly distanced (Wilfred Owen had adopted a somewhat similar stance in letters before he joined up, speaking of the possibility of the war effecting 'a little useful weeding'). Only when the war came home to him personally in the death of Robert Gregory did it elicit a poetic response and here his interest is not, essentially, in the conflict itself.

The insurrectionary poetry of 1916 provides some interesting parallels with First World War poetry. Specifically, Pearse's attitude to blood-sacrifice and his associated mythologizing have clear analogies in the work of the young English soldier-poets of 1914. The patriotic verse that greeted the outbreak of the war was not confined to the Rupert Brookes of England. Sassoon, the most determined of the realist/protest poets, was among the most idealistic and romantic in his early war poetry and even writers like Rosenberg and Owen seem to have been touched in the early part of the war by the blood-hunger that, it has been suggested, took hold of Europe in the early part of the century. In '1914' Owen could see the war as part of a natural cycle of death and renewal and write of 'the need/Of blood for seed'. Rosenberg, in 'On Receiving News of the War', was to call on this 'ancient crimson curse' to 'corrode, consume' and, thereby, restore to the universe its 'pristine bloom'. If such writers as these could express ideas not vastly different from those of Brooke it was in part because an atmosphere had been created in poetry that glorified death in war well before the outbreak of hostilities in 1914. And so, if Pearse went into the Dublin Post Office with the warrior Cuchulain alive in his imagination and mystical notions of Gaelic Ireland spurring him on, he was, in many ways, living an Irish parallel to the experience of many young Englishmen who went to war in 1914 – for if his imagination fed on Irish heroic myth, theirs was fed on mythologized icons of English heroism such as the Drake and Nelson of Newbolt's poems.

The 1916 experience, as Declan Kiberd reminds us in his essay here, was a very brief one. For Pearse and his fellow-rebels there was neither the attritional effect of long-drawn-out stalemate nor the time for reflection on the experienced reality of blood-sacrifice. In *The Singer* Pearse had contemplated the action he was to embark upon, the responsibility involved and the possible public blame. Such thinking about blood sacrifice in the abstract was, of course, different from seeing real blood shed as a matter of course month after month on the Western Front as evidenced in the changing poetry of Sassoon, and it is in fact with the poetry of 1914 in England that the work of the 1916 poets should be seen, not with that of the voice of experience in 1916–18. If historical circumstances precluded any transformation of 1916 poetry into the disillusioned protest of 1916–18 English poetry it was the non-combatants, Yeats and O'Casey, who offered a sustained examination of the questions of war and violence in relation to this and the ensuing conflicts of the next decade in Ireland. Hence their work in this connection is the subject of individual essays in this book.

The more protracted period of the Anglo-Irish War and the Irish Civil War, with its nerve-racking uncertainties, dangers and discomforts, gave Irish writers (notably O'Connor and O'Faolain) emotional experiences in some ways comparable to those that led to First World War protest poetry. A 1931 *Dublin Magazine* review of David Hogan's *Dark Mountain and Other Stories* describes it and its predecessor, *The Challenge of the Sentry*, as 'Ireland's war books' and 'a perfect justification of Ireland's war for independence', thus putting them in the category of 1916 writing – and, generally, Hogan's characters are to some extent touched by the idealizing note that allows the reviewer to see the book in such terms. In the final story in *Dark Mountain* however Hogan begins to probe seriously (if still from a rather romanticizing perspective) the effect of war and killing on the humane sensibility. Here, in fact, 1916 and the Great War are both influences. The central character is credited with heroic asceticism in the mould of Pearse; but he is also aware of the brutalising effects of action: 'the thing he feared most was the brutalising of his men . . . some of the stories from the great war frightened him.' Ernie O'Malley's *On Another Man's Wound* and *The Singing Flame* describe his experiences in the Anglo-Irish War and the Civil War respectively. The hardness of the single-minded pursuit of an objective typifies the tone of *On Another Man's Wound* though towards the end of *The Singing Flame* O'Malley permits the more humane aspects of his personality to show through in his response to the death of comrades and his willingness to question the position he had taken in the continued struggle.

It is from a more dispassionate viewpoint that O'Connor and O'Faolain consider their involvement in these wars. O'Connor recognizes that he had seen life 'through a veil of literature'. By the time the Civil War broke out the glamour had disappeared and he remarks that, though still young when they fought in it, he and his comrades were already 'hardened' by their involvement in the Anglo-Irish War. The short stories of both writers, however, are the products of disillusioned rather than hardened sensibilities. Both are concerned with the incompatibility of war and personal feeling. In situations of hostage-taking and reprisal shootings the brutality of war can be even more immediate and personal in its impact than in trenches separated by No Man's Land. In guerrilla war also, its participants living always on the edge of, never fully in, a community, the sense of isolation and deprivation experienced by the soldier can be intensified, and

O'Connor and O'Faolain are close to some of the moods of Sassoon's prose work in their use of images of isolation and exclusion from the warmth of human relationships, images that were to be central in fact to much Second World War British poetry.

The generation of young men who grew up in Britain in the 1930s felt the consequences of their fathers' war lengthening out to shadow their youth as developments in Germany made apparent the possibility that they too might be cheated of life like the 'lost generation' doomed in the trenches of 1914–18. As Roy Fuller famously put it, 'My photograph already looks historic' ('The Middle of a War'), indicating the mind-set of an apparently fated generation. For young southern Irishmen the situation, of course, was different in one obvious respect. No such threat seemed to hang over them. Yet, if we are to believe their own words, their mind-set had much in common with that of their British counterparts. They too felt themselves to be living in the shadow of a recent war; and as the 1930s began, the tone of articles in the *National Student*, the student magazine of University College Dublin, is telling. For example:

The present generation, we who are young, have seen life for the first time as the boys of Ireland have never seen it before. Our sympathies were given dearly in a war which must scar our minds for many years. Never had Irishmen fought each other so cruelly, so heartlessly . . . When we began to think and feel, life was already upon us, overwhelming; we are a generation born tired.

(Vol 11, no. 1, March, 1931)

In 1936 the Spanish Civil War appeared to many young men in England as not only a fight between the forces of democracy and fascism but a dress-rehearsal by the fascist powers for the next great European conflict. It aroused some heated debate in Ireland and generated some literary response, though in claiming the life of Charles Donnelly, a writer who combined socialist and internationalist principles with a poetic imagination which nevertheless remained unfettered by political dogma, the Battle of Jarama removed from the Irish scene one of its most promising young poets.

With the fact of Irish neutrality in the Second World War (and against the mental landscape outlined in the above quotation) it is not surprising to find, in December, 1944, R.M. Smyllie, the then editor of the *Irish Times*, noting in his Preface to *Poems from Ireland*, a collection of poems from the columns of the paper, edited by

Donagh MacDonagh, that: 'most of the poems have appeared
since the outbreak of war; yet it will be seen that those poets who
have been writing in Ireland have been almost wholly unaffected
by the impact of the world struggle'. The situation in the North
was obviously different, though here again war related writing
was not extensive. Robert Greacen depicts a lively literary scene in
Belfast, but one not dominated by discussion of the war, in his
autobiography, *Even Without Irene,* although he does recall
attendance at meetings of the Peace Pledge Union with Roy
McFadden. McFadden, in the Foreword to his *Collected Poems:
1943–95,* recalls his identification with English literary attitudes at
the time – 'with the anti-war poets' – and subscription to 'the
political anarchism of Herbert Read and Alex Comfort'. He was
also however aware of the legacy of the Irish wars and, in mid-
war, writes of the unresolved question resurrecting itself in the
'restless dream' of 1916 remembrance rituals. The major talent,
Louis MacNeice, of course, was elsewhere.

In the Foreword to his *They Go -- The Irish,* a selection of pieces
intended to give 'a composite picture of the Irish literary scene
laid in war-time England', Leslie Daiken writes: 'the instincts of
many Irish people have been peculiarly sound. They have rushed
to the aid, under arms, of fascism's victims. *They* do not sit on the
fence and await the outcome.' One contributor adduces the
intellectual state of neutral Ireland as her reason for going to
England rather than the sort of idealistic commitment Daiken's
Foreword envisages. While 'tremendous things were happening in
the world' she felt 'Dublin had become stifling, an intellectual
desert due no doubt to the erecting of mental barriers against
trends of thought and culture from outside'.[4] (Paradoxically,
Greacen in his autobiography gives as the reason for his wartime
decision to leave 'the general narrowness and philistinism' of
Belfast for Dublin a desire for 'new doors to open, new
opportunities'.) Daiken's major contributor, Sean O'Casey,
caustically introduces a wider Irish dimension with the reminder
that, in Easter Week, 'eight hundred men gathered in Dublin to
fight for Ireland, while four thousand, one hundred and eighty
men out of one battalion of one Irish regiment alone perished [in
the First World War] that England might live; and England in the
person of Henry Herbert Asquith roared out that Ireland stabbed
England in the back!' Though generally, as *Oak Leaves and Lavender*
suggests, his attitude to involvement in the Second World War is
of course much less narrowly nationalistic than that quotation
alone might suggest, on the responsibility for Irish neutrality he is

clear: 'the Ireland of to-day has been largely moulded by an English lord of misrule for the past thousand years; and this boyo is more responsible for her present-day neutrality than Ireland herself can ever be.' He returns therefore to the Great War to demand, in the words of Thomas Kettle, that, when the present war is ended, 'Soldier with equal soldier must we sit' to resolve finally the Irish question.

The really notable Irish writing of the war was produced by writers who do not appear in Daiken's anthology. As Beckett preferred France at war to Ireland at peace, so too did MacNeice decide to spend the war years in London. Elizabeth Bowen was also in England, her degree of commitment indicated in the work she was doing for the Ministry of Intelligence as indicated in Josette Leray's essay here. Both MacNeice and Bowen, in spite of their own choices, were nevertheless able to show moments of understanding of Irish neutrality – Bowen in her reports to the Ministry of Information (see Josette Leray's essay) and MacNeice, for instance, in a 1941 piece where he notes that 'De Valera's position is agonizingly difficult. Those who propose the application of the strong hand to Eire are forgetting their history.' Both writers, of course, were on the Home Front. In her Postscript to *The Demon Lover and Other Stories* Bowen says that 'both as a civilian and as a writer' she 'lived with every pore open . . . In war . . . I felt one with, and just like, everyone else. Sometimes I hardly knew where I stopped and somebody else began'. She notes the effects of the disintegration of the physical fabric of the known world: 'The violent destruction of solid things . . . left all of us, equally, heady and disembodied . . . Outwardly, we accepted that at this time individual destiny had to count for nothing: inwardly, individual destiny became an obsession in every heart. You cannot depersonalize persons.' In his prefatory Note to *Springboard: Poems 1941–44*, MacNeice notably says how 'Many of my titles in this book have the definite article, e.g. "The Satinist", "The Conscript". The reader must not think that I am offering him a set of Theophrastean characters. I am not generalising; "The Conscript" does not stand for all conscripts but for an imagined individual; any such individual seems to me to have an absolute quality which the definite article recognizes.' In this both writers are remarkably close in thought to the determination of young British combatant writers like Alun Lewis to retain the personal in face of the annihilation of war. In total war, where the home front was as likely to suffer the effects of bombing as the front line, the distinctions evident in 1914–18 poetry rapidly become blurred and war a more shared and general experience. Denis Johnston was closer than MacNeice and Bowen to actual battlefront experience as a war reporter with the BBC. With romantic memories of the 1916 rebels, some of whom he had come in contact with, Johnston is prepared to find war good right up to the experience of Buchenwald. In this he is not perhaps so isolated as one might think. The young Keith Douglas, in his account of his combatant experience in *Alamein to Zem Zem*, refuses to believe that the German troops whom he finds worthy opponents could be mixed up in the atrocities reported of the German set-up and insists that the administration must have a special set of thugs to carry out such acts.

If one considers the passionate and various involvement of Yeats over time, the divergent approaches of various Irish writers to the First World War, the ethically complex responses to the various Irish conflicts and the complicated questions of allegiance and ethical concern occasioned by the Second World War, the developing variety and complexity of Irish wartime writing begin to become apparent. In view of these diverse and individual standpoints it is clear that any critical approach has to be flexible and inclusive in terms of categories and boundaries. The kind of narrowness of definition supplied, for instance, by the Gravesian approach becomes increasingly inoperative and the expansion of the concept of 'war literature' has to extend to embrace not only non-combatant literature but complex shadings of allegiance and experience within that category. Julian Symons's 1942 definition – 'war poetry is not a specialised department of poetry: it is ... quite simply the poetry ... of people affected by the reality of war'[5] – is apposite. Yeats of course pre-eminently, with his life-long engagement with issues of violence and affiliation in times of insurrection and civil war, has laid down a powerful paradigm to counterbalance the exclusivity of the received First World War emphasis on the 'war poet'. The corpus of Irish 'war literature' therefore has its own distinctive configuration and has to be, as in the present volume, approached in an inclusive rather than a delimiting spirit. What follows therefore is a selection of essays by various critics on a range of authors. Coverage within the limits of a symposium-based selection of writers cannot of course be comprehensive. It is hoped, however, that the breadth, interest and variety of Irish war writing and the political, ethical and aesthetic choices involved are suggested within the accumulating scope of the book. The Symposium, designedly, had no pre-determined theoretical agenda and was exploratory in nature.

Hence it was in this spirit that individual contributors to the volume were invited to bring their own chosen approaches to bear on the authors and issues on which they write. Some notice is given of the literature of the Troubles, but the main focus of the volume (as of the Symposium) is essentially on the century's 'wars' in Irish literary experience.

IRISH PROSE WRITERS OF THE FIRST WORLD WAR

KEITH JEFFERY

This study is principally confined to a consideration of fiction, written by Irish writers who lived through the war and concerning Irish topics during the period of the conflict. Much of this material constitutes what might be classed as 'minor' prose work; it includes popular novels and other more ephemeral writing. For the historian, however, such writing can powerfully illuminate the period in question, and in many cases the 'fictional truth' contained in these works more accurately recounts their social and political context than more explicitly (and frequently self-consciously) 'literary' productions. In addition to the available fiction there is quite a large body of Irish prose writing in other genres which can be valuable for the historian. This includes memoirs by literary figures;[1] academics;[2] artists;[3] and others.[4] There are popular and propagandist works from the war and immediately after;[5] contemporary histories;[6] and, of course, regimental and unit histories[7] – prose works by Irishmen about Ireland's part in the war. There are also, inevitably, difficulties in establishing who exactly qualifies as an 'Irish writer'. One example may suffice: Robert Graves, son of an Irish poet, though long resident in England, described his own nationality at the time as 'Irish'.[8] Yet he embodied many of the attitudes inculcated in the English public school system, and served in a Welsh regiment. Does *Goodbye to All That* qualify as 'Irish prose writing'? And if it does not should we also exclude his father's predominantly Irish memoirs?[9]

Despite this apparent wealth of material, in terms of fiction there are actually rather few Irish 'war novels', especially in the sense of stories which are set on the battlefront itself. Only two writers of any note – Patrick MacGill and Liam O'Flaherty – produced work which drew on their own experiences in France.

1

Jocelyn Lee Hardy, an Ulsterman and regular officer who had served in the Connaught Rangers, wrote adventure stories in the 1930s, including one which drew on his personal experience of escaping from a prison camp in Germany.[10] Other Irish writers who served in the war, such as St John Ervine, Joyce Cary (in the West African campaign) and George A. Birmingham, did not incorporate their experiences in any of their novels,[11] although Birmingham did publish an autobiographical account of his service as an army chaplain.[12] No-one who lived through the war, and who did *not* serve on the battlefront, tried at any length to recreate the horror of the trenches in fiction.[13] There is no Irish Stephen Crane, although Sean O'Casey set the second act of *The Silver Tassie* 'somewhere in France'. One reason for Yeats' rejection of the play for the Abbey Theatre, indeed, was his view that it was impossible for a playwright successfully to recreate a situation of which he had no direct experience.[14] It would, besides, have been politically dangerous to put sympathetically-portrayed British soldiers on the Abbey stage in 1929.

At first sight the striking feature of the Irish literary response to the Great War is its comparative absence. This is in sharp contrast to the abundance of 'war literature' produced in other countries which participated in the conflict, as, for example, a glance at Philip E. Hager and Desmond Taylor's extensive bibliography of Great War novels will confirm.[15] The Irish response to the cataclysm of the war is a case, as it were, of 'the dog that didn't bark'. Why should this be so? It could be argued that Ireland's part in the war was more peripheral than that of other places. In geographical terms that was certainly true, though scarcely more so than the USA, Canada or Australia. In the absence, however, of conscription, proportionately fewer from Ireland served in the war than from countries where national service applied. Nevertheless a great many Irishmen – at least 210,000 – did serve, and over 27,000 died.[16] So the impact was not negligible. But, politically, except in Unionist Ulster, the experience of the war did not have the centrality which it had, say, in Great Britain or Australia. The war, the veterans and their organizations were politically and socially marginalised in the new independent Irish state.[17] The declining ascendancy class were the only social grouping, as a whole, for whom the impact of the war was fundamentally significant. The British notion of a 'lost generation' and of 'lost leaders' – or as one Englishman put it 'a generation was not decimated but decapitated'[18] – had simply no meaning in nationalist Ireland. Far from a generation of natural leaders being lost during the war years, the events of 1916 and afterwards produced an entirely new cohort of leaders. The losses of the war became largely irrelevant in the new Ireland. The environment, then, was not conducive to battlefront literature. In crude terms there was no popular demand for it and, if nothing else, the publication of war novels in Great Britain stimulated the market for such works.

This is not to say that the Great War is wholly absent from Irish fiction, although in some cases such an omission is remarkable. A substantial portion of Edward MacLysaght's Irish-language novel, *Cúrsaí Thomás*,[19] translated as *The Small Fields of Carrig*,[20] covers the period from the summer of 1914 until late 1918. The action takes place in Dublin, Limerick and the west of Ireland. There is, however, no mention at all of the war (or the Easter Rising), although the Dublin part of the book is set in 1914–15. The complete absence of the conflict is significant in a novel which celebrates the traditional verities of the land and Irish rural life and contrasts them with the dehumanising impact of urban living. It confirms, perhaps, the irrelevance of the war to one particular conception of Ireland.[21] Another novel with its heart in rural Ireland is Meta Mayne Reid's *The Land is Dear*.[22] Set over the war years in remote north Antrim, evidently near Bushmills, the conflict, which very occasionally impinges on the narrative, is essentially an irrelevance to the farming concerns and land obsession of the central characters.[23]

The greatest Irish novel written during the First World War was *Ulysses*. Understandably for a book set in June 1904 it makes no explicit mention of the conflict, but Jacques Darras has argued that the war provides an essential background to an understanding of the work. 'You cannot have James Joyce or Ulysses without a European war roaring in the background or across the Swiss border', asserts Darras. 'You may ignore it. You may pretend that it did not exist or that it were not worth mentioning. But facts are hard to beat.'[24]

I do not wish to dwell on novels which do *not* mention the war, but I do want to look at works, which, while not dealing with the actual fighting, treat Ireland, or Irish themes, during the war years. When considering the Irish literary response to the conflict we have perforce to look at novels about what might be called the 'home front' as well as the fighting. This is no bad thing. Many studies of 'war literature' ignore this aspect of modern conflict. Literary critics and cultural historians seem at times to have been as mesmerically attracted to the fighting itself as, we are told, were

the ill-starred volunteers of August 1914. It is as if what was
happening at home did not matter. But it did – and does – matter,
and we cannot begin to understand the impact – then and since –
of the Great War without addressing the home front. The war of
1914–18 was the first great 'total' war, when the whole strength of
the state, not just the fighting forces, was mobilised behind the
war effort. The war was a seamless robe which enveloped civilians
as much as servicemen and women, and more so in the First
World War than in any previous general conflict. So the absence of
much Irish battle front literature, and the concomitant existence of
a greater body of home front novels – which I suspect may
contrast with the relative balance of writing in English novels –
actually helps us to put the war in a clearer and historically more
accurate perspective. In any case, if we want to use the literature
about the war to inform us about its impact on a whole society or
nation, we must also remember that only a fraction of those
people physically fought in the war.

I want to concentrate on three main themes as expressed in the
literature: the initial impact of the war and the question of why
men enlisted; the battlefront experience; and the impact of the
continuing conflict at home.

The initial impact of the war and the problem of enlistment is a
natural starting point. The explanations of the various authors
about enlistment – explanations for the most part drawn from
their own personal or family experience – may help to answer one
of the most perplexing questions for the historian of the Great
War, which is why intelligent, rational, sensitive men, who
anticipated (or indeed already knew) the terrible horrors of the
Western Front, voluntarily joined the army. The date of writing a
novel is clearly significant in its depiction of the Irish response to
the outbreak of war. In August 1914, as the British Foreign
Secretary, Sir Edward Grey, remarked, the 'one bright spot in the
very dreadful situation' was Ireland.[25] The animosity between
nationalists and unionists, which in the summer of 1914 had been
threatening to break out into civil war, had apparently eased with
the onset of war. Both Carson and, perhaps more unexpectedly,
Redmond pledged their supporters behind the war effort. They
were both convinced of the justice of the conflict between British
democracy and Prussian militarism, and the fate of 'gallant little
Belgium' was held up as an example of what could happen to a
small country like Ireland.

George A. Birmingham's *Gossamer*,[26] a novel published early in
the war in which, unusually, the heroic qualities of international

banking are celebrated, reflects the willing enlistment of constitutional nationalists to the British war effort. Michael Gorman, an attractive, if venal, nationalist Member of Parliament, remarks that nationalists had 'rallied to the Empire at the very start and have kept on rallying ever since. It felt odd at first, but you get used to anything in time, even to being loyal' (p. 304). Gorman pompously expresses the politician's rationale for the war: '"The war", he said, "is for the liberation of Europe. It is a vast struggle, an Armageddon in which the forces of reaction, absolutism, tyranny, a military caste are ranged against democracy"' (p. 296). But the novel's narrator, Sir James Digby, disagrees. Digby is an Anglo-Irish Protestant who has sold his Irish estate under the recent land purchase scheme, thus becoming 'a man of no country' (p. 3). His motives for enlisting are fundamentally inarticulate:

'If you think', I said, 'that I'm going out to fight for the principles of democracy you're making a big mistake. There's nothing in the world I dislike more than that absurd democracy of yours . . . It's not patriotism. I have not got any country to be patriotic about. It's not any silly belief in liberty and democracy. I don't know why I'm doing it. I just have to. That's all.' (pp. 296–7)

The Belfast-born Birmingham was a Church of Ireland clergyman whose real name was James Owen Hannay. In 1916 he went to France as an army chaplain and himself took the 'loyalist' side in the war. His son served in the Irish Guards.[27] There is little serious or reflective political content in his novels, which are generally light comedies. In *Up, the Rebels!*,[28] however, he satirises Irish nationalists, in much the same way as he had treated Ulster Unionists in *The Red Hand of Ulster*.[29] *Up, the Rebels!* which was dedicated 'to any friends I have left in Ireland after the publication of this book', concerns a half-baked local rebellion raised in 1917 against the threat of conscription. The nationalists who support it are seen to have mixed and muddled motives. Birmingham makes his own position clear through his unpleasant characterization of an English pacifist journalist, Bettany, who has fled from conscription in Britain. But his underlying cowardice emerges when it appears that his new-found Irish allies are themselves quite prepared to employ violence. 'I didn't know these damned Irish were like this', he says. 'If I'd ever supposed for one instant that they really meant to fight, I wouldn't have gone near them' (p. 176).

Nationalists are also satirised in a couple of curious, slight fantasies about what might happen if the Germans actually occupied Ireland. *The Germans in Cork*,[30] by 'Baron von Kartoffel and others', attributed to Lady Carbery,[31] recounts events after the German conquest. As a reward for their services in support of the Germans, Sinn Feiners are offered small holdings 'on the salubrious shores of the Baltic' (p. 4). All men in Ireland between 17 and 35 years are conscripted into the German army, and trade unions are abolished, with all strikers punished by deportation to Prussia. The 'ancient faith of the Irish people' is swept away and replaced with Lutheranism (p. 112). In the much shorter, *The Germans at Bessbrook: A Dream*,[32] the author, James Richardson, one of a local Quaker mill-owning family, describes the 'longed for day [when] the reign of the bloody Anglo-Saxon was over in Ireland, and the domination of the spotless lily white Prusso-Saxon was begun' (p. 1). As with the Cork fantasy, the initial welcome for the invader soon cools. In Bessbrook, indeed, Protestants and Catholics unite to oppose a German scheme to demolish churches in order to build a fortification above the village. Eventually the 'German-Irish government' is brought down by Irish, Scottish and English forces and the author muses on 'the removal of the tyranny which came under the guise of freedom, as tyrannies often do' (p. 31).

The conflicting pressures of loyalty – personal and national – and cowardice are explored at length in St John Ervine's *Changing Winds*.[33] Much of the book is clearly drawn from Ervine's own experience. At the time of writing he was manager of the Abbey Theatre in Dublin and in the scenes at the end of the novel which depict the Easter Rising there is much which Ervine himself witnessed.[34] The plot concerns the close friendship between Henry Quinn, son of a modestly well-off Protestant landowning family in County Antrim, and three contemporaries from his English public school. While Quinn, at his father's insistence, goes to Trinity College, Dublin, the three English youths go to Cambridge. But they combine again to share a house in London where they move in mildly radical and socialist intellectual circles. Quinn becomes a novelist and one of the others a drama critic and playwright. The Belfast-born Ervine himself achieved success as a critic, playwright and novelist in London before 1914. He, too, moved in radical political circles and was a member of the Fabian Society with Rupert Brooke (a Cambridge man), to whose memory *Changing Winds* was dedicated. The title, moreover, is a quotation from 'The Dead', sonnet IV of Brooke's *1914* sequence.[35]

Two of Quinn's three friends join up at the start of the war, for conventional enough reasons. 'A chap must do his share . . .', says one, 'fighting's such a filthy job that it ought to be shared by everybody that can take a hand in it at all . . . I should hate to think that I let some one else save my skin when I'm perfectly able to save it myself' (pp. 415–16). Both friends are killed in 1915 and the third, who had held back on account of his wife and child, finally joins up as well. While Quinn accepts the rightness of the war – 'I know that if we lose this war, the world will be a worse place to live in than it is' (p. 517) – he procrastinates about enlisting, frozen by his own physical cowardice and his conviction that he also would die: 'In his heart he knew that he was afraid to go' (p. 504). He muses on the nature of patriotism, and the clearly sacramental quality of patriotic service:

Irrationally, impulsively, unaccountably one loved one's country. The air of it and the earth of it, the winds that blew over it and the seas that encircled it, all these had been mingled to make men, so that when there was danger and a threat to a man's country, some native thing in him stirred and compelled him to say, 'This is my body! This is my blood!' and sent him out, irrationally, impulsively, unaccountably to die in its defence.' (p. 525)

Through his experience of the Easter Rising Quinn finally overcomes his weakness. During the Rising he encounters John Marsh, a passionate nationalist republican who had been his tutor before he went up to Trinity. Marsh is out with the rebels at the General Post Office and is killed, dying, 'as he desired, for Ireland' (p. 568). Quinn, however, finds that in the experience of the Rising 'he had lived through a terror and had not been afraid'. He had, moreover, 'seen men immolating themselves gladly because they had believed that by so doing they would make their country a finer one to live in'. He finally accepts that 'In the end, nothing matters but that a man shall offer his life for his belief' (p. 569) – and sets off to enlist, and die. But Ervine is too canny to finish on quite such a conventional note, even in 1917. At the outbreak of the war Quinn's father – the most attractive character in the book – vehemently condemns the politicians who had made the conflict: 'old men sittin' in offices, an' making wars, an' then bidding young men to pay the price of them!' (p. 435). At the end of the novel Quinn reflects that, despite their differing loyalties (he is a moderate Home Ruler), both he and John Marsh 'had to pay for the incompetence and folly of old men who had wrangled and made bitterness' (p. 570).

Ervine himself joined up in October 1917, first as a trooper in the Household Cavalry and subsequently as a commissioned officer in the Royal Dublin Fusiliers, with whom he lost a leg on the Western Front in May 1918. He also lost his belief in Home Rule and became a powerful Unionist apologist. The tension between 'Irish' and 'British' loyalties also affected E. R. Dodds, another Protestant Home Ruler from the North. At the start of the war Dodds found himself 'immune' from the recruiting infection: it was not his war, and although he 'was missing an adventure on which others had staked their lives', he was still not prepared to offer his life 'on what was for me an alien cause'.[36] On the other hand, neither was he prepared to side with the republicans of 1916; the price of their dream was too high. He could not forget that many of his old friends 'were fighting for the English in the deadly mud of Flanders. Actively to take arms against them, save in the direst national need, was an intolerable prospect. I was a marginal man, caught between two irreconcilable loyalties.'[37] In *My Cousin Justin*,[38] Margaret Barrington, who lived in Ulster and Dublin during the war, observes that some other Ulstermen were equally reluctant to join up. At Lagan in Donegal, one Protestant, 'more bigot and more courageous than the rest', asked 'why our men should die fighting against "Protestant Germany for Catholic Belgium and Infidel France"' (p. 123). Cowardice also afflicts one of her characters, but unlike Ervine's Quinn it drives him to join up. 'I am a coward', he says, 'that's why I'm going. I'm joining the herd instead of going to jail as an anti-war propagandist' (p. 125).

We find equally divided loyalties in Catholic Ireland. In *The Wasted Island*[39] Eimar O'Duffy characterises the war as a shocking madness which has engulfed Europe. His protagonist, Bernard Lascelles, is the son of a prominent Anglo-Irish doctor, but his mother is Catholic and Bernard is educated at an English Catholic public school. By 1914 he has acquired advanced socialist and Irish nationalist opinions and refuses to join up and take part in a 'mere game of capitalist diplomacy' (p. 315). He sees, however, Redmond's National Volunteers enlisting and observes that 'nationalists of the middle and upper classes were, of course, the first to adapt themselves to circumstances' (p. 311). O'Duffy himself, like Lascelles, was educated at an English Catholic school (Stoneyhurst) and was thrown out of the family home by his father (who was 'dentist-in-ordinary to the Lord Lieutenant of Ireland') when he refused to join the British army in 1914.[40]

Kate O'Brien, who came from a prosperous Catholic background in Limerick, describes a similar family quarrel in *Mary Lavelle*.[41] When Mary's elder brother Jimmy reaches his eighteenth birthday in 1917 his father, a somewhat apathetic doctor, decides to get him a commission in the Munster Fusiliers. Jimmy declines the offer and, after a fierce row, leaves home for ever, later to join the IRA. By contrast, Mary Lavelle's stolid fiancé, John MacCurtain, 'taking his uncle's and John Redmond's advice', in September 1914 had gone off 'in private's uniform to the assistance of gallant little Belgium'. Although the war 'had proved hateful to him', he returned as a major with a DSO. (p. 27). Katharine Tynan, another middle-class Catholic writer, recalled that 'at least we started with utter enthusiasm for the War and its purposes', but 'one did not know all that would happen, how it would drag and drag, till weariness of it and longing for it to end overcame all other feelings.'[42] Her novel *The Golden Rose*,[43] is a romance set in the context of shifting Irish national attitudes and sharp social distinctions in the West of Ireland. Carmel O'Reilly falls in love with Beaufoy Molyneux, son of the local peer, Lord Creeslough. Carmel's father, a medical doctor, and her four brothers all enlist in the British forces at the start of the war. Dr O'Reilly is invalided out but loses his job as parish dispenser to a Sinn Fein supporter. Indeed, the ostracism of the 'Castle Catholic' family by local nationalists is paradoxically one spur to enlistment: Carmel realises 'that the war had been the boys' way of escape out of poverty, out of the strange unfriendliness of the country that had been so friendly' (p. 77). The O'Reillys suffer from the snobbery of the Anglo-Irish gentry, a situation which mirrored the author's own experience as the wife of a Resident Magistrate in Claremorris, County Mayo, from late 1914 to the end of the war. Her two sons joined up, one fought in Palestine the other in France. Both survived.

Unlike Ervine, most of the authors who considered the question couched the actual motivation for enlistment in strikingly unspecific terms. A man joined up simply because he 'had to'. Rex Pender, a sensitive soul, in Forrest Reid's *Pender Among the Residents*,[44] which deals with Pender's return after the war to his native Ballycastle, almost automatically enlisted when war broke out: 'I joined up. I didn't want to: I didn't even believe I'd be any good: but somehow I felt that I must' (p. 39). Emphatically not the military type, Forrest Reid himself did not enlist, but his account of Pender's motivation does not contradict one provided by Patrick MacGill, the 'navvy poet' from Glenties, County Donegal, who joined up in the great rush to the colours at the beginning of the war.[45] 'Why did you join?' asks one soldier in *The Red Horizon*. 'To save myself the trouble of telling people why I didn't', replies his mate.[46]

Patrick MacGill left a considerable body of war literature. Apart from a volume of poems, *Soldier Songs* (1917),[47] a journalistic potboiler, *The Diggers: the Australians in France* (1919), and a play, *Suspense* (1930),[48] he wrote two explicitly autobiographical works (sometimes described as 'novels'[49]), *The Amateur Army* (1915), in which he republished a series of articles he had written about the transformation of a raw 'rooky' into a 'finished fighter' (p. 7), and *The Great Push: an Episode of the Great War* (1916), which narrates the attack on the first day of the Battle of Loos in September 1915 in which the author was wounded. There are also four novels: *The Red Horizon* (1916); *The Brown Brethren* (1917); *The Dough-Boys* (1918);[50] and *Fear!* (1921). With the exception of *The Dough-Boys*, which is about American soldiers, and *Fear!*, all the prose writings deal with men in the London Irish Rifles, the regiment in which MacGill himself served. At the age of fourteen MacGill had migrated from Donegal to work in the Scottish potato fields. Later he became a navvy for the Caledonian Railway. In 1911, after the success of his *Gleanings for a Navvy's Scrap Book*, he was hired to write for the *Daily Express*. A very successful autobiographical novel, *Children of the Dead End* followed in 1914, by which time MacGill was employed editing ancient manuscripts in the Chapter Library of Windsor Castle. He had come a long way from his cabin in Glenties. He has, nevertheless, been regarded as a characteristic 'working-class novelist',[51] and of all the Irish prose writers of the Great War he has the humblest background. And yet his wartime work, while starkly realistic and described as 'bitter' and 'scathing', was not in any fundamental way subversive. *The Red Horizon*, indeed, attracted a foreword by Lord Esher, President of the County of London Territorial Association and Deputy Governor of Windsor Castle. Esher's contribution to the publication (which he privately described as 'a harmless book'[52]) was apparently solicited in order to forestall court-martial proceedings against MacGill for being too revealing in his published work.[53]

The Red Horizon follows the London Irish from their landing in France in the Spring of 1915 through to their time in the front line later that year. It is clear from the start that the unit is both Irish and British. Along with the Irish recruits are cheerful Cockneys and other Englishmen. When the battalion marches on parade to the local church, their pipes arrive at Mass playing *The Wearing of the Green*, and at the end of the service 'we sang the national anthem, ours, *God Save the King*' (p. 41). The Irish, though, are everywhere. Coming across a unit of the Scots Guards, the unnamed narrator hears 'the brogue that could be cut with a knife ... and the kindliness that sprang from the cabins of Corrymeela and the moors of Derrynane' (p. 83). There is much reflection about the German soldiers in the opposing trenches. 'How can I reconcile myself to this? ... Who are those men behind the line of sandbags that I should want to kill them, to disembowel them with my sword, blow their faces to pieces at three hundred yards, bomb them into eternity at a word of command?' (pp. 91–2) Nor does MacGill pull his punches in his graphic descriptions of terrible wounds, rotting corpses, shell-shocked comrades, and the penetrating, nauseating smell of the trenches. But the tale is not one of unrelieved horror, which no doubt explains why the censor eventually passed it, Lord Esher endorsed it, and it sold 37,000 copies by 1918.[54]

The war in *The Red Horizon* exists as an immutable fact of life and MacGill's characters accept it as such. They may not like the conflict – no sane man would – but theirs, classically, is 'not to reason why'. They respond to their shocking circumstances with resilience and a matter-of-fact acceptance of death. In a curious way the book celebrates the *joie de vivre* of the Irish and British soldiers, irreverent, cheerful and fiercely loyal to each other. Whatever might have been the case at the time of enlistment, the crucial factor holding the army together in the face of death at the battle front is not patriotism or commitment to some abstract high war aim, but *esprit-de-corps*. 'I am not far wrong in stating', wrote MacGill, 'that pride of regiment in an "old sweat" is much stronger than love of country'.[55] *The Red Horizon* concludes with a note of 'the romance of war', although lightened with a tinge of irony. We leave the 'gloriously weary' riflemen having left the trenches, now resting and smoking well away from the front line: 'There is romance, there is joy in the life of a soldier' (p. 306).

Army morale was evidently safe enough in the hands of Patrick MacGill. Indeed his reassuring portrait of the Expeditionary Force as fundamentally 'sound' reflects the historical truth. The British army in France (unlike the French army) was not riven with mutinies or widespread disaffection. Perhaps, then, MacGill's soldiers were as typical as he himself was not. Writing books clearly set him apart from the run-of-the-mill soldier, and his semi-autobiographical narrator in *The Red Horizon* was a cultured fellow, who found that 'Old Montaigne in a dug-out is a true friend and a fine companion' (p. 119). MacGill's strength as a writer, however, is that he tempers the reassuring qualities of his narrative with the unsettling and frightening realities of the war.

In *Brown Brethren*, Flanagan, a college-educated youth from the West of Ireland who had studied for the priesthood, with difficulty gets back to the trenches under an assumed name after having been invalided out of the service. He 'was a youngster who took eagerly to the life of war, its romance and roving'. What had attracted him back was the vitality of the front line, the (perhaps addictive) sense of living on the edge of great deeds. 'We've been living on the gods here', he explained, 'and I went back to live with ordinary mortals – I couldn't stick it' (pp. 115–16). But Flanagan is not long for this world. 'I saw 'im cop it', reported a colleague bluntly. 'Right froo the 'ead. 'E didn't say nuffin', just fell and stiffened' (p. 273).

There is no 'romance of war' at all in MacGill's sombre and neglected 1921 novel *Fear!* In an introduction it is explained that 'the blue pencil of the Censor was too busy during the War to allow a realist such as Patrick MacGill a chance of exposing the truth'. And it is a book with a message. 'Unconstrained by the thought of blue-pencil', MacGill 'has been able to write about war as war actually is'. The terrible realism of the story 'will bring home to all the conviction that such things must never be allowed to happen again' (p. 2).[56] The novel is narrated by Henry Arthur Ryder, sometime village barber and now a private soldier in France, who has written with the aim of 'the diverting of my mind from the horrors which encompass me here in France' and since it 'will help to ease the tedium of the trenches' (p. 9). Timid and with a weak constitution, Ryder is not one of those who enthusiastically enlisted at the beginning of the war. He had waited until he was conscripted towards the end of 1917, and he did not arrive in France until June 1918. He is fatalistic and does not concern himself in any way with war aims. After four weeks in France he remarks that 'I have not yet met in real life the Cockney who says that our cause is the right one, nor yet the clear-lipped boy who longs for an eternal war' (p. 109). The novel charts Ryder's progressive moral degeneration. On a trench raid he finds himself in a virtually psychopathic frenzy when it comes to using his bayonet: 'filled with a wild and wicked joy, I lunged the steel forward and caught the man on the face, shoving the bayonet through his gas-mask and through his head' (p. 139). He loses any belief he may have had in God; as a stretcher-bearer (which MacGill was) he has to step on bodies, living and dead; a colleague graphically describes the bungled execution of his mate for cowardice in the face of the enemy; he visits a prostitute (for the first time) but staggers off apparently before completing the job. 'I was', he writes, 'now a ship that had lost its anchor and was at the mercy of every buffeting wave' (p. 246). At the last – and surely very near the end of the war – he is killed in yet another pointless attack. The book is a very early example of a genre of grimly realistic and disillusioned writing which was to become quite widespread later in the decade. One critic has remarked that 'had *Fear!* been published in 1929 it might have achieved minor fame; coming as it did in 1921, it has been decently forgotten'.[57] All the same, the novel still sold quite well, achieving 16,179 copies by the fourth printing.[58]

The only other 'Irish' novel set wholly on the Western Front, Liam O'Flaherty's *Return of the Brute*, was published in 1929,[59] but it, too, has been 'decently forgotten'. Studies of O'Flaherty's writing do not tend to dwell on the work. Patrick Sheeran has described it as 'one of the worst [novels] ever published'.[60] The book presumably draws on O'Flaherty's own experience. Born on the Aran Islands and educated at Rockwell College, Blackrock College, the Holy Cross Seminary at Clonliffe and (briefly) University College Dublin, he joined the Irish Guards in 1915 and spent six months on the Western Front, culminating with his being shell-shocked at Langemarck (Flanders) in September 1917, and was later discharged from the army.

Return of the Brute is set in the mud of Arras in March 1917 and describes the events of a few hours during which all but one of a section of nine soldiers perish. The central character, Bill Gunn, is 'a huge fellow . . . with a spirit that hardship could not conquer', yet possessing 'a simple soul, which shone through his great, blue eyes' (p. 15). He had travelled from North America to join up at the start of the war, but had soon become disillusioned with the whole affair. 'I don't give a curse who wins this rotten war and I'd like to run my bayonet through the fellahs that started it', he asserts. 'We're just fighting for a gang of robbers . . . I've got my eyes open now, although I hadn't when I enlisted' (pp. 16–17). Representing the chief theme in the novel – the utter degradation and demoralization of the war – Gunn is progressively seized with a homicidal rage against Corporal Williams, the N.C.O. in charge of his bombing section. The book ends with Gunn throttling Williams to death with his bare hands and finally running off to his own end in front of the German machine guns. In the meantime all but one of the other soldiers have died in a variety of revolting circumstances: one drowns in a quagmire; another has his head blown off; a third has an artery severed by machine-gun fire while he is defecating; another apparently freezes to death, and so on. The (perhaps intended) effect of the work is to anaesthetise the reader to the horrors of the front; but it is gratuitous horror, 'like *All Quiet [on the Western Front]* without the sensitivity'.[61] Although individual scenes have, as one critic observed, a certain 'monstrous vigour',[62] there is no narrative development, and Gunn's rising madness is particularly unconvincing. As the *Times Literary Supplement* reviewer wanly remarked: 'there is hardly a soul in that bombing section less revolting than Gunn and the Corporal themselves. These people hardly require the war to make them repulsive.'[63]

O'Flaherty's short story, 'The Alien Skull',[64] more successfully evokes the moral degradation of the war. In this genre the author perforce has less opportunity to be self-indulgent towards the horror. Private Mulhall has been sent out into no-man's-land where he finds himself in a shell hole with a German soldier. The German is friendly and the men exchange bread and a cigarette. Mulhall, already a little unhinged, feels 'violently angry at not being able to hate the enemy and throttle him'. But when the German takes off his helmet his 'bare skull acted on his senses like a maddening drug' (pp. 173–4). Mulhall kills the other man and is himself shot dead shortly afterwards.

Both O'Flaherty's novel and the short story were published ten years after the end of the war, at a time when quite a few other such bleakly realistic and disillusioned works were being produced. Nothing of quite such power was published during the war, although as we have seen, there are elements of verismo in Patrick MacGill's writing. When considering the domestic impact of the war, the question which naturally arises is what did people think was going on in France? What did they *imagine* the war was like?[65] Apart from such literature as might have been available, there were also newspaper reports and letters home. Yet all three of these sources of information were subject to censorship, a factor which constrained MacGill. Letters home, in any case, were more often than not subject to self-censorship. In *Fear!*, MacGill's hero who waited to be conscripted and did not have a particularly jolly time at the Front, writes home to a sweetheart and while he mentions the 'carnage', he also remarks 'Though I grumble at times, I never regret having joined the Army' (p. 149). Among the most intimidating and unsettling manifestations of the war were the daily casualty lists which dominated the newspapers. Clearly, while they may have been spared some of the gruesome details, people at home soon came to appreciate the war's human cost. But this, too, had a brutalising effect which mirrored that which afflicted the soldiers at the front. In Ervine's *Changing Winds* the mother of one of Henry Quinn's friends remarks on 'how indifferent one becomes to the death lists'. 'And everywhere', muses Quinn, 'it seemed to him, that coarsening process was going on, a persistent blunting of the feelings, an itching desire for more and grimmer and bloodier details' (pp. 457, 458).

A similar point is made in Pamela Hinkson's *The Ladies' Road*,[66] one of the most impressive novels of the home front during 1914–18. The book is dedicated to Hinkson's mother, Katharine Tynan, who died a year before it was published: 'This last thing that we have shared'. Hinkson was in her mid-teens at the start of the war and spent much of the following years at Brookhill House, near Claremorris (County Mayo). The action of the novel moves between two family homes: 'Cappagh' in Ireland, modelled on Brookhill, and 'Winds' in England, idyllically sited on the Downs. The main character, Stella Mannering, is at school during the war. There she 'almost carelessly' turns to the casualty lists 'wondering if there was anyone she knew. There was a certain excitement about seeing the name of someone one knew.' But on this occasion she finds the name of her beloved cousin Philip, and 'she never turned to it [the casuality list] carelessly again' (p. 72).[67] The melancholy theme of the novel is that the women are victims of the war too. Stella, her sister, sister-in-law and aunt suffer terrible losses: both brothers and her uncle are killed (one in the early summer of 1918 on the Chemin des Dames ridge – from which the novel takes its title); her brother-in-law is taken prisoner; a cousin survives but has been badly gassed. Stella is less bewildered by this than her elders since 'she couldn't remember any other world than this. Or at least she had never lived in any other world' (p. 195).

In the face of the family's sacrifice Stella worries about being unable to contribute to the war effort, about being 'a useless mouth' (p. 80). Late in the war she incoherently tries to explain to a young officer about to go to France for the first time (where he is, inevitably, killed) how she could wish to go herself. 'But to go oneself', she says, 'not to be left behind and to see someone you love – and just wait. And if . . . It would be quicker anyhow and then it would be over. And it's lonely' (p. 197). Hinkson's mother makes the same point in her memoirs. In Mayo she and Pamela felt their 'alienation' and immunity from the war. Pamela 'envied even those who were under air-raids. Anything, anything, except the immunity (in a sense) which had been forced upon us' (p. 310). In *The Golden Rose*, too, Carmel O'Reilly wants 'to be somewhere where people were feeling the stress and suffering of the war. The poor people about them were hardly aware of the war except in so far as it affected prices' (p. 99).

Katharine Tynan writes movingly about the specific impact in Dublin of the disastrous landings at Gallipoli in the summer of 1915. Here the 10th (Irish) Division suffered terribly. It was the first action experienced by any of the three 'New Army' divisions raised in Ireland. 'So many of our friends had gone out in the 10th Division to perish at Suvla. For the first time came bitterness, for we felt that their lives had been thrown away and that their heroism had gone unrecognised . . . Dublin was full of mourning' (p. 178). In *Changing Winds* Ervine remarks that much of the well-documented public apathy with which the Easter Rising was greeted stemmed from the Gallipoli losses. 'Dublin', he wrote, 'was full of men and women mourning for their sons who had died at Suvla Bay . . . and were in no mood for rebellion' (p. 498). Margaret Barrington records simply (and inaccurately) that after Gallipoli 'no more men went'.[68]

What, then, could women do to 'play their part'? On the evidence of the books investigated, not much. They could encourage men to enlist, an activity which Henry Quinn's father excoriated: 'An' these wee bitches with their white feathers . . . ought to be well skelped'.[69] Margaret Barrington describes bereaved women bitterly demanding conscription so that everyone should suffer: 'They sent white feathers, wrote letters and talked hysterically. Let every man be taken.'[70] Pamela Hinkson's women are more reticent; their role is nobly to suffer and succour their men where possible. They offer hospitality to soldiers bound for France (though officers only). Among the most poignant, if highly sentimental, passages in the literature are those by Patrick MacGill about the women of France, for whom he has unbounded admiration. At Mass in a French church: 'The whole place breathed war, not in the splendid whirlwind rush of men mad in the wild enthusiasm of battle, but in the silent yearning, heartfelt sorrow, and great bravery, the bravery of women who remain at home'.[71]

The longer term impact of the war seems clear enough, at least so far as the Ascendancy class were concerned. Lennox Robinson observes that 'almost without exception, the big houses were emptied of all men of a fighting age'. It was, he continues, 'to be the last chapter in the history of many families'.[72] This is certainly true when the 1919–22 period is added to that of the war. Perhaps here there is a variation on the English 'lost generation' myth, but the old order would have passed away in any case – indeed it was already doing so – with or without the assistance of the Great War.

What does the literature *not* tell us? Apart from MacGill's books, it tells us virtually nothing about the working or peasant class experience of the war. I have found nothing in fiction about the response of working-class loyalist Ulster to the conflict.[73] Naturally enough the middle and upper classes are well represented in the works considered. But while the literature does usefully direct our attention to the home front, we learn very little of what the mass of the people were doing. Where it is particularly valuable is in recreating some of the forces bearing on the Catholic middle classes, whose conservative instincts biased them towards being loyal (or not 'disloyal') to the political status quo. When Ervine's work with its Ulster dimension is added to the corpus we also get a sense of the complexity of response in Ireland to the conflict. There were no simple answers depending on an individual's class or creed.

It may be that one reason for the paucity of Irish war literature is that the war actually had very little impact in Ireland. Enid Starkie in her memoirs recalls that in their comfortably-off-middle-class Dublin family they noticed very little change, at least for the first part of the conflict. The only marked difference was that there were no private dances, yet these were replaced by a great many more tennis parties than hitherto.[74] We do know that one impact of the war generally was to make Ireland, particularly rural Ireland, more prosperous.[75] So it may be that, for those not personally involved in the war through enlistment or in other ways, and for those who did not live in Dublin and were not directly affected by the Rising, the predominant 'impact of the war', such as it was, was that things got better. And maybe, then, Edward MacLysaght's 'war-less' novel, set in the years 1914–18, is not so far from the truth after all.[76]

1916: THE IDEA AND THE ACTION

DECLAN KIBERD

One summer Sunday, late in the nineteenth century, the poet and mystic George Russell stood on the esplanade at Bray and preached about the return of ancient Irish heroes. As it happened, among his auditors was that Standish James O'Grady whose *History of Ireland: Heroic Period* (1878–80) had made the exploits of Cuchulain available in English to a national readership. His object had been to provide in the ancient heroes exemplars who might reanimate the declining Anglo-Irish aristocracy. 'I desire', he wrote in his preface, 'to make this heroic period once again a portion of the imagination of the country, and its chief characters as familiar in the minds of our people as they once were'.[1] Watching Russell share this explosive information with a more downmarket audience of weekend holidaymakers, O'Grady felt a pang of dismay and foreboding: but there was nothing he could do to recall the genie back to the bottle.

It did not take him long to sense what would happen when Cuchulain was appropriated as a role-model by the clerks and schoolmasters massed before him. 'We have now a literary movement, it is not very important', he declared: 'it will be followed by a political movement, that will not be very important; then must come a military movement, that will be important indeed'.[2] O'Grady was but the first among many writers to witness with amazement what might happen when images and ideas crafted with care in the study took fire in someone else's head, and did so with an intensity which could express itself only in direct action. Years later, W. B. Yeats would ask 'Did that play of mine send out / Certain men the English shot?'[3] The conditions for theorizing a revolution were indeed no different from those for starting one. After it was over, Russell would gravely but proudly admit the link between the idea and the action: 'What was in Padraic Pearse's soul when he fought in Easter Week but an imagination, and the chief imagination which inspired him was that of the hero who stood against a host . . . I who knew how deep was Pearse's love for the Cuchulain whom O'Grady discovered or invented, remembered after Easter Week that he had been solitary against a great host in imagination with Cuchulain, long before circumstance permitted him to stand for his nation with so few companions against so great a power'.[4] And in lines from a late poem, Yeats asked a ringing question:

> When Pearse summoned Cuchulain to his side,
> What stalked through the Post Office? What intellect,
> What calculation, number, measurement replied?[5]

– and the answer was in due time: India, Egypt, Nigeria, and so on.

The rebels did indeed set headlines for men and women in those far-flung places: and the Soviet revolutionary V. I. Lenin had predicted as much when he wrote in 1914 that a blow against the British Empire in Ireland was of 'a hundred times more significance than a blow of equal weight in Asia or in Africa'.[6] English socialists were inclined to the rather patronizing belief that freedom could only be won by the colonies *after* they had gained power in the mother country. It never struck them that the fastest advances towards modernization might come from the periphery. But in 1916, along with the Irish insurrection, came attempts at rebellion in French Annam and the German Cameroons. The Irish were, if anything, ahead of their time, as Lenin later remarked: 'The misfortune of the Irish is that they rose prematurely, when the European revolt of the proletariat had not yet matured'. The world-historical events which might thereby have ensued have been spelled out by Conor Cruise O'Brien: had the rebels waited until 1918, when the country was united against the threat of conscription, a rising then with mass support would have called forth a British reign of terror, with the inevitable consequence of mutinies by Irish troops on the western front. By then, as a matter of fact, mass mutiny had taken Russia right out of the war, and the morale of both British and French armies was very low: so it would at least have been a possibility that the European ruling order might have collapsed.[7] James Connolly had foretold that 'a pin in the hands of a child could pierce the heart of a giant'. In the event, though the European order remained intact, the global order of British imperialism did not: those members of the British cabinet who saw the long-term implications for places like India and Egypt had their fears confirmed.

With hindsight, it is easy to see the 1916 rebels as an early instance of a decolonizing élite, and to advance the now-familiar analysis of economic frustrations and curtailed career opportunities which made the colony a factory of grievances. Modern educational reforms had produced a *cadre* of native intellectuals, not all of whom, by any means, could be drawn into the work of empire: but they also threw up new kinds of official, half-ashamed of the force by which they ruled. These self-doubts were sometimes visible to their more astute and restive subjects, and this had the effect of encouraging rather than mollifying rebels, who won more and more influential converts like Roger Casement and Erskine Childers over from the imperial side.[8] On Easter Monday 1916, when the rebels struck, the highest-ranking British officer on duty was an adjutant and the routine guards at the General Post Office had rifles but no ammunition.

Critics of the 'irrationalism' of the 1916 leaders point to the relative prosperity of Ireland during the years of the Great War, when high food prices caused large sections of the economy to boom. This is to forget, however, that revolution more often comes not in the darkest days of oppression so much as at a time when people have the luxury of being able to stand back a moment from their own condition and make a shrewd assessment of it. The leaders of the Easter Rebellion were many of them well-to-do: it would be hard to assign a strictly economic motive to the involvement of a headmaster such as Pearse, a university don like MacDonagh, or a son of Count Plunkett. Nonetheless, the ordinary Dubliners who marched behind them had known the consequences of dire recession in a city of chronic unemployment, and for them the high food prices were yet another outrage. The grievances of many rebels *were* economic and, as always, such men and women were glad to find leaders who could give them a spiritual and moral explanation. The frustrations of *all* the fighters were cultural: they wanted a land in which Gaelic traditions would be fully honoured. On that point, also, George Russell was an astute guide: just a year after the Rising, he accounted for its significance to still-baffled officials. Empires, he complained, destroy native culture, achieving 'the substitution therefore of a culture which has its value mainly for the people who created it, but is as alien to our race as the mood of the scientist is to the artist or poet'.[9]

Despite his cheerful pragmatism as a shaper of the agricultural co-operative movement, Russell could never cast the Rising in simply economistic terms: to him it was exactly the reverse, a plea for spirit as against dull matter, for imagination against empiricism (which to him seemed but a synonym for imperialism). The energy of life was its desire for expression: but the forms proffered by England, however well-intended, just did not fit. There is remarkably little anti-English sentiment in the writings of the Easter rebels for all that. Many of them revered particular English poets – Pearse admired and even imitated Wordsworth; MacDonagh wrote a fine thesis on Thomas Campion and devoted his very last class at University College Dublin to the virtues of Jane Austen, before marching out to prepare for insurrection; and Joseph Plunkett learned much from Francis Thompson. What they rejected was not England but the British imperial system, which denied expressive freedom to its colonial subjects. It was for this reason that Yeats said that 'no Irish voice has been lifted up in praise of that Imperialism which is . . . but a more painted and flaunting materialism; because Ireland has taken sides for ever with the poor in spirit who shall inherit the earth'.[10]

The 1916 leaders have often been accused of glorifying violence but, apart from one notorious speech by Pearse, they must have been the gentlest revolutionaries in modern history. They rose in the conviction that further involvement by Irish people in the Great War would lead to far more bloodshed than their Rising, which they hoped would take Ireland out of the war altogether. The British saw their action as treachery and shot its leaders as casually as they shot daily deserters on the western front. It took George Bernard Shaw to remind them that they should, under international law, have treated the men as prisoners-of-war: 'an Irishman resorting to arms to achieve the independence of his country is doing only what Englishmen will do if it be their misfortune to be invaded and conquered by the Germans'.[11] By the time he had written that, sixteen men were executed: and Yeats captured the new mood:

> O but we talked at large before
> The sixteen men were shot,
> But who can talk of give and take,
> What should be and what not
> While those dead men are loitering there
> To stir the boiling pot?
>
> You say that we should still the land
> Till Germany's overcome;
> But who is there to argue that
> Now Pearse is deaf and dumb?
> And is their logic to outweigh
> MacDonagh's bony thumb?[12]

To the British this Rising among a people who had not even experienced compulsory conscription seemed utterly inexplicable. To those Irish writers who sought to account for it in artistic terms, it appeared at first to be indescribable in any available language. This was initially a problem for the rebels themselves: how to express the unknown in terms of the known? MacDonagh and Plunkett's studies of mystic authors like Tauler take on an extra significance in this light, as if both men were hoping to find in the mystic's texts a solution to the technical problem. Indeed, MacDonagh wrote in *The Irish Review* of the challenge confronting 'the mystic who has to express in terms of sense and wit the things of God that are made known to him in no language'.[13] The rebels, likewise, sought a dream of which they could not directly speak: they could only speak of having sought it. The invention that was the Irish Republic was initially visible only to those who were the agents of freedom glimpsed as an abstract vision before it could be realized in history. In his poem 'The Fool', Pearse contemplated a point from which all outlines of the republic would become visible:

> O wise men, riddle me this: what if the dream come true?
> What if the dream come true? and if millions unborn shall dwell
> In the house that I shaped in my heart, the noble house of my
>   thought?[14]

From that vantage-point, many texts by Wilde, Shaw, Yeats, Synge and dozens of others might be seen to have represented, years earlier, a complex of ideas which found their fullest expression in the Rising of 1916. Yeats was the first knowingly to divine that connection when he told the young George Russell: 'absorb Ireland and her tragedy and you will be the poet of the people, perhaps the poet of a new insurrection'.[15] Ironically, in the event, Yeats himself filled the role which he had reserved for his friend. His play *Cathleen Ní Houlihan* (1902) cast the beautiful nationalist Maud Gonne in the part of a withered hag who would only walk again like a radiant young queen if young men were willing to kill and die for her. To the republican insurrectionist P. S. O'Hegarty, the drama became at once 'a sort of sacrament', to the rebel Countess Markievicz 'a kind of gospel'.[16] The Rising, when it came, was therefore seen by many as a foredoomed classical tragedy, whose *dénouement* was both inevitable and unpredictable, prophesied and yet surprising. Though it remained mysterious to many, the event was long in the gestation.

Year one of the revolutionists' calendar was 1893, because it marked the foundation of the Gaelic League. Even more striking than this, however, was the aura of the 1890s which clung to the characters caught up in the crisis, for many had been impressionable adolescents in the aesthetic decade. The rebels, Wilde-like, opted to invest their genius in their life and only their talent in their work, for they offered their lives to the public as works of art. Seeing themselves as martyrs for beauty, they aestheticized their sacrifice. Most of all, they followed the gospel which asserted 'the triumph of failure', the notion that whoever lost his life would save it. This idea underlies Thomas MacDonagh's play *When the Dawn is Come* and Pearse's *The Singer*, whose hero says:

One man can free a people as one Man redeemed the world. I will take no pike. I will go into the battle with bare hands. I will stand up before the Gall as Christ hung naked before men on the tree![17]

Equally, Joseph Plunkett's poem 'The Little Black Rose Shall be Red at Last' reworks the bardic image of Ireland as *róisín dubh* (dark róisín) into a nineties-ish mode:

Because we share our sorrows and our joys
And all your dear and intimate thoughts are mine
We shall not fear the trumpets and the noise
Of battle, for we know our dreams divine,
And when my heart is pillowed on your heart
And ebb and flowing of their passionate flood
Shall beat in concord love through every part
Of brain and body – when at last the blood
O'er leaps the final barrier to find
Only one source wherein to spend its strength
And we two lovers, long but one in mind
And soul, are made one only flesh at length;
Praise God, if this my blood fulfils the doom
When you, dark rose, shall redden into bloom.[18]

Here the Gaelic conceit of a ruler married to the land, whose relation is mediated by the poet, is replaced by the image of a poet whose body bleeds into the earth. This sexual congress will restore new life even though he dies, like the victim of a fertility rite, in the act. In his devotion to the Romantic Image which at once discloses and withholds its meanings, Plunkett provided yet another example of the age's penchant for the half-said thing, the symbol radiant with partially-articulated possibility.

The challenge of using the known to hint at the unknowable would eventually strike Yeats, the most articulate of all the poets of the nineties, as the artistic problem posed by revolution. It is the question broached in his play *The Resurrection*: 'What if there is always something that lies outside knowledge, outside order? What if at the moment when knowledge and order seem complete that something appears?'[19] That question, or a version of it, is embedded in many of Yeats's most visionary poems and plays: he is at his bravest and most vulnerable whenever he seeks to welcome the 'rough beast' of the unknowable future, without recourse to the props of the past for help or support.

The Easter rebels are sometimes depicted as martyrs to a text like *Cathleen Ní Houlihan*, but rather than reduce the living to a dead textuality, Yeats at his most daring asserts the power of texts to come to life. As a poet, he invents an ideal Ireland in his imagination, falls deeply in love with its form and proceeds to breathe it, Pygmalion-like, into being. It is hard, even now, to do full justice to the audacity of that enterprise.

The odds against it were massive. Karl Marx had complained of the lamentable tendency of persons on the brink of innovation to reduce history to costume drama by modelling themselves on some ancient Roman or Greek analogy, with the result that ghosts invariably appeared and stole their revolution. This was the mistake of all previous uprisings: to have presented themselves as *revivals*, so that the gesture of revolt could not be seen as such. Oscar Wilde's theatre had suggested that the self was plastic and that it could show a people how to refuse their assigned place and instead assume a better one. Its ultimate lesson, however, was that the imitation of any model, no matter how exalted, was slavery: the real challenge was to create a new, unprecedented self. One historian of culture has stated the problem very well:

Rebellions in *moeurs*, in manners broadly conceived, fail because they are insufficiently radical in terms of culture. It is still the creation of a believable mode of personality which is the object of cultural revolt, and, as such, the revolt is still chained to the bourgeois culture it seeks to overturn.[20]

The adoption of a pose was one step: what the second was might soon become more clear. The first stage demanded the violation of proprieties and the wearing of exotic clothes, but the second would move beyond that reactive affectation to an account of how a renovated consciousness might live. Such freedom had no precedent, except perhaps in the Thermidorean first years of revolutionary France, where the streets 'were to be places without masks' and where 'liberty was no longer expressed concretely in uniforms: now there appeared an idea of liberty in dress which would give the body free movement'. In the century after Thermidor, that barely-glimpsed freedom had been lost, but the experimental theatre of the 1890s, led by Wilde and Yeats, 'created an expression for the body which went beyond the terms of deviance and conformity' and which contrasted utterly with the restrictive costume of the streets. 'People turned to the theatre to solve the problematics of the street', writes Richard Sennett, 'to find images of spontaneity'.[21] Ordinary people, having lost belief in their own expressive powers, turned to artists and actors to do what they could not, and to teach them accordingly how to repossess their own emotions.

Whereas O'Connell's rapport with the people had offered a model for artists to emulate, now the artists were to be heroic exemplars for the politicians: but this was to involve no slavish imitation of external qualities. Yeats sought not to inspire imitation in others, preferring to teach them to become themselves: 'we move others, not because we have understood or thought about those others, but because all life has the same root'.[22] He saw that every Irish life was a ruin among whose debris might be discovered what this or that person ought to have been. His plays do not tell onlookers to be like Cuchulain, but to invent themselves: 'The greatest art symbolizes not those things that we have observed so much as those things that we have experienced, and when the imaginary saint or lover or hero moves us most deeply, it is the moment when he awakens within us for an instant our own heroism, our own sanctity, our own desire'.[23]

This was exactly the achievement of the 1916 rebels, who staged the Rising as street theatre and were justly celebrated in metaphors of drama by Yeats. All the mirrors for magistrates of ancient England had taught that 'to be fit to govern others we must be able to govern ourselves': and the rebels had done just that. During Easter Week's performance, they were enabled both to show feeling and to control it: and so, in the eyes of their audience, both Irish and international, they had literally governed themselves. This ultimately invested them with a power far greater than their power to shock. Yeats had always equated heroism with self-conquest, that ability of great ones under pressure to express some emotions while battening down still others held in reserve. This was the same tragic dignity admired in the rebel leaders by the English officer who presided over their execution. By such example, these leaders and their men urged all Ireland to do likewise, to conquer and so to express selves, to recover the literal meaning of the words *sinn féin*.

If there was an element of play-acting involved in the Rising, then that is best understood in existential terms. 'As soon as man conceives himself free, and determines to use that freedom', wrote Jean-Paul Sartre decades later, 'then his work takes on the character of play'.[24] The rebels' play was staged to gather an Irish audience and challenge an English one. In that sense, the Rising was a continuation of what had begun in the national theatre, which had among its audience 'almost everybody who was making opinion in Ireland'.[25] The early plays of the Abbey Theatre had taught that the conditions of life are open: the theatre can indeed be a place frequented by the 'low' as they study alternative possibilities for themselves, including ways in which they might usurp their masters. Though it seemed to conspire with carnivalesque disorder, the playhouse also provided the necessary antidote, for it encouraged a randomly-gathered crowd to sense its growing, cohesive power. Yeats often liked to quote Victor Hugo: 'in the theatre a mob becomes a people'. Indeed, the theory of tragedy propounded by Yeats – as the moment when casual differences between individuals are put aside for a communal solidarity of feeling – well captures that moment. So it was fitting that the printing press on which the Proclamation of the Republic was done should have been hidden in the Abbey Theatre. Many of the Rising's leaders had been initiated in theatrical methods by the Abbey: no previous Irish insurrection had been mounted in such avowedly theatrical terms. One of the first to fall was Sean Connolly, an actor with the company whom Yeats would recall in a late poem:

> Come gather round me, players all:
> Come praise Nineteen-Sixteen,
> Those from the pit and gallery
> Or from the painted scene
> That fought in the Post Office
> Or round the City Hall,
> Praise every man that came again,
> Praise every man that fell.
>
> *From mountain to mountain ride the fierce horsemen.*
>
> Who was the first man shot that day?
> The player Connolly
> Close to the City Hall he died;
> Carriage and voice had he;

> He lacked those years that go with skill,
> But later might have been
> A famous, a brilliant figure
> Before the painted scene
>
> *From mountain to mountain ride the fierce horsemen.*[26]

Every man and woman had been assigned a part in life: for Yeats, the question was not whether it was a good or bad one – rather it was whether he or she played it well. The actor could choose to resign the part, or to improvise as best he could in the absence of a clear set of instructions: however creative that improvisation, it would be based on a life-script appropriate to the actor's time and condition. Yeats, like Pearse, believed that each generation was set its own task and that theirs must fulfil a mission to renovate Irish consciousness. This destiny weighed all the more heavily on men and women who were still young when the century turned. To have embarked on life as the twentieth century began must have filled them with a sense of a divinely-ordained task. Pearse's own philosophy of Irish history was cyclical: the 1916 Proclamation noted that six times in the previous three centuries national rights had been asserted in arms. Some generations had surpassed others and carried out their life-task, but a generation which shirked the task would condemn itself to a shameful old age.

This complex of ideas – close enough to those propagated by Ortega Y Gasset in Spain at that period[27] – reflected a sharpened notion of *generation*, which emerged among European intellectuals after the turn of the century. This was partly a result of Freud's influential Oedipal theories, and even more a consequence of the pace of social change which was leaving the old and young no common ground on which to meet. Writers no longer seemed to address society as a whole: instead they fastened onto immediate contemporaries. It would be hard to find a better explanation of the styles of address adopted by Pearse, who repeatedly spoke to and for 'this generation', men and women in their twenties and thirties who had been to school in the Gaelic League. Left all but leaderless after the fall of Parnell, that generation had no choice but to father itself. It set out to define a new code, in the knowledge that if it did not achieve freedom, it would at least have provided its basis, and have left to successors a philosophy and a set of actions against which the next generation could define itself. Only if such were not done could the men and women of 1916 be deemed to have failed.

Such a view of history, though often denounced as fatalistic, has much in common with the Marxist definition of freedom as the conscious recognition of necessity, and it was dramatized, with his usual brilliance, by Yeats in *The Dreaming of the Bones*. Here, a rebel soldier escapes from the Post Office in 1916 and flees to the west, where he encounters the ghosts of Diarmuid and Dervorgilla who, it is alleged, brought the Norman occupiers to Ireland. They wish to consummate their illicit love in a kiss. Unfortunately, they cannot until they are forgiven by the soldier, and this is something which (despite the wishes of the audience) he cannot do. They are dead, of course, and he is living: though he might wish to set their troubled spirits free, he must accept his appointed part. There is no freedom but the freedom to weave the cloth of necessity unfolded by the musicians (the real protagonists) at the outset.[28]

Men may make their own histories, said Marx, but not under the circumstances which they might ideally have chosen: instead, they are confronted with the tradition of dead generations which weighs like a nightmare upon the brain of the living. How this works is interesting: when a crisis becomes absolute and a desperate man is compelled to choose the unknown, his act can never be his alone, for 'it takes place in circumstances directly found, given and transmitted from the past'.[29] The new act joins itself to the ghostly event: and the actors discover that their stage is filled with the spirits of buried men and dead heroes. These spectral appearances are conjured out of the anxieties which attend all acts of innovation: they offer themselves as known vessels into which the unknown quantities of the future may be poured. For it is a fact that every disruption of routine living for the sake of a new ideal is traumatic: 'every definite break with the past at once invites others and increases the strain upon everybody'.[30] To allay the fear of the unknown, even the most innovative may have to present it as the restoration of some past glory. As the French businessmen of 1789 portrayed themselves in the role of ancient Romans recovering democratic rights, so Pearse summoned Cuchulain to his side to validate his ideal – of a welfare state which would, so said the Proclamation, 'cherish all the children of the nation equally'. In reading out the Proclamation, as he stood before the Ionic pillars of the Post Office, to 'a few thin, perfunctory cheers',[31] Pearse was knowingly enforcing the classical analogies. He saw that in a traditionalist society, it is vitally necessary to gift-wrap the gospel of the future in the packaging of the past. This Connolly also did when he presented socialism as a return to the Celtic system whereby a chief held land in the common name of all the people. Joyce adopted a similar tactic when he concealed the subversive narrative of *Ulysses* beneath the cover of one of Europe's oldest stories, *The Odyssey*.

This is a further justification of the theatricality of the Easter rebellion: alas, it was ill-understood at the time, even by some of its more pragmatically-minded participants. Complaining that the events had 'the air of a Greek tragedy', Michael Collins sourly added: 'I do not think the Rising week was an appropriate time for the issue of memoranda couched in poetic phrases, nor of actions worked out in a similar fashion'.[32] Doubtless, as a volunteer, he was unimpressed by the choice of the Post Office as a military centre, since it left soldiers like himself exposed on all sides. As an act of dramatic symbolism, however, it was an inspired choice, since it cut across the main street of the capital city, paralyzing communications and forcing everyone to take notice. The selection of Easter Monday – when most British soldiers were on furlough at Fairyhouse Races – was not just a sound tactic, but another brilliant symbolization, since it reinforced Pearse's idea of the cyclical nature of history. Easter brought renewal, spring-time, new life to a dead landscape: and so it helped to justify and explain all previous abortive uprisings, for it wove them into a wider narrative, a myth of fall, death and glorious redemption.

It has become fashionable to portray the rebels as Catholic militants, because of the use of Easter symbolism. However, this is to read into their texts and actions a sectarianism which emerged only some time later, after the foundation of the Free State. The poetic imagery employed by Pearse and Plunkett was that of a generalized mystical Christianity rather than something specifically Catholic in overtone. In many ways, it took its cue from the Protestant notion of the 'life-task' which informed so much of the writing by soldiers of imperial Britain in the Great War. 'We cannot but be thankful that we were chosen, and not another generation, to do this work and pay this price'[33] was a refrain on the lips of the young volunteers who stood in line at recruiting offices with all the innocence of youths awaiting a great cricket match: and it was also the dominant idea of the Easter rebels. Such an attitude was possible only to a generation which had no first-hand experience of modern warfare with its mass graves.

Though British soldier-poets would soon know the hard realities and write anthems for doomed youth led to slaughter by callous age, the Irish case was different: the rebellion was short, its leaders (apart from de Valera) were shot, and so there was time for them to be glamorized in the long lull before the guerrilla war of independence began. Instead of a fearful revolution linked in the popular mind to a terror that devoured the revolutionary children, the Irish case was invoked by Pearse as an example of children devouring their own mother:

> Mise Éire
> Sine mé ná an Cailleach Béarra.
>
> Mór mo ghlóire
> Is mé do rug Cuchulain cróga.
>
> Mór mo náire,
> Mo chlann féin do dhíol a máthair.
>
> Mise Éire
> Uaigní mé ná an Cailleach Béarra.
>
> I am Ireland
> I am older than the Old Woman of Beare.
>
> Great my glory:
> I that bore Cuchulainn the valiant.
>
> Great my shame:
> My own children that sold their mother.
>
> I am Ireland:
> I am lonelier than the Old Woman of Beare.[34]

It was the death of the rebels, rather than that of their enemies, which would make a right rose tree, as Yeats retold:

> 'But where can we draw water',
> Said Pearse to Connolly,
> 'When all the wells are parched away?
> O plain as plain can be
> There's nothing but our own red blood
> Can make a right Rose Tree'.[35]

The imagery here is of the Liberty Tree, more Protestant than Catholic, with its roots in radical millenarian sects; and the notion that republican revolt is simply the political application of Protestant principles found sanction in the demeanour of the rebels. In the face of ecclesiastical condemnation, many simply bypassed the mandatory consultation with their confessors before rising: hence the prolonged sessions within the Post Office during which Pearse, Plunkett and Desmond FitzGerald filled lulls in combat with complex theological justifications of what they had done.[36] (The recital of rosaries might also be seen as a way of repudiating those ecclesiastics who said that the rebels were no longer Catholics.)

Pearse was a prototype of the revolutionary ascetic who renounces love, family ties and all sensual gratification: and it is this power over himself which gives the ascetic authority over others:

Fornocht a chonac thú,
aáille na háille,
is dhallas mo shúil
ar eagla go stánfainn.

Chualas do cheol,
a bhinne na binne,
is dhúnas mo chluas
ar eagla go gclisfinn.

Bhlaiseas do bhéal,
a mhilse na milse,
is chruas mo chroí
ar eagla mo mhillte.

Dhallas mo shúil,
is mo chluas do dhúnas;
chruas mo chroí
is mo mhian do mhúchas.

Thugas mo chúl
ar an aisling a chumas,
is ar an ród seo romham
m'aghaidh do thugas.

Thugas mo ghnúis
ar an ród seo romham,
ar an ngníomh a chím,
is ar an mbás a gheobhad.

Naked I saw thee,
O beauty of beauty,
And I blinded my eyes
For fear I should fail.

I heard thy music,
O melody of melody,
And I closed my ears
For fear I should falter.

I tasted thy mouth,
O sweetness of sweetness,
And I hardened my heart
For fear of my slaying.

I blinded my eyes,
And I closed my ears,
I hardened my heart
And I smothered my desire.

I turned my back
On the vision I had shaped,
And to this road before me
I turned my face.

I have turned my face
To this road before me,
To the deed that I see
And the death I shall die.[37]

In the *aisling* poems the gallant liberated the captive woman: in this instance, however, the hero-poet turns away from her. Like Plunkett, he will paradoxically liberate her only by dying, to prove his 'excess of love' (a phrase Pearse actually used, and which was repeated with an implication of moral accusation against the rebels in 'Easter 1916'). Such cold, marmoreal love is all that is possible to an ascetic who holds out to his followers something even better than victory – salvation. Pearse took Irish asceticism out of the monasteries and made it active in the political world: and his followers were repeatedly told that they were the elect, chosen for this redemptive task. The 'unprecedented inner loneliness' which assails all who wait for signs of divine election was endured by the rebel leaders in their theological debates.[38] Pearse, Plunkett, FitzGerald (and countless others, no doubt) were fast becoming their own priests.

None of this should seem in the least surprising. Modern revolutions have often been carried out by intellectuals who transmute the images and ideas of Christianity into a secular code. Marxism, insofar as it was a state religion, achieved much: but as a scientific theory of society, it would never have gone far. When Pearse called the people 'its own Messiah', he was simply repeating Rousseau's insistence that 'the voice of the people is, in fact, the voice of God'.[39] What made Pearse and his comrades rather different from other modern revolutionaries was that, in their utterances, the religious rhetoric was never occluded or buried, but remained visible and audible on the textual surface.

It will never be fully clear whether the resort to such language by insurrectionists is sincere or tactical: each case must be weighed on its merits. Christian imagery certainly helped to reassure hesitant well-wishers of the morality of the Irish rebels' actions: and, yet again, it allowed the materially-subordinate culture of Ireland to express its conviction of its spiritual superiority to England. Most of all, however, it permitted the rebels to embody the unknown in a language which had a high voltage for Irish people, especially for the poor. Conservative clericalist intellectuals were not slow to denounce such usage as blasphemous and distressing to ordinary Christians. The lawyer J. J. Horgan bluntly declared that the Rising was a sin and Pearse a heretic.[40] Yet what Pearse did was no different from what had been done by men like Yeats and Synge: he moved from faith in 'the kingdom of God' to faith in 'the kingdom of Ireland', employing the language of the former to launch his crusade for the latter. In effect, he equated patriotism with holiness. The revisionist historian and Jesuit, Francis Shaw, chose the fiftieth anniversary of the Rising to remark that 'objectively this equation of the patriot with Christ is in conflict with the whole Christian tradition, and, indeed, with the explicit teaching of Christ'.[41] It may indeed conflict with orthodox Catholicism: that, however, is not to say that it conflicts with Christianity as such, and many Protestant sects would have perfectly understood Pearse's equation of 'the people labouring, scourged, crowned with thorns, agonising and dying, to rise again immortal and impassible'[42] with the mystical body of Christ. If there is any substantive difference between the English revolutionaries of 1640 and the Irish insurgents of 1916, it is merely this: the English relied mainly on the Old Testament for their language, and the Irish on the New.

What troubled Horgan and Father Shaw in the 1916 writings was their unapologetic invocation of Wolfe Tone and, by extension, the 'godless' anti-Catholic rebels of the French Revolution. Father Shaw, citing clerical law, objected to Pearse's description of the Jacobin Tone as a prophet. There may indeed have been a calculated snub to ecclesiastical authority when Pearse wrote of being 'rebaptized in the Fenian faith', an organization which was itself under interdiction by the Catholic Church. However, most modern movements rapidly develop what has been called 'a secular equivalent of the church', often the primary system of education in decolonizing states, 'imbued with revolutionary and republican principles and content, and conducted by the secular equivalent of the priesthood',[43] i.e., teachers like Pearse.

Going even further back in history, a study of the art of the French Revolution would demonstrate a set of effects similar to those achieved by Pearse. David's famous painting of 'Marat Murdered in his Bath' explicitly linked the image to that of Christ in a *Pietà*, with the implication that the new martyr could fittingly replace the old.[44] There are two ways of viewing this manoeuvre. It might be seen as an attempt to extend and update a vibrant Christian tradition, to take a somewhat jaded form and animate it with real contemporary feeling; or it could be viewed as a subversive tactic, which converted the preceding Christian cult into an echo or parody of the more urgent and authentic contemporary image. With his synthesizing mind, Pearse saw an unbroken continuity from Cuchulain through Christ to Tone, and he would surely have preferred the first explanation, but there may have been among his comrades some – Connolly and MacDiarmada spring to mind – who favoured the second. The former usage could have been defended as retrieving Christian language from recent debased applications (as when English bishops blessed guns that went off to fight imperial wars); the latter might be seen as discrediting it entirely, once the latent content had emerged. The phase of self-invention followed hard upon the antiquarian phase, as the latent content of the revolution (a welfare state, a native republic) emerged from beneath its manifest symbols (Cuchulain, Jesus Christ).

The Edmund Burke who regarded revolution as a 'dramatic performance' and 'stage effect'[45] would have had little difficulty in making such a separation. Nor would he have been overly surprised at the difficulty which many students of 1916 have in separating the event from its mesh of defining texts. Many literary works, especially plays, had far greater an influence on the Rising than the event itself had on those like Sean O'Casey who came to write of it afterwards. There is a real sense in which *The Plough and the Stars* (1926) derives more from *On Baile's Strand* (1903, 1906) than from the Dublin streets: the notorious scene where Pearse's speechifying is juxtaposed against the prostitute Rosie Redmond plying her trade in a pub seems a deliberate reworking of Yeats's play, in which a posturing Cuchulain, at war with the waves, seems utterly irrelevant to the needs of a hungry fool and a blind beggar. But, no sooner has that been said than one is reminded that *On Baile's Strand* may have had far more effect on the Rising itself: after all, its scene where the proletarians mimic the antics of a self-defeating royalty seems an anticipatory version of the revolution (as well as a clear borrowing of the by-play of Hal and Falstaff in Shakespeare's *Henry IV(1)*). What is at issue here is a dialectical tension between an action and its representation, a tension most wittily captured in lines from a recent novel of the Northern Ireland conflict:

> 'But it is not like 1916.'
> 'It wasn't like 1916 in 1916.'
> There was a long silence.[46]

The whole event has been remorselessly textualized: for it – more than any of its individual protagonists – became an instantaneous martyr to literature.

YEATS AND WAR

JACQUELINE GENET

The powerful influence of history has long been a defining feature of Irish culture. Two versions of Irish history, a colonial and a native, compete with each other and the poet is caught between them. In Ireland, literature arises out of the attempt at resolution. This union of history and poetry in the quest for national identity and this tension created by two histories are present in Yeats's work. He is aware of division and exploits it for poetic purposes. His conception of war is founded on an antinomy. It is 'a terrible beauty':[1] 'terrible' because war means violence, death, bloodshed and therefore hatred, 'beauty' because it also involves heroism and possible rebirth. In this respect war can have an attraction for the poet so that war, like the sexual act, is a mixture of hatred and love. This paradoxical alliance is found in the mythic war of Troy, the archetype of wars in Yeats's poetical imagination, and is reflected in his conception of history – a conception conditioned not just by Irish conflicts but also by external wars such as the First World War, the Russian Civil War and the coming of the Second World War.

THE GREAT WAR

Ireland was only marginally involved in the Great War of 1914–18. Like so much else in this period Irish responses, first to the threat and then to the reality of the war, were contextualized within the nationalist debate. So, for many, the events of 1914–18 were one more occasion on which to demonstrate either commitment to, or rejection of, the Union with Great Britain. In the north, the Ulster Volunteers supported the English war effort by volunteering in large numbers for active service. In the south, all segments of the nationalist movement regarded the war as an English problem, a sideshow that might, as the banner in front of Liberty Hall announced, become 'Ireland's opportunity' for furthering independence. As a result, at least in the south, conscription was opposed, and the English government felt it unwise to implement a draft. Despite this opposition, many Irishmen from the south did in fact volunteer to fight although their numbers never approached those of the volunteers from Ulster, and their sympathies were not necessarily Unionist.

There is not much commentary on the First World War in Yeats's works. Though aware of its importance, he rarely mentions it. In 'Modern Poetry: a Broadcast', he says, 'established things were shaken by the Great War'[2] but his mood is one of almost total detachment. In response to a request passed on by Henry James to contribute to a collection of war poems, he sent one which originally opened:

> I think it better that at times like these
> We poets keep our mouths shut; for in truth
> We have no gift to set a statesman right.

In a covering letter he said this was the only thing he intended to write about the war and he proposed emulating the seven sleepers of Ephesus 'till bloody frivolity is over'.[3] On the outbreak of the war, Maud Gonne had written to him, 'You seemed to have escaped the obsession of this war – I cannot'.[4] In 1918, there was a threat that Britain might apply conscription to Ireland and Yeats wrote to Lord Haldane, giving his opinion that this would unwisely re-motivate revolutionary sentiment. Finally conscription was not attempted. Later his two Casement ballads poured angry scorn on the bad faith of England's rulers during the First World War. They conveyed a violent anglophobia and were much appreciated by those who had been his political enemies – de Valera's party. Yeats was publicly thanked.

THE 1917 RUSSIAN REVOLUTION

Yeats watched the repercussions of international events in Ireland and, in particular, of the 1917 Russian Revolution. England was involved in intervention to suppress the Bolshevik régime in Russia and Yeats feared that from sheer determination to oppose England Ireland might take the Bolshevik side. It has been said that the 'rough beast' of 'The Second Coming' could be Bolshevism called up by the 1917 Russian Revolution, two years old when the poem was written, and it is clear from the early manuscript drafts that Yeats had the anarchic state of eastern Europe in the aftermath of the First World War very much in mind. Stallworthy and Torchiana, who examined the early drafts, found references to the German army's march into Russia and to the murder by the Bolsheviks of the Tsar and his family. For Yeats, a strong opponent of Communism, this was the most potent instance of the 'mere anarchy' which was drowning the old imperial powers in a 'blood-dimmed tide'. In 'The Second Coming'

> Turning and turning in the widening gyre
> The falcon cannot hear the falconer

is a fine metaphor for what happens when the stable order of government breaks down. In normal times, the civil power (the falconer) is firmly in control of the weapons of force (the falcon). In time of war the military condition becomes a law, the falcon no longer responding to the falconer's call. It is difficult to believe however that, as the poem neared its final version, Yeats did not also have events nearer home in mind, seeing events in Ireland as in some way a foretaste of what all Europe was to experience some twenty years later.

THE SECOND WORLD WAR: THE FASCIST ATTRACTION

In the meantime, Yeats's political ideas became more and more reactionary. To Olivia Shakespear he wrote in May 1922, 'Out of all this murder and rapine will come not a demagogic but an authoritative Government'[5] and to Grierson in November of the same year: 'We are preparing here, behind our screen of bombs and smoke, a return to conservative politics as elsewhere in Europe . . . The Ireland that reacts from the present disorder is turning its eyes towards individualist Italy'[6] – or as we may understand it, fascist Italy (this letter was written just after Mussolini's march on Rome). He did not remain indifferent to the political turning of 1932 when de Valera triumphed at the elections. A good number of Cosgrave's supporters who did not accept their electoral defeat organized a movement on the fascist pattern, in the hope of regaining power. These were the Blue Shirts of General O'Duffy. Yeats became convinced that the sacrifices which permitted the formation of the free state of Ireland had been wasted; the upper classes now saw in Ireland but a place for sport, and as to the rest of the population, it was 'drowned in religious and political fanaticism'. The government was impotent; it was the reign of the mob and: 'If that reign is not broken our public life will move from violence to violence, or from violence to

apathy'.[7] *On the Boiler* and his correspondence well reflect his
sympathy for fascism. To Olivia Shakespear, he wrote on July 13th
1933: 'A Fascist opposition is forming behind the scenes to be
ready should some tragic situation develop. I find myself
constantly urging the despotic rule of the educated classes as the
only end to our troubles'.[8] However, six months later, he seemed
to have realized his mistake and he changed the first version of his
songs 'Three Songs to the same tune', initially composed for the
movement, 'that no party might sing them'.[9] The final disappointment that the fascist movement brought to him is reflected in
'Church and State'. Disillusioned, he proclaimed his renunciation
of politics: 'Do not try to make a politician of me, even in Ireland I
shall never I think be that again – As my sense of reality deepens,
and I think it does with age, my horror at the cruelty of
governments grows greater . . . Communist, fascist, nationalist,
clerical, anti-clerical, are all responsible according to the number
of their victims'.[10] That he was aware of his error is made clear by
his attitude at the time of the writers' congress in Madrid in 1937.
In his autobiography, Pablo Neruda testifies to the fact that Yeats
wrote to him expressing his regret at being unable, for reasons of
health, to attend this meeting which was held at the height of the
Spanish Civil War.

This is the context in which he foresaw the coming of the
Second World War. On April 8th 1936, he wrote to Ethel Mannin:
'If you have my poems by you, look up a poem called "The
Second Coming". It was written some sixteen or seventeen years
ago, and foretold what is happening' and he added, 'every nerve
trembles with horror at what is happening in Europe, "the
ceremony of innocence is drowned"'.[11] The poem 'Politics'
published in January 1939, says of the fears of the 'travelled man',
and the 'politician' only that: '. . . maybe what they say is true / Of
war and war's alarms', and *On The Boiler* makes it clear that Yeats
would have endorsed firmly de Valera's action in declaring Irish
neutrality and preparing to defend Ireland against all comers. His
chief concern remained with the Irish situation, with the wars
inside Ireland, the Easter Rising, the War of Independence and the
Civil War.

IRISH NATIONALISM: A LIFE-TIME CHOICE

Yeats, at an early age, embraced Irish nationalism and maintained
his allegiance to it in its multifarious forms for the rest of his life.
As a young boy lost in a London school, he became aware of his

nationality. The history taught him was not his own. Impatiently he looked forward to his holidays in Sligo where he immersed himself in those legends which, with nationalist enthusiasm, he was to revive. The acquaintance of O'Leary and Maud Gonne, and an historic event – Parnell's death – acted as catalysts in distinctive ways. The old Fenian, John O'Leary, had a twofold passion: politics and literature; and his political doctrine, nourished by five years in an English prison and fifteen in exile, echoed Wolfe Tone's theory: 'England's difficulty is Ireland's opportunity'. Yet he disagreed that the end should justify the means and Yeats was happy to reiterate his warning: 'There are things no man should do, even to save a nation'. Through him, however, he met Maud Gonne. Committed to the struggle against England, she exhorted Yeats to action. He accompanied her on her visits to the Irishmen of England and Scotland, listening to her impassioned speeches. If Maud urged him to act, Parnell's death inspired him to write. Parnell's affair contributed to turn away a great many minds from politics, to the profit of literature. In his speech delivered in Stockholm in 1925, Yeats stated: 'The modern literature of Ireland, and indeed all that stir of thought which prepared for the Anglo-Irish war, began when Parnell fell from power in 1891. A disillusioned and embittered Ireland turned from parliamentary politics'.[12]

HOW DID YEATS UNDERSTAND NATIONALISM?

The main task of nationalism is to give back to the country its genuine personality; in 1893, Yeats published *The Celtic Twilight*, contributing to the movement towards the Irish Literary Revival. The play *The Countess Cathleen* was written in order to persuade Maud Gonne, to whom he intended to give the leading part, of his own ability to participate, through his writings, in the movement towards national independence. Cathleen is the symbol of Ireland. She comes to the help of the starving people, in the same way as Maud who endeavoured to help the peasants of Donegal. As to *Cathleen Ni Houlihan*, also written for Maud, in 1902, it is undoubtedly one of the most significant contributions to the nationalist movement and it deeply impressed the young Padraic Pearse. One perceives the poet's anxiety, his sense of responsibility, together with a questioning of the value of a life entirely devoted to a political cause.

Yeats's nationalism, even in his most fervent periods, was not free from ambiguity. After the nationalist commitment, tinged with idealism, there followed a bitter disengagement. But he clearly declared his anglophobia all through his life. 'May the devil take King George!', is the original refrain of a poem which he first intended to include in the Crazy Jane series. He declared to Dorothy Wellesley, his English confidante in his last years: 'Your nation is nothing. It is only a stuffed lion'.[13] But at the same time he admitted his debt towards England. A passage from 'A General Introduction for my Work' (1937) clearly conveys his feelings: 'There are moments when hatred poisons my life and I accuse myself of effeminacy because I have not given it adequate expression'.[14] His hatred, he explains, was justified by the English persecutions: 'No people, Lecky said at the opening of his *Ireland in the Eighteenth Century*, have undergone greater persecution, nor did that persecution altogether cease up to our own day'. And yet he adds: 'I remind myself that ... I owe my soul to Shakespeare, to Spenser and to Blake, perhaps to William Morris, and to the English language in which I think, speak and write, that everything I love has come to me through English, my hatred tortures me with love, my love with hate ... This is Irish hatred and solitude ...' In a letter to Dorothy Wellesley, he repeats: 'How can I hate England, owing what I do to Shakespeare, Blake and Morris? England is the only country I cannot hate'.[15]

EASTER 1916

Nothing underlines more strikingly where Yeats's true nationality lay than the contrast between his almost ironic detachment from Britain at war and his reaction to the outbreak of fighting in Ireland with the Rising of 1916. While his response was not single-minded, he realized with the intuition of a great poet that Ireland could never be the same again. The Easter Rising was to prove the watershed of modern Irish history. When the Republic was declared on the steps of the General Post Office on April 17, 1916, it was done 'in the name of God and of the dead generations from which she (Ireland) receives her old tradition of nationhood.' Easter 1916 surprised him, like the majority of his fellow-men. It was an historical phenomenon from which he had been excluded. Probably he was slightly hurt that his advice should not have been taken, but the desperate heroism of the insurgents struck him deeply. We find him writing from his London club to Lady Gregory two weeks after the event: 'The Dublin tragedy has been a great sorrow and anxiety ... I had no idea that any public event could so deeply move me'.[16] The horror of the executions raised a general outcry. Yeats wrote to John Quinn in New York: 'We have lost the ablest and most fine-natured of our young men. A world seems to have been swept away'.[17]

The Poem 'Easter 1916' is a generous recantation of 'September 1913' in which 'Romantic Ireland' seemed to be dead. The personal quality of the poem is remarkable, in that the reader's access to the leaders of the Rising is mediated through their relationship with the poet: 'I have met them'. Most of the leaders' names were barely known to the general public, but there were several among those imprisoned or executed whom Yeats had known or been involved with personally. Pearse, MacDonagh, MacBride and Connolly had been shot after summary courts-martial, and Constance Markiewicz condemned to life imprisonment. His countrymen's heroism proved that he had misjudged them. In 'Easter 1916' he praised the leading figures of the Rising for becoming individuals as they emerged from the masses through their action. Before the Rising they had no individual identity as the use of pronouns shows: 'I have met them at close of day'. It was the futile comedy of life in which 'polite meaningless words' were exchanged. However, because of the Rising, 'All changed, changed utterly: / A terrible beauty is born.' This paradoxical refrain sums up his ideas. Forsaking comedy, the participants in the Rising had become involved in an attempt to modify the world. In the second section, Yeats still maintains the use of pronouns, but he provides sufficient detail for the reader familiar with the Rising to recognize Markiewicz, Pearse, MacDonagh and MacBride. Given the latter's marriage to and treatment of Maud Gonne, praising him posed particular problems for Yeats but, after the listing of MacBride's faults, there is an acknowledgement that 'he, too, has resigned his part / In the casual comedy'. In the eight sentences of the final stanza four are declarative while four are interrogative, with the most important question placed in the centre of the stanza. 'Was it needless death after all?' Most readers accept this line as simply a rhetorical question, but for Yeats the question was much more literal than that as he reflects when he writes in the next line: 'For England may keep faith / For all that is done and said'. Home Rule, which the Rising had as its objective, had been passed by Parliament; it had simply been suspended because of the war. Many assumed that England was simply looking for a way to retract Home Rule but Yeats dares to point out that, if England keeps its word, then the deaths were needless. However, despite his doubts about and reactions to the Rising, the British reaction – executing the leaders – horrifies him:

> I write it out in a verse –
> MacDonagh and MacBride
> And Connolly and Pearse
> Now and in time to be, . . .
> Are changed, changed utterly:
> A terrible beauty is born. ('Easter 1916')

Finally, he uses the names of the heroes of the Rising, rather than pronouns, to elevate them to the status of individuals. It is through their action that change has come over the world. In death, each of these men has found his real personality: 'Tel qu'en lui-même enfin, l'éternité le change'. So from anonymous beings, the participants in the Rising are raised to the level of individuals, then to that of heroes and finally of mythic creatures. In 'The Statues' Pearse will be assimilated to the demi-god Cuchulain: 'When Pearse summoned Cuchulain to his side, / What stalked through the Post Office?'

If Yeats admires their courage, he does not necessarily approve of their action. They have certainly sacrificed their lives to an ideal, but a fixed idea which hardens the heart is baneful. Yeats rejects political fanaticism as contrary to the perpetual renewal of a genuine life. This, the heroes of the Rising, who set themselves apart from the stream of life, did not understand. The changeless stone represents their inflexible sense of purpose:

> Hearts with one purpose alone
> Through summer and winter seem
> Enchanted to a stone
> To trouble the living stream. ('Easter 1916')

Yeats dreads this petrification of the heart: 'The stone's in the midst of all' or, again, 'Too long a sacrifice / Can make a stone of the heart'. (Subsequently, the image of the stone recurs in his political poems. The stone is one of those 'masterful images' mentioned in 'The Circus Animals' Desertion', which are used by the lyric poet to embody his themes.) At the end of 'Easter 1916' he does try to solve the contradiction between the change in Ireland and in the heroes' personalities on one side, and their constant aim on the other. They have changed because they have remained faithful to a cause – paradoxically because they have not changed. Doubt remains, adding to the ambiguity of the poem. Yeats is torn between his admiration for the greatness of the sacrifice and his condemnation of a life devoted to a political cause leading to violence and bloodshed. If death was perhaps useless, it was yet the result of an heroic dream, born of the love of Ireland, which has created this miracle of metamorphosis through sacrifice.

In his letter to John Quinn, Yeats continued: 'I keep going over the past in my mind and wondering if I could have done anything to turn those young men in some other direction'.[18] It was a thought that was to trouble him at the end of his life:

> I lie awake night after night
> And never get the answers right.
> Did that play of mine send out
> Certain men the English shot? ('The Man and the Echo')

Other poems pursue the mood of 'Easter 1916' in admiring the heroes' dedication and expressing bitter indignation at the British executions after the surrender. 'Sixteen Dead Men' takes up the theme of the change which has occurred in Ireland since the death of these sixteen men whom, in the last stanza, he associates with the heroes of Romantic Ireland. 'The Rose-Tree' mixes popular and symbolic elements. Using the form of the ballad, Yeats has Pearse insist that blood sacrifice is necessary to produce a 'right' rose-tree. 'On a Political Prisoner' again condemns abstract ideas, chiefly in women whose youth and beauty they ruin, as happened to Constance Markiewicz. Fanaticism had driven her mind until it had become 'a bitter, an abstract thing'.

The play, *The Dreaming of the Bones*, on which Yeats worked during 1917, is set just after the Rising. A young man, who has escaped from the Post Office, is found wandering on the Clare cliffs, awaiting an Aran fisherman's boat which will bring him to safety. He encounters an unhappy pair who prove in the dénouement to be the spirits of Diarmuid and Dervorgilla, names accursed in Irish tradition as those who first brought the Normans to Ireland. Their spirits can find rest only when one of the Irish race can forgive them. The young man weakens for a moment as he hears their plight, then comes the answer: 'O never, never / Shall Diarmuid and Dervorgilla be forgiven'.[19] The political message is that of adamant nationalism.

THE WAR OF INDEPENDENCE

When the Irish members met in Dublin in January 1919 and declared themselves the first Dail or parliament of an independent Irish state, when a provisional government was constituted with de Valera as president, the British did not recognize their claims. The first engagement of guerrilla war took place at Soloheadbeag on the day of the opening of the Dail and spread gradually over the whole country. Yeats clearly anticipated this war of independence. In May, 1918 he was planning to give a lecture in Dublin on war poetry, English and Irish, but on reflection he postponed this, saying: 'Times are too dangerous for me to encourage men to risks I am not prepared to share or approve'.[20] In a speech at The Oxford Union in 1921 he took the side of Sinn Fein against the Black and Tans. His letters recounted scenes of atrocity and became passionately concerned. In April, 1922 he described the situation to Olivia Shakespear in the following terms: 'All we can see from our windows (he was then staying at Thoor Ballylee) is beautiful and quiet and has been so; yet two miles off near Coole, which is close to a main-road, the Black and Tans flogged young men and then tied them to their lorries by the heels and dragged them along the road till their bodies were torn in pieces. I wonder will literature be much changed by that most momentous of events, the return of evil'.[21] Throughout the later stages of the struggle for the new state terrible events took place in the Irish countryside. We can read some of the gruesome detail in Lady Gregory's *Journal*. This disastrous situation roused Yeats's indignation.

He was horrified and his wrath turned into despair in the poem 'Nineteen Hundred and Nineteen' that he presented to Olivia Shakespear as 'thoughts suggested by the present state of the world . . . They are not philosophical but simple and passionate, a lamentation over lost peace and lost hope. My own philosophy does not make brighter the prospect, so far as any future we shall live to see is concerned'.[22] The poem's opening lament 'Many ingenious lovely things are gone . . .' adduces the example of Athens. Nothing remains of the masterpieces of Phidias' time and, though 'We too had many pretty toys when young', the Ireland which was that of Cathleen-ni-Houlihan has also gone. Yeats's ideal has collapsed. What Athens suffered, Ireland undergoes now. A violent tide spreads over the country. Terror rules over nights and days: 'Now days are dragon-ridden, the nightmare/ Rides upon sleep'. Visions of nightmare prevail:

> . . . a drunken soldiery
> Can leave the mother, murdered at her door,
> To crawl in her own blood, and go scot-free.

In a gathering mood of masochistic despair, the poet can envisage the destruction of this meaningless universe, his half-written page, his former dreams, since men have become weasels fighting in a hole. A delight in violence has succeeded honour and truth:

> We, who seven years ago
> Talked of honour and of truth
> Shriek with pleasure if we show
> The weasel's twist, the weasel's tooth.

Yeats's horror is so intense that he uses the first person plural 'we' as if speaking for all mankind. Human life is a failure and Yeats deflates all values by mocking the great, the wise and the good. Nothing is sacred. And when the sharp shaft of his destructive satire has reduced to naught what seemed to remain valuable, he turns it against himself, against mockers who do not act 'To bar that foul storm', thus giving free vent to his furious rage.

The storm bursts out in the final section, a symbol of the brutal anarchy which swoops over the world in an orgy of destruction, an Apocalyptic vision where 'the labyrinth of the wind' takes the place of that of meditation. All sense of bearing is lost: 'All turn with amorous cries, or angry cries / According to the wind, for all are blind'. 'Evil gathers head', represented by Herodias' daughters. The 'wind drops' as if dumb before the final vision of an evil spirit, 'That insolent fiend Robert Artisson', Lady Kyteler's incubus.[23] Evil is worshipped, the horrible has reached its climax. In these terms Yeats registers his horror and grief at this war.

THE CIVIL WAR

The Civil War broke out in April 1922 after the vote of the Government of Ireland Act in December 1920 which established the division of Ireland and after Griffith and Collins had agreed to sign the treaty which divided Ireland on December 6th 1921. They were disowned by de Valera. With a narrow majority, the wavering representatives rallied round the treaty. De Valera resigned, Griffith took his place and the Republican agitation began in April 1922. The Civil War between those who accepted the compromise settlement setting up the Free State within the British Commonwealth and those who wished to fight on for an independent republic was to last up to 1923. In December 1922, right in the middle of the Civil War, Yeats was appointed senator of the Dail by President Cosgrave. He accepted. He was plunged into action. As a senator on the Free State side, he was a potential target for assassination and was given an armed guard on his house. He wished for the reunification of Ireland but through legal means: 'I have no hope', he said in a speech to the Senate, 'of seeing Ireland united in my time, or of seeing Ulster won in my time; but I believe it will be won in the end, and not because we fight it, but because we govern this country well'.[24] During the Civil War, on January 4th 1923, he wrote from Dublin to Robert Bridges: 'Life here is interesting, but restless and unsafe – I have two bullet holes through my window'.[25] The poet was witnessing the birth-pangs of a new state: 'Here one works at the slow exciting work of creating the institutions of a new nation . . . Meanwhile the country is full of arms and explosives ready for any violent hand to use'.[26] Many of the remaining great houses went up in flames. In a letter to Olivia Shakespear on 7 December 1922, Yeats commented on the 'curious prophecies' of coming events he found in his own plays, as he prepared them for a collected edition. 'The Unicorn from the Stars', he wrote, 'is now being fulfilled in Munster where great houses are being burned. Some of the burners use arguments not unlike those of my wild men'.[27]

'Meditations in Time of Civil War' opens with an evocation of the settled order Yeats admired: 'Ancestral Houses'. We then witness the disintegration of this order. *A Vision* makes it clear that he saw his own age as one moving towards a catastrophic reversal. 'A civilization', he wrote there, 'is a struggle to keep self-control' and 'the last surrender, the irrational cry, revelation' is announced by 'the scream of Juno's peacock'.[28] It is this that we hear announcing the end of Ascendancy graciousness at the close of the third section of 'Meditations in Time of Civil War', heralding the coming desolation of section IV and the violence and turmoil of civil war that is to appear in sections V–VII. The chaos of the war seems to threaten his security: '. . . the key is turned / On our uncertainty.' He expounds his vision of contemporary events – 'Last night they trundled down the road / That dead young soldier in his blood' – in lines recalling a real episode of the Civil War which he witnessed. The walls of his tower, crumbling at the top, are the signs of this anarchy. Visions of violence and hatred follow one another. He climbs to the top of his tower, and 'Monstrous familiar images swim to the mind's eye' – 'the illusions that creep like maggots into civilisations when they begin to decline, and into minds when they begin to decay'.[29] First he has a vision of violence and hatred, that of a crowd crying 'vengeance for Jacques Molay'. He explains: 'A cry for vengeance because of the murder of the Grand Master of the Templars seems to me fit symbol for those who labour for hatred, and so for sterility in various kinds'.[30] This violence seems to be absurd and vain, as the repetition of 'nothing' emphasizes:

> The rage-driven, rage-tormented, and rage-hungry troop,
> Trooper belabouring trooper, biting at arm or at face,
> Plunges towards nothing, arms and fingers spreading wide
> For the embrace of nothing.

TROY, THE ARCHETYPAL WAR

Behind the real wars, outside or inside Ireland, there is the mythic war of Troy: 'We Irish are nearer than the English to the Mythic Age'.[31] Troy is, in Yeats's imagination, the archetype of the war which marks the turning of a civilization and embodies the reunion of contraries, hatred – love; death – rebirth. In one of his earliest poems, 'The Rose of the World', Yeats had announced his theme of Troy, linked with Helen-Maud Gonne:

> Who dreamed that beauty passes like a dream?
> For these red lips, with all their mournful pride,
> Mournful that no new wonder may betide,
> Troy passed away in one high funeral gleam,
> And Usna's children died.

'No Second Troy' sees Maud Gonne's agitations as part of the same historical destructiveness. She has 'taught to ignorant men most violent ways, / Or hurled the little streets upon the great' and Yeats asks: 'Why, what could she have done, being what she is? / Was there another Troy for her to burn?' Troy is also present in the Annunciation poems, in 'Two Songs from a Play' and in 'Leda and the Swan' in which we have the lines: 'The broken wall, the burning roof and tower / And Agamemnon dead'. The second stanza of 'Long-legged Fly' provides the link between Troy and Rome which is already hinted at in 'Two Songs from a Play':

> That the topless towers be burnt
> And men recall that face,
> Move most gently if move you must . . .

Here Yeats alludes, without naming her, to Helen of Troy by echoing the line from Christopher Marlowe's play *Dr Faustus*: 'Was this the face that launched a thousand ships, / And burnt the topless towers of Ilium?' Helen, in Yeats's poem, becomes the unnamed connection between Caesar and Michael Angelo. In Yeats's thought, Troy's fall stands at a turning-point in the gyres of history at which a new annunciation occurred. The precise moment of this turning-point is the conception of Helen, the product of a divine intervention in history like that which later produced Christ, and now, in the modern era, has given birth after two more millennia to the Anti-Christ of 'The Second Coming'. In Book V of *A Vision*, 'Dove or Swan', Yeats observes: 'I imagine the annunciation that founded Greece as made to Leda . . . and that from one of her eggs came Love and from the other War'.[32] The sonnet 'Leda and the Swan' focuses on that moment of annunciation. Our history issues from it, for love and war are generated here. Helen, though she is not mentioned, is the vehicle for the burning of Troy, the death of Agamemnon, and all that follows. Leda may have put on Zeus's knowledge as well as his power, but this is simply the knowledge that all things pass away, that the act of coition as well as war, consumes and extinguishes itself as it is consummated. Helen stands for the 'terrible beauty' which can destroy a civilization: she is war, love and hatred together. Her sexual energy is both destructive and generative. She is 'the female life-giving and life-removing power'.[33]

TERROR, HATRED, VIOLENCE

A survey of the poetic evocations of war in Yeats's works shows that he was both appalled and fascinated by the spectacle of violence. The three poems of Annunciation, 'Leda and the Swan', 'Two Songs from a Play' and 'The Second Coming' are visionary poems, conjuring up the nightmarish atmosphere of the end of a civilization. Images of death recur – that of Agamemnon in 'Leda and the Swan', Dionysus' in 'Two Songs from a Play' which also conjures up 'God's death'; and in 'The Second Coming' 'The ceremony of innocence is drowned'. Images of blood are found in the three poems: 'the brute blood of the air' in 'Leda and the Swan', 'Odour of blood' in 'Two Songs from a Play' and 'the blood-dimmed tide' in 'The Second Coming'. Images of brutality abound: 'tear the heart out of his side', 'Christ was slain' in 'Two Songs from a Play', 'a sudden blow' and 'terrified vague fingers' in 'Leda and the Swan', 'a gaze blank and pitiless as the sun', and 'rough beast' in 'The Second Coming'. The consequence is general anarchy and disturbance: 'Galilean turbulence' ('Two Songs from a Play'), 'the staggering girl' ('Leda and the Swan'), 'Things fall apart, the centre cannot hold', 'Mere anarchy is loosed upon the world' ('The Second Coming'). This is an apocalyptic vision and the world sinks into darkness: 'Out of the fabulous darkness', 'man's darkening thought', 'a fabulous, formless darkness' ('Two Songs from a Play'); 'the dark webs' ('Leda and the Swan') and in 'The Second Coming', 'The darkness drops again'. It is the vigour of his language that gives us the frisson of terror. In 'The Second Coming', the sense of a supernatural force is intensified by the bestial as well as slovenly associations of the verb 'slouches'.

Yeats advocated the building of armed forces. For him, 'the formation of military families should be encouraged'.[34] He wanted 'to throw back from our shores the disciplined uneducated masses of the commercial nations',[35] and in general he welcomed the approach of war as offering occasion, as the Irish Troubles had, for able, courageous men to move to the fore. Yeats believed that physical violence was a necessary and therefore desirable part of the historic process: '. . . good strong blows are delights to the mind'. ('Three Marching Songs') Evil should not be eliminated either but rather transformed. In 'A Bronze Head', Yeats expressed his belief that, in the modern era, only 'massacre' will save all that is worthwhile of 'this foul world in its decline and fall'. It is salvation through destruction.

Hatred pervades his poetry; the title of section VII of 'Meditations in Time of Civil War' runs: 'I see phantoms of hatred and of the heart's fullness and of the coming emptiness'. Its importance is emphasized at the end of *A General Introduction for my Work* in 1937: 'When I stand upon O'Connell Bridge in the half-light and notice that discordant architecture, all those electric signs, where modern heterogeneity has taken physical form, a vague hatred comes up out of my own dark and I am certain that wherever in Europe there are minds strong enough to lead others the same vague hatred rises; in four or five or in less generations this hatred will have issued in violence and imposed some kind of rule of kindred. I cannot know the nature of that rule, for its opposite fills the light; all I can do to bring it nearer is to intensify my hatred'.[36] The fictitious Ribh in 'Ribh considers Christian Love insufficient' has discovered that hatred can be a broom ('besom') to sweep the soul clean of its false convictions, so that 'From terror and deception freed it can / Discover impurities' and 'learn / A darker knowledge.'

There is for Yeats a wisdom that comes from terror itself. In a broadcast on 'Modern Poetry', in 1936 he said: 'I think profound philosophy must come from terror. An abyss opens under our feet: inherited convictions, the presuppositions of our thoughts . . . drop into the abyss. Whether we will or no we must ask the ancient questions: is there reality anywhere?'[37] War is both repellent and attractive. He repeats in *On the Boiler* a crucial passage he had included in *A Vision*: 'Dear predatory birds prepare for war, prepare your children and all that you can reach

... Love war because of its horror, that belief may be changed, civilization renewed'.[38]

LOVE AND REBIRTH

Side by side with the images of destruction that we have pointed out in the Annunciation poems, we find images of love and rebirth. 'Leda and the Swan' treats an act of love; 'Two Songs from a Play' conjure up 'love's pleasure'. The word 'heart' recurs in 'Two Songs from a Play' and Leda feels 'the strange heart beating where it lies'. Birth is suggested in 'Leda and the Swan' with 'A shudder in the loins' and clearly expressed in 'The Second Coming' with 'a rocking cradle'. 'God's death' in 'Two Songs from a Play' is 'but a play' in a cycle of rebirth. So hope persists '. . . the Muses sing / Of Magnus Annus at the spring'.

So all life is subject to the law of antithesis: the theory of opposites which governs human personality appears in the changes of history. Everything from the microcosm to the macrocosm is ruled by the opposition of time and eternity, human and divine, symbolized for instance by 'Leda and the Swan'. The conflict is par excellence Yeats's theme.

CYCLICAL CONCEPTION OF HISTORY

It is out of such hatred and hope, the sinister delight in apocalypse and the consoling sense of a permanence that reasserts itself through total change, that the poem 'Meru' finds its motive force. Named after the sacred mountain at the centre of the Hindu paradise, the sonnet sums up Yeats's philosophy of history. In *A Vision*, Yeats conceived of history as composed of two cones, rotating in opposite directions, the apex of each at the centre of the other's widest arc. One cone is widening as the other, whirling in the opposite direction, narrows. These spiralling motions are the gyres. The times of maximum historical turbulence are those when the gyres reverse their motions. These great historical reversals occur every cycle of two thousand years, at those moments when the previously expanding cone begins to contract and the previously contracting cone to expand. He saw the Irish events as a vivid microcosm of much larger events in world history. Central to his outlook was his cyclical conception of history. The later lines of the first stanza of 'The Second Coming' introduce the apocalyptic vision of mindless violence 'loosed upon the world' –

the note that is repeated in the closing sections of Yeats's other poems on the Irish Troubles. In each case, the reference to the local Irish situation with which the poems open is dropped by the end to evoke a condition of universal anarchy and violence.

His country is degenerating. The aristocratic values are disappearing; Coole is no longer a sanctuary; there is no place left for the 'Big Houses'. Money commands everything, art is disdained. For him, Cromwell symbolizes this degeneration.[39] To Dorothy Wellesley who questioned him on the political situation, asking which solution he advocated, he answered in a mood of despair: 'O my dear, I have no solution, none'.[40] Enlarging his vision, he discovered throughout Europe this same decadence of civilization, sinking into anarchy and violence. As early as 'Nineteen Hundred and Nineteen', Ireland is no longer alone in his mind; it becomes an image of the West. The sculptures of Phidias disappeared, though their beauty seemed imperishable, and all that modern man boasts of suffers the same fate. Similarly, the situation in Ireland is but the starting point of his vision in 'Parnell's Funeral' and 'The Curse of Cromwell'.

He even goes beyond the limits of the West and encompasses all contemporary civilization. The chaos of the Civil War in Ireland, the troubles in Europe, the spectre of the Second World War corroborated his opinion: our civilization is approaching its end, carried away in the cycles of history. He deals with the cosmic chaos, and presents nihilistic visions, gloomy landscapes, menacing and destructive winds. The swan of 'Nineteen Hundred and Nineteen' rushes into 'the desolate heaven'. Parnell's death which seems to assume a cosmic importance, conjuring up a sacrifice ordered by heaven, similar to Christ's, symbolically announces the transformation of an epoch, for 'An age is the reversal of an age' ('Parnell's Funeral'). Civilizations follow one another by opposing one another, antithetical then primary: 'So the Platonic year / Whirls out new right and wrong' ('Nineteen Hundred and Nineteen'). His theme turns into a cosmic philosophy of the rise and fall of civilizations.

Beyond the imminence of universal destruction, he had the assurance of a renewal. Even in the midst of chaos, man is capable of artistic creation as testified by Loie Fuller's Chinese dancers in 'Nineteen Hundred and Nineteen'; in spite of anarchy, men continue to act as artists: 'All men are dancers and their tread / Goes to the barbarous clangour of a gong.' Human mind will survive the general cataclysm. Yeats was convinced in the last years of his life, as he wrote in 1938 in 'Ireland after the

Revolution', 'that some tragic crisis shall so alter Europe and all opinion' that a new order will come into being which harks back to 'the civilization immediately behind that of Homer'. He looked forward enthusiastically to this new order. If our civilization approaches its end and 'irrational streams of blood are staining earth' ('The Gyres'), what matter, since another one will follow, announced by the monstrous beast of 'The Second Coming' which slouches towards Bethlehem? It will be for the next civilization, in 2000, what the annunciation of 'Leda and the Swan' was for Greek civilization and what the Annunciation of the Virgin Mary and the Dove was for Christian civilization. Each way of life disappears but life goes on, the soul survives:

> I came on a great house in the middle of the night,
> Its open lighted doorway and its windows all alight,
> And all my friends were there and made me welcome too.

This house, miraculously lighted in 'The Curse of Cromwell' is a symbol of the supernatural universe where the aristocracy of yore still lives on. The soul goes on living. Things and people '. . . both can and cannot be'. We are confronted only with metamorphoses:

> Conduct and work grow coarse, and coarse the soul,
> What matter? Those that Rocky Face holds dear,
> Lovers of horses and of women, shall,
> From marble of a broken sepulchre,
> Or dark betwixt the polecat and the owl,
> Or any rich, dark nothing disinter
> The workman, noble and saint, and all things run
> On that unfashionable gyre again. ('The Gyres')

This 'Rocky Face', like the 'rocky voice' in 'The Man and the Echo' and the lapis lazuli, represents eternity, changeless throughout all the cycles of man and history. This eternity is reached by human creatures through artistic creation, like the dancers in 'Nineteen Hundred and Nineteen'. Art triumphs over chaos for, even if its priceless objects disappear, man keeps the power of creating others. In the dance of history, he goes on dancing. The swan, a symbol of the poet, rides destructive winds undoubtedly, but remains inviolate in its pride and solitary beauty. Heraclitus whom Yeats quotes several times, in particular in *A Vision* and in *On the Boiler*, was right therefore: 'Opposites are everywhere face to face, dying each other's life, living each other's death'.[41]

THE ATTITUDE OF THE POET IN TIME OF WAR

In such a context, which should the poet choose: public life or private life – 'Perfection of the life or of the work' ('The choice')? Action or contemplation? The swordsman or the saint? What is the attitude of the poet in time of war? In 'Nineteen Hundred and Nineteen', solitude is a comfort to him. He withdraws into his tower for '. . . all triumph would / But break upon his ghostly solitude' and '. . . triumph can but mar our solitude'. The swan becomes the symbol of the poet's solitary soul which refuses all commitment. In the fifth section of 'Meditations in Time of Civil War', 'The Road at My Door', we discover Yeats's divided mood. The poet pictures himself standing at the door of his restored castle home while forces pass by and pause for a few idle words. He is jealous of the physical strength of the 'affable Irregular' – 'A heavily-built Falstaffian man' and of his indifferent gaiety in face of danger. He feels envious of the 'brown Lieutenant':

> I count those feathered balls of soot
> The moor-hen guides upon the stream,
> To silence the envy in my thought . . .

Then he questions himself: is not his contemplative life useless, compared to the activity of a soldier fighting for a cause? He 'Wonder[s] how many times I could have proved my worth / In something that all others understand or share'. But action is not for him: '. . . the abstract joy, / The half-read wisdom of daemonic images, / Suffice the ageing man as once the growing boy.'

The title of 'Vacillation' conveys man's excruciating condition, torn between opposing extremes. How far is it possible to reconcile the self and the anti-self, a conflict which takes place not only at the individual level, but also the national? How to approach that 'Unity of being' where all tension vanishes, where those two movements, respectively subjective and objective, as described in *A Vision*, are merged? Antinomies are central to Yeatsian politics, they account for their ambiguity and the alternations of commitment and non-commitment. The conflict between action and contemplation is solved through art, an art for which the Irish situation is but the starting point of the much wider vision which embraces his cyclical conception of history.

CONCLUSION

In a unifying spirit, Yeats endeavours, after the dialectical process, to transcend the antinomies. He believes in the Unity of Being, on the level of human personality, nation, art, philosophy. On the level of the nation, he tries to realize a politico-religious unity, founded on literature. *Four Years* ends on this significant passage: 'I had seen Ireland in my time turn from the bragging rhetoric and gregarious humour of O'Connell's generation and school, and offer herself to the solitary and proud Parnell as to her anti-self . . . and I had begun to hope, or to half hope, that we might be the first in Europe to seek unity as deliberately as it had been sought by theologian, poet, sculptor, architect, from the eleventh to the thirteenth century.[42] Yeats wants to act through literature. Therefore he chiefly dreams of Unity of Culture; thanks to it, a national unity will be achieved through art. It is intimately linked with the Unity of Being, for the absence of one in our time makes it very difficult to realize the other. The Unity of Culture, by giving back life to literary tradition and mythology, is connected for him with a belief in the race; if it is realized, the Irish race will become again: 'A chosen race, one of the pillars that uphold the world'.[43] In its turn, the Unity of Culture will be defined and conjured up by the Unity of Image for 'Nations, races, and individual men are unified by an image, or bundle of related images, symbolical or evocative of the state of mind which is . . . the most difficult to that man, race or nation'.[44] In other words, these images represent the 'anti-self', they spring from the Great Memory, the Collective Unconscious. So, beyond the event, the poet has led us from reality to myth and from Ireland to the world, to a conception of history, philosophy and aesthetics. From the national, we have reached the universal, the belief in the immortality of the soul, the perpetuation of the race and this 'artifice of eternity', artistic creation. That is why, amidst the contemporary chaos, Yeats's poetry leaves a hope. 'The blood of innocence has left no stain' ('Blood and the Moon'). His poems give us the 'tragic gaiety' of Shakespeare's heroes: 'Gaiety transfiguring all that dread' ('Lapis Lazuli'). 'What matter?' he exclaims in 'The Gyres': 'Out of cavern comes a voice, / And all it knows is that one word "Rejoice!"'

MAUD GONNE:
ROMANTIC REPUBLICAN

A. NORMAN JEFFARES

The recent publication of Maud Gonne's letters to W.B. Yeats[1] makes very clear how active and many faceted her life was. Many people have seen her as a goddess on a pedestal because of Yeats's poetic devotion and the magnificent love poetry he wrote out of his lengthy romantic obsession with her. Though her own autobiography,[2] and various biographies[3] have described her tumultuous life, they do not have the sheer and immediate impact of these letters which convey her different interests and activities very impressively indeed. Having spent some years working on the editing of these letters with Anna MacBride White, Maud Gonne's granddaughter, I thought I would suggest in this talk a tentative skeleton structure, an ordering of events in Maud Gonne's life that might form a basis for a new biography and enable us to see some pattern in her eighty-six crowded years, or, at least, to chart a passage through the material available to us. This process, partially because of today's limitations of time, will tend to emphasize particularly significant moments, but within what seem to be fairly well defined periods in her life. Her life would make a fine film or TV programme and I shall include one or two episodes which would lend themselves to such treatment.

The first phase might well be called *Her Father's Daughter*: it runs from Maud Gonne's birth, on 21 December 1866, to the autumn of 1887, almost, therefore, to her official coming of age at twenty-one. The Gonne family ancestors claimed Scottish origin from one of the Gunn Clan of Caithness, said to have settled in Kerry in Elizabeth's reign. A descendant or descendants of this Gunn moved to Mayo and from there a William Gonne, thought to have been disinherited by a second marriage, emigrated to Portugal sometime before the Lisbon earthquake of 1755. He entered the wine trade and his business prospered, with trading houses in Oporto and London. Maud's grandfather Charles Gonne was born in Portugal in 1800: some of his children were also born there, but Maud's father Thomas Gonne, generally known as Tommy, was born in London. Though he was educated with a view to his managing the continental side of the family business (which may explain his extensive knowledge of European languages) he joined the army instead, two of his brothers entering the family firm. He was a professional soldier, holding a commission in the 17th Lancers. He had attained his captaincy when he married Edith Cook, whose family had derived their considerable wealth from drapery (her great-grandfather was reputed to be worth over two million pounds in 1869).

A strain of tuberculosis ran in the Cook family, Edith dying of the disease in 1871 at the age of twenty-seven, when Maud was four and her younger sister Kathleen two. When Maud was born the family had been living near Aldershot, in Tongham, but an Irish posting followed and they lived in Floraville, a large house near Donnybrook on the outskirts of Dublin. They then moved to London to a house of their own where, shortly after they had settled in, Edith gave birth to a third daughter, Margaretta Rose. She died a few days later and the baby died a few weeks after that. Tommy had thought that he might have to give up his army career to look after his wife; indeed the children's nurse Mary Anne Meredith, known as Bowie, told Maud that he had intended to take the family to Italy, hoping the climate might be more suitable for his wife. Dying she made her husband promise not to send their daughters to a boarding school for, orphaned herself, she had loathed her boarding school. At the time of his wife's death Tommy Gonne instilled in Maud the idea that she should never be afraid of anything, particularly not even of death: it was a lesson she learned well, a lasting one.

After his wife's death Captain Gonne took a cottage near the Curragh Camp in County Kildare where he was stationed. Maud, however, developed a cough and he thought her health and Kathleen's would benefit from sea air, so he settled the girls in a house near the Bailey Lighthouse on Howth Head, the peninsula forming the northern arm of Dublin Bay; they were looked after by their nurse Bowie. They ran wild there very happily on the heather-covered hill. The effect of its natural beauty on Maud was strong and in later life she returned there from time to time, particularly at moments of severe stress. Another result of living on Howth was that the children met Irish people and appreciated the kindness and hospitality they received from the inhabitants of cottages on the peninsula. English and Anglo-Irish attitudes were ones of shock, however, when the girls failed to match the respectable norms of behaviour expected of them at a lunch in Howth Castle; eyebrows were raised; their father imported an English governess for them.

Contrast came in 1874 when the sisters were sent to Cook relatives in London while their father was again stationed at Aldershot. Their great-aunt Augusta Tarlton, a wealthy widow, was spectacularly mean while Emily, another aunt (their mother's favourite), a Portuguese who had married Frank Cook, was most generous to them – though she found this difficult, as her husband was also extremely mean (his second wife, Tennesse Clafin, an American stockbroker and strong advocate of feminism, socialism, spiritualism and free love in the magazine she and her sister published, later gave him his come-uppance). Emily Cook's best gift to the girls was her suggestion that Maud's lungs would benefit from a warmer climate: this led Tommy Gonne to move them to France, to the Villa Fleurie, on the Cannes-Grasse road, where they stayed till 1880. This was another beautiful place, the house surrounded by groves of orange and lemon trees. Here they had a French governess of strong republican views, possessing a highly developed belief in independence, which she passed on to Maud.

During their stay in France Tommy Gonne was military attaché in Vienna from March 1876 to October 1878; he was at home later in 1878 (having accidentally shot himself in the foot) but left for India in early December of that year, now Colonel of his regiment. He left his daughters in Cannes on the way to India; they had spent the summer of 1878 in Switzerland, returning to England for the autumn. Tommy Gonne left India in March 1881; retiring from his regiment, he became military attaché at St. Petersburg in April 1882 (he also stayed for some time in Bosnia) and returned in January 1883. It is likely that the family travelled in Europe during his leaves. When on a trip to Rome Maud, then seventeen, tall and spectacularly beautiful, received a proposal from a cousin, Charles Eyre, in the moonlight, at the Colosseum. She accepted, but her father, posted to Ireland again, decided this was decidedly a mistake and that the girls should stay with him in Dublin. He forbade further contact with the young man. Maud, however, carried on a clandestine correspondence with the cousin, using invisible ink: she showed this to her father, to demonstrate her independence. Laughter ensued, and the young man's protestations were in any case seen as tedious by her. What her father had also taught her – perhaps unnecessarily – was that will power could achieve anything. He and she got on very well together; he treated her virtually as a contemporary and she began to act as hostess for him in Dublin – no question of a chaperone for her.

Maud found the generals she met much more interesting than the young officers, whose conversation concentrated on racing and sport; officers' wives she tended to despise for being either dull or pretentious. When she was presented at court she caught the eye of the Prince of Wales, who escorted her to the royal dais. Her dress was magnificent: it impressed Oscar Wilde. It was the royal attention, however, that impressed a Gonne aunt, Mary, the Comptesse de la Sizeranne, who invited her to visit a German spa with her. The Gonnes were very unlike the Cooks: this great-aunt, twice widowed, at seventy-five had a young lover, officially her secretary. In her great-aunt's company Maud again met the Prince of Wales, but Colonel Gonne, arriving opportunely, took her back to Dublin at once, fearing the effect on his career if his daughter received royal companionship coldly, on her own reputation if she welcomed it. On another occasion he rescued her – at her telegraphed request – by sending a carriage to bring her home from a houseparty in County Cavan where she had been sickened by her host's description of his attitude to a homeless family, evicted by his agent because they supported the Land League. They were lying in a ditch, the wife ill and unlikely to last the night. These people, he told Maud, must be taught a lesson. In the autobiography, *A Servant of the Queen*, she traced her interest in Ireland's political situation to this incident.

Colonel Gonne died suddenly in Dublin of typhoid on 30 November 1886, when he was fifty-one and Maud twenty. This was an immensely severe loss to her. She had loved and deeply respected her father: that his death had brought to an end a generally very happy and carefree existence was quickly obvious. The girls had been left in the charge of their uncle, William Gonne, their father's sour elder brother, who did not reveal their favourable financial position to them. He gave them half a crown a week, which they had to account for in detail, telling them that as his brother's affairs had been very badly managed, there was virtually no money for them.

Maud's generosity, sense of fairness and loyalty to her dead father emerged when a woman called, to ask William Gonne for some financial support. She had had a daughter by Tommy Gonne, born six weeks before. On his deathbed he had insisted that Maud should make out a cheque to this woman, Margaret Wilson (she is called Eleanor Robbins in *A Servant of the Queen* where her daughter Eileen, Maud's half-sister, is called Daphne). Maud argued successfully with her stuffy uncle that there were commitments, and later she arranged that Mrs Wilson should take up a post as a governess in Russia,[4] and adopted her daughter, putting her in the care of Bowie, who had looked after Maud and Kathleen very devotedly, and remained their friend.

Maud and Kathleen decided to become independent of their uncle: with two cousins, May and Chotie, daughters of another uncle, Charlie Gonne, they planned careers for themselves. Chotie and Kathleen opted for the Slade, Maud and May for nursing. Maud's lungs, however, were not good enough to pass a health examination, so she found herself a role as an actress, and her uncle's sense of propriety was outraged when he saw her name as leading actress on posters advertising *Adrienne Lecouvreur* and another play. But her lungs gave way at the final stages of rehearsing and she began to spit blood. The Comptesse de la Sizeranne came to her aid, revealing that William Gonne had lied to his nieces, who would in fact be decidedly well off when they came of age: a trust set up in 1865 meant that they would inherit land, shares and diamonds. She brought the sisters to the French spa of Royat, near Clermont Ferrand, where Maud soon recovered her health.

At Royat a new chapter of her life began – it might be called *Ebullient Energy* – and extended from 1887 to 1900, dominated by Lucien Millevoye, a French deputy and committed Boulangist, who was sixteen years her senior; like her he had weak lungs and was also at Royat to recuperate. With the intensity of the tubercular, Maud thought that they had met before:[5] their infatuation developed quickly. As sensitive as she had earlier been to the atmosphere of Rome Maud was now affected by the dramatic thunderstorms and sultry heat of the Auvergne; she thought her destiny was driving her on, into an alliance with this French patriot against the British Empire. He was obsessed with the need to regain Alsace Lorraine for France; she with the need to free Ireland from English control. He saw her as Ireland's Joan of Arc, a role she was happy to take on. The fact that Millevoye was married did not matter to Maud. (Millevoye seems to have been involved in political life in Paris while his wife lived on the family estates in the country.) He did tell her at one stage in their relationship that he would divorce his wife and marry her. She had, however, no conventional wish for domesticity. Tommy

Gonne had encouraged her to want to be independent in mind and spirit and she now was about to have the material means to enable her to achieve that independence.

To a certain extent Millevoye inherited Tommy Gonne's influential position in Maud's life; but her father had shaped her character, and she had certainly inherited his capacity for travelling. After a month in Constantinople staying in the Embassy, the Ambassador's daughter being a friend, equipped with a revolver given her by Millevoye and accompanied by a monkey called Chaperone, she was summoned to Paris by him to be sent on a secret mission. It was all very exciting; she carried documents sewn into her dress to St. Petersburg for the Boulangists; these asked for support for their conspiracy against the French Government, and proposed a future treaty with Russia. Her journey was not without incident: held up at the frontier because she had no visa she persuaded a Russian diplomat travelling on the same train to telephone St. Petersburg to get permission for her to enter Russia without one: ironically he was carrying proposals from Germany for an alliance.

Maud now began her own self-appointed career as a worker for Ireland's independence, approaching the Irish Nationalist MP Michael Davitt at Westminster; she seemed (not for the last time) as if she might be a British spy, and Davitt was decidedly cautious in dealing with this ebullient, socially poised and independently-minded young lady. In Dublin she met Charles Oldham, and, through him, the old Fenian John O'Leary, now back in Dublin after serving some of his penal servitude, followed by enforced exile in Paris. He thought her energetic if not intellectual. A small landlord himself, he was not, however, impressed by any proposal for action against landlords which Maud favoured. After all, Parnell had six years earlier suppressed the Ladies' Land League run by his sister. The nub of the matter was that Irishmen did not really want women playing a full part in Irish political life. Maud and her friend Ida Jameson gave an Irish concert in Dublin with, daringly, no 'God Save the Queen' at the end but 'Let Erin Remember' instead; Maud's keen sense of the value of publicity was at work and she quickly set about establishing her presence in Dublin.

She met many of the livelier minds in Dublin through her hospitality, among them Douglas Hyde. A police report detailed her histrionic ability, her rifle practice and her habit of giving expensive suppers. But how was she to use her energy in any practical way? Refused entry as a woman to the Celtic Literary

Society and to the National League, she found a role – at the suggestion of Tim Harrington MP, the head of the National League – as a freelance in Donegal where a brutal series of evictions was taking place in 1888. (In February 1889 a police inspector was to be killed while attempting to arrest Father MacFadden in Gweedore.) Maud and her cousin May went there, along with Dagda, her Great Dane who needed leather boots for his feet, cut by keeping up with his mistress as she rode around the area which had been made miserable by the activities of Colonel Olpherts, an oppressive landlord. This reconnaissance was followed by actions: endless letters to newspapers, publicity pursued vigorously and accompanied by the practical aim of providing shelter for the homeless, all pushed through with pertinacity.

In London on 30 January 1889 she swept into W.B. Yeats's life, and what he called 'the troubling' of his life began. To her he was Willie Yeats, an art student, whose original ambitions of writing about Irish places (particularly Sligo, as Allingham had about Donegal), and of describing folk belief, added to by his increasing knowledge of Irish literature to which Katharine Tynan and John O'Leary had introduced him, were now expanding into a wish to create an Irish awareness of Ireland's past Gaelic heritage. To her he was another of the many and diverse people who wanted a new kind of Ireland: he was shy, kind, gentle, an idealist. To him she seemed goddess-like, unattainable: he fell completely in love with her but though she was like one of his ideal heroines, one of Shelley's wild revolutionaries, he asked himself what wife would she make for a poor student.

Her intimate thoughts, however, were focussed on Millevoye. She was on her way back to Paris: there, less than a year later, on 11 January 1890, she had a son by him, Georges Silvère. The child's existence did not prevent her continuing her political activity: he was left in charge of a nurse while she discovered her oratorical powers, successfully supporting a Home Rule candidate in Barrow-in-Furness. Despite a recrudescence of her lung trouble she returned to work in Donegal. Millevoye, who had thought her efforts in Ireland were a 'side issue', had followed her, against her wishes, and fell ill in Dunfanaghy. Weak and feverish, in a damp hotel bed, he had to be nursed back to health and sent back to France, where she followed him later when she heard there was a warrant out for her arrest. Her sympathisers arranged that a train should stop in the middle of the countryside at night to pick her up and enable her to avoid being apprehended. A spell at San

Raphael restored her health, but her relationship with Millevoye was disillusioning. In Dublin in July 1891 she told Yeats of some unhappiness: a few days later, when he had gone off for a holiday with the Johnson brothers in County Down – they were releasing fire balloons and chasing them over the fields – she wrote to him telling him she was sad: she had dreamed of some past when he and she had been brother and sister and had been sold into slavery. He rushed back to Dublin and proposed to her, to be refused in the terms she was to use on similar occasions afterwards; she would never marry; she had reasons; but she asked for his friendship using words 'that were not of a conventional ring'. The world would thank her for not marrying him, she told him, but he should go on writing her such lovely poetry.

In September she relied on him for comfort, arriving, clad in black from head to foot, on the mail boat that brought Parnell's body back to Ireland. She, however, though she attended his funeral in Glasnevin, was secretly mourning the death of her son, who had died of meningitis on 30 July 1891 at 5pm in her apartment, 66 Avenue de la Grande Armee (the death certificate does not give his parents' names; he was nineteen and a half months old when he died). She described him to Yeats as an adopted child. In November Yeats persuaded her to join the Order of the Golden Dawn in London, hoping an interest in occultism might occupy her attention rather than politics, and that she might come to share his interest in mystical matters. He also involved her in his plans for the Irish literary movement, which gained momentum in 1892. As members of a sub-committee of the National Literary Society they worked on plans for setting up reading rooms and libraries in Ireland, to make Irish material more widely available in conjunction with a programme of lectures. The scheme was not well administered, and Yeats's own plans for a series of Irish books ran into difficulties, the direction of it being given to Sir Charles Gavan Duffy.

Maud's desire for activity led her to pursue a more vigorous public life. Her lecturing in France on Irish affairs with a strongly anti-Westminster attitude was recorded in over two thousand articles in the French press, as Yeats proclaimed in an article. Despite her deep grief for her dead son – she tried to induce sleep by taking chloroform, to which she became addicted for a time – she had the energy to turn her attention to the plight of the treason-felony prisoners in Portsmouth Gaol in 1892; she was horrified by the conditions there when she managed to visit them.

Working for the Amnesty Association, she involved herself in a vast correspondence about them, her letters occupying eight hours of her day. She again became seriously ill, this time in Dublin: in charge of Dr Sigerson, she was moved on a stretcher back to London by her cousin May, and then returned to France where Millevoye's career was in ruins. Their affair sparked up again – earlier she had been disillusioned, not unnaturally, by Millevoye's idea that she should become the mistress of someone he wished to influence. She suggested he should edit *La Patrie*. She now became influential in Paris, Millevoye with *La Patrie* and Drumont with *La Parole* encouraged by her to express anti-British sentiments in their journals. Her apartment on the Avenue d'Eylau developed into a lively centre for discussion of Irish and French affairs. On 6 August 1894, Iseult, also a child of Millevoye, was born, conceived, the lovers thought, in the mausoleum that Maud had erected in memory of Georges Silvère, and with the hope his spirit would be re-incarnated in another child.

Maud's belief in reincarnation had been supported by talk in George Russell's house in Dublin in September 1891. While she had not remained a member of the Order of the Golden Dawn for long, thinking it tainted by Freemasonry (from which some of its rituals were derived) and also despising the dreariness of its English middle-class members, she was, however, very sympathetic to Yeats's dream of creating an Irish Order of Mysteries. When staying with Douglas Hyde he had seen an uninhabited castle on Lough Key in County Roscommon and thought it could become 'A Castle of Heroes', where members of the proposed order could withdraw, meditate and recruit their spiritual strength. Maud helped him in preparing rituals and made drawings and designs for them. They exchanged accounts of visions; they experimented with hashish to see if it would enhance their capacity to experience such visions; and he continued to write her lovely poems. In France he helped her with the affairs of L'Association Irlandaise in 1897; and she founded a paper, *L'Irlande Libre*. This journal was praised by Millevoye, but their relationship was now less close.

By 1897 preparations to celebrate the revolution of 1798 were in hand and Maud became involved in them. She planned to make a lecture tour in the United States, to raise funds for the proposed memorial to Wolfe Tone in Dublin. But she found, to her surprise and annoyance, that the planning committee would not agree to her visit. Yeats, however, called a meeting (both he and Maud were members of the IRB) in London to authorise it. The negative reaction was partially due to a split within the Clan na Gael, the American Fenian organisation, but there was probably also an element of anti-feminism in it (for instance, Maud's name was removed from the National Literary Society in Dublin of which she had been a founder member). Yeats, wanting to prove himself more than a dreamer, now became President of the Wolfe Tone Association of Great Britain and France, with the idealistic aim of uniting the various Irish political factions and calling a Convention which would be in charge of policy, and would eventually replace Irish membership at Westminster. It did not, however, impress Maud much as a plan, nor did his behaviour on the occasion of the riots that occurred in Dublin at the time of Victoria's jubilee. Maud had made an inflammatory speech: she and Yeats joined a procession organised by the labour leader James Connolly, a demonstration which drew police baton charges; and later Yeats refused to let her leave the National Club in Rutland Square, pocketing the key when there was a disturbance outside and an old woman was killed. Afterwards she told him firmly that he should keep out of the hurly burly of politics:

Our friendship must indeed be strong for me not to hate you, for you made me do the most cowardly thing I have ever done in my life. It is quite absurd to say I should have reasoned & given explanations.

Do you ask a soldier for explanations on the battlefield of course it is only a very small thing a riot & a police charge but the same need for *immediate action* is there – there is no time to give explanations. I don't ask for obedience from others, I only am answerable for my own acts. I less than any others, would be capable of giving lengthy explanations of what I want & I intend to do, as my rule in life is to obey inspirations which come to me & which always guide me right.

For a long time, I had a feeling that I should not encourage you to mix yourself up in the *outer* side of politics & you know I have never asked you to do so. I see now that I was wrong in not obeying this feeling more completely & probably you were allowed to hinder me on that comparatively unimportant occasion to show me that it is necessary you should not mix in what is really not in your line of action. You have a higher work to do – With me it is different I was born to be in the midst of a crowd.

To return to the unfortunate event in Rutland Square everyone who remained in the club & did not go out to the rescue of the people who were batoned by the police ought to feel ashamed of themselves, owing to their action, or rather their *inaction,* that poor old woman Mrs Fitzsimon was taken to hospital on a car & allowed to fall from that car by a half-drunken, wholly mad policeman. This would not have happened if I had been able to do my duty.

Do you know that to be a coward for those we love, is only a degree less bad than to be a coward for oneself. The latter I know well you are not, the former you know well you are.

It is therefore impossible for us ever to do any work together where there is likely to be excitement or physical danger & now let us never allude to this stupid subject again.

(*L.* pp. 72–3)

After this excitement Maud again needed to recruit her strength and went to Aix-Les-Bains with her cousin May. There she won a lot of money at the Casino, which she decided to use to defend the people arrested in the Dublin riots. She then gave lectures in Paris, London, Dublin and Cork as well as in Scotland and the Midlands. Yeats chaired some of these meetings but, while his unrequited devotion to her intensified, he was becoming disillusioned with the actual process of political struggle while Maud throve on the stimulus of it all. This ebullience continued during her American lecture tour where she collected £1000 for the Amnesty Association and the Wolfe Tone fund.[6] Then she went to the West of Ireland to join in organising the '98 celebrations there. She went to Castlebar, Ballina, and Balderrig, where there was a famine and where she organised an effective protest against inadequate relief rates, to be followed by the erection of a fish-curing plant there, for which she lobbied successfully in Dublin. By April she again needed rest: her powers of recuperation were constantly tested: this time a fortnight in bed cured her bronchitis and set her up for more public speaking in France before a return to Dublin where she broke an arm in June as the result of a horse which was drawing her car falling when she was speaking at a demonstration.

The foundation stone for the Wolfe Tone monument was laid in Dublin on 15 August. Maud (who had spoken at a meeting chaired by Yeats at St. Martin's Hall on 10 August) did not speak on this occasion but, with a French delegation,[7] received a magnificent welcome in Ballina and Castlebar. She and Yeats had incurred the enmity of several people. Charles MacCarthy Teeling, an eccentric who had been expelled from the Young Ireland Society for refusing to accept a decision of the chairman, John O'Leary, and throwing a chair at him, had been circulating various accusations and slanders in Dublin to the effect that Maud was spying for the English. In answer to her enquiry Yeats told her in March 1897 of what was being said against her. Later that month, at Maud's request, he wrote to the Comte de Cremont, who was secretary of the St. Patrick's Association in France, to tell him that Teeling was not a member of the Young Ireland Society and not fit to hold an honorary office in the French Society of St. Patrick. Both Michael Davitt and Tim Harrington also supported her. Teeling stepped up his attacks in July, calling her 'a vile abandoned woman who has had more than one illegitimate child' and adding that the French suspected her of supplying information to the English. Frank Hugh O'Donnell, another eccentric, equally unstable, was to attack them both damagingly later.

Yeats, who had spent his first long summer at Coole in 1897, was worn out with the strain of his hopeless passion for her. Having had his first experience of sex with Mrs Shakespear in 1896 in his thirty-first year he was devastatingly frustrated when she realised that he could not escape his obsession with Maud, and their affair, which had brought him much happiness, came to an end. (On one occasion Maud, possibly aware of his involvement with Mrs Shakespear, had written to him to tell him that he had appeared to her when she was in a hotel in Dublin and that they had later gone together to the Howth cliffs.) At Coole he poured out his sorrows to Lady Gregory, who damped down any enthusiasm he might have had for the plan Maud and James Connolly had formed of urging tenants in Kerry to kill their landlords and take food by force,[8] telling him it would be for those who were above the people in means and education to teach them, were there a real famine there, rather 'to die with courage than to live by robbery.' He took the point and said he would try to dissuade Maud from the project. Politically he and she were beginning to drift apart; he had been deeply shaken by the violence of the Jubilee riots in Dublin and the period of his work, chairing meetings and speaking at them and sitting on committees, for the '98 centenary – however valuable the practical experience of politics was to be to him in later life – made up, he said, the worst months of his life. In mystical matters, however, Maud and he shared their interest increasingly and despite their energetic commitment to politics, his promotion of the literary movement and his fresh interest in the possibility of bringing an Irish theatre into being, their work on Celtic mysticism developed during 1898 in London and Paris.

In Dublin in November there was a dramatic change in their relationship. One morning when he called on her in her hotel Maud asked him if he had had a strange dream: he told her that he had dreamed she had kissed him for the first time. In the evening she told him that the evening before, after falling asleep, she had seen a great spirit put her hand in Yeats's and say to her that they were married. After telling him of this, she then kissed him (for the first time), but next day apologised: she could never be his wife. She then revealed her secret life to him: her pact with the devil made a fortnight before her father's death, which she thought meant she had sacrificed her soul for freedom to live as she chose; her relationship with Millevoye, the birth and death of Georges, the birth of Iseult, and her dislike of sexual love – since Iseult's birth, she told him, she had lived apart from Millevoye though she felt it her duty to support him in his political ideals. Yeats was deeply shaken by these revelations, but out of them came the mystical marriage with its complementary dreams and projections of personalities. Maud heard a voice saying she was to receive the initiation of the spear: a double vision ensued. 'She thought herself,' Yeats wrote, 'a great stone statue through which passed flame, and I felt myself becoming flame and mounting up through and looking out of the eyes of a great stone Minerva.'

Maud's political alliance with Millevoye was given fresh life when the Boer War began. Here was an active war against England, and she wanted to help the Boers. An Irish Brigade was formed to fight alongside the Boers and Maud became a member of the Transvaal Committee, joining vigorously in an anti-enlistment campaign. When Chamberlain, then Colonial Secretary, visited Dublin to receive an honorary degree from Trinity College Maud played a leading part in the protests. Her letter to Yeats describing this is racy:

I arrived on Saturday night at 9.30 in Dublin after a fearfully rough crossing. I at once went to Committee meeting & found a crowded room & great enthusiasm on account of the proclamation forbidding [the] meeting which a detective had just come & delivered. Willie Redmond said instead of one we would have a dozen meetings & if necessary he was prepared to address the people from the top of a lamp post!!! It was decided that all the speakers should meet at Mr O'Leary's at 12.30 & a brake should drive in from there to Beresford Place. Next day W. Redmond called for me at 12. He seemed nervous & talked about arrests & also said he had been told the Govt would not only baton, but shoot down the people & we must be careful to prevent such needless sacrifice. Arrests I thought possible but the shooting idea quite absurd, England does not want to proclaim to the world that she is at war in Ireland.

Davitt was with O'Leary when we arrived, & after a few moments awkward pause explained that he & Mr O'Leary considered it would be foolish & senseless going to Beresford Place, all our purpose was served by the proclamation of the meeting. Mr Redmond only half agreed & said some meeting ought to be held in a hall. I entirely disagreed & said I should go to Beresford Place whatever happened as when a meeting was announced it must be held or attempted at any cost so as not to set an example of cowardice to the crowd. Mr Davitt said his wife was only confined a week & it might kill her if anything happened to him, & rather in contradiction a few moments later said of course WE would risk nothing by going to Beresford Place, but he would not wish the crowd getting batonned. O'Leary agreed with Mr Davitt. Mr Redmond appealed to me for the sake of unity & appearance to first join with them in a meeting in the Celtic Literary Society rooms & then I was free to do what I liked after. The brake & committee arrived & great was their consternation when matters were explained to them. The M.P.s & Mr O'Leary decided it would be foolish & risky to drive down to the Celtic rooms in the brake, – they would each go separately.

I went in the brake & we drove to Beresford Place which was very strongly guarded. We forced an entrance & the crowd broke in on every side but the police were too strong they charged & succeeded in surrounding the brake & arrested our driver & marched the brake & all of us to the Police station an enormous crowd followed & cheering wildly. The police must have had orders not to arrest me, for they suddenly let go of our horses & Connolly took the reins & we drove all around the town, halting for passing our resolution in front of Trinity College & the Castle & waving Transvaal flag. The crowd was as numerous & as enthusiastic as at the Jubilee. The cheering for the Boers was deafening. They got out the mounted police & charged our brake, but didn't venture to arrest anyone. Finally we returned to the Celtic rooms & found Mr O'Leary presiding a meeting composed of 5 reporters & the M.P. orators. The moment I left the brake & got inside the Celtic rooms the police seized it & arrested Connolly so I went out again to try & bail him out. I returned in time for end of meeting, a few people possibly 80 had assembled. To appease & please me Davitt told me he had arranged to have several effigies of Chamberlain burned in the town.

I had arranged for one to be burned, but hearing Davitt's friends had undertaken this work, I at once counter ordered ours, as it was useless to risk my friends, if the thing was already arranged for, & I had no money in my hand to pay for defenses & fines in the case of more arrests. I regret to say that as far as I have heard No effigy of Chamberlain was burned. Moral – never trust to others to do what one can do for oneself.

(*L.* pp. 115–16)

She had become friendly with Arthur Griffith and his journal the *United Irishman* gave her a useful platform. In the beginning of 1900 she went on another lecture tour in the United States, to support the Boers' cause and to collect funds for Griffith's journal. 1900 was a strenuous year for her. She produced a special number of *L'Irlande Libre*, attacking Victoria as the Famine Queen; she won a libel action against the editor of the Dublin *Figaro* who had suggested she was receiving money from the English government; she organised the famous Patriotic Children's Treat in Clonturk Park in Dublin which over 20,000 children attended; she resigned (as did Yeats) from the IRB after the collapse of her work in France caused by the betrayal of a member of French Military Intelligence, a Colonel 'L', whom she had introduced to the IRB in London, and by the interception of funds she had sought from and been sent by the Transvaal representative in Europe, which were to pay for the concealment of IRB bombs in British troopships. Both fiascos were the work of the malevolent Frank Hugh O'Donnell. She had parted from Millevoye (who had a new mistress) in what seemed a final meeting at Chamonix, though later he had met her in Paris with a member of French Intelligence about the revelation of the identity of Colonel 'L'. But the great achievement of 1900 was her formation of Inghínidhe na hÉireann, the Daughters of Ireland, a group of women of which she became president. This group became part of Cumann na nGaedheal and so Maud at last was no longer a freelance but could operate within and through a nationally recognised body. She was thus to liberate many other women into a larger scope of activity – not least, incidentally, in the areas of education and art. It was, for instance, Inghínidhe na hÉireann which was to stage Yeats's explosive *Cathleen Ni Houlihan* for the first time, with Maud in the title role, in 1902. 1900 marked the end of Millevoye's influence: she had told Yeats she would always be as a sister to him, and she felt herself under the protection of the god Lug (Lugh). It was a year which resembled a whirlwind, but she wrote to Yeats 'in the midst of that whirlwind is dead quiet calm which is peace too'.

The calm was shattered in the next period of her life, extending from 1900–1905. It could be called *The Married Activist*; it is dominated by Maud's relationship with John MacBride. Accompanied by his friend Arthur Griffith, she had met him in Paris (since obviously he could not return to Ireland) on his return from South Africa in November 1900: in her eyes he was a hero: he had been actually fighting the British Army. H.W. Nevinson had realised on meeting Maud in 1899 that she longed for action, not theorising talk: he commented that 'the first man of resolute action whom she meets will have her at his mercy'. Something had to be arranged for this man of resolute action to do, and MacBride undertook a lecture tour in the US. He was not a good lecturer and she went out to America to help him in February 1901, returning after two months, having refused a proposal of marriage from him, telling him marriage was not in her thoughts while a war was on. But in June 1902, in Dublin (where she now rented a small house in Coulson Avenue, Rathgar) having played Cathleen in Yeats's *Cathleen Ni Houlihan* with such devastating effect, she had decided to become a Catholic and to marry MacBride who had 'a stronger will' than her own. The news when it hit Yeats had an overwhelming effect and he wrote to beg her to change her mind; he wrote out a passage from one of his diaries referring to their 'dealing with spiritual things' and reminded her of how she had told him in 1898, at the beginning of their spiritual marriage, that she was brought away by Lug and her hand put in his, and that she was told they were married:

Your hands were put in mine & we were told to do a certain great work together. For all who undertake such tasks there comes a moment of extreme peril. I know now that you have come to your moment of peril. If you carry out your purpose you will fall into a lower order & do great injury to the religion of free souls that is growing up in Ireland, it may be to enlighten the whole world. A man said to me last night having seen the announcement in the papers 'The priests will <all triumph over for you> exult over us <us for generations> all for generations because of this'. There are people (& these are the great number) who need the priests or some other masters but [there] are a few bid me write this letter. You possess your influence in Ireland very largely because you come to the people from above. You represent a superior class, a class whose people are more independent, have a more beautiful life, a more refined life. Every man almost of the people who has spoken to me of you has shown that you influence him very largely because of this. <You are> Maud Gonne is surrounded with romance. She puts <away> from her what seems an easy & splendid life that she may devote herself to the people. I have heard you called 'our great lady'. But Maud Gonne is about to pass away <you are going to do> something which the people <did> never forgave James Stephens for doing, though he was a man for whom it mattered far less, you are going to marry one of the people <you are>. This [?weakness] which <has> [?thrust] down your soul to a lower order of faith is thrusting you down socially, is thrusting you down to the people, <you will have no longer any thing to give only

those who are above them can [indecipherable] you to> [?] rob & them
of robbing you>. They will never forgive it – This [?they] [are] most
aristocratic minded <people> the most thirsting for what is above them
& beyond them, of living peoples. You have lived so much & you are of
those for whom surrender of any leadership not that of their own souls
is the great betrayal, the denial of God. It was our work to teach a few
strong aristocratic spirits that to believe the soul was immortal & that
one prospered hereafter *if one laid upon oneself* an heroic discipline in
living & [?to] send them to uplift the nation. You & I were chosen to
begin this work & <just> just when <you> I come to understand it fully
you go from me & seek to thrust the people <down> further into
weakness further from self reliance. Now on <on> a matter on which I
must say <say all> speak if I am to say & believe <that it is not many
[?my]> that some are more than man [?know/now] now I appeal, I
whose hands were placed in yours by eternal hands, to come back to
yourself. To take up again the proud solitary haughty life which made
[you] seem like one of the Golden Gods.. . . . it is not only the truth &
your friends but your own soul that you are about to betray.

(L. pp. 164–66)

It was not only Yeats who was opposed to the marriage.
MacBride's family and friends, like Maud's, thought it unsuitable,
and Maud thought her father appeared to her as she was packing
up and clearing her apartment in Paris and said 'Lambkin, don't
do it. You must not get married'. But marry she did, on 21
February 1903. The honeymoon seems to have been spent not only
in Normandy (where Maud had used a legacy to buy Les
Mouettes, a house at Colleville sur Mer which had a garden
running down to the sea) but also in Spain. This involved a slow
journey south which was to act as cover (Maud acting as decoy to
draw off the police who were shadowing them) for a plan that
MacBride should assassinate Edward VII who was to visit
Gibraltar. This fell through because of MacBride's excessive
drinking with some friends at the time he was meant to carry out
this mission, which was probably linked with the Clann na Gael in
America, with John Devoy involved in it. He came back to the
hotel drunk and refused to say what had happened.

The touch of farce about the failed assassination plot[9] was
partially redeemed in what was called 'the Battle of the Rotunda'.
It became known that Dublin Corporation would be asked to pass
an address of welcome to the King when he visited Dublin in July.
Maud organised resistance to this at a meeting of the Irish
parliamentary party when she led a party on the stage at the

Rotunda to present a statement. Edward Martyn's nerve failed him and Maud took the paper he was to read and demanded if the Lord Mayor was going to welcome the King. He refused to answer and the meeting erupted in violence, described by George Russell to Yeats as 'the most gorgeous row Dublin has had since Jubilee time'. There followed another farcical situation, known as 'The Battle of Coulson Avenue' which occurred when Maud flew a black petticoat from a broom handle to mark, she said, the death of Pope Leo VIII. This enraged her neighbours, flying Union Jacks to celebrate the King's visit to Ireland.

Maud's son by MacBride, Jean Seagan (later Seán) was born on 26 January 1904 at Passy. In February 1905 she sued for divorce in Paris. She was granted a separation, not a divorce, because of legal complications about MacBride's domicile. She fought the case strongly but it was a most distressing time for her as her letters to Yeats show very clearly.

A new period in Maud's life began – it could be called *Isolated Domesticity* – in 1906. The divorce case seemed to have put an end to her political activity in Ireland. She did not want to cause political dissensions like those which had arisen in the case of Parnell. She now stayed in France at Colleville for the summers; for the winters she lived in Paris, fearing that MacBride might lay claim to Seán if she brought the family to Ireland, where MacBride had obtained a post. Something of the puritan feeling that had assailed the new drama in Ireland had also turned on Maud, vilified by MacBride's partisans, when she attended the Abbey Theatre in 1906, accompanied by Yeats. Their friendship, strengthened by the support he (and his friends Lady Gregory and John Quinn) had given her during the long drawn-out divorce proceedings, became closer again and the mystic marriage was renewed in 1908. It seems more than likely that they had a brief sexual relationship at the end of that year. After 1909, however, they seem to have still drifted apart somewhat and did not meet frequently, though they still wrote to each other at intervals[10] and Yeats was still writing poems to her and about her.

In Paris Maud studied painting; she sold some paintings and illustrated books, notably the *Celtic Wonder Tales* of Ella Young, a friend and member of Inghínidhe na hÉireann. She took part in the relief work necessitated by the severe flooding of Paris in 1910 and next involved herself in a movement to provide meals for poor school children in Dublin, which got under way in the winter of 1911 with 250 children fed in St Audeon's parish, a number which doubled the following year. A free feeding bill had been

passed at Westminster but was not extended to Ireland: this was
something for which Maud lobbied energetically in London. In
1912 she was working on this campaign in Dublin and Brussels. In
1913 she helped the poor in the Dublin lockout, having brought
Iseult there with her on a brief visit.

When the First World War broke out in 1914 she and Iseult
nursed wounded soldiers at Arrens in the Pyrenees, where she
had brought the family for a holiday in the summer. Refused a
passport to return home to Ireland, she and Iseult were given the
rank of Lieutenant. She wrote to Yeats of trying to drown in this
material work of nursing 'the sorrow and disappointment of it all'.
In her heart was growing 'a wild hatred of the war machine which
is grinding the life out of these natures [nations?] and reducing
their population to helpless slavery and ruin'. The greater part of
the wounded were 'resigned to the inevitable, they accept patriotic
duty, but all pray for the end of the war and hope it will be before
they are recovered, and in the hearts of some there is a terrible
secret bitterness'.

In 1915 Maud was nursing in Paris-Plage and Paris. At Easter
1916 the family was back in Colleville, where Yeats joined them
about two months after the Rising in Dublin. Maud learned from
the press in early May that MacBride had been shot and
commented to Yeats that he had died for Ireland. Yeats spent the
summer at Colleville and proposed to Maud again, to be refused
in the usual terms. She was, however, not a little surprised when,
a week afterwards, he asked her permission to propose to Iseult,
but told him he could, but that the child would not marry him.
Iseult enjoyed flirting with him during the summer; he proposed
to her again the next summer and accompanied Maud and the
family to London, where Iseult finally refused him.

In 1916 another phase in Maud's life had begun which could be
called *The Imprisoned Mother*; it lasted until 1922. She had been
given permission to travel from France to England but not Ireland.
Yeats described her to Lady Gregory in 1917 as being in 'a joyous
and self forgetting condition of political hate the like of which I
have not yet encountered'. In London she resumed her painting
and illustrating work, and then, disguised, went to Dublin in
January 1918. There she bought 73 St. Stephen's Green. While
Yeats, who had married Georgie Hyde Lees in October 1917, was
living in Ballinamantane House in County Galway (which Lady
Gregory had lent the newly married couple while the tower at
Gort that Yeats had bought for £35 in 1917 was being made
habitable) Maud was arrested. An alleged treasonable conspiracy

with the Germans was proclaimed by the authorities, who rounded up the leadership of Sinn Féin and the Volunteer Movement. Maud was moved to England and placed in Holloway Gaol. This was indeed a traumatic experience. She wrote to Yeats:

I need hardly tell you that the German plot exists only in the panic disordered imagination of the English Government. Outside my cell is a card *unconvicted prisoner* yet here are kept Countess Markievicz, Mrs Clark and I *au secret*, no visits, no solicitor allowed, no charge made. I live, eat and sleep in a cell 7 feet by 13, a small window so high one can't see out, only about 1/2 foot air opening.

(*L.* p. 395)

She was 'wild with anxiety about Seagan' whom she had last seen running beside the police van that had carried her off to the Bridewell in Dublin when she, Seán and an English MP, Joseph King, were walking to her house in St. Stephen's Green. Yeats and his wife took charge of the fourteen-year-old Seán in the summer.

In the autumn a strong campaign was mounted for Maud's release. Yeats, fearful for her health, saw the Chief Secretary and persuaded him that an independent doctor should be allowed to see her. As a result of this she was sent to a nursing home, from which she went to Yeats's rooms at Woburn Buildings in November, Dr. Tunnicliffe reporting some improvement in her condition. She again disguised herself, got to Dublin and arrived at her house in St. Stephen's Green which she had lent to Yeats and his wife, who was expecting her first child. Fearing the effect of possible police or army raids on his wife who was seriously ill with pneumonia, Yeats refused Maud entry, without telling his wife. A violent quarrel blew up, which was not settled easily, though the Yeatses moved out and Maud was back in her house by Christmas: sometime after that, however, Yeats and Maud were again on friendly terms.

When he returned from a lecture tour in the United States, which lasted from January to May 1920, he came to Ireland to help Maud since Iseult's marriage to Francis Stuart was not going well and Maud thought he would be more effective than she in dealing with the problems that arose. His sensible suggestions were accepted. Maud worked for the Department of Publicity of the Government of the Republic under the direction of Desmond Fitzgerald who was in hiding after the outlawing of Sinn Féin in 1919. When he was arrested Maud asked Yeats to intervene on his behalf so that his wife could see him and he could exercise in the open air. She worked for Fitzgerald's successor Erskine Childers, and she helped to organise relief work – this eventuated in the establishment of the Irish White Cross. She also acted as a judge in the Sinn Féin courts. Meanwhile Seán, officially a law student, was a member of the IRA. He had been imprisoned for breaking the curfew in September 1920 but was released after two days.

Eventually a truce was arranged in the summer of 1921. Maud was hopeful that the Treaty which brought the twenty-six county Irish Free State into being would be a useful basis on which to proceed to full independence, and it seemed to her an improvement on the earlier Home Rule Bill. Her attitude had changed as a result of her experiences in France; she had not had the violently militant outlook of, say, the Countess Markiewicz who had fought in 1916; the ending of bloodshed was a benefit she welcomed. But she may also have hoped that young men such as Seán, now high in the ranks of the IRA, would survive to make their careers in the new state. And she had faith in Arthur Griffith, now President of the Irish Free State.

These attitudes changed soon after the Treaty was signed. The next phase in Maud's life could well be called *The Disillusioned Republican*: it extends from 1923 to 1937. Though she represented Ireland at the Irish Race Convention in Paris in January 1922, sent there by Griffith, and though she was again in Paris on publicity work, she dashed back to Ireland in June when the Free State Government shelled the anti-treaty IRA forces in the Four Courts. Seán was one of those fighting and was detained in Mountjoy Gaol with one hundred and seventy-nine others who surrendered. The fighting continued. Maud and many other politically active women joined together to act as a peace committee. They met the government and the republican forces separately but failed to achieve peace. After Griffith's death in August – Collins was to die in an ambush shortly afterwards – Maud no longer had a close relationship with the new Irish government, now controlled by Cosgrave, Mulcahy and O'Higgins. Her attention turned to the plight of prisoners – her son-in-law Francis Stuart was also interned now – and she realised that organization was called for; she formed the Women's Prisoners Defence League. Charlotte Despard, a cantankerous and at times embittered Englishwoman, an idealistic socialist, pacifist and feminist (and, ironically, the sister of Lord French, a Field Marshal who became Viceroy of Ireland from 1918 to 1921) whom Maud had first met in 1917, was brought into the nationalist cause by enlisting her aid in creating relief for women and children. She became President of the Women's Prisoners Defence League, which was banned in 1923.

She shared the purchase of a house in Clonskeagh, a Dublin suburb, with Maud; this was Roebuck House, which had large gardens, and provided a refuge for many who were in need or on the run. (Before Maud left 73 St. Stephen's Green the house was twice raided by Free State government troops; on the second occasion they burnt all her papers in the street – these included letters sent to her over the years by Yeats.) Both Maud and Mrs Despard organised demonstrations and processions which ended on Sunday mornings in O'Connell Street and which took place despite the banning of public meetings and governmental attempts to suppress them by armed force.

Maud's personal war on the Irish Free State became more outspoken. Arrested and kept in Mountjoy Gaol for a night in January 1923, she and Mrs Despard made good use of this detention for propaganda against the regime and attacked the conditions within the prisons as more political prisoners who opposed the Treaty were incarcerated. Yeats had become a Senator and she wrote to him the day before her arrest to say if he 'did not denounce the government she renounced his society for ever'. He wrote to Iseult to offer to help with the authorities 'in the matter of warm blankets', thinking he could not effect her release. She was, however, arrested again on 10 April and this time she began a hunger strike in Kilmainham Gaol. Mrs Despard heroically and stoically sat outside the prison gates for the twenty days and nights that Maud was in confinement. Yeats urged Cosgrave, the President, to consider her age (she was fifty-seven) but Cosgrave thought the women prisoners could not be considered 'as ordinary females'. The Civil War ended in May 1924, and Maud, who had taken a long time to recover from her hunger strike and imprisonment, launched herself into anti-government campaigning in the election that was held in August 1924. Her next work was on the Released Prisoners' Committee.

Seán MacBride, who had escaped from detention in 1922, was on the run and involved in work for the IRA until 1937 (when he was called to the Bar); he was married in 1926, was overseas for a year but then came back to Ireland in 1927, ostensibly to run the jam manufacturing industry that Mrs Despard had set up in Roebuck House in 1924. This was taken over by Seán MacBride and his wife. In July 1927 he was arrested on suspicion of murdering Kevin O'Higgins. He had a clear alibi, but was detained for some time none the less. Maud asked Yeats to intervene to get him leave to see Josephine, an old nurse, who was dying of cancer. Yeats, however, was unable to get permission and he and Maud exchanged letters defending their personal political attitudes, Yeats telling her on 7 October 1927 that he hadn't answered her last letter because they would never change each other's politics. Seán was again in prison in 1929.

After de Valera's defeat of Cosgrave's government in 1932, an outcome for which Maud and Mrs Despard, along with members of the Women's Prisoners Defence League, had fought strenuously, there was a brief moment when she thought progress could occur in the way she hoped. But soon she was denouncing the new regime as repressive, particularly distressed at the increasing number of political prisoners and their treatment in Irish gaols. She edited *Prison Bars* from 1937 to 1938, a monthly newsheet which largely dealt with prisoners' welfare. The Women's Prisoners Defence League continued to take much of her energy – she still recuperated in spells at various French spas, very severe rheumatism now being the main problem – but she was largely responsible for getting a wide hearing for a pamphlet about Michael Conway, sentenced to death in 1936, which may probably have helped to bring about his release in 1938.

Maud was getting old, but she had written to Yeats in 1928:

On how you hate old age – well so do I, I see no redeeming features in it, but I, who am more a rebel against man than you, rebel less against nature & accept the inevitable & go with it gently into the unknown – only against the sordidness & cruelty of small ambitions I fight until the long rest comes – out of that rest I believe the Great Mother will refashion beauty & life again.

(*L.* p. 445)

She couldn't resist replying, characteristically, to his comments that a book he had sent her, and several letters to other people, had gone astray:

You mustn't feel puzzled about letters not arriving – Free State methods in the post office as in all these departments are British in brutality but minus the efficiency.

Did you ever know a time in Ireland where one felt certain one's letters were not opened & read by the police?

(*L.* p. 446)

And she told the former Free State Senator 'though you voted treason bills & flogging bills for them, they don't trust you'.

Although the Free State she hated was to vanish, becoming Eire, or Ireland, in the Constitution de Valera carried by referendum in 1937, she found the new basis of the state unacceptable in its attitude to women, vastly inferior she thought, to the 1916 Proclamation of the Republic, which had announced equal rights and opportunities for women. The new Constitution seemed to confine women to the home; and Maud had earlier experienced the difficulties of operating in a masculine-dominated political climate in which distrust of women meant their exclusion from full political or indeed economic freedom on the grounds of preserving their social welfare.

Out of the Mainstream might well serve as a title for an account of Maud's last sixteen years from 1937 to 1953. Writing her autobiography *A Servant of the Queen* had occupied her; it was published in 1937 and gave a racily written selective picture, mainly of high-lights of her life up to her marriage. It is an idiosyncratic life, romantically presented, sometimes inaccurate or vague as to dates and ordering, largely because of the destruction of her papers by the Free State soldiery. But it exudes immense vitality and shows how she had devoted herself to the cause of gaining Ireland's freedom from British rule. That is one way of putting it, but ultimately one which is too restrictive, because her concern was for the poor and the underprivileged as well, and her sympathies were instantly engaged by instances of injustice and unkindness. Her own incarcerations, in Holloway, in Mountjoy and Kilmainham gaols, had strengthened her hatred of the cruelties of the penal system: it was particularly disturbing for her to discover the new independent Ireland was even worse than England in its treatment of prisoners. And then there was the matter of the border: was a twenty-six county republic a fully independent Ireland? At the age of seventy-two Maud spoke most effectively at an anti-partition meeting in County Donegal in 1939; that year Yeats died at the age of seventy-three and Mrs Despard (whose funeral oration Maud delivered at Glasnevin Cemetery) at the age of ninety-five.

Maud's attitude to the Second World War was in some ways complex. She was strongly in favour of neutrality, and had written in support of it in an article in *The Kerryman* in June 1938. She thought the world's troubles were caused by international capitalism. Dating back to the German aid in attempting to provide arms for the insurgents in 1916 and the vain effort to raise an Irish force among the Irish prisoners of war to fight on the German side was the view that England's enemies were Ireland's friends. And her attention was focussed on Ireland, though there was a background awareness of the sheer waste of war; indeed she thought that Orangemen might prefer neutrality if American aid brought about the end of partition. After the war was over characteristically she turned her attention to the plight of children, urging shipments of food to Germany. She was now largely bedridden, her heart weak; though hoping no more young lives would be sacrificed, she could no longer herself campaign actively on behalf of prisoners, as a letter she wrote to the *Irish Times* reveals: 'Those unable to serve can *demand* nothing; therefore I, who am so and almost bedridden, make my last request.' Seán MacBride, however, continued her fight on behalf of the Republicans, who were judged by military tribunals, through the courts. At the inquest into the death of Sean McCaughey, for instance, who died on hunger strike in 1946 after being held for five years, he was able to make clear the conditions under which prisoners were being held. He formed a new party, Clann na Poblachta, and was elected a TD; in the ensuing coalition government he became Minister of External Affairs, and the Taoiseach, John Costello, repealed the External Relations Act, taking Ireland out of the British Commonwealth.

Maud found old age trying; she broke a hip; she had pneumonia and influenza; and she found writing a second volume of autobiography to be called *The Tower of Age* too much to complete as she contemplated some of the sadness of the past. She did, however, give a number of impressively vigorous radio talks on the fiftieth year of Inghínidhe na hÉireann. While she enjoyed the company of her family – Seán and his wife and their two children lived in Roebuck House – many of her former friends were now dead, and she found the restrictions increasing enfeeblement of body imposed on her akin to the frustrating helplessness of being imprisoned. Her heart muscles had weakened so much that she now spent her time in bed. Her father had brought her up not to fear death (something she passed on to her son) and by the eighty-sixth year of her eventful, exciting life she was more than willing to liberate herself from the material world into what she believed would be the freer life of the spirit.

O'CASEY AT WAR

CHRISTOPHER MURRAY

O'Casey's attitude to life was from first to last combative. His autobiography in six books begins with the birth of a child (John Casside) determined to fight for life in a context of suffering; it ends with an old man (Sean O'Casey), having endured many transformations as a result of socio-political conditions, shouting 'Hurrah!' in the face of death itself. Yet one cannot read far into O'Casey's plays, prose and letters without discovering a personality steeped in the joy of life and impatient with nay-sayers of any kind. We find a fighter who loved peace; a humanist who was a socialist; a communist whose vocabulary was enduringly Christian. He was, as the saying goes, a tissue of contradictions.

His career as playwright falls into several phases which can be clarified through a consideration of O'Casey's attitude to war. In his early days as a writer, before 1914, O'Casey was an ardent nationalist and a supporter of the militant aims of the Irish Republican Brotherhood (forerunners of the IRA). Many of these early publications, articles and poems, have been collected in *Feathers from the Green Crow*, edited by Robert Hogan (1962), and they make surprising reading. They are as naive as they are patriotic. Even after the Dublin railway strike of 1911, which he was to dramatize first in *The Harvest Festival* (unstaged, written 1918–19) and later in *Red Roses for Me* (1943[1]), O'Casey was not yet in favour of international socialism. He hoped instead for an alliance between workers and republican separatists. The Dublin lock-out of 1913 changed his mind. Thereafter socialism began to take precedence in his world-view, although it was not until after the Russian Revolution of 1917 that he saw what this meant: that Yeats's 'terrible beauty' was born not in Dublin in Easter 1916 but in Russia.[2] Thereafter, as writer, he made the 1916 Rising the centre of his artistic statement. In condemning the 1916 Rising he was turning his back on militant republicanism and, indeed, on war. Many years were to pass before he could take a fresh look at war and, by a process of hindsight fused with fantasy, a justification for violence is found. These two distinct phases of O'Casey's career, with their contradictory attitudes towards war, provide the main subject of this essay.

It is necessary before proceeding to discuss O'Casey's dramatization of 1916 and the wars which followed to explain a little further how it was that he came not to be involved in the 1916 Rising in the first place. The simplest explanation is that he was ill at the time, but, of course, that has little to do with the matter. He had long severed direct association with the militants. Desmond Greaves says it was because of O'Casey's mother, for whom O'Casey was caring at the time, and Greaves implies that this explanation was, in turn, a cloak for O'Casey's lack of physical courage.[3] Once again, such simple reasons are beside the point. For since the Dublin lock-out of 1913 O'Casey's politics had undergone a sea-change.

The labour leader Jim Larkin had founded the Irish Transport and General Workers' Union, to which O'Casey gave allegiance, and in August 1913 the employers, notably the owner of the Dublin tramways William Martin Murphy, locked out the unionized workers. Through the months of hardship which followed the city was polarized. The middle classes demanded public transport and made use of scab labour on the trams and elsewhere. O'Casey formed the view that the nationalists with whom he formerly sympathized were strike-breakers. Moreover, he witnessed the brutality of the forces of law and order against his fellow workers. O'Casey was appointed secretary of a relief committee. Then a workers' defence was formed, the Irish Citizen Army; O'Casey drafted its constitution and became the first secretary. He was to be its historian in a few years' time (*The Story of the Citizen Army*, 1919), but that was after he had left in serious disagreement with policy. 'The Army stood for the absolute unity of nationhood, and the rights and liberties of the world's democracies. No scab or blackleg could be one of them, and every member, whenever possible, had to be a member of a trade union, recognized by the Trades Union Congress.'[4] In November 1913 the National Volunteers were founded, the group destined to be the main fighting body in 1916. 'O'Casey was antagonistic to them from the start; with some reason, for their supporters included many people who had been anti-worker during the 1913 strike.'[5] He tried to have a motion passed which would prevent an alliance between the Irish Citizen Army and the Volunteers. He failed and resigned as secretary. He took no further part in the gathering of the political storm which broke in 1916. As O'Casey saw it, and as he makes clear in his history of the Citizen Army, the labour movement betrayed itself by allying with the republican nationalist movement. He later blamed James Connolly, who took over leadership of the Citizen Army when Larkin went to the United States in October 1914, for this decision and for making joint-cause with Padraic Pearse, leader of the Volunteers. Thus to O'Casey, sixty or seventy years before the revisionist historians made the case, the 1916 Rising was a tragic error. The only hero of this episode, he claimed, was the pacifist Francis Sheehy-Skeffington, 'the living antithesis of the Easter Insurrection'.[6] It is logical enough for *The Plough and the Stars* (1926) to be seen, consequently, as a pacifist statement, but this is true only because the cause, in O'Casey's view, was wrong. Of course, all of the foregoing represents O'Casey's 'invention', his re-structuring and re-interpretation of events, perhaps thirty years after their occurrence. This alerts us to the fact that O'Casey was an artist and not a historian: as he re-made himself imaginatively (in the *Autobiographies*) so too he re-made the history of his time and transformed it into drama (and in the later plays into myth).

In the text of *The Plough and the Stars*, which provides the key to the three great Dublin plays, Pearse and Connolly are the only signatories of the proclamation (of the Irish Republic) to be mentioned by name. This is deliberate. O'Casey is providing an analysis of events which is simplified but coherent. The fatal alliance was between the Irish Citizen Army (whose emblem was the plough and stars) and the Irish Volunteers (whose emblem was the tricolour signifying union of green and orange interests): Connolly and Pearse represented this alliance. In the cast of characters all but one are working-class (the soldiers among them being members of the Citizen Army); the one exception, Lieutenant Langon, a civil servant, is a member of the Volunteers.

Langon, in the minority though he is, has as spokesman the Figure in the Window, whose speeches are culled from those by Padraic Pearse, 'The Coming Revolution' (1914), 'Peace and the Gael' (1915, two excerpts), and the oration at the graveside of O'Donovan Rossa (1915). In the first production, the actor making those speeches imitated Pearse 'in almost his very accents'.[7] They are bloody and blood-curdling words, such as, 'Bloodshed is a cleansing and sanctifying thing, and the nation that regards it as the final horror has lost its manhood', or 'Such august homage was never offered to God as this: the homage of millions of lives given gladly for love of country', or 'War is a terrible thing, but war is not an evil thing [...] When war comes to Ireland she must welcome it as she would welcome the Angel of God!'[8] Langon echoes these sentiments when he and the two members of the ICA, Clitheroe and Brennan, run into the public house for a drink: his are the most incendiary comments of the three, although all three utter similar blasphemies: 'Th' time is rotten ripe for revolution . . . Ireland is greater than a mother . . . Th' time for Ireland's battle is now – th' place for Ireland's battle is here . . . Wounds for th' Independence of Ireland!' (*CP*, 1, 213–4). It is appropriate that it is Langon who is graphically and painfully wounded during the Rising as depicted in act 3: 'Everyone else escapin', an' me gettin' me belly ripped asundher!.. [. . .] Me clothes seem to be all soakin' wet . . . It's blood . . . My God, it must be me own blood!' (*CP*, 1, 234). And Langon becomes an icon of war's realistic violence and pain.

If this train of consequences from Pearse's romantic bloodlust to Langon's exhibition of panic at the realization of impending death were not enough, O'Casey provides Nora Clitheroe's reaction to the men fighting at the barricades. In the first place she repudiates the notion that her protest at her husband's involvement is in any way cowardly, as she was told: 'Me who risked more for love than they would risk for hate . . . He is to be butchered as a sacrifice to th' dead!' (*CP*, 1, 220). As a pregnant woman she asserts the greater risk she takes 'for love' than the soldiers take 'for hate', and thereby Nora establishes a debate between fertility and war. This opposition forms part of the general imagery in the play of 'home' and its protection from assault or invasion established in the opening scene, where we find Fluther Good installing a lock on Nora Clitheroe's door to secure her home in all its associations. In act 4 Nora has lost both her baby and her home when news is brought of Jack Clitheroe's 'heroic' death: the irony here is matched only by that of the British soldiers' joining in the song, from World War I, Ivor Novello's 'Keep the Home Fires Burning', as the play ends. In act 3, however, O'Casey is intent upon his *agon*, his fierce denunciation of a pointless and costly battle. And so Nora moves on to assert, in the second place, that it is the fighting men themselves who are afraid, but 'afraid to say they're afraid!' (*CP*, 1, 221). She instances a dead body she saw in the street, and so describes it that it stands metonymically for all killed in battle. The details are expressionistic in their exaggerated, nightmarish intensity:

An' in th' middle o' th' sthreet was somethin' huddled up in a horrible tangled heap . . . His face was jammed again [st] th' stones, an' his arm was twisted round his back . . . An' every twist of his body was a cry against th' terrible thing that had happened to him . . . An' I saw they were afraid to look at it . . .

(*CP*, 1, 221).

This focus on the particularities of death under gunfire is found again in act 4 when the British soldiers come under attack from a sniper on the roofs of the tenements. Here the expressionism which was to find its full force in *The Silver Tassie* is tentatively on offer again: '*Voices in a lilting chant to the left in a distant street*, Red Cr . . . oss, Red Cr . . . oss! . . . Ambu . . . lance, Ambu . . . lance!' (*CP*, 1, 241). When this cry is repeated Corporal Stoddart reacts with revealing passion: 'Christ, that's another of our men 'it by that blawsted sniper! 'E's knocking abaht 'ere, somewheres. Gawd, when we gets th' bloighter, we'll give 'im the cold steel, we will. We'll jab the belly out of 'im, we will!' (*CP*, 1, 250). In the event, Stoddard and Sergeant Tinley succeed only in shooting Bessie Burgess, whom they mistake for the sniper: 'Well, we couldn't afford to toike any chawnces.' (*CP*, 1, 260). Such is the logic of warfare, as O'Casey repudiates it.

Although *The Plough and the Stars* covers historic ground anterior to the settings of *The Shadow of a Gunman* (1923) and *Juno and the Paycock* (1924) it comes last in the order of composition. It is necessary, however, to consider *The Plough* first, because the roots of O'Casey's anti-war feelings are most in evidence there. If one accepts the analogy of Shakespeare's history plays – and O'Casey's three Dublin plays are in their own specific way history plays – one might point out that these were not written in chronological order either: the *Henry VI* plays, set after 1420, were written and staged before *Richard II*, which is set in 1399 and contains the clue to the whole series of history plays which culminate in *Richard III*. Shakespeare finds the roots of disorder and civil war in the act of assassinating the deposed King Richard II. In a comparable way, O'Casey was to trace the wars which lasted until 1923 to the primal error of the 1916 Rising. *The Shadow of a Gunman*, set in 1920, dramatizes the chaos dominant in Dublin during the period when the notorious Black-and-Tan regiment brutally attempted to suppress the Sinn Fein guerilla forces. *Juno and the Paycock* is set in 1922 when the IRA, or 'Die-hards' as they are called in the play, are engaged in civil war with the supporters of the Treaty and the newly established Irish Free State. Captain

Boyle comically uses the refrain, 'The whole worl's is in a state o' chassis', meaning *chaos*, and this refrain underlines the serious, political themes of the play, the breakdown of loyalties and the moral disorder associated with irresponsibility. O'Casey provides the correct gloss on these later plays when he says in *Inishfallen, Fare Thee Well*: 'The cause of the Easter Rising [of 1916] had been betrayed by the commonplace bourgeois class, who laid low the concept of the common good and the common task, and were now decorating themselves with the privileges and powers dropped in their flight by those defeated by the dear, dead men.'[9]

The attitude to war presented in *The Shadow of a Gunman* is that war is no longer a simple, romantic setting but a complex site of instability and danger. If O'Casey foregrounds the comedy inherent in the antics of Shields and Davoren, underlined by the absurdity of another would-be writer, Mr Gallogher, with his letter of complaint to the IRA (which Davoren is invited to admire and the audience both to mock and to parallel with Davoren's own efforts at composition), the tragic elements in the background force themselves into the central space so that comedy yields to tragedy and a bitter irony is conceived. Just as Maguire, the inoffensive little man thought to have gone catching butterflies in Knocksedan, leaves a bag of bombs in Shields's room which eventually exposes the cowardice of Shields and Davoren in a comic way and leads to Minnie Powell's heroic if futile act of sacrifice, so Adolphus Grigson exhibits a double response to the raiding Black-and-Tan soldiers. As a loyalist and an Orangeman he is cocksure of his safety; as a drunken Irishman he is terror-stricken before the out-of-control invaders of the tenement. Grigson is both ridiculous and a realistic measure of the uncertainties to be feared. When Mrs Grigson reports to Shields how the Black-and-Tans teased Grigson by forcing him to sing a hymn while they drank his whiskey the combination of comedy and the deadly serious which is the keynote of the play is once again sounded: 'there's torture for you, an' they all laughin' at poor Dolphie's terrible sufferins'. (*CP*, 1, 150)

The voice could be the voice of Beckett. But O'Casey uses this absurdity only to press home the point of the insecurity of civilians in a world where public danger invades private peace (a recurring pattern in the play). Grigson says: 'You're sure of your life nowhere now; it's just as safe to go everywhere as it is to go anywhere. An' they don't give a damn whether you're a loyal man or not.' (*CP*, 1, 142) Shields, a Catholic from the other side, so to speak, has a similar comment to make: 'It's the civilians that suffer; when there's an ambush they don't know where to run. Shot in the back to save the British Empire, an' shot in the breast to save the soul of Ireland.' (*CP*, 1, 132) Ironically, this is just how Minnie Powell is killed at the end of the play. The Black-and-Tans, having arrested Minnie, are ambushed by the IRA; as Minnie tried to 'jump off the lorry she was on' (*CP*, 1, 156) she was caught in crossfire and shot 'through the buzzom' (thus, probably by the IRA: she had her wounds, like Young Siward in *Macbeth*, in front). The absurdity of her death is plain to the audience, aware as Minnie was not that Davoren was not worth saving.

What O'Casey does, then, in *The Shadow of a Gunman* and *The Plough and the Stars* is to demythologize the romantic, heroic ideal of blood-sacrifice. He has the cheek to counterpose Yeats in this matter. With *Cathleen Ni Houlihan* (1902) Yeats and Lady Gregory had defined in dramatic terms the ideal of sacrifice unto death for the sake of Ireland, allegorized as an old woman whose youth can be renewed thereby. By the end of this one-act play the old woman has become a young girl, with 'the walk of a queen',[10] a veritable goddess of nationalism. *Cathleen Ni Houlihan* was to become associated with the 1916 rising, as Padraic Pearse formulated a doctrine of necessary blood-sacrifice quite close to the symbolism of Yeats. By 1920, however, terror had replaced romance in the streets of Dublin, a city under curfew, and in the countryside. Seumas Shields puts it thus:

The country is gone mad. Instead of counting their beads now they're countin' bullets... An' you daren't open your mouth, for Kathleen ni Houlihan is very different now to the woman who used to play the harp an' sing 'Weep on, weep on, your hour is past', for she's a ragin' divil now, an' if you only look crooked at her you're sure of a punch in th' eye.
(*CP*, 1, 131–2)

Where Yeats, prior to 1916, had romanticized war – or at least the commitment to rebellion – O'Casey, after 1916, issued a counter-statement. O'Casey, after all, wrote his Dublin plays while the national consciousness was still in formation, and he threw into question the validity of an armed struggle which exposed all sides and both sexes to the dangers of modern street-warfare.

The tone of *Juno and the Paycock* is less strident in this regard. One can see why long queues formed around the corner of the Abbey Theatre for the first production in March 1924. With actors of the calibre of F.J. McCormick as Joxer Daly, Barry Fitzgerald as Captain Boyle and Sara Allgood as Juno audiences were in for a treat of pure, comic Dublinese. To an extent they were rewarded, and their expectations fulfilled. At the same time they had to put up with some searing anti-war sentiments. O'Casey introduced this serious material through the marginal character, Johnny Boyle, virtually an icon of the folly of warfare. Having lost his arm in the fighting of 1916 Johnny had a leg shattered in the subsequent war of independence. Now he wants out of the whole business but is in terror that his old comrades will catch up with him for betraying Robbie Tancred, with whose reported death in an ambush the play opens. O'Casey had wanted to entitle *The Shadow of a Gunman On the Run*,[11] to focus on Davoren's supposed IRA involvement, but the title would better suit *Juno*. For Johnny Boyle is a portrait of a real man on the run, and O'Casey originally intended to make him the central character.[12] Johnny is modern, dispossessed, alienated man, whose crippled bodily state records a psyche shattered through the effects of war. To Juno's complaint that his panic-driven state is his own fault, 'sleepin' wan [one] night in me sisther's, an' the nex' in your father's brother's – you'll get no rest goin' on that way', Johnny replies with bleak acceptance of his fugitive status: 'I can rest nowhere, nowhere, nowhere.' (*CP*, 1, 41) Johnny's terror is palpable, and his life seems as uncertain as the flame before the holy lamp, the extinction of which throws him into hysteria. At the end of act 2 when a member of the IRA comes to summon Johnny to an IRA meeting we see how inescapable Johnny's position is:

Johnny. I'm not going', then. I know nothing about Tancred.

The Young Man [at the door]. You'd betther come for your own sake – remember your oath.

Johnny [passionately]. I won't go! Haven't I done enough for Ireland! I've lost me arm, an' me hip's desthroyed so that I'll never be able to walk right agen! Good God, haven't I done enough for Ireland?

The Young Man. Boyle, no man can do enough for Ireland!

(*CP*, 1, 60)

The insatiable appetite of militant republicanism is here dramatized. Inevitably, as the play draws to a close, Johnny is taken away for execution. O'Casey wanted to show the execution scene on stage, as he told Gabriel Fallon,[13] but the Abbey directors cut the scene. Fallon (who played Bentham in the first production of *Juno*) thought the directors right, on the basis that Johnny's fate is made abundantly clear. But when one reads the chapter entitled 'Comrades' in *Inishfallen* one begins to regret the loss of the scene (whatever happened to it in manuscript). That horrifying episode culminates in the Dublin mountains where a young republican soldier is tracked down by a Free-State Colonel:

– I'm an old comrade of yours, Mick, the young man pleaded.

– Sure I know that well, said the Colonel heartily, and I'll say this much – for the sake of oul' times, we won't let you suffer long.

– Jesus! whimpered the half-dead lad, yous wouldn't shoot an old comrade, Mick!

The Colonel's arm holding the gun shot forward suddenly, the muzzle of the gun, tilted slightly upwards, splitting the lad's lips and crashing through his chattering teeth.

– Be Jasus! We would, he said, and then he pulled the trigger.[14]

This is quite close to the dialogue in act 3 of *Juno*:

Johnny. I'm an oul' comrade – yous wouldn't shoot an oul' comrade.

Second Irregular. Poor Tancred was an oul' comrade o' yours, but you didn't think o' that when you gave him away to the gang that sent him to his grave . . .

                                                              (*CP*, 1, 84)

O'Casey's instinct was to show rather than merely to narrate; arguably, a scene showing the violent execution would have carried cathartic shock values and added to the tragic intensity of the ending of *Juno*. It was because of this need to show 'the garlanded horror of war'[15] and not merely to narrate it that O'Casey went on to write *The Silver Tassie* (1929) with its controversial second act.

                                   2

With *The Silver Tassie* O'Casey entered a new phase of his playwriting career. To what extent it was clear to O'Casey himself that he was doing so is a moot point. He was now in London, newly married to a glamorous actress, and although the new play was written for the Abbey (and with specific actors in mind) and first submitted to the Abbey it was breaking new ground. By the time he wrote *Rose and Crown*, the fourth book of the autobiography, however (1952), it was quite clear to O'Casey himself that with *The Silver Tassie* he was going in a new direction: 'There was no importance in trying to do the same thing again,

letting the second play imitate the first, and the third the second.'
(*Autobiographies*, 2, 270). But even then, in 1952, O'Casey failed to
recognize that *The Silver Tassie* marked a divide with his preceding
subject matter. Up to this point, his attention was focused on the
development of the nationalist consciousness and its conflict with
a socialist vision of a new republic. Coherence was given to the
incoherence of contemporary history by means of this commitment
to a point of view. But now O'Casey turned his attention to the
1914–18 war and its terrible desecration of human life, without
providing any analysis of the Irish attitude towards this war: there
is no Man outside the Window in *The Silver Tassie* to contextualize
the action. O'Casey could have found such a figure in John
Redmond, leader of the Irish Parliamentary Party, who encouraged Irishmen to volunteer for service in the 1914–18 war, on
the (mistaken) assumption that Home Rule, on hold ever since the
outbreak of the war, would be ensured by a good-will policy of
support by the Irish for the British war effort, *'wherever needed'*.[16]
No such argument finds its way into O'Casey's play. He ignores
the politics of Home Rule; *The Silver Tassie* transcends nationalist
concerns. O'Casey was extending his dramaturgy to a wider,
humanistic brief: the issue of world war in a so-called civilized,
Christian era.

This is one reason why Yeats failed to appreciate the greatness
of *The Silver Tassie* – for it is a great play, even though a flawed
and over-ambitious one. Yeats wanted O'Casey to stay in the
groove the Abbey had made for him. To Olivia Shakespear he
wrote after he had rejected O'Casey's play: 'The play is all anti-
war propaganda to the exclusion of plot and character . . . Of
course if we had played his play, his fame is so great that we
would have had full house for a time, *but we had hoped to turn him
into a different path*.'[17] That path, essentially, was the path of Synge
(d. 1909). O'Casey had obviously felt the pressure to go down and
stay down that path, because in January 1926 he wrote in some
exasperation to Lennox Robinson, one of the three directors of the
Abbey board and manager/producer at this time:

I am sorry, but I'm not Synge; not even, I'm afraid, a reincarnation.
Besides, things have happened since Synge: the war has shaken some of
the respectability out of the heart of man; we have had our own
changes, and the U.S.S.R. has fixed a new star in the sky . . .[18]

The new direction O'Casey was groping towards was
expressionism. O'Casey later insisted that he knew nothing about
expressionism in 1928. 'I never consciously adopted "expres-

sionism", which I don't understand and never did.'[19] The matter has been much debated but there is no doubt that O'Casey saw expressionist plays staged by the Dublin Drama League before 1926, in particular Ernst Toller's *Masse Mensch* (*Masses and Man*).[20] Gabriel Fallon adds that O'Casey 'professed, too, a great regard for Strindberg's *The Dream Play* which he had read but which the League had not done' (p. 47). Strindberg's *A Dream Play* (1901) is commonly regarded as the first expressionist play, and Strindberg's note may be taken as outlining the new principles involved:

> In this dream play the author has [...] attempted to imitate the inconsequent yet transparently logical shape of a dream. Everything can happen, everything is possible and probable. Time and place do not exist; on an insignificant basis of reality the imagination spins, weaving new patterns; a mixture of memories, experiences, free fancies, incongruities and improvisations. The characters split, double, multiply, evaporate, condense, disperse, assemble. But one consciousness rules over them all, that of the dreamer; for him there are no secrets, no illogicalities, no scruples, no laws. He neither acquits nor condemns, but merely relates.[21]

Post-war expressionism, emanating initially from Germany, was full of bitterness, disillusion and despair. One of the first examples of this new form in English was Eugene O'Neill's *The Hairy Ape* (1922), which O'Casey knew and admired: 'O'Neill's loud shout on a first advent to the Drama.'[22] Thus we find O'Casey easily referring to these authors as early as 1924, when he wrote to Lady Gregory about Upton Sinclair's *The Singing Jailbirds*:

> The Play is not comparable to either O'Neill's 'Hairy Ape', or Toller's 'Masses & Men.' The sentiments expressed seem to be to be the old lust for martyrdom, as dangerous in the Labour Movement as it is in Politics.[23]

It may be inferred, then, that O'Casey adopted expressionism without fully realizing what he was about. Yeats, however, was floored by *The Silver Tassie*. All Yeats could see were the warning lights of propaganda, a dreaded word in his lexicon. Thus, in the famous letter rejecting *The Silver Tassie* (20 April 1928), Yeats could only argue that O'Casey had 'no subject' because he was writing, not of Irish history and politics, but of a war which he had not personally experienced, 'and so write out of your opinions. You illustrate those opinions by a series of almost unrelated scenes , as you might in a leading article . . .'[24] Yeats went on to insist that O'Casey's dramaturgy was unacceptable because, in effect, he had ceased to write as Aristotle had prescribed in the *Poetics*. Of course, Yeats had not the faintest idea what expressionism was and so was no help whatever to O'Casey here. In August 1928 Lady Gregory read Denis Johnston's expressionistic play, later entitled *The Old Lady Says 'No!'*, to Yeats at Coole; Yeats disliked it, and Lady Gregory added:

> Yeats had said 'I told G.B.S. the other day I perhaps ought not to judge plays but give place to someone else, as I don't know much about impressionism [*sic*], and he said "There is nothing in it, in impressionism"'.
> I asked Yeats then 'What is impressionism?' and he said 'No law' – and I said 'all jaw', and he said 'Just so'. And that certainly describes this play.[25]

Apparently it described *The Silver Tassie* also.

The Silver Tassie depicts war as obscene, sacrilegious and absurd. It does this in two distinct ways: by presenting the case history of Harry Heegan, an athlete who ends up in a wheelchair, and by illustrating the horrors of modern warfare through the experimental means used in act 2. The characterization of Harry Heegan is an extension of the symbolism used in depicting Johnny Boyle in *Juno*. This time we see before and after. We see Harry in act 1 at the peak of his physical powers, on leave from France, a footballer who champions his winning team, 'a herculean young athlete and infantry soldier', as David Krause calls him.[26] Harry is a manual worker, indeed, a stage direction says, '*a typical young worker, enthusiastic, very often boisterous, sensible by instinct rather than by reason. He has gone to the trenches as unthinkingly as he would go to the polling booth.*' (*CP*, 2, 25) We have, therefore, a working-class Adonis about to be sacrificed on the altar, roughly speaking, of a bourgeois conspiracy. The class question is only faintly impressed on the play but it is important nevertheless. In act 2, where Harry does not actually appear, the weary soldiers on view in the war zone are mostly non-ranked, and presented anonymously and in 'masses'; the officer class is by contrast privileged and pampered. An officer has Barney punished for stealing a cock while he himself was fornicating: the soldiers, sympathetic to Barney, scorn the 'Brass-hat' as a decorated non-combatant who "as to do the thinking for the Tommies!' (*CP*, 2, 49). The Visitor, some sort of a politician, who comes to see the war for himself, is mocked likewise as a coward who nevertheless patronizes the fighting men. He is not pleased when the Corporal makes little of Barney's crime:

Visitor [*reprovingly, to the Corporal*]. Seriously, Corporal, seriously please. Sacred, sacred: property of the citizen of a friendly State, sacred. On Active Service, serious to steal a fowl, a cock. [*To Barney*] The uniform, the cause, boy, the corps. Infra dignitatem, boy, infra dignitatem.

(*CP*, 2, 41)

The Visitor is soon exposed for the self-interested party he is: he will take 'no unnecessary risks', (*CP*, 2, 47) and flees as quickly as he can when battle threatens.

In this regard, in O'Casey's treatment of the First World War from the point of view of the common soldier, *The Silver Tassie* must be contrasted with R.C. Sheriff's *Journey's End* (1928). The latter, set in the trenches in 1918, dealt with war from the officers' point of view, and with young Laurence Olivier in the lead it did so well on the London stage as to infuriate O'Casey. When it was revived in 1939 O'Casey was to call *Journey's End* 'That backboneless & ribless play' (a view expanded in *Rose and Crown*), and felt vindicated, 'for when it came out first, I ventured to say it was no good, &, England's heart stopped beating. I got into an infernal row, for all said I said it because of *The Silver Tassie* being a war-play too; &, of course, I was jealous of *Journey's End*. Well, time has shown I made more than a guess.'[27] Sheriff dramatized the horror of war, but O'Casey also showed the victimization of the masses. In order to press home this point O'Casey depicted the aftermath.

When we see Harry again, in act 3, he is in hospital in a wheelchair. His anguish over his paralyzed state is contrasted with the indifference of the doctor from another class, Surgeon Maxwell, ominously depicted as unable to keep his hands off the nurses. While Harry holds on to the faint hope that an operation might restore him to health so long as nobody says to him 'While there's life there's hope!', Surgeon Maxwell reveals his cynicism:

Harry [*after a pause*]. I'm looking forward to the operation to-morrow.
Surgeon Maxwell. That's the way to take it. While there's life there's hope [*with a grin and a wink at Susie*]. And now we'll have a look at Twenty-six.
[*Harry, when he hears 'while there's life there's hope', wheels himself madly out left; half-way out he turns his head and stretches to look out into the grounds, then he goes on.*]
Susie. Will the operation to-morrow be successful?
Surgeon Maxwell. Oh, of course; very successful.
Susie. Do him any good, d'ye think?
Surgeon Maxwell. Oh, blast the good it'll do him.

(*CP*, 2, 68)

In act 4, some time later, the crippled Harry is shown, alongside the blinded Teddy, as incapable of accepting his role on the margins of society. Here O'Casey seems to draw on the war poetry of Wilfred Owen, and especially on 'Disabled', which begins:

> He sat in a wheeled chair, waiting for dark,
> And shivered in his ghastly suit of grey,
> Legless, sewn short at elbow. Through the park
> Voices of boys rang saddening like a hymn,
> Voices of play and pleasure after day,
> Till gathering sleep had mothered them from him.[28]

The speaker in the poem, too, was once a footballer and recalls being 'After the matches, carried shoulder-high', as Harry Heegan was in the first production in act 1 of *The Silver Tassie*.[29] The speaker, too, joined up 'after football, when he'd drunk a peg', without forethought: 'He wonders why'. In his paralyzed state the speaker experiences what Harry experiences in act 4:

> To-night he noticed how the women's eyes
> Passed from him to the strong men that were whole.

(p. 76)

In *The Silver Tassie*, however, the paralyzed man is not content to sit and feel self-pity. With blazing fury he attacks those he sees as having betrayed him, Jessie and Barney, and crushes the trophy, the silver tassie, under his wheelchair in a rage of self-identification. But because he fails to identify and target the real source of his destruction, among the societal forces which engaged in war in the first place, Harry merely alienates himself further. Jack Mitchell argues that here O'Casey 'holds his working people responsible for their own actions, because he knows them to be the only shapers of history',[30] but this is untenable. Why should the likes of Surgeon Maxwell and Susie Monican assume the status of approved commentators at the end of the play? To be sure, life must go on and those who cannot dance must step aside, but the form of the play leaves unchallenged the right of these two shallow creatures to articulate anything which we can accept as adequate to the tragedy of war. The text sidesteps the casualties of war and endorses the dance of life. This leaves unresolved the question of responsibility for war and its destructiveness.

As is well known, *The Silver Tassie* marks a major turning point in O'Casey's career. The rejection by the Abbey cut him adrift from a theatre within which he could work, and for ten years made O'Casey turn his back on his real subject-matter, Ireland and Irish socio-political affairs. True, *The Silver Tassie* was eventually staged at the Abbey, in 1935, and O'Casey made his peace with Yeats; but the row which broke out over this production (in 1935), while not at all on the scale of the riots which had greeted *The Plough and the Stars* in 1926, did nothing to persuade O'Casey that his proper place was with the Abbey. He never again offered the Abbey a new play.

Four years were to pass before he had another play staged in London. This was *Within the Gates* (1933), which had an important American première (in a different and better production) some months later. For all its faults (it is over-long, with too many characters even in its revised, 'stage', version, and tries to incorporate too many themes), *Within the Gates* is an extraordinary play. It holds post-war England up to scrutiny and finds it totally wanting, spiritually, intellectually and politically. It is a latter-day morality play in the guise of expressionism. Heinz Kosok insists that *Within the Gates* 'shows no influence at all of the drama of German expressionism', but he does not mention Strindberg.[31] In April 1925 O'Casey saw and admired *The Spook Sonata*, produced by the Dublin Drama League. His friend Gabriel Fallon played Old Hummel. He described how O'Casey, 'who was obviously impressed by the play, professed to understand it ten minutes after its production, when I found him waiting for me as usual in the Green Room.'[32] All Fallon could get out of O'Casey's was 'It's a great criticism of life', but this in itself is revealing. It implies that Strindberg was a poet (for Matthew Arnold had defined poetry as, at bottom, a criticism of life), and this is what O'Casey now aimed to be: a poet in the modern theatre. This did not mean writing in verse, although there is verse in *Within the Gates* as there was in *The Silver Tassie*, but the use of the stage in a symbolic and anti-realistic style.

Within the Gates is set in a large city park, clearly modelled – because of Speakers' Corner – on Hyde Park. Each of the four scenes takes place in a different season, beginning with spring and ending with winter, and at a different time of day, beginning with early morning and ending with dark night. The action seems continuous but these time specifications ensure that a montage effect is achieved; O'Casey first envisaged the story as a film, and the techniques he used indicate a debt to film.[33] Lighting effects, accordingly, become quite important. In particular, a war memorial is variously lit in the four scenes, so that its significance can be emphasized. Here, in fact, is the link with the theme of *The Silver Tassie*.

Within the Gates unfolds a story of a young woman, dying like the age she lives in from the effects of neglect and exploitation (a Mollser in a new guise, or a Rosie Redmond with a bad heart), who is in search of salvation and peace. In the park she does not want for advice and intellectual argument but the main contenders for her soul (her body being already in the public domain since she is a prostitute) are the Dreamer (a poet), the Bishop (her natural father, it emerges), the Atheist (her step-father) and the Salvation Army Officer. The Young Woman's mother, simply called Old Woman, alcoholic and prematurely aged, follows Young Woman around and unwittingly brings to light the paternity of the Bishop. Since everything in the play is symbolic (as O'Casey himself insisted),[34] one must see the struggle for Young Woman's salvation or deliverance as part of a socio-political argument. The clues are in the text. As scene 3 opens a band plays 'Land of Hope and Glory'; it is an autumn evening; two Attendants discuss the music and ask, 'Why aren't we part of the 'ope en' the glory?' (*CP*, 2, 177). In the background is heard the chant of the Down-and-Outs, 'We challenge life no more, no more, with our dead faith, and our dead hope'. (*CP*, 2, 196) It is the era of the Depression, the early 1930s. The Down-and-Outs, with their defeatist chant, represent the greatest danger O'Casey could imagine to the human spirit. Yet the Bishop calls them 'God's own aristocracy, the poor in spirit!' (*CP*, 2, 196). They will get the Young Woman in the end, he threatens. O'Casey's aim is to make crystal clear, through images, music and dance, not only the tragedy underlying this predicament but its relation to the war just fought and won.

Thus scene 4 opens in winter, in darkness, with the 'Last Post' sounding in the background. The whole world, we are told, is upside down. Or as the Old Woman puts it, 'Everything golden is going into the bellies of the worms.' (*CP*, 2, 213) She becomes the key figure to the post-war climate. Her husband was killed in the war, and she brings a wreath to lay at the base of the war memorial presiding over the space where the action takes place. In the first scene the war memorial is described as: *'in the form of a steel-helmeted soldier, the head bent on the breast, skeleton-like hands leaning on the butt-end of a rifle.'* (*CP*, 2, 117) He could be out of act 2 of *The Silver Tassie*. In scene 4 he glows (from a light behind him) *'like burnished aluminium; and the bent head appears to be looking down at the life going on below it.'* (*CP*, 2, 203) Disgusted with the absurd talk of the Man with Umbrella, the Old Woman comments: 'And to think that all our hero soldiers died that such as you might live!'

This is the key to the whole play. She then lays her wreath, 'as a signal of shame unto those who've forgotten the dead.' (*CP*, 2, 214) The semiotics of her action should not here be missed. Usually, a wreath is laid at a monument to *commemorate* the dead; hence, indeed, Poppy Day or Remembrance Sunday. O'Casey makes a reversal in the meaning of the sign, just as in *The Silver Tassie* Harry Heegan (in act 4) relates the silver cup to the chalice of the Eucharist but replaces the word 'remission' with 'commission': 'red like the blood that was shed for you and for many for the commission of sin!' (*CP*, 2, 92). Just as Harry's reversal is an accusation that war is a sin and not a sacrifice, so the Old Woman's reversal of *remembrance* is an accusation that the war was a total waste.

The question remains whether O'Casey is able successfully to relate this general accusation to the theme of the particular, individual case of the Young Woman's salvation. He has no clever gimmicks to offer, as Shaw had at the end of *Major Barbara*. O'Casey is, after all, writing for the age after *Heartbreak House*. All he knows is that for him as for Shaw (whom he admired this side idolatry) discouragement or disillusion was not to be tolerated. Though the Down-and-Outs come for her in a body, with '*a menacing hum, like that of a swarm of wasps*' (*CP*, 2, 228), the Young Woman withstands their chant and vows to 'go the last few steps of the way rejoicing; I'll go, go game, and I'll die dancing!' And so she does, like the drunken Nannie in *Nannie's Night Out* (1924). The music to which she and Dreamer dance before she dies is '*as if the tune was heard only in the[ir] minds*' (*CP*, 2, 228). Such music has to come from within. And so O'Casey is saying that the imagination alone creates the means, the symbols, for courage and salvation. The supplier of this energy within the play is Dreamer, a convenient if not altogether convincing character. He sees from the start that 'No one has a right to life, who doesn't fight to make it greater.' (*CP*, 2, 121) And there, finally, it is. Fighting is necessary for change, if the Down-and-Outs are not to inherit the earth. It was but a short step from this assertion of independence to the position wherein O'Casey could champion war as necessary and approvable, when the cause is right. Hence the propagandistic *The Star Turns Red* (1940).

3

The shift from *Within the Gates* to *The Star Turns Red* took five years, 'the longest fallow period of [O'Casey's] life', according to his biographer, Garry O'Connor.[35] It seems clear that O'Casey's political attitude underwent another sea-change during this period, especially with the rise of Fascism and the outbreak of the Spanish Civil War. He suddenly became an outspoken advocate of Communism, and moved away from the 'artistic elitism' of *Within the Gates*.[36] After all, in that play it is a poet and poetry only which are offered as the answer to the ideological state apparatus. The Dreamer is Donal Davoren revisited, but Davoren as instructed by Seumas Shields: 'I think a poet's claim to greatness depends upon his power to put passion in the common people.' (*CP*, 1, 127) The Dreamer, however, puts passion only in the Young Woman, Jannice, so that she defies the Church in the person of her father the Bishop. O'Casey now moved on to an allegory uniting Irish history *c.* 1913 and European events *c.* 1937. *The Star Turns Red* is a play set in the future: 'To-morrow, or the next day' and is thus meant to be apocalyptic.

The Star Turns Red found a form to vindicate a hero, and it paved the way – as a transitional play – for a far better play, *Red Roses For Me* (1943). *The Star Turns Red* presents a crude and violent opposition between forces of the left, working men led by Red Jim, and forces of the right, working men in Fascist uniform supported by the Catholic Church. Red Jim, the hero, somewhat unconvincingly triumphs in his fight for equality: 'We fight on; we suffer; we die; but we fight on.' (*CP*, 2, 352) And again, with the last line of the play, 'He fought for life, for life is all; and death is nothing!' (*CP*, 2, 353). This is to go beyond history.

It has been pointed out that O'Casey here created 'A model victory-situation which includes strong elements of actual situations which in life ended in defeat.'[37] We must bear in mind that the play was finished in early 1939, published in February 1940 and staged in London in March 1940, that is, while the Second World War was bursting into reality. The time was ripe for a hero who could stand up to Fascism, and who could make clear the alliance between Church and militarism in this area. Small wonder that the Lord Chamberlain refused a licence for a professional performance[38] (its première was by Unity Theatre, an amateur, workers' theatre), and that publication was refused by Macmillan of New York. *The Star Turns Red* is an explosive and subversive play. James Agate, reviewing the première in the *Sunday Times* in 1940, described it as 'a masterpiece', no doubt ironically.[39] But it is a far better play than a plot summary might suggest, as a belated production at the Abbey Theatre in 1978 revealed. Nevertheless, its primary interest today, in the wake of the collapse of Communism, is in every sense historical, not least in relation to the history of O'Casey's development: from the negative analysis of war to the positive defence of war as the means of engineering change.

The Star Turns Red, then, justifies violence and warfare in the cause of workers' rights. From here on, using fantasy as part of his dramaturgy, O'Casey was to accept the concept of 'hero' and its attendant notion of sacrifice for a cause violently fought for. *Red Roses for Me*, in this context, marked a significant return to O'Casey's earliest attitudes. *The Harvest Festival*, submitted to the Abbey in 1919 and rejected, is the only early play by O'Casey to survive. It was published in 1980.[40] The text shows how O'Casey's use of a belligerent, working-class hero in *The Harvest Festival* was abandoned in *The Shadow of a Gunman* and the following plays for the depiction of the modern anti-hero. We thus find, in *The Star Turns Red* initially but more obviously in *Red Roses for Me*, a reversion to and a renewal of faith in the hero and his necessary sacrifice. *Red Roses for Me* is a rewriting of *The Harvest Festival*; it also revises radically O'Casey's earlier opinions on war.

Red Roses for Me creates a new, self-conscious idea of martyrdom in O'Casey. Ayamonn Breydon is an autobiographical and idealized portrait (as may readily be seen by comparing 'Johnny' in *Pictures in the Hallway* (1942), written at the same time as *Red Roses for Me*). The play fuses a number of diverse issues: it deals with a railway strike in Dublin in 1911[41] in which O'Casey took part; it presents a conflict between culture (Shakespeare), nationalism and socialism; it dramatizes the love-story of a Protestant (Ayamonn) and a Catholic (Sheila) in a context which re-examines the love story of Jack Clitheroe and Nora; and it brings together questions of religious belief and practice and political responsibility in such a way as to provide an approved fusion of sacrifice and revolution. The result is an ending which is fantasy but which imagines, through its use of the symbolism of Easter and the imagery of martyrdom, a workers' revolution with the spiritual aura and implications of 1916. In other words, O'Casey transforms history by the power of the imagination. (Transformation is a key part in the dramaturgy: Dublin and Dublin's poor are transformed through Ayamonn's inspiration in act 3.) Ayamonn's being received in the church in the end signals a victory over bigotry as well as over oppression (the opposite happened at the end of *The Harvest Festival*). The rector, receiving the body at his church, chants 'All our brother's mordant strife / Fought for more abundant life;' (*CP*, 3, 224): his death is perceived as an inspiration, and the cause he espoused once the call came to altruism lives on as the play ends.

O'Casey could thus imaginatively rewrite the tragedy he experienced of the alliance of labour and nationalism, 1914–16, so that his earlier depiction of the people as marginalized, duped and exposed to random warfare is now radically revised. Martyrdom was now seen as meaningful. Expressionism and fantasy had to come into play to achieve this end; naturalism would have been tied to the facts of history. From here on, O'Casey dramatized what might have been, in order (ironically) to produce a Yeatsian land of heart's desire. With only one exception his plays now were all to return to Ireland, to the question of freedom, to Cathleen ni Houlihan and her increasingly thorny ways. The exception was *Oak Leaves and Lavender* (1946), a play about World War II. But here, too, the new O'Casey is to be found.

O'Casey subtitled *Oak Leaves* 'A Warld on Wallpaper', an ironic reference to something Yeats had said about *The Silver Tassie* when he rejected it: 'the whole history of the world must be reduced to wallpaper in front of which the characters must pose and speak.'[42] Yeats's claim rankled. O'Casey disagreed violently, for his tendency was to foreground history as an active force. By the time he came to write *The Star Turns Red* O'Casey was in favour of fighting fire with fire: history could be invoked as imagery to legitimate social revolution. As O'Casey insisted, *Oak Leaves* must be seen as a product of its time: 'it was a Blood-thirsty time; the gods were athirst.'[43] The play is set in Cornwall in and around the Battle of Britain, summer 1940, a critical moment in modern European history. Two young pilots are killed in the play, one Irish and one English, one Marxist and the other aristocratic and as politically unfocused as Harry Heegan in *The Silver Tassie*. The premise of the play is that history, symbolized by the eighteenth-century Prelude and Epilogue, must fuel opposition to tyranny and be seen as containing the power to transform the everyday into the visionary. Thus history energizes sacrifice, and O'Casey can now approve of sacrifice in a nationalist cause. The justification is contained in the young socialist Drishogue's assertion, 'death is but a part of life' (*CP*, 4, 29). When the two pilots die, a crowd of local people recognize that 'They died for us all'. The women in *Oak Leaves*, in stark contrast to the women in the early, Dublin plays, also recognize and approve this spirit of sacrifice. Therefore, violence is presented as necessary, and conscientious objection to war as intolerable. As late as 1959 one finds O'Casey defending *Oak Leaves* thus: 'Life must become brutal in strife, otherwise it wouldn't be any damned good.[. . .] However, the last wasn't a war for us – it was a fight for life, & it had to be waged; & if we had lost it, whatever good there was in man – and there was a helluva lot – would have gone.'[44] That 'we' records the loss of O'Casey's objectivity. This attitude persisted in O'Casey side-by-side with a strong opposition to war in general and the possibility after 1945 (as the *Letters* of those years show) of a nuclear war in particular.

Thus we see O'Casey significantly changing his tune between *The Plough and the Stars* and *Oak Leaves and Lavender*. If one takes *The Harvest Festival* (written 1918–19) into account one could say there was no fundamental change: O'Casey approved of violence if the cause was socialist. Yet that explanation will not really do for *Oak Leaves*, where the principle of self-defence transcends ideology. Ever a fighter, O'Casey was not against aggression among nations (he approved of the Russian invasion of Hungary in 1956, after all). The various phases into which his work falls, then, make clear the contradictions in his attitude towards war.

FRANK O'CONNOR'S 'WAR BOOK': *GUESTS OF THE NATION*

ELMER ANDREWS

1

O'Connor's writings about his 'war' experiences follow a classic pattern, exemplified by other such different 'war' writers as Ernest Hemingway, Stephen Crane and Sean O'Faolain. The pattern is one of youthful idealism succeeded by crushing disillusionment, in O'Connor's and O'Faolain's case, a disillusionment not only with revolutionary violence *per se*, but with the new Ireland which was being ushered into existence through their efforts. As O'Connor ruefully declared: 'every word we said, every act we committed, was a destruction of the improvisation and what we were bringing about was a new Establishment of Church and State in which imagination would play no part, and young men and women would emigrate to the ends of the earth, not because the country was poor, but because it was mediocre'.[1] In O'Connor's writings, both autobiographical and fictional, his 'war' experiences are constructed as a youthful rite of passage, a progression from innocence to adult experience.

2

At the time of the 1916 Rising O'Connor was twelve. When the Civil War ended he was twenty. With the encouragement of his mother and his old schoolteacher, Daniel Corkery, he joined the Volunteers in 1919, and acted as a dispatch-carrier, researcher and scout for two years until the armistice. 'The Irish nation and myself', O'Connor famously remarked, 'were both engaged in an elaborate process of improvisation. I was improvising an education I could not afford, and the country was improvising a revolution it could not afford' (*OC*, p. 184). At first, playing at war was better than a provincial boredom exacerbated by a 5 pm curfew. 'If it was nothing else', O'Connor declares in *An Only Child*, 'it was a brief escape from tedium and frustration to go out the country roads on summer evenings, slouching along in knee breeches and gaiters, hands in the pockets of one's trench-coat and hat pulled over one's right eye' (*OC*, p. 202). As his biographer James Matthews writes, O'Connor along with other young men of the time was 'completely caught up in the romance of rifles and uniforms and press releases'.[2] The Anglo-Irish Treaty signed on 11th July 1921 precipitated civil war between the Free Staters under Collins and Griffith who accepted the Treaty, and the Republicans under de Valera who refused to take the oath of allegiance to the Crown and refused to concede the six counties of Ulster. O'Connor joined the Republicans, that being, in his view, the 'party of imagination': 'We were acting on the unimpeachable logic of the imagination, that only what exists in the mind is real' (*OC*, p. 210). At this time, he says, he saw life 'through a veil of literature' (*OC*, p. 211).

As the fighting wore on, O'Connor quickly 'tired of war and wanted to go home . . . And after all the nonsense I had read about the excitement of one's baptism of fire, I was finding it intolerably dull. It just went on and on' (*OC*, p. 221). In his *Paris Review* interview, he reminisces on his days in the IRA:

My soldiering was rather like my efforts at being a musician; it was an imitation of the behaviour of soldiers rather than soldiering. I was completely incapable of remembering anything for ten minutes. And I always got alarmed the moment people started shooting at me, so I was a wretchedly bad soldier, but that doesn't prevent you from picking up the atmosphere of the period. I really got into it when I was about fifteen as a sort of Boy Scout, doing odd jobs for the I.R.A., and then continued on with it until finally I was captured and interned for a year. Nearly all the writers went with the extreme Republican group. People like O'Faolain, myself, Francis Stuart, Peadar O'Donnell, all the young writers of our generation went Republican. Why we did it, the Lord knows, except that young writers are never capable of getting the facts of anything correctly.[3]

War, he was being forced to conclude, was the antithesis, not the expression, of 'the imaginative concept of life' (*OC*, p. 240). He refused to take part in the killings of unarmed soldiers out with their girls, but the demand that he do so only confirmed for him his feeling that 'the romantic improvisation was tearing right down the middle' (*OC*, p. 240). After four months on the run he was captured in February 1923, and during the year he spent in prison, first in the Women's Gaol in Sunday's Well and then in Gormanstown, his disillusionment deepened. He tells of visiting a prisoner who had been beaten to a 'lump of dough' by his captors for trying to burn down an old woman's house. The 'romance of self-determination', O'Connor laments, had degenerated into a terrible brutality: 'I was beginning to think that this was all our romanticism came to – a miserable attempt to burn a widow's house, the rifle butts and bayonets of hysterical soldiers, a poor woman of the lanes kneeling in some city church and appealing to a God who could not listen, and then – a barrack wall with some smug humbug of a priest muttering prayers' (*OC*, p. 243). Echoing the closing line of his story, 'Guests of the Nation', O'Connor writes of the effect on him of witnessing the 'lump of dough' in the prison cell: 'certainly, that night changed something for ever in me' (*OC*, p. 244).

In Gormanstown, he sought escape from boredom by teaching Irish and German and learning French. He repudiated martyrdom ('I shouted . . . that I was sick to death of the worship of martyrdom . . . I didn't want to die. I wanted to live') (*OC*, p. 254) and 'mystical nationalism' (p. 262) and refused the discipline imposed by his fellow internees: 'it was probably the first time I had ever taken an unpopular stand without allies' (*OC*, p. 257). The sentimental high-mindedness, he felt, went hand in hand with an extraordinary inhumanity. Having himself refused to take part in a hunger strike, he recalls being approached by another prisoner the day the men came off their strike: '"Well, professor," he said gleefully, "the pigs feed", and I turned away in disgust because that was exactly what the scene resembled, and I knew it was the end of our magical improvisation' (*OC*, p. 270). Gormanstown camp, O'Connor concludes, 'was a grave of lost illusions' (*OC*, p. 271).

Even in prison, in his stand against the demands of his fellow-internees, he asserted the primacy of personal freedom and the need to define the self against conventional expectation and the pressure of circumstance. Seeing the dangerous excesses of romantic nationalism, he became increasingly uneasy about the relationship between Irish nationalism and the Romantic Movement. Imagination, which provided the original impetus to revolution, when it is detached from rational mind, can lead to sterile and self-destructive fantasy: 'It was clear to me that we were all going mad, and yet I could see no way out. The imagination seems to paralyse not only the critical faculty but the ability to act upon the most ordinary instinct of self-preservation' (*OC*, p. 240). In Gormanstown, he reacted strongly against 'Shelley and his followers', 'the harmless, sugary, nineteenth century dying of Tennyson or Christina Rossetti that always moved me to tears' (*OC*, pp. 253–4). The imagination, he could see, must be kept in close and creative relationship with practical judgement and rational mind if it is to serve an authentically liberating purpose.

Whilst in prison, O'Connor discovered grammar. This was a discovery not unrelated to his growing disillusionment with the romance of war and his developing realism and concern with the role of authority:

Maybe it was the grammar that started me off, or maybe the grammar itself was only a symptom of the emergence from a protracted adolescence, but I was beginning to have grave doubts about many of the political ideas that I had held as gospel.

(*OC*, p. 251)

Grammar was associated in his mind with the male principle, deriving from his father's energetic regimentalism (his father was an ex-bandsman in the British army), in contrast to the feminine side of his personality, deriving from his mother's unself-conscious, unworldly innocence:

Grammar is the bread-winner of language as usage is the housekeeper, and the poor man's efforts at keeping order are for ever being thwarted by his wife's intrigues and her perpetual warnings to the children not to tell Father. But language, like life, is impossible without a father and he is forever returning to his thankless job of restoring authority.

(*OC*, p. 251)

The characteristic tension of O'Connor's entire *oeuvre* becomes apparent here, one which is represented by the need to balance his mother's influence so lovingly described in *An Only Child* (1961) with acknowledgement of a contrary inheritance adumbrated in the title of his posthumous work *My Father's Son*. (The maternal/feminine and the paternal/masculine were, O'Connor confessed in *An Only Child*, 'the two powers that were struggling for possession of my soul'.) In other terms, it is the conflict between 'instinct' and 'judgement', the heart and the head, imagination and reason, romance and realism. As James Matthews put it: 'Like his mother perhaps, O'Connor believed that he could make the world more palatable. That he always tried is testimony to his romanticism; that he knew in the end that the reach exceeds the grasp is the mark of his realism'.[4] It is not all that hard, then, to appreciate the way O'Connor was drawn to those paradoxical historical figures such as Michael Collins who combined a romantic idealism with ruthless pragmatic realism. To O'Connor, Collins was 'the big fellow' in a Lilliputian world, the ontological hero opposed to tyranny in general, 'the man of genius who embodies the best in a nation'.[5]

In literature, O'Connor favoured the nineteenth century realists whose work represented a 'domestication of literature', a literature of the 'Dutch interior', opposed to the mythological or historical or romantic, 'a mirror in the roadway'[6] reflecting the lives of ordinary people and charged with a moral passion. Jane Austen's art represented a 'flight from fancy', Stendhal's a 'flight from reality'.[7] Austen shows 'the temper of the true novelist who is always reacting against romanticism in fiction' (*MR*, p. 18). 'The judgment and the instincts are always at war in her' (*MR*, p. 26), and this is the source of her artistic strength. Her 'judgment' keeps her 'imagination' under strict control, and her 'truth' depends crucially on that balance. Stendhal, on the other hand, fails to demonstrate a proper intellectual detachment, consequently robbing his novels of their 'emotional impact' (*MR*, p. 54). O'Connor may underestimate the subtlety and intensity of Stendhal's handling of the tension between 'emotion' and 'judgment', but he is correct in the observation that it is out of the civil war within ourselves that true art is made.

From his earliest writings in *Guests of the Nation*, one feels the struggle to accommodate both 'emotion' and 'judgment', romance and realism. Temperamentally, he felt himself to be a romantic. As a child he was well known as a dreamer, and later in life, in a letter to his close friend Nancy McCarthy, he confessed: 'Russell is right about me; I am a romantic and the realism is only a kink. Realism be damned! It's only a sort of spiritual cold storage'.[8] At times like this he bridled under the constraints of realism, but he was always alert to the dangers of romantic excess, and it was out of the tension between realism and romance that he was to produce his best work. The short story, he believed, was the classic form of an adversarial individualism. 'Always in the short story there is this sense of outlawed figures wandering about the fringes of society'.[9] The short story 'remains by its very nature remote from the community – romantic, individualistic and intransigent' (*LV*, p. 21). His own early persona in *Guests of the Nation* is that of the outlaw, the fugitive IRA man. But the special tension in these stories comes from the equivalent assertion of the existence – however shadowily or inexactly – of ordinary society, and of traditional humanistic values, the ties of family and community, love, the sanctity of human life.

3

Shortly after his release from Gormanstown, O'Connor began turning his new experiences into poems, prose sketches and eventually, between 1929 and 1930, short stories. It was AE who recommended him to Macmillan in London:

> May I supplicate attention for his mss. He is a young man of very great talent, an admirable poet and something of a scholar. His translations from the Gaelic are the best I know. His stories are I believe about the civil war in Ireland and he had exceptional opportunities for gathering intimate knowledge of this dark period in our history. But his interest in writing these stories is in the characters not in the political situation.[10]

The volume of stories which Macmillan eventually published under the title *Guests of the Nation* O'Connor described as his 'war book'.[11] In O'Connor's opinion, 'the two most remarkable story-tellers of the First World War were Ernest Hemingway and Isaac Babel' (*LV*, p. 187) (though Babel is mainly a writer of the Russian Civil War), and he acknowledges the particular influence of Babel's most famous work, *The Red Cavalry*, which appeared in English in 1926:

> The man who has influenced me most, I suppose, is really Isaak Babel, and again with that natural enthusiasm of mine for imitating everybody, 'Guests of the Nation' and a couple of the other stories in that book are really imitations of Babel's stories in *The Red Cavalry*.[12]

In his introduction to Babel's *Collected Stories*, Lionel Trilling eloquently describes Babel's essential quality:

> At that first reading it seemed to me – although it does not now – that the stories were touched with cruelty. They were about violence of the most extreme kind, yet they were composed with a striking elegance and precision of objectivity, and also with a kind of lyric *joy*, so that one could not at once know just how the author was responding to the brutality he recorded, whether he thought it good or bad, justified or not justified.[13]

O'Connor shares Trilling's fascination with Babel's violence, and also his unease at the author's apparent failure to incorporate an adequate moral perspective on the events he describes. Like

Trilling (and indeed most readers), O'Connor was intrigued by the conflict in Babel between the Jewish intellectual and the Soviet commissar. Babel was clearly a paradoxical figure, a Jew fighting in one of the notoriously anti-Semitic Cossack regiments; an intellectual, habitually pacific and humane, who threw himself into the passionate life of the bold and violent Cossacks. Indeed, O'Connor finds 'two personalities' in Babel's stories, and 'while one seems to say one thing the other often says the opposite' (*LV*, p. 192). Babel's fantasy of power and violence, O'Connor felt, contradicts the sensitive, intellectual 'Jewish' side of his character. While recognizing that Babel's 'romanticisation of violence' drew its intensity from this conflict between the Jewish intellectual and the Soviet officer, O'Connor believed that the two sides of Babel's personality were never properly integrated: 'In his enthusiasm for Cossack violence Babel has denied his ancestry' (*LV*, pp. 198). The stories are deficient because they 'contain more poetry than storytelling . . . Passion can never rule the universe of the storyteller; it leaves too many things unexplained' (*LV*, p. 200). Babel is always 'most moving' when he writes out of 'the conflict in himself, when he juxtaposes the two cultures – the barbaric culture of the Communists and the humane one of the Jews – and shows them to us in antithesis' (*LV*, pp. 198–9). He is least satisfying when the romanticization of violence is allowed to obliterate the moral conscience.

O'Connor doesn't actually discuss Babel's story 'My First Goose', but we can imagine it is the kind of story that would gain his approval. It describes a rite of passage, the test of an intellectual newcomer to the brigade, who must prove himself ready to kill before he is accepted by his comrades. By killing an old woman's goose in a particularly brutal manner he overcomes their hostility and becomes one of them. But the struggle to achieve such inhumanity is clearly acknowledged: 'We slept, all six of us, beneath a wooden roof that let in the stars, warming one another, our legs intermingled. I dreamed: and in my dreams saw women. But my heart, stained with bloodshed, grated and brimmed over'.

Other stories leave O'Connor 'confused' (*LV*, p. 192). In 'After the Battle', a Cossack rages against the narrator because he had ridden into battle with an unloaded revolver. The story ends with the narrator's prayer to 'grant me the simplest of proficiencies – the ability to kill my fellow-men'. One can appreciate O'Connor's difficulties in knowing the precise degree of irony present here, especially in light of another story, 'The Death of Dolgushov', in which the narrator during a retreat finds a mortally wounded man who begs to be dispatched before the enemy tortures him, shrinks away from the terrible responsibility, and is set upon by his best friend, who having killed the wounded man, says to the narrator, 'You guys in specs have about as much pity for chaps like us as a cat has for a mouse '.

'With Old Man Makhno' is another of the stories O'Connor specifically criticises for the 'confusion' it arouses. A Jewish girl is being raped by six Russian soldiers in succession. She would have been raped by a seventh only Kikin, the seventh, realizes that one of the other rapists is syphilitic. O'Connor criticises Babel for not clarifying his own attitude to the event. 'The SS Cow-Wheat' is also criticised for apparently asking the reader to admire the conduct of Comrade Makeyev who reluctantly executes the drunken skipper of a boat that has been commissioned to bring urgently needed wheat to Moscow. O'Connor concludes that Babel's stories give us an image of 'an extraordinary attractive mixed-up Jewish kid' (*LV*, p. 94).

Clearly, Babel is attracted by a primitive energy, the glory of conscienceless self-assertion, a fantasy of personal animal grace, which he celebrated in the Cossack ethos. In 'The Brigade Commander' he speaks admiringly of Kolesnikov's 'masterful indifference of a Tartar Khan' and in 'My First Goose' of another brigade commander, Savitsky, whose manly power elicits a similar boyish hero-worship. Contrast these portraits with O'Connor's picture of the brigade commander, Jeremiah Donovan, in 'Guests of the Nation'. The possibility of grace, which was part of what Babel saw in the Cossacks, is never entertained by O'Connor in his portrayal of Irish Republicanism. Where Babel invokes a Lawrentian mystique of manly power, the image of the Noble Savage, O'Connor's war stories give us, at their most exhilarated, the boyish thrill of playing dangerous games, and chart a process of paralysing disillusionment. Romance is continually being subjected to realistic judgement. O'Connor is as interested as Babel or Stephen Crane or Ernest Hemingway in boyhood and in the drama of the boy's initiation into manhood, but the question O'Connor puts to himself is not the one which means so much to the Russian writer, nor even the one that is important to the two American writers. Babel asks if he can endure the killing; Crane and Hemingway ask if they can endure being killed, if they will be able to meet danger with honour, show grace under pressure. O'Connor asks if there are not other virtues to be exalted than physical courage.

As Trilling emphasises, Babel's stylistic means *does*, of course, embody a moral point of view. Certainly, there is no doubt that Babel knew the terrible reality of violence in his own life. Trilling adduces Babel's childhood memory of seeing his father, a poor shopkeeper, 'on his knees before a Cossack captain on a horse, who said, "At your service", and touched his fur cap with his yellow-gloved hand and politely paid no heed to the mob looting the Babel store'.[14] As a member of a Cossack regiment, Babel served what was ultimately to destroy him: arrested in 1937, he died in a concentration camp two or three years later, possibly shot. The controversial form in which he cast his stories – their detachment and objectivity, the indifference to 'meanings' and 'values' – necessarily implies an intense moral concern, an intuition of a harsh, unyielding, ironic universe in which morality converts to strict aesthetic form. In contrast, O'Connor's stories emphasise the possibility of change and process, and display a more traditional moral/humanistic preoccupation: 'moral passion', O'Connor wrote in *The Mirror in the Roadway*, 'is literature's main contribution to the arts' (*MR*, p. 12). The great task facing him was to find the means of presenting the experience of adolescent romanticism with all its unselfconscious exuberance and at the same time incorporate a more mature judgement upon it. In O'Connor's stories, too, there is evidence of two personalities, that of the bookman and 'old-fashioned humanist' on one hand and, on the other, the boyish adventurer and IRA activist. The remainder of this essay will consider the formal procedures O'Connor employed in an attempt to accommodate these different levels or modes of experience, and offer some assessment of the extent to which his stories in *Guests of the Nation* represent an effectively integrated narrative, a more coherent personality, than that which O'Connor found in Babel's stories.

4

The title story of *Guests of the Nation* is set during the Anglo-Irish war and concerns two Englishmen, Belcher and Hawkins, who are held captive by two Irishmen, Bonaparte, who is the narrator of the story, and Noble. The four strike up a close and easy friendship until the command comes that the two Englishmen must be shot in reprisal for the shooting of two Irishmen earlier that day. Duty must come before personal feeling. At the end the narrator is left numbed and lonely, confronting the eternal silence of the infinite spaces, which is all there is left when trust and friendship have been betrayed.

The first part of the story emphasises a pervasive process of osmosis, a kind of personal, linguistic and cultural crossing. In establishing the friendly atmosphere and camaraderie amongst the four men, O'Connor dissolves the usual divisions between English and Irish. Conventional categorisations are broken down, symbolising the subordination of the political to the personal, the abstract to the concrete. The four play cards, carry on a friendly banter and behave like a typical O'Connor family unit with Belcher helping the cantankerous old woman of the house like any good son would help his mother. The two prisoners need little guarding – 'you could have planted that pair down anywhere from this to Claregalway and they'd have taken root there like a native weed. I never in my short experience saw two men take to the country as they did'. The simile suggests that the two Englishmen are more 'native' than 'foreign', or even 'guest'. Hawkins knows the countryside better than the two Irishmen. The two English soldiers are included in the Second Battalion's social evenings and have become a recognised part of the local community. Hawkins passes messages to Bonaparte from the local girls and has learnt to dance Irish dances, indicative of English freedom and confidence in contrast to Irish chauvinism and insecurity: 'he could not return the compliment, because our lads at that time did not dance foreign dances on principle'. Nevertheless, English linguistic usages, such as the use of the word 'chum', have crossed over for, as the narrator remarks, 'we had picked up some of their curious expressions'. As far as Hawkins the amateur Marxist is concerned, the line of division is more deeply drawn between capitalists and labour than it is between English and Irish. There is a palpably closer bond between the two Englishmen and the two Irishmen than there is between the two Irishmen and their commanding officer, Jeremiah Donovan. From the beginning Donovan broods over the action like a malignant shadow. He 'would come up and supervise the game' and 'shout at him [Hawkins] as if he was one of our own'. Donovan is not 'one of our own' in that 'Noble and myself used to make fun of his broad accent, because we were both from the town'. On this basis the narrator proposes greater similarity between Donovan the hardline Irishman and Belcher the English prisoner: Donovan was 'a sober and contented poor devil like the big Englishman'. There are an infinite number of ways, O'Connor is suggesting, in which individuals may be grouped and identified, and nationality may not be the most meaningful one.

The story is set in the dark, among the ashes: 'At dusk the big

Englishman, Belcher, would shift his long legs out of the ashes'. Belcher, with his uncommon lack of speech, is a spectral presence, 'walking in and out like a ghost'. These proleptic symbols of 'ghost' and 'dusk' and 'ashes' establish the mood of tragedy, the imminence of death. The game of cards is also prognostic of the tit-for-tat economy of the political world: 'He [Belcher] could have skinned myself and Noble, but whatever we lost to him, Hawkins lost to us, and Hawkins only played with the money Belcher gave him'. The other figure apart from Donovan presiding over the action is the old woman. If Donovan, the 'big farmer', is representative of masculine force and patriarchal authority (he is given O'Connor's father's family name), the old woman is the domestic muse, Mother Ireland, who at the end is appalled by the inhumanity perpetrated in her name. O'Connor takes the feminine side, in revolt against the barbarism of the father, the 'majesty of the law'.

The crucial dispossession in the story is not the historical dispossession of the Irish by their English masters. It exists at the more personal level of the Englishman, Belcher's, final tragic dispossession from the 'home' he has made and enjoyed amongst the Irish: 'I like the feeling of a home, as you may have noticed'. He says this as he is led to his death by the very same people who had earlier made him feel at home. The awful deed is done and the story moves to its famous poetic ending implying the sheer sadness of life, a vague loneliness:

I pushed my way out past her and left them at it. I stood at the door, watching the stars and listening to the shrieking of the birds dying out over the bogs. It is so strange what you feel at times like that that you can't describe it. Noble says he saw everything ten times the size, as though there were nothing in the whole world but that little patch of bog with the two Englishmen stiffening into it, but with me it was as if the patch of bog where the Englishmen were was a million miles away, and even Noble and the old woman, mumbling behind me, and the birds and the bloody stars were all far away, and I was somehow very small and very lost and lonely like a child astray in the snow. And anything that happened to me afterwards, I never felt the same about again.

The narrator removes himself from his historical frame by the use of a hypnotic, rhetorically heightened romantic discourse. The story shifts to the level of the abstract, the emotional and the personal. Widening his angle of vision, O'Connor moves beyond the boundaries of the room in the house, the patch of bog which fills Noble's vision, towards a panoramic and panchronic position, a point in the future from which he can sum up his experiences. On the way, he indulges a dangerously sentimental metaphysics. Attention shifts from actual atrocity to a highly subjective experience of alienation ('It was all mad lonely') and *ostranenie* ('It is so strange...'). It is the experience of the orphan removed from the mother, alone in a dark universe, 'astray in the snow'. The passage, in moving away from the clean well-lighted place out into the metaphysical void, symbolised by the snow-filled wastes, represents an avoidance of adult responsibility and the world of historical reality. We think of another equally famous ending to an equally famous story: Gabriel Conroy's thoughts moving from his wife (who has fallen asleep) to ponder the snow and the West and the ghost of Michael Furey in Joyce's 'The Dead'. Irish landscape again functions as a distraction from the failure of human relationship. When the human crisis reaches its climax the narrative slides into sentimentalism and generality. Both stories are converted into an old Irish narrative of the romance of failure. Joyce's image for this failure is the entire landscape of Ireland covered in snow, an image reiterated by O'Faolain in one of his finest stories 'A Broken World': 'under that white shroud, covering the whole of Ireland, life was lying broken and hardly breathing'.

In O'Connor's scenario we have the child as well as the snow. Childhood, one is tempted to think, has been the inspiration of the nation – of Joyce in *Dubliners*, of Patrick Pearse in his writings, of Yeats in 'Easter 1916' where the Rising leaders are children named 'as a mother names her children', of de Valera's vision of an Ireland of comely maidens and athletic youths romping in a Gaelic Eden. For O'Connor, the short story in its essence deals with life's victims – the insulted and injured, the forlorn and alienated, and the concentration on defeat and alienation, on life's victims, leads naturally to concern with forms of consciousness that are exceedingly limited: children and those in a low state of cultural development. In 'Guests of the Nation', he appeals to ritualized emotions, habitual associations, and retreats behind a mask of innocence and pathos rather than questioning the real historical meaning of the events which have occurred. In removing himself from history and freezing his experience into a modern myth of numbed disorientation and failure, the narrator denies the possibility of interpreting and controlling the changing world. He prefers to assume the role of helpless child astray in the snow.

In the last two lines a final shift takes place expressive of the narrator's (half-hearted) desire to re-enter history and giving the story its final form as the narrator's 'remembrance of things past'. The internal focalizer (the narrator who experiences the events as they occur) becomes the narrator-focalizer (who stands outside the frame of the main narrative, retrospectively assessing his story). Such a shift is a form of 'transgression' that Genette calls metalepsis – an 'effect of strangeness'[15] marked by an unexpected transition between one narrative level and another. Narrating instance slips into narrated event. In a final unexpected twist the narrative is internalised to fit the narrator's artistic needs, thereby turning the story of the guests of the nation into a story of the narrator's rite of passage. Bonaparte's final attempt to reassert the authority of his narrative presence on the text resonates with O'Connor's own anxiety about the nature and status of his narrative.

O'Connor's struggle to satisfy the dual demand of 'instinct' and 'judgment', enactment and assessment, is discernible again in his next story 'Attack'. The narrator and his friend Lomasney are on a night-time mission to blow up a police garrison. Until the attack begins they hide out in an isolated cottage belonging to an old couple, the Kiernans, whose son, Paddy, was smuggled out of the country to America five years earlier to escape the rigour of the law after he accidentally killed a man in a brawl in a pub. The two IRA men discover that old Kiernan is hiding his outlaw son in his loft. To Kiernan, his two visitors are mere 'children playmaking', and indeed neither Lomasney nor the narrator says or does anything to disabuse him (or us) of this opinion. However, old man Kiernan changes his tune when Lomasney takes charge of the situation and shows how Paddy can be saved. With the elimination of the local constabulary, Paddy will be able to take his place once again in the community. Old Kiernan's delight at Lomasney's ingenuity knows no bounds. Lomasney believes he will be 'our best recruit' – this of the old man whose new-found revolutionary enthusiasm stems entirely from personal interest rather than the least political principle.

The narrator and his friend are little more credible. Both are presented as excruciatingly naive, politically and morally. Lomasney, when recalling the time of Paddy's emigration to America, thinks how 'stupid' the idea was, not because it was a futile flouting of the rule of law but because it was showing an unnecessary fear of and respect for the law: 'he cleared out. It was a stupid thing to do – I know that now – but we were frightened of the law in those days'. Five years on, the sign of maturity is apparently the anarchic readiness to take the law into your own hands, in personal as well as political matters. And then there is the question of the justification of revolutionary violence. For Lomasney, its validity is confirmed by the completely irrelevant consideration of the personal case of Paddy Kiernan. Knowing that he is going out to blow up the policemen for the sake of his old friend as well as for Ireland gives a marvellous boost to Lomasney's confidence: 'I never went out on a job with a clearer conscience', he blithely declares. But it is the narrator's justification for the projected attack which is most revealing of the childishness of so-called patriotic motive:

But for a long time now this attack of ours was being promised to the garrison, whose sense of duty had outrun their common sense. Policemen are like that. A soldier never does more than he need do, and so far as possible he keeps on good terms with his enemy; for him the ideal is the least amount of disorder; he only asks not to be taken prisoner or ambushed or blown up too often. But for the policeman there is only one ideal, Order, hushed and entire; to his well-drilled mind a stray shot at a rabbit and a stray shot at a general are one and the same thing, so that in civil commotion he loses all sense of proportion and becomes a helpless, hopeless, gibbering maniac whom in everybody's interests it is better to remove. That at least was how we thought in those days, and the garrison I speak of had been a bad lot, saucy to the villagers and a nuisance to our men for miles around. Oh, it was coming to them – everybody knew that.

As moral reasoning this is risible. Violence is a boys' game. Old Kiernan's remark 'And I thinking ye were only like children playmaking' is not far off the mark.

There is, however, a complex focalisation at work in the story. The narrator steps outside the boyish naivety, distances himself from the attitudes of the past: 'That at least was how we thought in those days' – a remark which gives explicit moral perspective to the romance of violence and acts to subvert the boyish enthusiasm of the narration. It has the same status and function as the statement which closes 'Guests of the Nation': 'And anything that happened to me afterwards, I never felt the same about again'. Both place the narrator in a chronological position of full, or at least greater knowledge, and identify the narrative as a retrospective view of an earlier ignorant self. Genette's concept of 'transgression' points to the way in which a writer breaks the frame of his narrative and violates normal literary expectations. In 'Guests of the Nation' and 'Attack' O'Connor's transgressive tactic is an interpellation of information beyond that which is immediately accessible to the focalising centre at the time of the action. The information constitutes a move beyond a position of ignorance or limitation or confusion to that of interpretation. This breaking of his own narrative system suggests a tell-tale stress point where the writer's moral purpose comes up against the boundaries of conventional form. We glimpse the profound tension in O'Connor's aesthetic.

Where the culminating experience towards which the narrative of 'Guests of the Nation' moves is the traumatised psyche's hysterical regression and contraction to childhood, 'Attack' represents an opposite movement away from the feelings and attitudes of a child. This is largely achieved through the handling of narrative tone, which implies a consistent ironic detachment from the boyish attitudes that are presented. There are two kinds of Law in this story – the civil authority of the policemen, removal of which will restore life to Paddy, the man in the attic, the popular transgressor who has been quite literally 'silenced' and 'submerged'. His 'submergence', in fact, began years ago at the hands of his father: it is old Kiernan who is the other oppressive authority-figure in the story, for Paddy, we read, had been 'kept down at home by his father' and 'would have been crushed ... if he'd stayed at home'. At a stroke, Lomasney the giant-killer aims to transform the condition of oppression, both personal and public, through a redemptive act of violence. He will enact a young man's dream of freedom, including the youthful Michael O'Donovan's desire to escape the law of the father. The story's narrator, however, who is even more closely to be identified with the developing author, embodies a more complex, comprehensive vision in which youthful enthusiasms are tempered by a more adult sense of responsibility.

In 'Attack' O'Connor is interested in uncovering the impurities and contradictions of the motives governing political action. 'Jumbo's Wife' is another study of the unreliability, the unruliness and contradictoriness of human motive. The story is composed out of a network of ironic reversals and betrayals. The wife who had often thought 'she would do for him' unwittingly betrays her informer husband to the Volunteers and then does all she can to try and save him when they close in for the kill. The story emphasises the way human individuality continually escapes system and expectation and consequently renders itself liable to the charge of betrayal in the eyes of conventional morality. The human always undermines the political, which depends on conformity to a programme or a system. Political action is therefore always ironic – as in the story's final line: 'They [the Volunteers] had squared her account with Jumbo at last.' This echoes an earlier reassurance the Volunteers had given Jumbo's wife when she first came to them looking for a champion. The Volunteers' language is the language of accounting (ironically reminding us that the original dispute between Jumbo and his wife was over money) euphemistically encoding the act of murder, which is justified as a promise faithfully fulfilled on the part of the Volunteers. The statement masks the fact that the Volunteers' action against Jumbo was prosecuted entirely for their own ends: it was their own account they had settled with Jumbo at last. As far as Jumbo's wife is concerned, their action was not merely irrelevant but tragic, a ruthless defiance of her wishes. Once caught up in the political action, Jumbo's wife quickly loses all control over her husband's fate. The fact that she does not have a name implies her impotence and insignificance. In the political world there is precious little room for the personal life. The power-brokers' glib cliché conceals the awful human tragedy which O'Connor makes the substance and burden of his story.

After the excitements of the chase and the intense personal feeling of 'Jumbo's Wife', O'Connor shifts to a quiet, painterly mode in 'Nightpiece with Figures': 'Preluded by one short squeak of its hinges, a door opens slowly and quietly into a dark and empty barn. Framed in the doorway is the glow of an autumn night . . .' The use of the present tense and indefinite article marks the emblematic nature of the story. As in Plato's cave, a 'shadow show' is played out in the barn, the figures discernible only in 'dim silhouette'. In this womb-like hiding place, three hunted IRA men are joined by two nuns, one a jolly, resilient old woman who clings to memories of the heroic past, the other 'a visionary, enchanted youth', a dishevelled aisling figure. The story is an image of the emergence into consciousness of dim thoughts and fears. In the dark, the conversation tells of 'desire and loss'. Where 'in the old days we were all united', the people now are 'indifferent' or hostile. The story reflects the disillusionment of the times and the author's own awareness of the ever-widening gap between the ideal and the real: 'Where is the sovereign Irish people we used to hear so much about a year or two ago? . . . We haven't any heroes left, but we can always find you a few informers'. Like the men of the cave in the most famous of the Platonic myths, O'Connor's IRA men confront the unreality of their lives. They ponder the collapse of the national dream. As at the end of 'Guests of the Nation', we are left with a profound emptiness and melancholy. And another lost 'child' in the figure of the demoralised young nun.

Demoralised she may be, but the child-nun reminds the men of what they have been fighting for. She is the nation's inspiration. O'Connor widens the angle of vision as he had done at the end of 'Guests of the Nation', and the story gives way to abstraction and sentimentality. In 'Guests of the Nation', the sense of estrangement produced by the narrator's traumatising experience of killing pushes him outside the language of all the available discourses ('It is so strange what you feel at times like that that you can't describe it'): similarly, in 'Nightpiece', there are no words for the men's bitter-sweet experience of the young nun:

They are all happy as though some wonderful thing had happened to them, but what the wonderful thing is they could not say, and with their happiness is mixed a melancholy as strange and perturbing, as though life itself and all the modes of life were inadequate. It is not a bitter melancholy like the melancholy of defeat, and in the morning, when they take to the country roads again, it will have passed.

But the memory of the young nun will not pass so lightly from their minds.

The farther removed from the simplicity, serenity and beauty that made up the idea of 'Holy Ireland', the more intense becomes the nostalgia. O'Connor's ending recalls that of the Irish-American Scott Fitzgerald's great masterpiece *The Great Gatsby* where the strenuous lyricism expresses a powerful nostalgia for the American paradise which, in the story of Jay Gatsby, had just been lost again.

The sense of disillusionment and defeat continues into the next story, 'September Dawn', which, like 'Nightpiece', also invokes a countering female image of life and love. 'September Dawn' is a story about disbandment, disintegration, the dissolution of a political force and the tentative discovery of something more meaningful and satisfying than violence. The world O'Connor presents in 'Nightpiece' and 'September Dawn' is one in the throes of entropy, of everything running down, moving towards eventual homogeneity. 'Entropy', a term taken from physics, refers to an increasing disorder of energy moving at random, finally arriving at total inertia. This final unhappy state is one where the capacity for fresh idiom or direction or momentum is absent. 'Entropy' haunts the modern imagination, preoccupied as it is with the defeat of the individual and the doom of present civilization or society. Part 1 of 'September Dawn' tells of the dismantling of a flying column, the dispersal of the men back to their homes and families after a hectic chase across the countryside: 'It was a sort of game a schoolboy would play with a beetle'. Again, war is a schoolboy's game. The life of the soldier is stripped of the least vestige of romance. O'Connor emphasises hardship, disappointment and grinding defeat. After the excitement of action comes a terrible psychic dislocation. Keown, seeking escape in drink, sleeps fitfully. Woken by the howling wind, he thinks his pursuers have finally caught up with him and his friend Hickey. Hysterical from the fear of death, he screams like a child and asks Hickey to hold his hand: 'Hickey took his hand, and seeing him quieter lay down again beside him. After a few moments Keown's free hand rose and felt his arm and shoulder, even his face, for company'. Hickey's own feeling of insecurity, disorientation, and especially alienation, is just as overwhelming. Assailed by doubt and loneliness and melancholy, he is just as desperate for human contact: 'suddenly it became clear to him that his life was a melancholy, aimless life, and that all this endless struggle and concealment was but so much out of an existence that would mean little anyhow'. The feeling both Keown and Hickey experience at the end of the fighting is recognizably that of the little boy lost which the narrator in 'Guests of the Nation' came to experience after the killing of the two Englishmen. Hickey recalls the tantalising vision of love he had seen earlier in the day when he was on the run, the appearance of a girl in white: 'At that very moment he had felt something explode within him at the inhumanity, the coldness, of it all. He had wanted to wave to her; what was that but the desire for some human contact?'

The dawn brings a new day and new hope. The entropic process is arrested, perhaps even reversed. The wind has stilled. Light and warmth persist in the September dawn: 'Light, a cold, wintry, forbidding light suffused the chill air. The birds were singing'. The title, with its autumnal reference balanced against the promise of new day, encodes the story's central tension. Seeing the girl of the house lighting the fire, Hickey goes to her and kisses her:

She leaned against his shoulder in her queer silent way, with no shyness. And for him in that melancholy kiss an ache of longing was kindled, and he buried his face in the warm flesh of her throat as the kitchen filled with the acrid smell of turf; while the blue smoke drifting through the narrow doorway was caught and whirled headlong through grey fields and dark masses of trees upon which an autumn sun was rising.

Hickey exchanges a dead and futile politics for 'warm flesh'. He discovers love which, like the 'seed of fire' the girl kindles in the hearth, inspirits the future. The new values affirmed at the end of the story involve a similar opening out of the narrative perspective as we find at the end of 'Guests of the Nation', but where it is a vast emptiness that fills the mind in that story, the snow spread over all, in 'September Dawn' the blue smoke which drifts across the land is the sign of warmth, domesticity and new life. After the shootings in 'Guests of the Nation', Bonaparte and Noble return to a kitchen which was 'dark and cold', and an old woman appalled by what they have done. 'September Dawn' ends with the lighting of the fire and the young girl, silent, pliant and receptive, a male fantasy of erotic love, the convenient cypher of male desire, both comforting mother and sexual female, with no more individual human life than that permitted traditional images of Irish femininity that have doubled as symbols of national identity. The story, that is, ends with a routine idealism. It demonstrates a continued reluctance to re-enter history that we noted in 'Guests of the Nation'. The bankruptcy of old ideals leads to only partial realism, an incomplete emergence from Plato's cave. The new consciousness is, at best, only half-born. To get beyond the perennial idealising habit of mind would be the ultimate 'dawning' for such as Hickey, the 'old celebate' whom Keown ribs for his lack of knowledge of women: 'You hate and fear women as you hate and fear the devil'. The story is loosely based on O'Connor's own experience. In *An Only Child*, he tells how, in August 1922, when Cork was invaded from the sea, he and his friend Sean Hendrick (to whom the story was dedicated when it first appeared in a magazine) fled, eventually to a farmhouse in Reannarree, a wild, Irish-speaking area in the mountains around Macroom. Here, O'Connor fell in love with the farmer's daughter: '[her] gentle, blond, lethargic beauty was as breath-taking as her Irish, and she spoke that as I had never heard it spoken before, with style. Unfortunately, I had no notion of how to make love to her, because she appeared to me through a veil of characters from books I had read' (*OC*, p. 231). Something of that 'lack of knowledge of women' is incorporated into the story, though it must be said, without any trace of irony, such is the intensity of the desire for an antidote to despair.

A 'flippant attitude' dominates a few of the stories, as the blurb on the 1993 Poolbeg edition of *Guests of the Nation* indicates. This is true of 'Machine-Gun Corps in Action' and 'Laughter', both of which raise the question of the nature and purpose of O'Connor's humour. 'Machine-Gun Corps in Action' tells of a rogue machine-gunner, a little ragged man in an old check suit and a pair of musical-comedy tramp's brogues who is travelling the country causing havoc with his machine-gun wherever he goes. The tramp represents an anarchic force outside the jurisdiction of military order. A wildly quixotic figure, he refuses to conform until his wife turns up to take responsibility for him. It is she who tames him and takes him back to her little house and shop in the town. Where Synge's tramp attempts to lead Nora or Pegeen out of an oppressively conventionalised social world into the realms of nature and romance beyond society, O'Connor's tramp, embodiment of a similarly wild, unruly energy, is eventually contained within the bounds of marriage, law and respectability. As in 'Jumbo's Wife', O'Connor wants to emphasise the perpetual residuum of human life which makes a mockery of social control and regulation, and, in the manner of O'Casey, he asserts a powerful female influence while converting the male world to music-hall. Synge's Romance is absorbed by O'Casey's Realism. In contrast to 'Jumbo's Wife', the decisive force for order in this story is the wife not the brigade commander who is continually cheated of his quarry and even forced to pay to get the machine-gun. It is the individual who emphatically determines the course of history, not the other way around, as in the classic revolutionary text. 'Machine-Gun Corps in Action' offers a highly comic view of the Troubles, and in O'Connor's wild carnival sense of the world we detect the unresolved conflict in the author between 'imagination' and 'judgment'. A 'Boys' Own' Romanticism dominates the narrative, which is haunted by the 'Invisible Presences' (*OC*, p. 156) from the pages of *The Gem* and *The Magnet* which, by O'Connor's own account, filled his imagination up to the time he discovered Corkery.

The laughter evoked in the next story, which is entitled 'Laughter' is more controlled. Here the laughter is examined and explained. Only by carnivalizing violence, we come to understand, can it be made manageable. Carnival is one of the Russian theorist Mikhail Bakhtin's key terms. It is associated with masquerade, an upsetting of the firm structures and strict rankings of the 'official' or military life by an assumption of masks and false identities (*vide* the machine-gunner), which blur the boundaries between high and low, 'official' and 'provisional'.

O'Connor's writing is a carnivalistic overthrow of 'respectable' modes of discourse, a form of irreverence, such as has already been noted (though less scandalously) in the various narrative tactics employed in 'Guests of the Nation' to suspend normal categories and undercut conventional values. Laughter is an eruption of wildness, of all that is normally inadmissible and kept repressed. It is a disturbance of normal hierarchical boundaries, a decentering of authority, exerting a 'centrifugal'[16] pressure on the text. O'Connor's 'Laughter' includes a variety of images of this momentary breaking down or dissolving of conventional relations as a form of release from unbearable tensions. The first kind of laughter is that of the mother and daughter who are entertained by Stephen's story of Hair-lip, the local would-be IRA man, while they all wait for the other members of an IRA raiding party to assemble. Stephen's story is really Alec Gorman's story, and Stephen honours Alec's story-telling talent: the story 'needed Alec's secretive excited way of telling it'; 'it was a treat to see Alec take off this gesture'. Such performance skills are essential if the conversion of violence into laughter is to take place successfully. Then, when the daughter Mary thinks the knock at the door means that they have all been discovered by the authorities, she 'staggered and burst into a shriek of excited laughter.' Thinking she must finally confront the Law, Mary disintegrates in hysterical laughter. The main action is the ambush carried out by the four IRA men. Crouching in the wet darkness, waiting for their target, a lorry, to come into range, the protagonist, Stephen, experiences a strange, exciting disorientation. Reality seems to lose its solidity:

But whether it was his spectacles or his nerves that were at fault, he saw only three shadows that might not have been men at all. He could no longer distinguish them, and as he looked more closely, they seemed to dissolve and disappear into the dark and empty background of the fields.

He felt himself alone there, utterly alone. Once more he dabbed furiously at his glasses, and now two of the figures took shape again and seemed to come to life for a moment.

The experience of being 'utterly alone' is similar to that of the child astray in the snow in 'Guests of the Nation', but in 'Laughter' violence is exhilarating ('It had happened too quickly to be taken in; he wanted more of it, and still more until the flavour of it was on his tongue') and produces, not melancholy, but an equally paralysing hysterical laughter: 'there was something strange in that laughter, something out of another world, inhuman and sprightly, as though some gay spirit were breathing through them both'. Laughter marks a process of 'making strange': it is a refusal of the despotism of circumstance.

Fleeing from the scene of the attack, Stephen and his friend Cunningham meet an old woman who asks if there has been a shooting. Cunningham 'seemed to Stephen that he could no longer control himself. He shook with laughter and looked at the old tramp woman with wild, happy eyes'. His facetious reply that there was no shooting, only the sound of an old woman bursting paper bags, reassures the old woman that amidst the darkness and death there persists a playfully defiant, essentially life-affirming human spirit: 'She looked at him for a moment and laughed . . . "Young devil! Young devil!" she yelled merrily after him'. In contrast to the old woman at the end of 'Guests of the Nation' who is the voice of conscience and responsibility, the old 'mother' in 'Laughter' is the ancient hostess of carnival. The tragic muse is exchanged for the comic.

Many of the stories are structured on an archetypal rite of passage. 'Jo' presents such a process, ending, as 'Guests of the Nation', 'Nightpiece with Figures' and 'September Dawn' end, with the discovery of new value and a shift in allegiance. Returning to the use of the first person narration and a retrospective point of view that we find in the first two stories in the book, the story quickly establishes the distinctive character of the narrator through a vigorous, chatty vernacular. He emphasises his embeddedness in a particular community and culture with his references to 'our lads', 'our war', 'our Jo'. This makes his eventual gesture of independence all the more remarkable. The anxiety to assert belonging is accompanied by suspicion of the 'other', in particular of the Marshal who, as the son of a British soldier, 'wasn't the sort of man that people like you or me would care to chum up with'. 'Our Jo' has a 'wild streak' and is regarded by the narrator with something approaching hero-worship. In the way he recalls such 'daft schemes' of Jo's as the one to steal an express train and post overnight to the fighting in Dublin, the narrator both reveals his enjoyment of Jo and suggests his desire to be seen as a rather more responsible (or timid?) individual. Jo is kin to that other delinquent and maverick revolutionist, the machine-gunner of an earlier story, and is just as dangerously irresponsible. After the rout at Passage, Jo and the narrator relieve their disappointment by getting 'mad drunk' and shooting up the town: 'I was told after that I split one man's head with the butt of my revolver'. The narrator's idiom, in its young man's jaunty insouciance, bears the marks of Jo's questionable influence: 'We lost the war again at Passage – the most lamentable day of my life, I must admit, because my best pal was killed there, and because our lads, that were as fine a lot of soldiers as ever did right wheel on a parade ground, were being blown right and left like sheep without a shepherd.' Jo is 'an imaginary man', paranoid and fond of independent action. To him, violence is a boys' game, something 'to wile away the time'; 'fighting was better than lonesomeness'. About one of the 'jobs', he tells the narrator that he 'couldn't wish for a better fight'. Tearing up railway lines is being 'usefully employed', something to be done 'as a matter of principle' since they had spent so much time drinking that it was 'too late to do much damage'. The attitudes and feelings of both young men are enormously childish. They are no more grown-up about matters of the heart, falling out over a girl and refusing to speak to each other, until one night Jo 'whispered into my ear' that he 'wanted to be friends again', whereupon the narrator says he was 'very pleased, and we shook hands heartily on it'. The moral basis of their actions is continually being undermined. Jo's concern about finding that the Marshal had looted watches and silver spoons is juxtaposed with the comment that 'the same night Jo sniped a bottle of booze out of the local public, and the three of us drank it together'. Jo eventually shoots his old friend the Marshal for deserting to the enemy, and describes the incident with shockingly unfeeling gusto: 'I took my aim as cool and determined as if he was only a cockshot at a fair. I fired three times running, and before I could fire a fourth Babyface was down on top of me like a sack of meal. I had to jump out of his way or he'd have knocked me flying'. After the shooting, Jo goes to offer his condolences to the Marshal's father. As he leaves the father's house he meets the narrator and tells him to hurry up: 'Go on in now before you're too late. They're drinking the dozen of silver spoons inside.' The narrator's reply indicates his withdrawal from the sickening violence, the emergence of conscience, a moral and emotional growth: '"I will not," said I a bit short . . . somehow I could never bring myself to be pally with Jo again'. In the course of the story, the narrator's voice has been heard less and less and Jo's has tended to take over. This makes the ending all the more effective, for it is only after letting Jo have his full say, only after showing the brutalization of human feeling that war entails, that the narrator exchanges the ironic method that has been used up to this point for a straightforward culminating statement of his own attitude. Re-entering the narrative, he re-defines his relationship with Jo, moving it beyond adolescent hero-worship of the 'wild man'.

The next three stories in the book are all versions of the rite of passage theme in which the narrator or protagonist progresses from innocence to experience. 'Alec' is another story taking its title from the name of a local hero who is the object of the narrator's boyish admiration. As in 'Jo', the narrator is again cast as a callow youth attracted by the wild adventurer and popular story-teller, and the story charts his change in attitude towards his hero. Both Alec and the narrator get embroiled in a running feud between two local women, this story, like so many of the others, insisting on personalising and domesticating the world of politics. The image of community O'Connor offers in 'Alec' is even more negative than in previous stories. Here, he emphasises the back-biting, the malicious gossip, the constant suspicion and allegation of spying or informing, the imagined slightings, the conflicts between mother and son and between father and son. The community is crossed and divided in all sorts of ways, the personal tensions mirroring the larger conflict between the IRA and the Free Staters. The story, which is composed out of a network of stories, rumours and reports, gives us the impression of a volatile, shifting world with no secure foundations. The first person narration enforces the sense of relativism and subjectivism. There are stories within stories within stories. The narrator rehearses Alec's story of the origins of the feud between old Kate Nagle and her neighbour Najax: 'By his [Alec's] account . . . old Kate had been putting it about in her malicious way that Najax was a Free State spy . . .' 'These were the words of Najax as reported to Alec by Kate Nagle'. Najax seeks an ally in the narrator, Larry, who is struck by the childishness of the whole situation: 'She [Najax] was very like a child'; she listens to his advice 'with childish acquiescence'. When confined in prison for his political activities, the source of Larry's news of the outside world are the unreliable newspaper reports and stories from newly arrived prisoners. A curious note from Najax 'confirmed our worst suspicions' that Alec had turned informer to gain his freedom. Eventually, Larry hears from one of the other prisoners that Alec, once on the outside, has been more active than ever: giving his guards the slip, he has proceeded to burn down the house where he and Larry were captured, half killing the caretaker who, it is rumoured, had informed on them. The proliferation of rumour and counter-rumour constitutes a pathology of culture which subverts any political idealism.

Stories such as 'Jo', 'Alec' and 'Machine-Gun Corps in Action' celebrate the vital energy of the 'wild' and resourceful individual while questioning his dubious morality. Thus, the maverick machine-gunner is criticised because of his quixotic chivalry, and Jo and Alec because of their capacity for a quite ruthless brutality. The prisoner's story of Alec's deeds on the outside concludes: '"There!" said the innocent with a triumphant glance, "there now! He [the caretaker] is not expected to recover. What do you make of that?"' With that last question O'Connor makes the whole story vibrate, for the speaker's triumphalism is not the only response the question might elicit. That question, coming at the very end, poses a ringing challenge to the narrator, and thus represents a deftly ironical incorporation of a self-reflexive dimension into the story. Larry must decide to what extent he is going to connive in conventional expectations, and to what extent he is going to follow the promptings of his own conscience.

In 'Soirée Chez Une Belle Jeune Fille' it is a young girl's acquisition of knowledge in a sternly masculine world that the story details. At first Helen thinks of the world of political struggle as 'a world of youth and comradeship and adventure' and is pleased to have escaped the 'old stuffy, proprietary world she had been reared in'. But the world of the revolution disappoints. Employed as a courier for the IRA, she finds that her colleagues are not all the dashing heroes she had imagined, and that her hard efforts are rewarded with the barest recognition. On delivering a dispatch to Michael Redmond, who has been staying at the house of an old schoolfriend, May Crowley, Helen comes 'perilously close to tears', so little notice is paid to her: 'It was her first experience of headquarters work and already it was too much'. Helen's experience closely echoes that of O'Connor himself, who likewise acted as an IRA courier. In *An Only Child* he describes Childers, one of the supposedly 'great romantic figures of the period', as 'disappointing' (*OC*, p. 212), and when Childers sent him to Buttevant with dispatches for the divisional commander, Liam Deasy, Deasy 'disappointed all my expectations by ignoring the despatches, telling me I looked very tired, and putting me to bed' (*OC*, p. 216). In the story, what Helen finds most difficult to come to terms with is the relationship between Republicans and Free Staters when they meet on a personal level. Like the unidentified farmhouse in O'Connor's first story, 'Guests of the Nation', May's house is 'No Man's Land', a place withdrawn from the main action where warm and intimate relations persist amongst individuals who are supposedly enemies. May refuses to let politics interfere with old friendships. Not even Redmond expects May to reject old friends because of their politics: 'No one expects impossibilities'. The main event in the story is a dramatic enactment of the contradictions: Jordan, the IRA man who is 'The Hero of All Dreams', is offered the opportunity to visit his wife and family in the town and guaranteed a safe passage back if he will help Dr Considine, 'a tall young man in the uniform of the Regular Army', to transport a dead body which Considine has in his car outside. It is the body of a man Jordan had boasted to Helen and May of killing earlier in the day. In May's eyes, Jordan's placing his role of family man above that of revolutionist shatters his romantic charisma. By the end, Helen has much to think about, for this is a story about the growing awareness of uncertainty and the dissolving of fixed ideas; about the abandonment of adolescent romanticism and the need to face life's contradictions.

The next story, 'The Patriarch' also tells of a rite of passage, a process of disillusionment in which the narrator who starts out as a protegé of 'the patriarch', Michael Callanan, gradually comes to view the old man in a more realistic light. The story charts a trajectory of revolutionary commitment from juvenile fascination and hero-worship through growing disenchantment to full awareness of the tragic sense of life. It is essentially O'Connor's own experience of war, and of his relationship with his early mentor, Daniel Corkery. The process of disillusionment described in the story is, in some measure, a projection of O'Connor's outgrowing Corkery's influence. It was Corkery who introduced O'Connor to the Irish language and to revolution, and who undertook an attempted polemical revision of the Irish literary heritage. In the story, the Patriarch is a man with an obsessive interest in the Irish language, he introduces the narrator to the language and to 'volunteer work', and he is engaged in a process of discursive manipulation, determined that the old songs should be interpreted to give them a contemporary political relevance. In labouring to convert traditional Irish culture to Republican polemic, the Patriarch renders himself an absurdly comic figure. He is continually being undermined, as when the narrator discovers that the Patriarch himself doesn't know any Irish.

As a young man fighting for Ireland, the narrator thinks the Revolution was 'all thrilling and wonderful'. A pernicious romanticism, encouraged by the Patriarch, imbues his whole life. But by the end of the Anglo-Irish war the narrator is aware that he has changed and is more than a little impatient with the Patriarch's sterile idealism:

We were innocent in those days, and yet strangely, when the armistice came and there was no longer anything for us to do, we woke and found ourselves hardened, almost grown up, a little sly, a little given to bragging, a little contemptuous of people like the Patriarch who indulged in what we thought false sentiment.

During the time of 'the Treaty squabble', the narrator's disillusionment with both the war and the Patriarch deepens. Civil war has quickly lost any romantic glamour it might have had: 'after the first flush of enthusiasm has died away, fighting of this sort is a filthy game in which obstinacy and the desire for revenge soon predominate'. It is a time of unrest and uncertainty in which the Patriarch seems more and more of an anachronism. Even he is broken with guilt when one of his protegés ends up dead. Weak, incontinent, female-dominated, dying, the Patriarch moves out of the public arena altogether and is confined to his room and his bed. The squabbling of the outside world, however, continues in the private world, as seen in the constant bickering and hostility between the old man and his housekeeper: 'it was all so strange: here was death – here the hero of my boyhood, and I was listening only to a display of senile hatred of his housekeeper'. The 'dignity' of a previous time has degenerated into selfish, childish 'obstinacy and the desire for revenge'. The old man dies, and as the narrator looks out of his bedroom window over the countryside, he feels engulfed by a pervasive darkness and evil. As in 'Guests of the Nation', O'Connor ends by pulling back from the human drama and re-establishing the larger context. Here, it is the storm-filled night, rain, the sound of sniper-fire, the housekeeper's prayers – 'all magnified into something terrifying, remote and cruel'. The narrator is again brought to the point where the normal world is made strange and suddenly appears alien and threatening. Looking through the bedroom window, he confronts the terrifying infinite spaces of which Pascal spoke, and the story moves to the familiar culminating sense of impotence, lostness and desolation.

The last four stories in the book are not 'war' stories, but they continue many of the themes and motifs of earlier stories. 'The Patriarch' dramatised the position of the 'old guard', clinging to the old-fashioned, outworn values and ambitions of the past, unable to adapt to change. This concern with the past and the challenge of the present extends into the next two stories, 'After Fourteen Years', which offers an image of what Brian Friel calls 'fossilisation', and 'The Late Henry Conran', in which the protagonist, through the good offices of a friend and the loving ministrations of his wife, is coaxed out of the past and into present reality. 'After Fourteen Years' tells of Nicholas, who, out of a paralysing sense of personal weakness, longs for the security of the past, to be able to live only in memory as a way of protecting himself against harsh reality. Romance, passion, innocence, all belong to the past and it is to that other country that he wishes to return. The story repeats something of the feeling of 'Nightpiece with Figures'. It is written out of a sense of impotence and disillusionment with the present, a sense that vitality has passed from the world and that life is an enforced and miserable compromise amidst uncertainty, loss and death. O'Connor understands the contemporary disenchantment, but shows the desire to escape to the past as a contemptible failure of courage, a denial of life. Nicholas is a pathetic figure and is unable to command any respect even though O'Connor's gentle, melancholic lyricism is obviously intended to canvas some sympathy for him. Through the handling of tone the claims of the heart and those of the head are subtly balanced.

'The Late Henry Conran' is also about facing change, the longing for the past, the desire for stasis and fixed identity. It is about coming to terms with post-revolutionary Ireland and about the emergence of a petit bourgeois, post-colonial order bent on suppressing an embarrassing older generation. Where Nicholas in the previous story returns in remembrance to his idealised earlier life, Henry Conran returns in person to wife Nellie and family after twenty-five years in America. Henry, like Nicholas, laments change – the disappearance of the Mollies and the All-for-Irelanders, but is particularly bitter that in the announcement of his son's wedding he was referred to as 'the late Henry Conran'. Henry fights for his life, and for the past. He refuses to let his ambitious son and flashy new wife write him out of existence. Much of the comedy lies in the way the 'wild' man Henry is manipulated by his wife who pacifies him, gets him ready for bed as if he were a baby, and brings him to a state of acceptance and resignation. Henry protests to the end, but the virulence subsides: there is a great relief from the trauma of change and marginalisation in the personal values of friendship, love and domesticity.

The last story, 'The Procession of Life', brings the book to a close on a note of triumphant self-discovery and self-assertion, and makes it clear that O'Connor's fight for freedom is a fundamentally ontological, rather than a merely political, enterprise: 'my fight for Irish freedom', he wrote in *An Only Child*, 'was of the same order as my fight for other sorts of freedom' (*OC*, pp. 201–2).

Instead of hankering after a lost past, 'The Procession of Life' looks forward confidently to a bright new future. It tells of a young man's progression from innocence to experience, his breaking free of the tyranny of the father. His mother is dead and his father has locked him out of the house. Down by the darkened city quays the boy, Larry, encounters 'the procession of life'. Both 'miserable and elated' by his new freedom, a lonely, frightened outcast in the city which has suddenly become unfamiliar to him, he recalls Synge's Christy Mahon, another boy seeking independence from his father and similarly adrift in a hostile world until he finds romance with Pegeen. In O'Connor's story, it is reality that Larry discovers with the help of a prostitute. Before that, the boy has had to evade another representative of authority, the policeman; and come to terms with the unsettling figure of the watchman. The watchman is an ambiguous character, at first contemptuous of the boy for not standing up to his father and for being so inexperienced with drink, girls and pipe-smoking (as Old Mahon was contemptuous of Christy), then criticising the boy for not respecting his elders. He boasts of his own violence to his father, yet mouths concern about reputation and morality and a desire to protect the boy from the likes of the prostitute. Marvelling at Larry's timidity and innocence, in the next breath he violently rejects the boy out of a shamelessly hypocritical moral scruple: 'Am I going to have it said I gethered all the young blackguards of the city about me'. His crooked morality is coded in his name, 'Squinty'. The watchman turns out to be as inflexible and tyrannical as the father. He is capable of a horrifying brutality ('If you don't go away I'll strangle you and drop your naked body in the river fo the fish to ate. Be off with you, you devil's brat!') yet is easily mollified and is soon making tea for the boy.

O'Connor plays with light and darkness as he did in 'Nightpiece', another vaguely allegorical story. 'The Procession of Life', as the title implies, has something of the typological quality of morality play and pageant: an emblematic, instructional art. O'Connor resolves the characteristic tension in his work between 'instinct' and 'judgement' by (loosely) structuring the sense of swarming human life in terms of medieval allegory. The action, which takes place in a pool of light from the watchman's brazier, the characters appearing from the darkness and then disappearing back into it, offers an image of the dark underside of society and consciousness. The night-time truth is different from the clarities of the daylight world. In the darkness nothing is certain. The watchman is sinister and unpredictable, both weak and dangerous. The policeman is equally unreliable, and even more oppressive, as the language used to describe him insists: 'heavy footsteps thudding along', 'y'ould ram', 'thundered', 'interrupted heavily'. Instead of offering the reassurance of law and order, he is motivated by dark personal impulses, takes the prostitute away from Larry for his own pleasure, and attempts to make the boy feel better by giving him whiskey. A prostitute possesses whatever human warmth and honesty there are in the story. She is a 'mysterious woman', 'magical and compelling', who initiates the boy into the mysteries of sex, coaxing him into prohibited experience: taking her proffered hand, Larry 'wasn't even certain that he might lawfully hold it at all'. She is the representative of both disruptive libidinal pleasure and matriarchal comfort and security. In the end, the boy, like Christy Mahon, attains independence of father and female, of Law and Libido, 'a likely gaffer in the end of all', who has seen into the hypocrisies, ironies and instabilities of life and learnt the value of self-reliance. He overcomes 'fear' and 'lonesomeness' and faces into the city 'jauntily', his development mirroring that of his creator.

With this last story, itself telling of a rite of passage, O'Connor completes the larger pattern of personal and artistic development that the collection as a whole represents. For *Guests of the Nation* is clearly designed as a unified volume, like Corkery's *A Munster Twilight* or Joyce's *Dubliners* or Moore's *The Untilled Field*. O'Connor's last story is particularly reminiscent of Sherwood Anderson's last story in *Winesburg, Ohio*, a book which O'Connor much admired,[17] and which is also about a young man's improvising an education for himself. In Anderson's final story, 'Departure', the hero, George, is propelled beyond the restricted confines of his mid-west home town, 'going out of his town to meet the adventure of his life'. O'Connor ends with a similar Joycean anticipation of flight and potency, having brought us from the 'ashes' and 'dusk' and sense of confinement at the start of the first story to the dawn and the ships and the feeling of release – 'the faint brightness over the hill [which] showed clearer and clearer, until at last the boy could distinguish the dim outlines of riverside and ships and masts' – at the end of the last one.

SEAN O'FAOLAIN'S
MIDSUMMER NIGHT MADNESS AND OTHER STORIES:
CONTEXTS FOR REVISIONISM

PATRICK WALSH

Maurice Harmon's recent biography provides us with the following snapshot of an episode in the life of the ageing Irish writer:

He talked freely with Elfreda ... He never revealed his background, presented himself as sophisticated, as one who had lived in Italy, had an affair with Honor Tracy, had a homosexual experience ... He was, he told her, deeply ashamed of having belonged to the I.R.A. and was very reluctant to allow Constable to reprint stories from *Midsummer Night Madness*. He liked Englishness, liked being published by Constable which he regarded as a very British kind of publishing house with an old Etonian at the helm.[1]

The comments on the IRA are exceptional and, despite O'Faolain's thorough-going and well-known revision of the period of his political and military involvement with Republicanism, his analysis of the physical force tradition was usually presented carefully from the standpoint of one who had known it from within, of one who knew its limitations but who was also aware of the complex social, historical and political landscape within which it was situated. The context of 1977 and a lunch with an employee of an English publishing firm suggests an explanation connected with the recrudescence of political violence in the North of Ireland: polite assuaging noises about contemporary horrors. There is an implicit suggestion also that the homosexual experience (a bizarre note, in that it is unrelated to anything else in the biography) is of a similar nature: the garrulity of a flirtatious, ageing writer in the company of a young, influential, cosmopolitan figure he is eager to impress. Harmon makes it clear that, in his old age, O'Faolain had established a pattern in this respect, particularly with young female employees of English publishing houses.[2]

In a vivid, if anecdotal, way the incident highlights a fractious issue in Irish letters: the relationship between the writer and the audiences for which he is writing, both the immediate Irish one and that of the wider international community. The issue was foregrounded by O'Faolain right at the start of his career. Edward Garnett, the influential writer and reader for the publishers, Jonathan Cape, was an early patron, and their relationship has been described by Maurice Harmon as 'the most important in Sean's entire literary life.'[3] He wrote a provocative introduction to O'Faolain's first collection of short stories in which he described the Irish as 'the most backward nation in Europe' and 'most indifferent to literature and art, and least aware of critical standards.'[4] While O'Faolain went to some lengths to tone down some of the more anti-clerical of Garnett's incendiary remarks[5] – and it is clear that their tone had much to do with the damage that the Censorship Act of 1929 was beginning to inflict on the careers of Irish authors – nevertheless, as an introduction to a first book in such circumstances, it is astonishingly combative and singularly lacking in strategic acumen. The alliance with sympathetic overseas publishers was one that O'Faolain continued throughout his career and, while it advanced his writing career abroad, it left him exposed at home in Ireland. One is reminded wryly of his old mentor Daniel Corkery's gibe about Frank O'Connor on the occasion of their last meeting on a street in Cork in the mid-50s: 'Well, if it isn't Mr. Frank O'Connor who only writes for American magazines now.'[6] The comment could have been applied just as readily to O'Faolain. One doesn't have to subscribe to Corkery's narrow conception of the role of the Irish writer – to write primarily for an Irish audience – to see that the matter does highlight a problematic area in O'Faolain's career, namely the paradoxical character of his fierce engagement with Irish society which produced both the obsessive, regionally focused intensity of his opposition to the socially conservative southern state in the '30s and '40s and a growing resignation (in the final decades of his life) to the social forces that produced that state – at the same time as he began to devote more of his life and work to the broader world outside Ireland, principally Europe and America.

Recently historians have begun to turn their attention to the processes by which modern historiography has evolved in Ireland this century. While T.W. Moody and R. Dudley Edwards were central figures in the creation of the conditions in Irish academia that would help give birth to the complex intersection of history writing and contemporary politics that has been named revisionism,[7] it was Sean O'Faolain who had explicitly mapped out its agenda long before the historical phenomenon was distinctive enough to be named. Recent writers have tended to subsume the O'Faolain of the early years into the contemporary context within which the revisionist controversy is situated without any close examination of the tensions or difficulties which are raised. For example during the recent period there was a public reticence on the part of O'Faolain in relation to the Northern Troubles: this is curious given the oracular status he had achieved within Irish cultural and political life. Addressing this conjunction of silence and crisis helps us to address one of the major obfuscations that surround the revisionist debate: namely the tendency to ignore the importance to the development of this debate of the sharply differentiated political contexts of the partitioned states into which its contentious energies were released. A result of this was that the otherwise central dynamic of the social and political conjuncture created by partition was obscured and marginalised in the revisionist project. It was primarily out of the political and academic conditions of the southern state that revisionism emerged, and the suffocating, officially sponsored, nationalist orthodoxy, which it initially set out to subvert, was fundamentally a phenomenon of that state: its northern variant, while bearing the family likeness in most other respects, was an oppositional phenomenon antagonistic to the established structures of power. The outbreak of the Northern Troubles in the late 60s interrupted this process and provided a radically altered political context for its development. While much attention has been given to the perceived impetus that the sectarian ugliness of the conflict gave to the revisionist project little attention has been paid to its corollary – the establishment in violent, unignorable terms of an all-Ireland context for the debate. In addition the modernization of the southern and northern states in the context of the penetration of both international capital and political radicalism provided a sharply differentiated social landscape. When the assumptions and mind-sets of the earlier period within which O'Faolain's ground-breaking polemics were situated are applied without elaboration or qualification to the later period, tensions become apparent, tensions that are unresolvable if this change in context is not recognised.

We can concretise these observations if we note the relationship between a key, early revisionist text and O'Faolain's polemics of the 30s. In 1936, in a wide-ranging attack on the work and influence of Daniel Corkery, he had been particularly scathing on the influence of what has become Corkery's most enduring and influential book – *The Hidden Ireland*. One of the harshest sections of the article attacks the consequences of the idealization of the peasantry which he perceived as being contained in this work: it is a barrier to modernity; the Celtic World is 'now dead and forgotten' in the minds of the peasantry who 'threw it all aside to build up, for themselves, and for the first time, a world of their own in the hovels to which that ancient curse the Celtic state, had by its inefficiency reduced them.'[8] This could be seen almost as a manifesto for similar ideas which he adumbrated at greater length later in *The Bell*. O'Faolain also explicitly points the way for the modern historian. Of *The Hidden Ireland* he writes: 'It is a book which needed to be written. But it should have been written by a historian; and as it stands – with no historian willing to engage his energies in challenging and disproving so many elaborate generalizations – it has had and will continue to have a profound effect on modern Irish (uncritical) thought'.[9]

The Hidden Ireland's version of the past provided powerful cultural underpinning to traditional nationalist history which became, in the 1930s, the educational orthodoxy of the new state. Although a response to an earlier period – the rise of the Gaelic League and Irish Ireland, and the cultural challenge they thus posed to the provincial culture of the Protestant Anglo-Irish Ascendancy – Corkery's book emerged at a time in partitioned Ireland when this eclectic radical current was being subsumed into this orthodoxy. In a state where power had passed to the Catholic middle-class the elision of Gaelic, Catholic and nationalist history was an important obfuscation that helped the fragile, social structures of the state to cohere. The disruptive energy of radical republicanism was managed by the emergence of Fianna Fail and the alliance it constructed with the conservative forces of the institutional church. Corkery's work, and cultural nationalism generally, was imbued with the analytical weaknesses of the decayed tradition of nineteenth century romanticism which left it open to this assimilation. The genesis of revisionist historiography lies in the revolt against the stultifying pieties that this tradition drew over the southern state in the years after partition. This process has quickened over the last three decades as the economic changes of the 1960s and the subsequent rapid industrialisation which followed provided a new social pressure which gave urgency to the dismantling of these pieties.

Louis Cullen's seminal 1969 article 'The Hidden Ireland: Reassessment of a Concept' takes up the invitation extended by O'Faolain and is a key text in modern revisionism. Attacking *The Hidden Ireland* as history, it characterises it as simplistic, impoverishing our view of the processes by which 'Irish nationality and the sense of identity' accumulated, 'seeing it in the context of settlement and oppression and not in the rich, complex and varied stream of identity and racial consciousness heightened in the course of centuries of Anglo-Irish relations.'[10] However, the real terms of this controversy were set by Corkery when he published *Synge and Anglo-Irish Literature* in 1931. Before that *The Hidden Ireland* had been received largely as a necessary corrective to Ascendancy history, towards which the surviving English written sources were naturally skewed. *Synge and Anglo-Irish Literature* provided a more disturbing sectarian context for the earlier book. Corkery's work was consequently reacted to with hostility by both the survivors of the Revival generation and younger more iconoclastic writers such as O'Faolain and O'Connor. In the '30s, '40s and '50s the terms of this debate were principally set by the repressive social agenda of the southern state, around issues such as the anti-divorce and censorship laws. Cullen's article, however, appeared in the politically momentous year of 1969 when the social processes to which these political issues were addressed were once again posed in a framework which transcended the containing bounds of the partitioned states. The sectarianism that some perceived *Synge and Anglo-Irish Literature* to be an expression of, was now posed in a more deadly way. The contradictions that partition had contained now emerged in malevolent form. It became difficult to address the social tensions of either state without reference to wider parameters that transcended the borders of the partition settlement. Because the concerns mapped out by O'Faolain were principally concerned with the social climate of the southern state and largely ignored the all-Ireland social and political context which had shaped them, their application by a later generation of historians and writers contributed to the fierce polemical character of the revisionist debate. Just as the re-emergence of partition as a critical, immediate issue on the Irish political stage produced an uncharacteristic silence from a figure whose polemical combativeness had done so much to shape him as a writer, the application of his ideas by contemporary historians produced a historiography that proved controversial when applied to an Ireland that was grappling painfully with the violent consequences of its division. As Louis Cullen's article sought to revise and provide a critique of the continuities of nationalist versions of history, with their emphasis on 'settlement and oppression', events in the ghettos of the North were moving to confirm them.

Just as it has been argued that it is critically important to acknowledge the different contexts within which O'Faolain's proto-revisionist critique of the '30s and '40s and the contemporary revisionist debate are situated, so it is equally important to register a similar disjunction between the setting of his stories depicting the War of Independence and Civil War, and the actual context in which they were written and published over ten years later. O'Faolain's first book *Midsummer Night Madness and Other Stories* is not a contemporary record but a reflection on a period of his life and a period of Irish history that was already beginning to recede into the past. Paradoxically, the most important context for an understanding of these stories is not the period with which they deal but the period in which they were written, when the social and political institutions of the southern and northern states were beginning to bed down into seemingly immovable, monolithic fact. The mood of these stories is shaped both by the excited exaltation of many of the young activists which they portray and the bitter disappointment of the period of suffocating reaction out of which they were created. This duality can be detected in their structural and thematic concerns.

Versions of some of the stories in the volume had appeared in the years before their publication as part of a collection, but together they offered the writer an opportunity to present a broader view of the conflicts in which he had participated. The whole book is permeated by images which offer a critique of the naivety of his early involvement. Counterposed to the activities of the revolutionaries is the private world of the self – a richer, warmer, more authentic and inviting world symbolised throughout the collection by the female and sexuality. This is indicated most emphatically by the final story, 'The Patriot'. The early naive ardour of Bernie, a young Republican activist, is described and juxtaposed with a vivid account of his final weeks with the exhausted, disorganised Republican forces and his eventual capture by the Free Staters. In the earlier part of the story, set in the seaside town of Youghal, he is depicted as hopeful and enthusiastic, 'seated high up on a lorry, with his rifle across his back and his coat-collar turned up, and his cap thrown back

and upwards from his forehead to let his curls free to the wind.'[11]
He falls in love with Norah, a childhood acquaintance, and their
young, innocent love is described with lush romanticism. Months
later, a disillusioned hunted fugitive in the mountains, 'he
remembered how lovely Youghal had been, and how lovely
Norah, and he hated to look up at the cold naked mountains.'[12]
Contrasted with this fecund relationship is the figure of Edward
Bradley, a middle-aged, unmarried Sinn Fein propagandist and
fiery orator. The character is a conflation of prominent Cork
Republicans of the period – perhaps two of Corkery's friends and
collaborators, the Republican martyrs, Terence McSwiney and
Tomas MacCurtain: the young Bernie declares defensively to his
disapproving aunt, 'Some day that man will be Lord Mayor of
Cork and then you'll sing a different song.'[13] However, as
Corkery's most recent biographer has noted, in the detail of the
character there is more of the confirmed bachelor Corkery than of
his two dead friends.[14] Introduced as Bernie's teacher, 'Old
Bradley', he speaks words 'with a terrible passion against
England,'[15] firing the two young people's nationalist conviction.
Later, when Bernie is released from imprisonment, he marries
Norah and they return to Youghal for their honeymoon. The town
is blooming and lovely and by chance they encounter Bradley
again as he addresses a Sinn Fein public meeting: 'the terrible
passion of the man blazed like the fire of burning youth.'[16]
Unaffected, the excited lovers return to their hotel room. Before he
pulls the curtains, Bernie sees the 'old bachelor, the patriot,
driving out of the town into the country and the dark night . . . But
that wind would not for many miles cool the passion in him to
which he had given his life.'[17] Drawing the curtains on Bradley's
barren fanaticism he turns towards the bed where his young wife
lies smiling and waiting. Positioned at the end of the book the
story's didactic intention could not be clearer, and it represents the
most trenchant statement of the position O'Faolain had now
reached in relation to the conflict. It is also a valedictory gesture
indicating a clear break with the past and indeed his later fiction is
largely concerned with the world that came into being as a result
of that conflict, the world of the independent Irish State.

'The Patriot' completes explicitly a series of motifs that are part
of the implicit themes of his first collection. Each of the stories
portrays young activists caught up in the whirl of events that
constitutes the Irish revolution. Each also traces an arc of
disillusion, a learning process that is dearly bought. The fertile
world of the sexual and female beckons the young fighters away

from the cold, inhuman world of revolutionary fanaticism to a more intimate domestic world of companionship, growth and renewal. For example, the young guerrilla in 'Fugue' traverses the harsh mountains at the end of his tether whilst the figure of a young woman who has given him and his companion shelter haunts his journey. Her smile, her softness and – as an insistent image of the fecund, nurturing essence of the feminine – her breasts are constantly before him:

I might have been the last human creature to crawl to the last summit of the world waiting until the Deluge and the fortieth night of rain would strain him upwards on his toes while the water licked his stretched neck. Yet everywhere they slept sound abed, my dark woman curling her warm body beneath the bed-clothes, the warmer for the wet fall without, thinking if she turned and heard the dripping eaves – that the winter was at last come.[18]

In 'The Small Lady' this juxtaposition of the public world of revolutionary commitment and the private, interior world of sexual intimacy is ravelled with a more complex, ambitious intent. An Anglo-Irish woman, a reputed informer, has been selected as a hostage by Sinn Feiners. The reality of the events (based on a real incident in the Anglo-Irish war[19]) is juxtaposed at the start with a stereotypical Republican ballad:

> The name she had was the Small Lady
> Five foot in her scarlet gown;
> God's curse may light upon her
> And fall from heaven down
> For she sold our boys to England's Tans
> So they fell without a blow
> Face to face with a firing squad
> All standing in a row.[20]

In O'Faolain's story the woman, Bella Browne, is sophisticated, sexually experienced and widely travelled. Resigned to her fate, yet alive to the vibrantly beautiful countryside through which her abductors escort her, she aches for life and freedom:

She would not care if they made her spend the night wandering over the mountains – she even laughed quietly to herself to think of the game rising against the moon, the little fishes darting out of their sleep – she would not care if they sate the night out watching the embers dying in some farmer's kitchen, not even care if they then shot her in the dawn for 'a cursed English spy.' Only she must have a few more hours of

beautiful and passionate life, and then, 'O Goddam all, good-bye green
fields, blue sky; off I pop into the great Has-been!' Yet when the gentle
fall began to trickle across her lips and down the channel of her breasts
she shivered: it was cold up here even where the sun still shone, cold
with the coldness of the sweating earth, and when she turned to look at
her captors she thought they looked like homeless animals clustered in a
storm.[21]

Desperate for human companionship she responds to the
innocence and physical beauty of the young man Denis, one of her
captors:

She let her eyes wander over his long tapering hands that clasped his
rifle, his waist like a colt or a greyhound, back to his eyes that looked at
her with a frank and open look, and at once she felt she could speak to
this boy.[22]

They stop for a night in a monastery and there amidst the cold,
empty corridors she takes the young man to her bed and makes
love to him. The shivering piety of a drunken resident of the
monastery is juxtaposed with their tender and passionate closeness:

They remained in one another's arms for so long that she lost all feeling
of time, and it was at last a wild cry that broke the charm, rising time
after time in the corridor outside where the drunkard ran howling past,
beating with his fists on their door and every door, crying out in the
horrors of drink, 'O Lord God have mercy on me a sinner, Lord God!
Lord God! For all Eternity, for all Eternity, for all Eternity!' and so he
cried until somebody dragged him away by main force, perhaps some
of the guerrillas in their shirt-tails, and there was silence again but for
the dull murmurs of the choir below and their own breathing in the
dark, except when stopping his mouth with hers, she kissed him long
and slow, and even then the choir was silent, until they breathed
again.[23]

In the morning she is 'Mrs Browne' again and later the boy
confesses his 'sin' to a priest. Bella is eventually executed and the
band of Republicans is surprised by a pursuing group of Tans.
Amongst them, acting as their guide, is an old RIC constable,
Denis' father – a rather intrusive and awkwardly developed ironic
touch. The end of the story sees Denis escaping with a companion
over the mountains and his youth and vitality are counterposed to
the cold finality of Bella's fate. The companion informs him that he
knows 'a domn fine girrl down there will give us a warm bed for
the night.' By the time they reach the girl's door, 'they were in a

gay mood, rejoicing in the loveliness of the night, and their own youth, and the promise of infinite days yet to come.'[24] This terse, effective, coolly observant ending is at odds with the story's dominant schematic tendency to treat Bella and Denis as representative of historic native Catholic and Anglo-Irish Protestant formations in the Irish social landscape. This dichotomy between an engagement with the subjective and psychological in the experience of his characters, and the conflicting tendency towards a more didactically oriented presentation of them as social types, represents a disabling tension in the story, one which was present in O'Faolain's writing generally and which he only rarely resolved.

Here, as on many occasions in this first collection, O'Faolain juxtaposes the harsh realities of suffering and death with a vivid, sensual romanticism that is embodied both in the sometimes harsh, sometimes lush beauty of the country through which the fighters move, and in images of the fertile, female figures whose human warmth haunts their imaginations. When he tips this carefully judged balance for heavy, didactic purposes the effect of his writing is diffused. Some of the stories are also over-ambitious, straining towards the varied events and multiple characterisation of the novel and out of the constraints of the short story. For instance, there are a number of connecting names and incidents that reach from one story to another. The drunken, sullen, IRA activist Stevey Long of the opening story later gets his come-uppance in 'The Death of Stevey Long.' Escaping from prison, murdering in the process a deserting English soldier who has assisted him, he returns foolishly to a night-time Cork City which is under curfew. Pursued by the British he takes refuge in a deserted house where he finds a dead woman seated in an armchair. The manner of the woman's death has been narrated in another story, 'The Bomb Shop', and, unknown to Stevey Long, the house has been evacuated by the IRA because it has become too dangerous. The dead woman has been presented as a Cathleen Ni Houlihan figure presiding over the activities of the bomb makers. She has been killed by a stray shot from the gun of one of them as they squabble and fight in the overheated atmosphere of the bomb-shop. Now, with more heavy irony, the brutal, callous Stevey Long happens on this house as a final place of refuge only to seal his own fate, for it is soon raided by the British and he is captured and executed. These cumbersome structural links illustrate the ambitious aspiration of the young writer – a comprehensive portrayal of the struggle which, though its focus is primarily on isolated individuals, gestures towards a breadth of presentation.

O'Faolain also strives for a social complexity that is only intermittently successful. For example, in 'The Small Lady' Bella's past life is sketched in rather stereotypical terms. Attempts to deal with her experiences outside the events of the abduction are broad and unconvincing. Similarly, the semi-autobiographical touch of the young activist's RIC father overloads the story. Strains are evident also in another ambitious story which aims to engage with a social landscape more varied than the milieu of Catholic, Republican militants. 'Mid Summer Night Madness', the opening story from which the collection takes its name, resembles 'The Small Lady' in that it attempts to deal in emblematic terms with the intersection of different layers of Irish society at the moment of revolutionary flux. The use of the Anglo-Irish experience in this story, which like 'The Patriot' is also strategically positioned in the book, demonstrates most clearly that in this first collection the writer is as much engaged with the debate about the nature of Irish culture and society that was part of the '30s polemical engagement as with the recent past of the revolutionary years.

The narrator, a young Republican organiser, puts the City of Cork behind him and heads out into the summer countryside on a mission. He is returning to an area that he knows well, his mother's home village, and is to be billeted in the big house of the district: 'I might even see and meet, if he were still alive, its strange mad owner whom as children we thought more terrifying than any of the ogres in the fairy books – Old Henn of Henn Hall.'[25] Henn is a representative figure of the Ascendancy – isolated, rakish and profligate, he has been a figure of scandal for the Catholics of the district: 'Clearly, a man who lived by the things of the body – women, wine, hunting, fishing, shooting.'[26] This half-mythical ogre has presided over the dreams and nightmares of the youth of his mother and many like her. When the IRA organiser arrives at the hall he finds installed there the local commandant, Stevey Long – the drunken braggart who, as we have noted, reappears in another story – and a sensuous, female figure, a half-civilized gypsy woman who has divided her sexual favours between Long and the old rake, Henn. Stevey is crude and sensual and the woman is drawn to him because of his youth and virility. He treats her roughly in front of the embarrassed narrator:

'She has great titties, John,' said Stevey coarsely, and she slapped his face for that, and as I went on with my supper I heard him kiss her in return.[27]

The ogre, old Henn, turns out to be a more sympathetic figure. Dissipated and impotent, even to control visitors to his own household, he worships the lazy sensuality of the indifferent gypsy. She has come to represent all the receded, unattainable carnality to which he had devoted his youth. Stevey is stung into activity by the arrival of the young organiser and burns the house of the Blakes, a neighbouring gentry family. Once again, emblematically, this house contains archetypal figures – two aged maiden sisters and their father, representative, like Henn, of an isolated, decaying class. They take refuge with Henn and, in the story's baroque climax, the drunken Long, anxious to conceal his own complicity, confronts Henn over Gypsy's pregnancy in front of a crowd of his fellow incendiaries. Threatening to burn the house, he demands that Henn shoulder his responsibility and marry her. Thus an odd, incongruous union – between youth and age, peasant and gentry, native and Anglo-Irish – is effected. The last paragraph of the story provides us with a glimpse of the ill-matched pair in a bizarre parody of a European tour:

But I find it too painful to think of him, there in Paris, with his scraps of governess-French, guiding his tinker wife through the boulevards, the cafés, the theatres – seeing once more the lovely women and the men gay in their hour. Life is too pitiful in these recapturings of the *temps perdu*, these brief intervals of reality.[28]

O'Faolain is engaging overtly in this story with one of the major cultural controversies of the 30s, one that had been given concrete, disputatious shape by the publication of Daniel Corkery's *Synge and Anglo-Irish Literature* – namely the nature of the relationship between Anglo-Irish Protestant culture and that of the native Catholic, the Irish Ireland version of which was beginning to entrench as the educational orthodoxy of the new state. O'Faolain sided emphatically with Yeats and his associates, breaking decisively from the influence of Corkery in the process. The year of publication of *Midsummer Night Madness and Other Stories* has, in retrospect, come to be seen as an important moment in the political and cultural history of Ireland. The year of the Eucharistic Congress and the formation of de Valera's first government, it was also the founding year of Yeats' ambitiously conceived Irish Academy of Letters. Corkery was offered membership by Yeats but declined on the grounds that such an academy, so named and principally including English language writers, was a contradiction in terms. The encounter, with its almost ceremonial ritualism has, in retrospect, taken on an emblematic quality: on one side was a declining world represented by Yeats and the Revivalists, a pre-independence Ireland where a largely Protestant literary culture interacted with and partially provided leadership for an emergent Irish democracy. On the other side was independent, Catholic Ireland represented by Corkery; beginning now to entrench, it was ousting the last vestiges of ascendancy. With the shrewdness that was as much a characteristic of the ageing poet as the dreamy absent-mindedness much noted by his friends, Yeats, when forming his academy, had one eye on the past and another on the future. While its core was made up of great names of the Revival period (e.g. A.E., George Moore) it also welcomed younger people such as O'Faolain and O'Connor. Yeats saw them as important representatives of the generation that would inherit the achievements of the Revival: '"You", he said to O'Connor, "will save the Abbey Theatre and O'Faolain will save the Academy."'[29]

It is in such a context that we should see O'Faolain's collection of 'war stories' offered in 1932. The period of his own commitment was already the subject of his revisionist scrutiny and he presents the revolutionary intensity of that period – the 'madness' – as fanatical and inward looking. Old Henn and Gypsy, bedraggled and ridiculous figures though they are, carry with them to Europe the imaginative sympathy of the young writer. The reference to Proust's great novel is fleeting, but telling. The 'lost time' of his youth is conceived specifically in European terms. Many years later the same opposition is expressed acutely in his autobiography:

Long after, twenty years after, when I had disciplined myself for this wagging world, and begun to travel in Europe I read what others – most of them my contemporaries and some of them my friends – had been seeing, thinking and doing in France, Austria, Italy, Greece, Asia Minor, the far Orient, such men and women as Robert Byron, the Sitwells, Morgan Foster, Elizabeth Bowen, Harold Acton, Christopher Sykes, Raymond Mortimer, V.S. Pritchett, Cyril Connolly – in those fabled Twenties when you could travel often and widely for a few pounds. As I read I was often tempted to bewail my Twenties, which I had spent arguing politics with young men, talking Gaelic to old men, in sun and rain, cowering under dripping hedges, sitting by cottage fires among the mountains. Was I mad to have spent my youth like that?[30]

Henn and Gypsy's peregrinations offer a positive example, as well as a lament for lost opportunities. It is towards Europe that the exhausted bickering traditions of Ireland must turn for new life and inspiration. In the years that followed O'Faolain's fierce critique of the narrowness of the cultural underpinnings of the Free State accumulated into an impressive, sustained body of writing that probed the narrow foundations of the social and political reality of that state. His first book should be seen as one of the earliest documents of that process and not indiscriminately as the contemporaneous record of the experiences of a young Republican activist. Paradoxically, making this distinction highlights also features of his thinking that were limited by the very terms of his polemical engagement and illuminates the process by which the parameters formed by the recently settled boundaries of the southern state limited the effectiveness of his critique. For all the coruscating insight that he brought to this task, and which is most impressively documented in the pages of *The Bell*, a disabling irony dwelt within it. Alongside the polemical activism of his youth he had laid down a vision of the state that included not only a myopic, romantic intensity but also a sense of the significance of the precise procession of political events out of which it had been created. Even as he railed against the narrow reality of this state to a remarkable degree his imagination was enclosed by the immediate political situation in which he was situated in the 30s. For instance the North only rarely intruded in his writing as a constituent part of the social geography of his world view. Even then it was handled gingerly as 'different,' even foreign. For example the following passage which is taken from 'The Six Counties' chapter of his 1941 travel book *An Irish Journey* is shaped by a heavy, stereotypical concept of 'Protestant Ulster'[31] and does less than justice to the complex social and historical mesh that has produced the Protestant and Catholic community of south west Ulster:

It [Enniskillen] is a town with a very pleasant flavour, and like all Northern towns it has the sturdy, clean, smart, efficient air of an English market town. It has the same reticence, too, and the same heaviness. The contrast between it and, say, Sligo is the contrast between two foreign countries.[32]

The North is different but to obsessively focus only on this difference is to produce an attenuated account of its culture, and the corollary of this, which is germane to our immediate point here about the parameters which formed the world view of O'Faolain, is that seeing the North in this way also produces an incomplete view of the South. Buried under the weight of the monolithic actuality of partition was an all Ireland political context that was vital to an understanding of its political and social dynamic. By representing difference as foreignness, and substituting polarities for the continuities of complex regional nuances, partition not only effected a radical truncation of the historical experience of Catholic Ireland but that of Protestant Ireland also.

O'Faolain's last full collection of stories, published in 1976, was entitled *Foreign Affairs and Other Stories* and, while its ironic title focuses primarily on love affairs in a European setting, in a comment on the stories O'Faolain makes clear that the foreignness he refers to is a more unsettling internalised reflection on how the individual mediates the internal 'self' in relation to the 'other' which lies outside the self:

I did find out (I think) that nobody is ever 'free' except when absorbed by some thing or body other than oneself which forces submission on us ... this sort of thing is the struggle between the 'foreign' and the 'gregarious' in all of us ... what we both seek is a something, a light, a land not 'theirs' – ours[33].

Recognising the 'foreign' confirms what is 'ours' and not 'theirs'. Ultimately the foreignness of the 'other', whether it is the Protestantism of Ulster or the cultural variousness of the European, provides a measure by which the boundaries of what is 'ours' can be established. For O'Faolain the boundaries of that 'imagined community,'[34] the southern state, eventually defined the limits of even the broadest and deepest of his political imaginings.

ROADS TO SPAIN: IRISH WRITERS AND THE SPANISH CIVIL WAR

KATHLEEN DEVINE

If for a central body of left-wing writers in 1930s England the outbreak of the Spanish Civil War in July, 1936 seemed to present an obvious challenge to react in terms of ideological positions previously embraced, whether by literally taking the road to Spain or by offering literary support from home, the case did not seem so clear-cut in Ireland. With an independent status so recently won and the memory of civil war at home a still unhealed wound, it is unsurprising that opinion in the largely Catholic southern state substantially fell in with the body of clergy supporting Franco, a conservative instinct, ironically, supporting rebellion. Republican and socialist organizations were much harassed in the Free State; moreover, preoccupied as they were with the local situation, support for Spain was not their first priority. In Ulster memory of recent Irish history was also raw and the political coloration of the forces associated with the Spanish Republican Government would obviously have been a matter for suspicion (the Students' Union of Queen's University in Belfast banned Peadar O'Donnell from speaking to the Literary and Scientific Society after his return from Spain).[1] Writers however as different as Louis MacNeice and Peadar O'Donnell, or Ewart Milne and Charles Donnelly, did, with varying degrees of commitment, take the road to Spain.[2] The result in the first three cases is a literature of honest witness, rising, in the case of O'Donnell and MacNeice, to episodes of humane identification. In the case of Donnelly, however, we have an ideologically committed activist who becomes a combatant, but who as a writer produces poetry which transcends the immediate events to achieve a broader perspective on war. In this respect, the direction his work was taking is comparable to that of the soldier poets of World War II such as Keith Douglas and Alun Lewis who, conscious of larger

147

continuities in war literature and war experience, showed a similar ability to treat the specific historical moment within a universalising perspective.

Amongst other writers the conflict created no marked excitement and, for instance, Sean O'Faolain's reply to the 'Authors Take Sides' questionnaire organized through the *Left Review* indicates the distance felt from the political heat generated by it in English literary circles. Irascibly he wrote: 'If you want to know, I do think Fascism is lousy. So is Communism, only more so. But there are other ideas in the world besides either of them – thank God (whom neither of you believe in).'[3] Beckett's cryptic '!UPTHEREPUBLIC!' embodied subtle ironies at the expense of the exercise not acknowledged by the survey's organizers, suggesting in its run-on form the mindless roar of the converted at a political meeting. Yeats, although his letters show him to be alert to the situation,[4] did not engage directly in his poetry with the Spanish question, preferring instead the perennial themes of sex and age in 'Politics' where he is the observer of other men's political passion:

> How can I, that girl standing there,
> My attention fix
> On Roman or on Russian
> Or on Spanish politics?[5]

O'Casey's political sympathies may have been clear but there was an obvious element of mischief in the expression of them (his addressee was Harold Macmillan): 'I am praying to God that the Spanish Communists may win. I wish I could be with them. However, if I haven't manned a tank, or fired a rifle for the cause of Communism, I have, at least, in my day, fired stones at the police.'[6] Belfast-born Louis MacNeice, domiciled in England, responded more soberly to the *Left Review* questionnaire: 'I support the Valencia Government in Spain. Normally I would only support a cause because I hoped to get something out of it. Here the reason is stronger; if this cause is lost, nobody with civilized values may be able to get anything out of anything', and in his poetry he acknowledged honestly the distance he felt from events recognized as important but beyond his immediate personal purview.

MacNeice visited Spain with Anthony Blunt at Easter, 1936. His position as holiday-maker provides an appropriate persona to suggest his distanced, uninvolved reaction to the Spanish situation when, in section VI of *Autumn Journal*,[7] he writes of the experience. The role of the tripper for whom the rain can be worse than the political atmosphere allows scope for registering the outsider's array of impressions, where flippancy ('And we thought the dark / Women who dyed their hair should have it dyed more often') can interweave with an astute sensitivity to an atmosphere 'ripe as an egg for revolt and ruin'. As will be seen however he did ultimately find his own personal axis of sympathy and identification. Behind the device of the 'tripper' persona, however, there lies a deeper cultural alienation which, though less personally felt than in the earlier 'Carrickfergus', reasserts itself here through the deployment of similar emblems of power and victimization. These are again embodied in church artefact and practice: the candles of entreaty lit by the victimized poor and the monumentary sculpture of the dead repressor. In 'Carrickfergus' '. . . the Irish Quarter was a slum for the blind and halt' as alien to MacNeice as the 'candles of the Irish poor' from which he felt himself 'banned forever', while, emblems of the structures of power and privilege, 'The Chichesters knelt in marble at the end of a transept / With ruffs about their necks, their portion sure'. In Spain he finds:

> The old complaints
> Covered with gilt and dimly lit with candles.
> With powerful or banal
> Monuments of riches or repression.

More strongly than the persona of the tripper these recurring images assert MacNeice's essential isolation from the Spanish ethos but, as in his view of the socio-religious world evoked in 'Carrickfergus', he is a compassionate observer. As cultivated tourist, he might note how 'With fretted stone the Moor / Had chiselled for effects of sun and shadow' but, as Thirties poet, he notes against such aesthetic effects the incongruous '. . . shadows of the poor, / The begging cripples and the children begging'. One of the central concerns of the Thirties writers, the question of the artist's power to effect change, emerges in the sombre reflection on Goya's royal portraits: 'Goya had the laugh – / But can what is corrupt be cured by laughter?' In the prose account of this visit, in *The Strings are False*,[8] MacNeice is more straightforwardly the tourist, and the treatment more loosely discursive. Here, his response to the Prado's art treasures is expansive and, although juxtaposed with a critique of Marxist art criticism and principles, is not, as in the poetic treatment of the visit, focused on the topical question raised for him as artist by the Goyas.

MacNeice returned to Spain in New Year, 1939 before the fall of Barcelona. This time the detachment in the prose account in *The Strings are False* is that of the journalist. Only when he is back in France after his visit does personal feeling surface in the New Testament image used to condemn the non-intervention policy of England and France – those guilty of 'passing by'. Typically, MacNeice's clear-sighted logic extends the condemnation to himself: 'It was all only too understandable but I still found myself hating them . . . And then, very logically, I found myself hating myself'.[9] Again, the poetry of *Autumn Journal* (in Section XXIII) presents a more clearly focused ethical response. Since his previous stay the significance of the Spanish conflict has become clear and his own attitude to the issues involved has been further defined, not least by the personal and public stocktaking which has constituted the dialectical progress of the poem. Now the issues are '. . . plain; / We have come to a place in space where shortly / All of us may be forced to camp in time'. He finds the visit inspiriting, feeling now a solidarity with the embattled inhabitants of the city:

> And it appears that every man's desire
>   Is life rather than victuals.
> Life being more, it seems, than merely the bare
>   Permission to keep alive and receive orders.

For all this, however, there is no suggestion that he should become actively involved in Barcelona. He is still the visitor, his identification with the inhabitants fuelled by his recognition of their grace under pressure. And it is that rather than ideological commitment that touches his conscience. His more general concern is now with the impending war in Europe. He concludes however with a salute to the qualities he has witnessed in the Barcelona populace, and though there is (as more emphatically in the prose account) an element of self-accusation here ('The cocks crow in Barcelona / Is it the heart's reveille or the sour / Reproach of Simon Peter?'), the keynote is challenge rather than guilt:

> . . . these people contain truth, whatever
>   Their nominal facade.
> Listen: a whirr, a challenge, an aubade –
>   It is the cock crowing in Barcelona.

This section of *Autumn Journal* is therefore at one level, an act of expiation though, logically, he feels no guilt. Dignified in their human qualities, Barcelona's citizens are not victims in need of his intervention but positive exemplars of human qualities which he, and others, may need in the uncertain future. His mind clarified by the visit, he feels freed to go.

Peadar O'Donnell was on holiday in Spain when hostilities broke out, having been speeded out of Ireland by the desire to escape politics, at least for a time. IRA man, then founder member of the Republican Congress with George Gilmore, Michael Price and Frank Ryan, his socialist views brought sufficient opprobrium for him to seek a quiet place in which to pursue his literary career – something, he humorously admits, he might have done years before were it not that:

... there's a touch of St. Peter in me. I get missions; ask any of the Irish bishops ... crowds had got into the habit of singing hymns at me and hurling bottles.[10]

It is thus lightly that O'Donnell refers to his own political activities in Ireland at the beginning of *Salud! An Irishman in Spain*, but his treatment of his countrymen's attitude to political and other disputes will, subsequently, indicate a 'mission' to persuade them to adopt a more open minded approach to such matters. Forced to leave Achill by a local dispute in which he had been caught up, he humorously remarks that 'you could not write books amid such crashing of worlds'. Like Kavanagh, he is ironically aware how a 'local squabble' can take on the proportions of epic and, rather naively perhaps, he seeks in Spain the neighbourliness of home without the political complications in which he cannot help but get involved in his own country. He finds not peace but civil war, and his book is intended to combat propaganda that might lead to disaffection among those of his own political persuasion in Ireland: 'I am writing ... because of the uproar which the news from Spain caused in my own country where it kindled the antagonisms of our own Civil War.'

The humorous, kindly persona O'Donnell projects in his narrative is that of the Irish countryman, garrulous, temperamentally incapable of remaining aloof from the life around him – the man who, though political activity and literary interests may have given him another perspective on life, yet retains his feel for the simplicities of the life of the community that earns its living from the sea or land. He is also, of course, a man who has seen active service in a civil war at home in the previous decade and who now tries to see the pattern of human grievance, greed, fear and suspicion that underlies and links all conflict, whether it be on the scale of a village squabble on Achill or of a nation-wide war at home or in Spain.

O'Donnell has been accused of romanticizing the Spanish conflict and of failing to penetrate the political nuances of the situation as did Orwell and Borkenau. This is partly true and while no-one would deny the limitations of his political insights in the book it is only fair to note that his is a disinterested romanticism, honestly avowed and not employed in the service of his political sympathies. His romantic sympathy, therefore, may, on occasion, at one level be caught by the spirit of the 'old Spain' of the rebelling officer class or directed towards the peasant whom he believes to be at one with the land; and, by the same token, the defenders of the Republic with whom he is politically at one are more objectively observed. If he does not give the same insights into the political and historical forces at work as does Borkenau, the homely style and strongly subjective nature of his narrative do not set up expectations of that sort of analysis. Primarily interested, for instance, in the rural areas and the life of the small farmers, he shows no sympathy for the urban-based doctrinaire socialism that fails to understand the argument for simply reforming rather than destroying the existing social structure, an argument based on the experience of the peasant, 'the real voice of the countryside' whose 'ideas went deep into the soil, into history.' It is the episodes illustrating the gulf between peasant and 'doctrinaire revolutionaries' that most clearly differentiate O'Donnell from the ideologically-committed left-wing English writers on Spain.

In describing actual events he experienced at first hand O'Donnell's romanticism is kept in abeyance. So close is his bond of sympathy with the Republicans' cause that, seemingly instinctively, he uses the first person plural when speaking of those with whom he had contact. With admirable integrity however he sticks to his reporter's brief and, early in his account, describes two episodes which other observers of like sympathies might well have omitted, the sacking of the village church and the execution of three young men found guilty of carrying documents to the enemy. Describing the former, he is disarmingly honest about his own mixed, human reaction:

I have rarely been in such a flux of indecision . . . The attack on the church was without a trace of justification: the village was in our hands so that there could be no question of the church being used as a Fascist post . . . The effect of the attack was also against the interests of the anti-Fascist struggle in the village . . . A steadily mounting rage was my main reaction though I could not be quite sure whether my temper drew its heat from revolt against the dark backwardness of what was taking place or from alarm at the bewilderment which such outrages must cause among Catholic masses who are sincerely anti-Fascist.

(*S* p. 72)

The passion of decency informing his attack on the spurious reason later given for sacking the church is followed by the awakened political consciousness as he fears that, with such 'darkened minds' to the fore, 'hooligan elements' will take over.

A different style is employed to recreate the outbreak of hostilities in Barcelona, an episode presented in vivid, impressionistic terms:

Who was it first saw and shouted? Some bothered soul, restless that the night watch had been abandoned? Some old body without the strength to keep a strong grip on sleep? . . . Anyway there was a shout. A room leaped to life and roared. A house leaped to life and roared. A street leaped to life and roared. No speeches, for men and women looked and knew, saw and struck. An avalanche of life . . . Barricades.

(*S* p. 59)

Imaginatively caught by a drama he did not actually witness, he permits the novelist to replace the objective chronicler required by his avowed aim in the book.

In contrast, when confronted by the reality of civil war in the execution of three young men, O'Donnell's humane sensibility is so attuned to the three in their last moments that it is a 'shock' to see the crowd, bright-faced and smiling at the execution. Inevitably reminded of the execution of Republican prisoners in Mountjoy Jail, and of the sombre mood of the waiting Irish crowd, he is clearly disturbed to find a response to execution so different from his own in people with whose cause he is in sympathy. His own feelings are not easily put away: 'you find yourself remembering the tilt of a young man's head as he got to his feet. In the roots of us all there is a pity which is all-embracing, a deep, eternal pity which kindles on a love of life for all things that walk in the sun' (*S* p. 92). The crowd's smiles belie such an optimistic philosophy. The man who had hoped to find the 'neighbourliness' of an Irish fishing village without its complications is finding in Spain only too many of the factors that complicate and darken human relations.

O'Donnell's fundamental decency (and his own prison experience) is again evident in his uneasiness about visiting Fascist prisoners as an observer; in fact, throughout the narrative, his moments of greatest empathy are reserved for prisoners, irrespective of the fact that they are men who fought against the principles in which he staunchly believed. Where he is notably lacking in empathy is with those who might seem its most obvious recipients, the air-raid victims. Their fear evokes the response:

In an instant we were back in far-off days when a sudden convulsion in nature seemed the fury of an angry god to the dim minds of men . . . One felt ashamed without knowing why; why must there be always a touch of shame in seeing a blind instinct to escape death rob man of his dignity.
(S p. 204)

This is followed by a graphic, cinematic treatment of the suffering as he zooms in on one victim:

Into the whole pandemonium came one screeching note that seemed to take all the fear and madness of the village into itself for you only heard it alone, all other sounds standing back as an accompaniment. A girl swung round the corner and came into clear view. One side of her face was blood dark, and black spots showered down her grey-white frock, but you scarcely noticed anything, except to listen for one stretched second. The screech snapped, an abrupt break like that of a steam-whistle, only cleaner. The screech seemed to stand by itself in the air for a second, so piercing its note and so sharp its end. And then, as though she knew people were dashing towards her, and that she belonged to the fading scream, she let go, folding inwards as though her body would leave itself ready to be put away.
(S p. 205)

It is disconcerting to find this vivid image of pain followed by 'When the dead are gathered together what is an air raid but a few bodies . . . what remains is that conflict of voices clawing at one another: men and women with all the lights of reason gone out.' It would seem that O'Donnell, the romantic, who had reacted to the sacking of the church with the fear that 'darkened minds' might control the people's cause, can have no sympathy with that 'darkness', whether it manifests itself in the implementation of 'the new [political] ideas which should have lit up a new to-morrow' or in the primitive fear of those enduring an air-raid.[11]

O'Donnell's book then, suggests a highly subjective response to the Spanish experience. Initial enthusiasm is tempered by recognition of factors he finds reprehensible and, as the narrative progresses, one senses a personal distancing from the events he describes. Unable to condone all that he observes, yet constrained by his integrity to report it, O'Donnell gives us a book in which his own generous, unsophisticated narrative persona is what leaves the most lasting impression as he tries to come to terms with a situation in which imagined event (the citizens' reaction to the Barcelona rising) and observed reality (executions and acts of vandalism) are at odds. He is a romantic in Spain, as his account shows, but a disappointed one. Yet disappointment does not lead to the angry disillusion evident in, e.g., Ewart Milne's work and the personal integrity evident in his response to the vandalising of the church is the informing voice of a narrative that, for all his occasional intrusions of philosophising and political comment, remains essentially on the level of personal anecdote and reportage.

Unlike O'Donnell, Ewart Milne went to Spain in direct response to events there. His level of involvement however echoes his ambiguous attitude to the politics which led other men to join the International Brigades. He never made the full commitment of taking up arms, opting instead for work with the Spanish Medical Aid Committee, at first in London and then driving ambulances and medical supplies to the Republican lines. His comments in the foreword to *Drums Without End* suggest that it was his experience of events in Spain that had led him to rethink his political allegiances:

... that curiosity which caused me to question the peasants and waiters and so on ... to find out *which* side they were on, and to learn that mostly they did *not* support the then Government of socialists and communists, caused me to think again, and led finally to a rejection of the whole set-up, although I held my tongue about my conclusions, as I think others did also. Even then I was beginning to tramp a long road back and away from socialism ...[12]

Despite the claim in 'Gun Runner' that he had been 'pretty well-doped' in political terms, Milne's writing about the Spanish experience is never that of the totally committed political activist.

In the prose pieces set in Spain Milne never treats of the Spanish situation as such. Rather the work is an attempt to articulate his own uncertainties about his role in Spain, his attitude to the politics that led him there, and his feelings about the English exponents of those politics who also went to Spain. His protagonists are English-speaking volunteers, sometimes accompanied by the associated figure of a female reporter. In 'Tomorrow' a sardonic narrative voice describes the central figures – a woman 'reporter' and two 'lorry drivers', describable thus only

temporarily, ... for the civil war duration ... they were young men of what is known as good family whose temperaments had sent them haring off to Spain's conflict to be on the side of oppressed persons and peoples, but it wasn't working out so well, because the persons and peoples were getting rid of their oppressions too quickly here and naturally that didn't suit the two drivers of good family.

In such volunteers Milne finds more than a little of the evangelical imperialist zeal that had fired earlier, more selfish, English ventures overseas. He is not a sufficiently competent writer of the short story to let this emerge through character and action but interjects a heavy-handed narrative commentary. The driver, Twomey, exemplifies a sense of cultural superiority ('in his heart disliking the people he had come to free or help or something') while Charles, the other driver, reflects a more complex but essentially romantic attitude. Decent and curious (as Milne professed himself to be) about the attitudes of the Spaniards he meets, he would, at one level, reject change in order to preserve valued picturesque qualities. This however sits ill with the sense of justice that brought him to Spain. The real virulence of Milne's criticism of the motives of those from 'good families' who involved themselves in the struggle of people of a nation and class not their own, and for whom they had no real empathy, is expressed in the character of the woman, a shallow, self-deceiving character:

She was the girl reporter, wasn't she? Doing her best to get her stuff published and in Right-wing papers at that, which was much more effective, because the best people read the Right-wing papers and her articles were bound to have some effect on them . . . Oh God, I'm bored, I'm bored, what do I want? Shall I never . . . ?

These characters embody Milne's criticism of the vacuum in English life of the thirties in which he sees contradictory impulses and liberal decency leading to indecision and paralysis.

In 'Medley in Spain' Milne most directly confronts his personal moral discomfiture about his role in Spain in a first person narrative. He seeks to 'get clear' and find release from the tensions the situation creates. His need is for the utter simplicity that the war cannot offer him as it seemed to do for so many whose political sympathies he, to some degree, shared. Feeling demands being made of him by the situation which he is incapable of satisfying he retreats to the position of the isolated artist:

Life to me was a series of wonderfully intricate patterns, no single pattern could predominate for long. I drank in the confusion, the bloodshed, the chaos thirstily, like the animal I was, but very soon I would want to lie down lazily and digest my meal, the meal that had begun thirty-four years ago.

It is the clearest statement yet of his personal position and is pitiless in its laying bare of the artist's impersonal response to the immediate. Listening to talk of refugees' suffering he feels no empathy:

their talk was like a scene on a painted stage to me . . . Doubtless many of those refugees would have been wandering the roads whether or not there was a civil war, since they might as well starve one place as another, and machine-gunning from the air only encouraged them to die quickly . . .

The apparent callousness is repellent but the rest of the sentence shows its real thrust to be a self-punishing refusal of the self-indulgence of empathetic emotion for a situation he was not going to share: 'but it seemed a bit too easy to identify oneself with their suffering, and in the next breath as it were to identify oneself with the rich, indeed luscious food of the Valencian hotel' (where he was to spend the night).

   Like MacNeice (who will employ a similar phrase in relation to his own situation in the Second World War) Milne, in his desire 'to get clear', is conscious of the need for individual thinking in situations where mass propaganda prevails, and he expresses this in his response to the men of the Thaalman Brigade, men whom he admires for their discipline but whose willing abnegation of their own will in the service of an ideology he finds abhorrent. He admires the individual heroic act (like that of his swashbuckling friend, Lewis Clive, walking into a hail of bullets swinging his cane) but cannot reconcile himself to heroism that is harnessed and dictated by an ideology. In the poem 'Thinking of Artolas' his genuine feeling for Charles Donnelly and Kupchik, following on the conventionally elegiac treatment of the dead tankist, is specifically directed towards them as individuals. Begun in disaffection with the whole outside journalistic involvement (and, of course, his own) in the situation, it deliberately affronts the expectations of elegy or political aggrandisement in the crude, alienating address to the reader:

I set them together, Izzy Kupchik and Donnelly;
And of that date with death among the junipers
I say only, they kept it: and record the exploded
Spreadeagled mass when the moon was later
Watching the wine that baked earth was drinking.

> Such my story, Sirs and Senoras. Whether you like it
> Or pay a visit to your vomitorium, is all one . . .

Milne's dilemma finds crude expression in his prose and is a disruptive force in his poems. A humane impulse intrudes the urge to participate on the artistic need for isolation and freedom, yet he knows he has neither the physical courage he admires in others nor the fixed certainty of political belief that would enable him to commit himself totally. Personal conflict jars throughout the prose, finding its outlet in a harsh sardonic treatment of his fictional characters or in the deliberate, antagonizing brutality of that passage on refugees. The result is a small body of work in which the disturbed personality of the writer is what leaves the most lasting impression, an impression not altered by his final story of the conflict, 'Gun Runner', written in 1982, which, in its murky, spy-thriller atmosphere, provides a bitterly disillusioned endpiece to his period of 'political activity'.

One young Irish writer of real promise made the full commitment to action in Spain that Milne found so problematic. Charles Donnelly died on the Jarama front in February, 1937.[13] His road to Spain began in a profound dissatisfaction not only with his own country's social structures but with its intellectual and cultural life that, as he saw it, displaced the poet and his values. His early prose work poses a world, barbaric, philistine, which has no place for, nor apprehension of, beauty. Always the isolated consciousness in this early work, Donnelly's poet figure is perceived in highly romanticized terms. The first piece, 'The Death Song',[14] seems to take its central idea from aisling poetry (with Gray's 'The Bard' thrown in), its poet figure a combination of expected saviour and bard who sings the maiden Eire's woes. Projected as the very image of pure, unselfish high-mindedness, the poet, powerless to save her, can only ensure that she remain undefiled by the grandiose choice of oblivion, flinging her, with himself, into the abyss. That the tale has intentional contemporary relevance seems clear from 'Philistia – An Essay in Allegory',[15] his next published piece, where contemporary Ireland is seen to be as much in need of saving from the oppressive forces of philistinism as the maiden of the previous piece from her would-be defilers.

Donnelly's first poems published in the student magazine of University College, Dublin, show a similar youthful, romantic ardour. The hopeless fury of the first two prose pieces soon abates however as romantic influences rapidly give way in the verse to a more modern idiom. Stylistic devices adopted aim to create an air of impersonality. The result can appear strained and mannered, particularly in the omission of the article (or the related stylistic habit of substituting the definite article for the possessive). His work developed rapidly, however, his handling of such devices becoming more deft as in 'The Flowering Bars', written on the imprisonment of Cora Hughes (a fellow-member of the Republican Congress with whom he was emotionally involved), at a time when poetic experimentation together with deep personal feeling and political commitment replaced earlier sub-Romantic posturings.

Donnelly's intense concern for social justice however soon became so all-absorbing that he abandoned poetry, putting all his energies into the organization of protest marches, making speeches and writing articles for the *Republican Congress* paper in Dublin and its London version, *Irish Front*, in which he was editorially involved. His articles were not confined to protest against social deprivation but were actively concerned with the setting up of a workers' republic. The idealism that had taken an aesthetic path in his earliest work was now directed to consider the steps necessary for the realization of the socialist dream.

When the Spanish revolt threatened democracy Donnelly reacted in both poetic and political terms. As poet his response was not the high-minded gesture envisaged in the early 'The Death Song' any more than it was to put his poetry at the service of his politics as several of his English contemporaries did. Now, with the prospect of action, poetry found its role as instrument for the imagination's exploration of the confrontation with death and the individual's ability to deal with it. Nor, as politically-aware activist, was he inclined to the role of the romantic young David throwing himself against the Goliath of fascism for the sake of the Spanish people as such. His naivety took a different turn and he reacted as an internationalist with an eye to the future who felt this was the struggle that would one day be re-enacted in his own country. His remark (before he left for the war) to Ewart Milne about going to Spain to study tactics is in accord with the memory of another acquaintance who recollects him enthusiastically demonstrating military tactics for the conduct of the Spanish campaign with match-sticks on the table of a trade union club.[16] Donnelly's rapid development as a poet in the light of all this can be traced in the last three poems of his small *oeuvre*.

'Poem' was written in London in 1936 for George Gilmore who visited Donnelly there prior to his intended participation in the Spanish conflict. (His plans were in fact thwarted.) It gives the young poet the opportunity to present as an objective meditation on another man's actions and probable fate his feelings and conjectures about his own. The poem looks, with remarkable detachment, at the two aspects of war that must concern any young soldier: his ability to act with courage under fire and the prospect of death. It opens in a studiedly plain style as the poet explores the difficult question of one's response to the test of action – the test that was to be so strong a feature of the imaginative experience of those of his generation in Britain who were to become embroiled in the Second World War. No romantic vision is allowed; rebellion is a matter, not of Yeatsian Cuchulains striding through the contemporary world of action, but, more austerely, as befits a young socialist of the 1930s, of 'private study'. The dilemma about the private self, its ability to translate theory into practice, can only be resolved in the public field of action. There can be no prop in preconceived ideas or existing images of heroism because, as he realizes, the testing will occur 'under circumstances different from what you'd expected'. Only the field of action will show the quality of the man: 'Whether at nerve-roots is secret / Iron, there's no diviner can tell, only the moment can show'.[17]

The implicit questioning of self involved in 'Poem' has affinities with that of the English soldier-poets at the outbreak of the Great War. The language however shows a poet for whom the innocence of the early period of that war is no longer possible. While young men like Herbert Asquith had at that time looked to the past to find a pattern for present action in the concept of the heroic, finding temporary sustenance in images of tournament, lance and Roman legion, Donnelly, like Keith Douglas in the Second World War, looks to a future in which he may have no existence outside the sentimental heroising of popular oratory. The poem's recognition of the forces, benign and malign alike, that militate against truth, and his now more complex concept of selfhood, align him with such soldier-poets of World War II as Douglas and Alun Lewis. The single concept of self in the early 'The Death Song' has given way, in 'Poem', to one acknowledging multiple identities making up the composite private and public man. Thus, 'unclear' though the moment envisaged in the first stanza may be, it is utterly decisive, not only in determining one's response to the test of physical courage but in loss of self in at least one of its manifestations. There can be no going back to the private world once 'Your flag is public over granite' for, in that moment, you have declared yourself, given yourself into the public domain and, thereby, have become its property. Hence

> Whatever the issue of the battle is, your memory
> Is public, for them to pull awry with crooked hands,
> Moist eyes. And village reputations will be built on
> Inaccurate accounts of your campaign. You're name for orators.

The objectivity with which Donnelly stands apart from himself to contemplate the results of the action he is about to take shows an independent poetic personality whose potential will be evident in 'The Tolerance of Crows' and 'Heroic Heart'. That the poem is written to another is, of course, a useful distancing device but, for all that George Gilmore was its confessedly embarrassed recipient, the intensity derives from a deeply meditated projection of the results of the poet's own proposed course of action.

In none of the possible circumstances of death envisaged in the poem is the individual the deciding force, any more than he can be in creating his posthumous reputation:

> In a delaying action, perhaps, on hillside in remote parish
> . . . sniper may sight you carelessly contoured,
> Or death may follow years in strait confinement . . .

In war, one does not die by the book – nor according to the conventions of the heroic. Nor can the activist's manual any more confine the imagination of the poet-volunteer than it can assure a particular military outcome, and Donnelly's imagination reverts to his own people, not in Brookean sentiment but in ironic recognition of their chameleon response to their public men: '. . . you'll be with Parnell and with Pearse'. Donnelly's achieved objectivity here is akin to that of Keith Douglas who, like him, envisages a future in which, dead himself, he will still have an existence in the memory of others. Neither imagines death in terms of the intimate memories of friend or lover but in terms of reputation and in the knowledge that reputation is a thing externally created, not something the dead can control (Douglas was, of course, writing in the aftermath of the First World War, Donnelly in that of Easter, 1916 as well).

In the final stanza Donnelly approaches an awareness of the dilemma that was to preoccupy Alun Lewis in World War II, that of maintaining total self-integrity in action required of one by outside agencies:

> Skilful in minor manual turns, patron of obscure subjects, of
> Gaelic swordsmanship and mediaeval armoury.
> The technique of the public man, the masked servilities are
> Not for you. Master of military trade, you give
> Like Raleigh, Lawrence, Childers, your services but not yourself.

With this tribute to Gilmore he acknowledges the need to maintain the individuality of the man involved in political or military roles that seem to demand total self-abnegation. Here, of course, he faces the dilemma Milne experienced but transcends the frustrated anger of his response. The stanza strives towards a recognition of the complexities in human life that cannot be resolved by simple acceptance of any one system of values.

'The Tolerance of Crows' and 'Heroic Heart', like 'Poem', show Donnelly's remarkable ability to deal with profoundly personal and immediate experience in an unemotive and impersonal manner. Centrally, in both, he confronts the reality of what, formerly, had been abstract tactical problems of study. 'The Tolerance of Crows' is a meditation on death in modern warfare. As in the later 'Heroic Heart' there is an intensely imaginative engagement with the subject – the young activist has come from the abstract study of tactics to a contemplation of the reality that results from putting that study into action. Tactics are now no longer only '... solved / Problems on maps' (or games with matchsticks on a club table). They are the dispensers of death, manipulating 'tools' that are its servants and enablers. No longer the great victor of First World War poetry, death is here the 'innocent' creature of the solvers of 'Problems on maps'. Unleashed, however, it destroys not just flesh but the power that called it into action through war, the human mind. Donnelly's concentration of language almost obscures his meaning in the lines:

> And with flesh falls apart the mind
> That trails thought from the mind that cuts
> Thought clearly for a waiting purpose.

We seem here to have a transference of the graphic physical imagery typical of late World War I poetry to the sphere of mental evisceration as thought 'trails' from the mind as the flesh 'falls apart'. It is an interesting example of Donnelly's ability to take what his predecessors had to offer while transforming it utterly to his own purposes.

Hard though the truth the poem embodies, the overall tenor of the piece is strangely emotionally satisfying. The final line, with the now successful omission of the definite article affording a universalizing perspective, quietly, unemphatically, underlines the tragedy of war-death in an image that lifts it above any particular war:

> Body awaits the tolerance of crows.

The linguistic play on the word 'tolerance' (which at one level simply indicates the indifference of the carrion bird to the provenance of the food it finds) subtly reminds us of a humane quality unavailable to men opposed in battle. The quietude of the line, its impersonal yet strangely intimate feel, is the utterly satisfying resolution to what has been an intensely individual meditation on death in war.

'Heroic Heart' (written in Spain) looks to the moment of maximum terror in an attack when the speaker finds himself 'under a storm of 'planes'. Courage is expressed, not in traditional rhetoric, but in terms that suggest that Donnelly is aware that Wilfred Owen's 'hearts made great with shot'[18] had disqualified forever the notion of the manly heart in a white heat of Brookean courage, avid in a cause. Here the 'heroic heart' is of 'ice', its effects seen, not in terms of personal bravery, but of the natural world, and Donnelly's sense of the intensity of the experience of battle is expressed in the surprising but effective word 'ludicrously':

> Ice of heroic heart seals plasmic soil
> Where things ludicrously take root
> To show in leaf kindness time had buried
> And cry music under a storm of 'planes.

This suggests an alert intelligence responding to a new situation that reveals its truth experientially. That truth is bizarre – battle, the excitement of which Julian Grenfell had candidly confessed could 'Take(s) him by the throat and make him blind'[19] here creates an experience that Keith Douglas would later suggest could only be expressed in terms of the world of Lewis Carroll: 'It is tremendously illogical – to read about it cannot convey the impression of having walked through the looking-glass which touches a man entering a battle'.[20] All previously normative experience revises and re-defines itself in the light of an experience that can make the processes of creation and growth seem 'ludicrous', and where normalcy has become the abnormal. Yet at the same time, normalcy can reclaim the ice-bound heart as nature's processes 'show in leaf kindness time had buried'. Restored, however temporarily, the being of the soldier regains something of its humanity: '. . . intent mouth recall[s] old tender tricks'. This vision of the dehumanizing effects of war and of the healing and restorative effects of the natural world on the denatured and desensitized being of the soldier had begun to be felt in the late poetry of Wilfred Owen and was to be central to the work of Donnelly's exact contemporary, Alun Lewis, in the Second World War.

In these final poems Donnelly, like Keith Douglas in World War II, shows a remarkable blend of objectivity and compassion. 'The Tolerance of Crows' reverberates with a sense of his own relation, as intended combatant, to those already dead. As Douglas, noting the activities of the scavenging wild dogs of the desert battlefield in 'Dead Men', knows how close he is to the 'actors' on death's stage as the still living 'figure writhing on the backcloth',[21] so, too, Donnelly knows how close he is, potentially, as intending participant, to experiencing the impersonal tolerance of the carrion bird of the battlefield. It is that awareness, by a highly intelligent young man whose approach to experience is intellectual and intensely imaginative rather than emotional, that gives depth and resonance to these poems. The work shows the deepening vision of a novice in war who, so quickly crystallising an intelligent and compassionate response to it, could, on the existing evidence, undoubtedly have become one of the important war poets in the English language had he survived. He remains in touch with the humane values, does not become a 'party' poct, a mouthpiece, and, in this, he shares with the other Irish writers of left-wing sympathies who went to Spain a common integrity not easily achievable in the heated political atmosphere of the time.

LOUIS MACNEICE AND
THE SECOND WORLD WAR

TERENCE BROWN

For Louis MacNeice, as for so many, 1939 was a year of journeyings. Hitler's invasion of the Sudetenland and the feeble response of the international community, as well as the involvement of the great powers in the Spanish Civil War, the horrors of *Kristalnacht*, had alerted the world to the imminence of a major conflagration in Europe. So last holidays abroad were enjoyed before once again the lights would go out all over the continent, hurried exiles were arranged as individuals and families sought sanctuary in regions and countries which might escape the nightmare to come. Urgent messages were carried from country to country in the hope that the disaster might be averted. It was, in Cyril Connolly's words, 'Closing time in the gardens of the west'. For many writers, accustomed to easy travel in a decade in which air as well as railway transport had made the crossing of international borders a natural thing, the prospect of being unable to enjoy such freedom was a fact which began to concentrate their minds in precise ways. Ezra Pound travelled in 1939 to his native United States in a vain attempt to influence governmental economic policy but chose to return to Italy to the tragic fate which awaited him there. Francis Stuart would wait a year before in 1940 his dark angel would take him to Berlin and a complicity with the regime there that none of his subsequent writings nor the special pleadings of his apologists have quite been able to expunge. By contrast Samuel Beckett heard the declaration of war in the Dublin suburb of Foxrock where he had spent the summer and hurried back to Paris, preferring as he said, France at war to Ireland at peace, where he would eventually be honoured by the French Government for distinguished war service in the resistance to the Nazi tyranny.

Louis MacNeice was also on holiday in Ireland on the 3rd of

September 1939. He spent the day following at the All-Ireland Hurling final between Cork and Kilkenny (in his record of the match MacNeice mistakes Kilkenny for Kerry).

I was alone with the catastrophe, spent Saturday drinking in a bar with the Dublin literati; they hardly mentioned the war but debated the correct versions of Dublin street songs. Sunday morning the hotel man woke me (I was sleeping late and sodden), said, 'England has declared war'. Chamberlain's speech on a record was broadcast over and over again during the day. I went to Croke Park in the afternoon to watch the All-Ireland hurling final – Cork in crimson against Kerry in orange and black. Talk of escapism, I thought . . . There was a huge crowd of Gaelic Leaguers, all wearing their *fáine*, one-minded partisans.[1]

Escapism of course was much on MacNeice's mind in September and October of 1939. In January his friend W.H. Auden had emigrated to the United States with Christopher Isherwood. Furthermore MacNeice himself had decided to abandon his lectureship in Classics at Bedford College in London and America was beckoning. There was too the possibility of a chair in English literature in Trinity College, Dublin, which had just become vacant. About this MacNeice wrote in September to his friend and mentor, the classical scholar E.R. Dodds 'I dare say this will scandalise you as being a kind of escapism but I can't really see that I should be doing any more for civilisation by what they say the intellectuals must do – propaganda work'.[2]

For MacNeice of course the decision about what he might do in the imminent war was complicated by his Irish nationality. For although throughout the Thirties he had written deprecatingly in his poetry about much that irritated and repelled him in Ireland north and south, MacNeice had no doubt that his patrimony was an Irish one. The MacNeices hailed from the west of Ireland and his father had even served in the Church of Ireland in County Waterford in the 1930s, further complicating his son's Northern Irish provenance. And his mentor E.R. Dodds (who had given him his first job in Birmingham), a Banbridge Protestant who had acted as secretary to Yeats in the Lane Committee in Dublin and had edited the *Journal and Papers of Stephen MacKenna*, was an Irish nationalist of marked individuality. Indeed in 1914 he had decided that 'this was not my war'.[3] And while the Rising of 1916 was not his rising either – 'Its price was in my view too high'[4] – he remembered in his memoirs, reflecting on Yeats's 'celebrated palinode':

I could not remain unaffected by the surge of sympathy which that poem immortalizes. It was impossible to withhold one's admiration from the heroic dreamers in the Dublin Post Office. And after the executions any notion of again putting on a British uniform, even in the harmless capacity of a hospital orderly [in which role Dodds had briefly acted in Serbia in 1915], became invincibly repugnant. If, as was threatened, an attempt were now made to impose conscription on the Irish people against their will, I was, like many others, determined to resist by force if I had no other option.[5]

In 1939 it is almost certain that MacNeice would have felt as an Irishman that it was not necessarily incumbent upon him to enlist in the British forces to fight against Germany. In 1941 he was to write after he had decided to return to London from the United States 'I have never really thought of myself as British; if there is one country I feel at home in, it is Eire'.[6] Dodds, his older friend, would have understood, whatever his English contemporaries might have felt. For Dodds had remained in Oxford as a student until 1917, stubbornly expressing sympathy for the rebels of 1916 in the midst of world war. When he graduated in 1917 he took a post as a teacher in Kilkenny College and then at the High School in Dublin where he remained until 1919. It is this context of Irish nationalist scruple about service in the King's uniform that gives meaning to MacNeice's letter to Dodds in October 1939 from Dublin where he ponders the possibility of enlistment:

Down here one gets quite de- (or dis)orientated. It all sounds like a nightmare algebra which you have to change back into people being killed. It is all very well for everyone to go on saying 'Destroy Hitlerism' but what the hell are they going to construct? I am now falling into a sort of paradox which is: – if the war were a rational war leading somewhere, I should want to stay out of it in order to see where it led to: but if it is a hopeless war leading nowhere, I feel half inclined to take the King's shilling & escape – more likely than not – the frustration to come.[7]

As Irishman he reckons he has a perfectly honourable choice in the matter. No Englishman could justifiably censure him for disloyalty in not rallying to the colours. Indeed he understands that from the nationalist point of view the war is England's war. By November 1939 we find him writing in even more troubled terms to Dodds from Belfast on precisely the issue that had confronted Dodds in 1914: 'the tiresome corollary of this from my point of view is that, *if* it is my war, I feel I ought to get involved in it in one of the more unpleasant ways'.[8]

In the new year (1940) it wasn't yet his war and he set out for America and a teaching post at Cornell. In Peter McDonald's words 'to all appearances he had joined Auden, Isherwood and the rest in "escapism"'.[9] But of course he hadn't, as McDonald in his excellent study of MacNeice from which I have quoted these extracts from the poet's correspondence, understands, even if he fails fully to grasp how for MacNeice, the Irishman, the question whether the war was his war, was a real one.

There was however something in what Ireland represented for MacNeice which he knew he must resist. In the sequence poem he composed in August and September 1939 which he published as 'The Coming of War' in *The Last Ditch* (the only book of his to be published in Ireland; it was published in Dublin by the Yeats family's Cuala Press in 1940) and which appeared in edited form as 'The Closing Album' in *Plant and Phantom* in 1941, he calls it 'Forgetfulness'[10] ('Cushendun'). He could he feels hide his 'head / In the clouds of the west' ('Running away from the war').[11] Yet even in Ireland war intrudes – 'But Mars was angry / On the hills of Clare' ('O the crossbones of Galway')[12] – and the country only offers a tantalisingly beautiful but essentially deceptive haven from responsible action and 'doom all night... lapping at the door', ('Why, now it has happened')[13] or at best a place that gave him 'time for thought' ('Dublin').[14] Ireland therefore represented for MacNeice in the war years an image of an impossible condition in which history and its demands could somehow be avoided, a state of mind and feeling in which the self could indulge in a lotus-like forgetfulness of real, complex issues of loyalty, duty, responsibility. I therefore think it wrong to read his often quoted poem of 1942 'Neutrality' too literally. Certainly the death of MacNeice's close friend Graham Shepard on a convoy in the North Atlantic gives an edge of real bitterness to its final stanza where the poet advises a neutral island:

> look eastward from your heart, there bulks
> A continent, close, dark, as archetypal sin,
> While to the west off your own shores the mackerel
> Are fat – on the flesh of your kin.

> (*C.P.* 203)

But it seems unlikely that the man who in 1939 and 1940 could agonize in his letters to Dodds over the question as to whether the war was his war, could completely fail to understand Ireland's neutrality in the conflict. Certainly in 1941 he insisted after a three week stay in Ireland 'I have no wish now to bring up the undying (though chameleonic) Irish Question but I would ask you to remember that the feeling in Eire is now predominantly pro-British (though still opposed to participation in the War), that the pro-German minority is extremely small and that De Valera's position is agonizingly difficult. Those who propose the application of the strong hand to Eire are forgetting their history ...'.[15] Accordingly in 'Neutrality' he associates 'The neutral island facing the Atlantic' with a human *universal*, 'the neutral island in the heart of man', and both with the archaic mythical landscapes of an imagined west which represents a powerfully attractive narcotic when the challenges of reality are too great:

> Look into your heart, you will find a County Sligo,
> A Knocknarea with for navel a cairn of stones,
> You will find the shadow and sheen of a moleskin mountain
> And a litter of chronicles and bones.
>
> Look into your heart, you will find fermenting rivers,
> Intricacies of gloom and glint,
> You will find such ducats of dream and great doubloons
>   of ceremony
> As nobody to-day would mint.

> (*C.P.* 202)

The topography and the allusions here are obviously Yeatsian. MacNeice deems Yeatsian romanticism, its aristocratic celebration of ceremony, as complicit with a kind of escapism which must be resisted however appealing it may be. Indeed the stanzas I have quoted are compact of nostalgia and a recognition that there is something deathly about such solipsistic imaginative self-regard in face of war.

This poem is of course only one aspect of MacNeice's complex response to Yeats whose poetry and achievement he confronted in his book *The Poetry of W.B. Yeats*, which he began working on in 1939 and which he completed during his time at Cornell in 1940 at the same period as he was wrestling with the moral and personal demands of the war.

Journeying to the United States the poet remembered, in the long autobiographical essay he wrote in the months immediately following his return to London, how 'for five months' he had been 'tormented by the ethical problems of the war. In Ireland most people said to me "What is it to you?" while many of my friends in England took the line it was just power politics'.[16] America like Dublin in 'Running away from the war' gave him 'time for thought': 'I thought I could think things out there, get myself clear before I went into the maelstrom'.[17] Indeed the fact that MacNeice titled his autobiography (which was published posthumously, since he decided at the time not to publish a work which might have offended his father and step-mother), *The Strings Are False* suggests that MacNeice himself saw this work as a kind of prelude to battle. For in Act IV, Scene III of Shakespeare's *Julius Caesar*, in Brutus' tent before the battle of Philippi, Brutus' boy Lucius, a musician, stirs in his sleep after Brutus has seen the ghost of Caesar. He murmurs 'The strings, my lord, are false'. Indeed the whole structure of the work as we have it suggests that MacNeice reckoned his essay a study of the moment before the outbreak of conflict. It opens with the poet aboard ship, returning to England, and ends at the moment he had left for America on an earlier, short visit at Easter 1939 before war had been declared.[18] And a protracted central section deals with his stay in Barcelona during the siege, just before the final struggle for the city had begun. *The Strings Are False* is therefore an account of an *entr'acte* in which the poet had sought 'clarification', which as he insists 'may be too much to demand of most people but a writer must demand it of himself'.[19]

Not that the essay arrives at any very great clarity: 'It is, as I said, the same boat that brought me over. That was in January 1940 and this is December 1940. But before all that? I am 33 years old and what can I have been doing that I still am in a muddle?'[20] But he had decided that England was the place to be since, as he reported in a letter to his father, he 'thought [he] was missing history'.[21] And in *Horizon* in 1941 he confessed:

While I was in America I felt a very long way from Europe, though not so far away as I felt during the autumn of 1939 in Ireland . . . From June on I wished to return, not because I thought I could be more *useful* in England than in America, but because I wanted to see these things for myself. My chief motive thus being vulgar curiosity, my second motive was no less egotistical; I thought that if I stayed another year out of England I should have to stay out for good, having missed so much history, lost touch.[22]

In reacting in this way MacNeice displayed an acute artistic self-awareness. For his surest achievement of the 1930s had been *Autumn Journal*, an intimate, immediate response to an historic moment. As artist he couldn't afford to miss history. And his writings in the next four years indicate how wisely he had acted, for the war years were to be one of the most productive, creative periods of MacNeice's life, when his work expressed a complex, rich view of the world. It was a view that his critical engagement with Yeats's poetry did much to stimulate.

For MacNeice Yeats's poetry posed a very special challenge. Throughout the 1930s MacNeice in his published essays and reviews had espoused a critical position which deemed poetry to be a matter of communication, that it was of necessity about something and if it was to be of social utility, as the poet believed it should be, that something had to be significant. Yeats's with its magic, Irish nationalism and aestheticism seemed to fly in the face of such prescriptions; yet MacNeice could not deny that if he were 'making a general anthology of shorter English poems, I should want to include some sixty by W.B. Yeats. There is no other poet in the language from whom I should choose so many . . . I like re-reading Yeats more than I like re-reading most English poets'.[23] So this demanded some explanation in view of MacNeice's earlier critical nostrums. War is the defining reality as MacNeice shifts his ground. 'I had' he tells us in chapter one of his study of the recently dead Yeats 'only written a little of this book when Germany invaded Poland':

On that day I was in Galway. As soon as I heard on the wireless of the outbreak of war, Galway became unreal. And Yeats and his poetry became unreal also.

This was not merely because Galway and Yeats belong in a sense to a past order of things. The unreality which now overtook them was also overtaking in my mind modern London, modernist art and Left Wing politics. If the war made nonsense of Yeats's poetry and of all works that are called 'escapist', it also made nonsense of the poetry that professes to be 'realist' . . . For war spares neither the poetry of Xanadu nor the poetry of pylons. I gradually inferred, as I recovered from the shock of war, that both these kinds of poetry stand or fall together. War does not prove that one is better or worse than the other; it attempts to disprove both. But poetry must not be disproved. If war is the test of reality, then all poetry is unreal; but in that case unreality is a virtue. If, on the other hand, war is a great enemy of reality, although an incontestable fact, then reality is something which is not exactly commensurable with fact.[24]

Yeats's poetry like the challenge of war provoked a crisis of faith in which the problem of value became central in MacNeice's mind. It was no longer a question, in face of war, whether Yeats's poetry was more or less valuable than that by MacNeice's exact contemporaries, but whether poetry itself was of any value.

Bound up with the question of the value of poetry was the even more fundamental question as to the value of human life itself. This becomes a recurrent theme in the poet's writings during the war in a body of work which, including graphic prose accounts of the blitz on London, radio plays and poems, constitutes one of the most impressive records we possess of Britain at war (Henry Moore's series of sketches of the underground world during the bombings come to mind as an equivalently memorable achievement) – a body of Irish writing to be compared surely with Francis Stuart's record of his Berlin years.

For MacNeice the war as he experienced it most directly in the Blitz (he served as a fire-watcher) was a great force of negation, a terrifying unleashing of elemental energies that would destroy everything which makes human life livable. In 'The Morning After the Blitz' in May 1941 he wrote of a bombing raid as being 'like the banging of all the tea-trays and the loosing of all the fireworks and the rumbling of all the tumbrils and the breaking of all the oceans in the world. Just one long drawn-out lunatic symphony'.[25] Yet even pure destruction, what he called in his poem 'Troll's courtship' 'utter negation in a positive form' (*C.P.* 199) could be oddly exhilarating, as if the destruction of London clarified issues in a demanding, exacting way: 'When the All Clear went I began a tour of London, half appalled and half enlivened by this fantasy of destruction. For it was – if I am to be candid – enlivening'.[26] It was also compellingly dramatic. This is MacNeice's extraordinary description of a raid on May 10th 1941 when the poet watched the city burning from the dome of St. Paul's which had narrowly escaped a direct hit:

When the day came up and the planes had gone, London was burning still; you could stand on top of the dome and warm your hands at it. I had never before realized the infinite variety of fire – subtleties never attained by any Impressionist painter. These fires were a wedding of power with a feminine sensuous beauty. A glowering crimson power mottled with black; a yellow liquid power – a kind of Virgin Birth – which is sheer destruction; a cracking, a hissing, and an underground growling. But up above were the softest clouds of smoke – soft as marabou – purple and umber and pink and orange which spread out and shaded off to blue. Looking at these fires from above I got them in perspective. When the fire takes over a new building, first of all it is the building that is on fire, but later it is the fire that is the solid object, the building is just a gimcrack screen that the fire has folded around itself.[27]

These experiences were the basis of three of MacNeice's most memorable war poems 'Brother Fire', 'The Trolls' and 'Troll's courtship'. They share with the prose descriptions a chill ecstasy, as if the overwhelming experience of mass destruction had induced an elevation of mood for which mythical, metaphysical and religious categories are the only possible means of represen-tation. Tonally these poems are remarkable for their insouciant courting of nihilism, a debonair zest for a terror which is stripping reality of its essences and imposing absolute demands on a consciousness for which the issue of value is all that remains when 'Brother Fire' has done his worst. After the raid on May 10th which MacNeice watched from the cathedral he wrote:

All the same I know we should ask ourselves every so often whether, living in these conditions, we are still seeing straight. I find that I vacillate as to the answer; sometimes I say to myself 'This is mere chaos, it makes no sense,' and at other times I think 'Before I saw wartime London I must have been spiritually colour-blind'. 'There is plenty of degradation – the cheapness inevitable in a world that involves so much short-term propaganda – and plenty of squalor, but there is also an exaltation and, when I say that, I do not mean anything in the nature of Rupert Brooke heroics or last ditch bravado, I mean something much bleaker and, in one sense, humbler, something like the feeling you get on top of a mountain on a cold, grey day . . . There is, in some quarters, an understandable swing-back to religion but the revival of religion (with its ordinary connotations) is something I neither expect or desire. What *is* being forced upon people is a revival of the religious sense. And after the hand-to-mouth ethics of nineteenth century liberalism and the inverted and blinkered quasi-religion of Marxism and the sentimentality of the cynical Lost Generation – after all that, we need all the senses we were born with; and one of those is the religious.[28]

So in 'Brother Fire' he addresses, with Franciscan humility, the principle of negation at work in the fires looting the city, reckoning it a force of purgation and spiritual renewal: 'Which gluttony of his for us was Lenten fare'. Fire is that by which

> were we weaned to knowledge of the Will
> That wills the natural world but wills us dead.

(C.P. 196)

The fire is simultaneously creator and destroyer, an elemental energy sometimes contained in the grates where the folkloric dogs stand guard, sometimes 'having his dog's day / Jumping the London streets with millions of tin cans / Clanking at his tail'. 'O delicate walker' apostrophises the poet,

                    babbler, dialectician Fire,
          O enemy and image of ourselves,
          Did we not on those mornings after the All Clear,
          When you were looting shops in elemental joy
          And singing as you swarmed up city block and spire,
          Echo your thoughts in ours? 'Destroy! Destroy!'

                                                              (*C.P.* 196)

For MacNeice the question of the value of poetry and of life itself, so keenly pressed by the experience of the London blitz, involved him in the philosophic problem of reductionism. As MacNeice was agonising about where he should spend the war and after he had plunged into a life in England of intense work – producing articles, features for the BBC, developing the genre of radio drama – he was also brooding, in a way he had not done since his undergraduate years in the 1920s, on essentially metaphysical problems, now given an immediate edge by the possibility of his own death. War it seems raised the question of value in powerful yet precise terms. It seemed an undeniable, determining force beside which poetry and human feeling, life itself, were insubstantial, dubious things. War in the most cruel fashion possible seemed to confirm what the 1930s poets in general had tended to believe in a rather superficial manner, that forces as great as the *zeitgeist*, history, the dialectic, the iron laws of natural selection and biology, were the determinants of individual consciousness which deluded itself that it possessed meaningful autonomy. War made such theorising all too real as society was caught up by a process over which the individual seemed to have no control whatsoever. So MacNeice writes of a conscript in the poem of that name, as one who is, apparently, wholly determined:

          Being so young he feels the weight of history
          Like clay around his boots; he would, if he could, fly
          In search of a future like a sycamore seed
          But is prevented by his own Necessity,
          His own yet alien, which, whatever he may plead,
          To every question gives the same reply.

                                                              (*C.P.* 203)

The conscript is not the only figure in the poems of the war years caught in his own necessity. MacNeice writes of character types in 'Bottleneck', 'The Mixer', 'The Libertine', 'The Satirist' as figures for whom character is destiny. He writes compassionately too of the victims of the war itself, refugees especially, cast up on foreign shores by the inevitable tides of war. One of his key images of these years, in the poetry and the prose, is the Atlantic crossing, a tunnel which ships enter and must negotiate if they are not to perish: 'No Euclid could have devised / Neater means to a more essential end' ('Convoy', *C.P.* 200). Nature also reminds of determinism and ineluctable law:

> The whale butting through scarps of moving marble,
> The tapeworm probing the intestinal darkness,
> The swallows drawn collectively to their magnet
> These are our prototypes . . . .
>
> ('Explorations', *C.P.* 194)

'And yet', continues this poem. It is that 'and yet' which philosophically concerns MacNeice in the war years. Poetry and life may be explicable in terms of determining forces but MacNeice recurrently resists the idea that to explain something is to explain it away. A phenomenon cannot be reduced to its causes.

The challenge war presented to Yeats's work and by extension to all poetry demanded that MacNeice develop a philosophy of life and death that could sustain art and existence through the ultimate crises they faced. To satisfy MacNeice's intelligence such a view had to resolve the philosophic dilemmas posed by reductionism and determinism. Consequently in the Preface to *The Poetry of W.B. Yeats* MacNeice worries about the relationship of poetry to life, introducing his anti-reductionist concerns:

We still tend to think that, because a thing is in time, its value can only be explained by an abstraction from the thing of some supposedly timeless qualities; this is to explain the thing away. That a rose withers is no disproof of the rose, which remains an absolute, its value inseparable from its existence (for existence is still existence, whether the tense is past or future) . . . Life – let alone art – cannot be assessed purely in terms of utility. Food, for example, is useful for life but what is life useful for? To both the question of pleasure and the question of value the utilitarian has no answer. The faith in the *value* of living is a mystical faith.[29]

In chapter one, 'Introductory' he expands at length on this perception, responding to critics who 'often tend to write as if a condition were the same thing as a cause'.[30] Again he offers a definition of life and crucially of poetry which rescues them from reductionist and utilitarian explanation: 'Life for living creatures is not something which you merely have or have not; it is something plastic; it *is* what you make it. The sense of values governing this conscious or unconscious creation of life (presumably unconscious

among the lower animals, partly conscious among human beings)
is not utilitarian, it can only be described as mystical'.[31]

This outlook, developed as he was working on his book on
Yeats, finds frequent expression in MacNeice's poems of the war
years, making them by and large more positive in overall tone,
more celebratory than anything he had produced before. There is
much to fear, much to deprecate in a world at war but even the
conscript is allowed the possibility:

> though on the flat his life has no
> Promise but of diminishing returns,
> By feeling down and upwards he can divine
> That dignity which far above him burns
> In stars that yet are his and which below
> Stands rooted like a dolmen in his spine.

(*C.P.* 203)

'Prospect' expresses with lyrical élan this new mystical response
(there is nothing like it in the pre-war poetry) to life:

> Though Nature's laws exploit
> And defeat anarchic men,
> Though every sandcastle concept
> Being *ad hoc* must crumble again,
>
> And though to-day is arid,
> We know – and knowing bless –
> That rooted in futurity
> There is a plant of tenderness.

(*C.P.* 213)

What saves MacNeice's anti-reductionist stance from sentimentality in the poems he wrote in the early 1940s is the fact that he
combines this positive note with an immediate, almost existential
awareness of the fact of death. It is the mystery and glory of
consciousness which makes humankind unique for MacNeice; it is
hoping and despairing that makes us 'the final / Anomaly of the
world' ('Explorations', *C.P.* 195). And in these years death as the
end of consciousness was a daily present possibility for the poet
and his friends as it was for all the citizens of London. The shutter
could fall 'Congealing the kaleidoscope at Now' ('The Casualty',
C.P. 245) as it did in mid-Atlantic for Graham Shepard, for whom
he wrote the powerful elegy from which this phrase comes. Death
as intimate reality in the war years gave a zest and intensity to life
that informed the experience of conscious existence with an

almost religious quality.

Critics have noted a similar mystical empiricism as an effect of desperate conditions in Francis Stuart's *Black List Section H.* MacNeice in a meditative manuscript written in 1941 (and only recently published) brooded on the knowledge of death which the war had brought:

Death in its own right – as War does incidentally – sets our lives in perspective. Every man's funeral is his own, just as people are lonely in their lives, but Death as a leveller also writes us in life. & Death not only levels but differentiates – it crystallizes our deeds.

We did not need a war to teach us this but war has taught us it. Before the war we wore blinkers. Applied science, by increasing comfort & controlling disease, had – geared to a 'liberal' individualism – encouraged us to think of death as a pure negation, a nuisance. But applied science, by shattering a town overnight, by superimposing upon ordered decay a fantastic but palpable madness, has shown us the integral function of death. Death is the opposite of decay; a stimulus, a necessary horizon.

& this will affect our conception of Freedom . . .[32]

In 'Prayer in mid-passage' written about 1943 MacNeice draws on such thinking to produce one of his most haunting poems, which links the trope of a sea voyage, the Atlantic Tunnel, with the Dantesque moment of mid-life crisis (the poet was thirty-five in 1943). He addresses his own death as the source of the faith which allows him to break silence with meaningful song in the midst of war:

> We were the past – and doomed because
> We were a past that never was;
> Yet grant to men that they may climb
> This time-bound ladder out of time
> And by our human organs we
> Shall thus transcend humanity.
>
> Take therefore, though Thou disregard,
> This prayer, this hymn, this feckless word,
> O Thou my silence, Thou my song,
> To whom all focal doubts belong
> And but for whom this breath were breath –
> Thou my meaning, Thou my death.
>
> ('Prayer in mid-passage', *C.P.* 212)

BECKETT AND WORLD WAR II

In memoriam Samuel Beckett, 1906–1989

JOHN FLETCHER

The Republic of Ireland, as is well known, adopted a policy of neutrality in World War II, and Samuel Beckett, who always kept his Irish citizenship, was on a family visit to Dublin when hostilities broke out. Since however the Trinity graduate was by then permanently domiciled in Paris, he hurried back there, preferring, as he was later to put it, France at war to Ireland at peace. For a while of course nothing much happened, but when the 'phoney war' came abruptly to an end in the summer of 1940 and Paris was occupied, his life changed completely, as did everyone else's. His Irish passport protected him from internment as an enemy alien, and he could have sat out the war in the relative safety of his Paris apartment, sharing the privations of the French, but not otherwise exposed to any particular risks. But he chose instead to throw in his lot with the Resistance. At the end of the war he was decorated by the French Republic for his services in the defence of freedom. He was later to dismiss his clandestine activity as 'boy scout stuff', but it was inherently dangerous, and had the Gestapo caught him (as on at least one occasion they nearly did) his citizenship would not have saved him from deportation at best and at worst from the firing squad. Others died for offences as trivial as concealing or carrying tracts, so his fate would hardly have been much different.[1]

The full story of Beckett's participation in the Resistance still has not been told: for that we await James Knowlson's authorised, definitive biography.* But we do know why he opted to join the underground rather than continue with the safety and relative ease of *la vie de bohème*. He was a man of republican sympathies: he may not have found the theocracy of his newly-independent

* Now of course published, 1996 (ed.).

178

mother country much to his liking – he who could see no valid reason for banning books in Ireland, or condoms either for that matter[2] – but he had no quarrel with what would now be called 'Brits Out'.[3] So he was emphatically not the sort of intellectual who embraced authoritarian ideologies: not for him the *führerprinzip* and the cult of the *übermensch*. The secular, libertarian and egalitarian ideals of his adopted country were entirely to his taste, and he had no hesitation in throwing in his lot with those who were determined to defend them and it against the invader. He had nothing against Germany as such: in fact he had lived there, spoke the language fluently, and had the highest regard for its composers (Schubert and Beethoven especially), its writers (notably Fontane), and its philosophers (particularly Schopenhauer). But the Nazis were another matter: he could not stomach the way they banned the work of writers and composers of Jewish descent and highjacked any philosophy (like Nietzsche's) which could be pressed into service to give spurious intellectual respectability to the racist and militaristic ideology of their regime.

But Beckett had personal reasons too for forswearing the neutrality of his passport. His close friends were in danger: Paul Léon, Joyce's secretary, because he was Jewish; Alfred Péron, who helped Sam translate *Murphy* into French and to whom the translation is dedicated, because of his left-wing views and activities. Beckett's friendship with Péron dated from the later 1920s, when Alfred had been exchange *lecteur* from the Ecole Normale Supérieure during Sam's senior undergraduate years at TCD, and it continued when Beckett went to Paris immediately afterwards as Trinity's exchange lector at the Ecole. It was natural that, ten years later, he and Péron should be active in the same Resistance group. When that group was infiltrated, Péron was arrested. Beckett was warned just in time, leaving his apartment in the rue des Favorites with only half an hour to spare. (Paul Léon was not so lucky: he was picked up in one of the French police sweeps of Paris Jews, interned locally, and then deported to an extermination camp in the east.) Beckett was not to return to his apartment for four years; miraculously, when he opened the door, nothing had been disturbed, and he was able to get back to normal life and down to work at once. It was then that he wrote *Molloy* and the rest – of which more later.

Once arrested Péron was deported by the Gestapo, and died in 1945 soon after his liberation from Mauthausen concentration camp. He had been a brilliant *agrégé d'anglais* of great promise. As Beckett was to say in different ways many times in his writings, what terrors can ordinary misery hold for anyone who has known such extremities of pain? Still more friends, however, were to die, directly or indirectly, from the conflict. One whose loss was felt particularly keenly by Beckett was Dr Arthur Darley, a colleague at the Irish Red Cross Hospital at Saint-Lô in Normandy. Beckett was interpreter and storekeeper there in 1946, and Darley died of tuberculosis in the unit he had come from Ireland to set up to treat civilian victims of the battles for the liberation of France. The poem 'Mort de A. D.' is Beckett's elegy written in his memory.[4]

In between escaping from Paris and returning there after serving with the Irish Red Cross in newly-liberated Normandy, Beckett lay low in the countryside near Avignon, helping out in the vineyards, meeting regularly with other refugee friends like the painter Henri Hayden, and writing *Watt*, his last full-length work of fiction in English, undertaken, as he later said, to take his mind off the war and the occupation. He needed to: he was working as an *agent de liaison*, collecting from a variety of sources information about troop movements, supply dumps, and other pieces of intelligence valuable to the allies. He edited, translated into English and typed out this material for onward dispatch to London. Had he been caught with it in his possession, he would have been tortured and shot. 'Boy scout stuff' it perhaps seemed to him, but in no imaginable circumstances does learning to tie reef knots carry the death penalty. Fortunately he was not discovered, and when the region was liberated he returned to Dublin to visit his mother. Getting back to France was not easy since the country was still on a war footing, but the gift of a hospital by the people of Ireland to the suffering inhabitants of the devastated city of Saint-Lô provided the opportunity.

It also inspired Beckett to write poetry, not only the lament for Arthur Darley, but also the quatrain entitled 'Saint-Lô', which in my opinion is the finest piece of verse he ever composed:

> Vire will wind in other shadows
> unborn through the bright ways tremble
> and the old mind ghost-forsaken
> sink into its havoc

(Poems, p. 32)

Probably the only gloss which the reader needs on this poem is that Vire is the name of the river which runs through Saint-Lô. The 'other shadows' are perhaps those which will be cast when the war-torn city is rebuilt and new walls produce a different shade. However that may be, the general sense of the poem is clear enough: the town, which in rubble is a fair reflection of the metaphysical anguish the poet feels about life in general, a kind of objective correlative of his state of mind, will one day rise again from the ashes and the Vire wend its way, as it has done for centuries, through other shadows and different – yet probably not greatly dissimilar – forms of pain and grief. The poet, however, will continue, the more effectively for having been deserted by the 'ghosts' haunting him in these ruins, to sink further into his personal havoc, a state which no bombardment brings about and so no bulldozer can clear away.

This is a poem about loneliness, the incurable kind which reconstruction and rebirth serve only to highlight and exacerbate. Vire will wind again through a rebuilt Saint-Lô, but the city will remain a place of shadows despite the 'bright ways tremble'. 'You're on earth, there's no cure for that', Hamm points out in *Endgame* (p. 37). In 'Saint-Lô' the poet is saying that war may be terrible, but life is worse: the as yet 'unborn' waters of the ever-running Vire are a promise, but a deceitful one, of refreshing succour. Beckett's pessimism is profound, perhaps best expressed by Estragon's sour twist in *Waiting for Godot* of the wise saw, first formulated by Heraclitus, that one never steps twice into the same stream, that existence is a continually renewed and therefore potentially exciting phenomenon. It is hard to despair, after all, if life seems to be in constant movement, since better days may be just round the corner. Estragon deflates such happy optimism when he asserts, with characteristic forthrightness, 'It's never the same pus from one second to the next' (p. 60). 'Saint-Lô' reveals how deeply Beckett grieved over the state of war-torn Europe while maintaining his characteristic scepticism about whether postwar reconstruction would modify the basic existential problem, that is, whether life in cities rebuilt to a high standard of comfort would be any less profoundly pointless than life in a landscape of ruins.

Alfred Péron and Arthur Darley were not the only friends of Beckett affected by the world war. There was also Georges Pelorson. He is of particular interest because he stood at the opposite end of the political spectrum from Péron and therefore of Beckett himself. He too was a student at the Ecole Normale Supérieure, and he too went to Dublin as the Ecole's exchange lector. His period of secondment there corresponded to the time when Beckett was assistant lecturer in French at TCD, and the two men got on well, even to the extent of writing together a skit on Corneille's heroic drama *Le Cid* which they called *Le Kid*.[5]

We tend to think of the elite Ecole Normale Supérieure as being exclusively left-wing, if only because Jean-Paul Sartre and Paul Nizan were famous graduates, but there were people of the extreme right who went there too. Perhaps the best known of these is Robert Brasillach, a militant fascist and fanatical antisemite who was shot at the Liberation for his inflammatory propaganda activity in support of the Axis powers. So it was perfectly possible for the same college to contain, side by side with fascists or anti-republican monarchists, intellectuals who were communists or crypto-communists. Before the war students' political agitation was harmless, and was savagely debunked as such by Paul Nizan in his novel *The Conspiracy* (1938). But during the war boys who had bandied dangerous ideas about in the dorms of the Ecole became men who suddenly found themselves in a position where they could exert a direct influence on events. The feverish talk in smoke-filled rooms was no longer ineffectual adolescent posturing; it got printed in German-financed news-papers. It cost lives: the lives of Jews, Communists and opposition intellectuals of all persuasions, who were fingered in the collaborationist press by Brasillach and his kind.

Georges Pelorson was of a similar political persuasion, but he escaped the worst rigours of the Liberation purges because he did not write for the pro-German, anti-Gaullist sheets. But he did work for the puppet Vichy regime, albeit in a subordinate capacity and only for a short time. In 1942 he was appointed assistant to the head of the youth section of the Vichy ministry of education, and was put in charge of moral, civic and professional training, as well as of the propaganda which the youth section put out in Paris. For about a year Pelorson passionately advocated a form of spiritual nationalism which claimed to be based on Christian values but was in fact strongly tinged with fascism and racism. Advocating 'national revolution' and state authoritarianism on the Nazi model, coupled with France's full participation in the new (Nazi) European order, he tried to get youth organizations to adopt an oath of allegiance to the head of state, Marshal Pétain, in which their young members would swear that they were true Frenchmen by virtue both of their birth on French soil and of their impeccable racial history. The purpose of this, insofar as it had a rational purpose – fascists being notorious suckers for anything that involves parades, banners and loyalty oaths – was no doubt to flush out the Jewish children who were known to be protected by certain youth groups (which explains why some young Jews survived even though their parents were deported). But the oath was not widely adopted, and Pelorson's own creation, the so-called 'national teams', failed to mobilise the mass of French youth.

There were two main reasons for this. The first was the hostility of the Catholic Church, which clung fiercely to its traditional dominance of French youth movements; it was not impressed by the extreme right's highjack of Christian values, and it was able, through Pétain's wife 'Madame la Maréchale', to prevail on the dictator and his entourage – which was ultra-conservative rather than fascist – to block moves to replicate the Hitler Youth in France. The other reason was the Nazis' own agenda. The occupation forces were not interested in giving French fascists their head; all they cared about was France's continued supine collaboration in the German war effort. French youths were conscripted into a forced labour scheme and sent to work in German armaments factories. This was hardly likely to encourage them to join any youth organization which swore allegiance, however indirectly, to the Germans who were only out to exploit them. Vichy's decision to raise a paramilitary force, the Milice, to fight the maquis, in what had by then become to all intents and purposes a French civil war, put paid finally to Pelorson's efforts to organise French youth voluntarily on fascist lines; the political situation had become too polarised, and he left the ministry, his mission unaccomplished and his achievement distinctly limited.[6]

After the war he embarked upon a career as a literary journalist, frequently writing on Irish literature in general, and on Samuel Beckett in particular, under the pseudonym Georges Belmont.[7] It was characteristic of Beckett that he remained loyal to Pelorson in spite of the latter's problems with the authorities at the Liberation. This showed real magnanimity on the great writer's part, for while Pelorson had been enjoying official approval in occupied Paris, Beckett was living in danger and some hardship in the south of France.

Critics agree that World War II marks a watershed in Beckett's *oeuvre*. Although he does not make the war the subject of his creative work, it is undoubtedly the case that his experience and knowledge of what happened in Europe in 1939-45 coloured his vision in a clearly discernible way. His last major prewar composition, *Murphy*, is a comic masterpiece written in densely-tapestried Anglo-Irish in which wit is not an occasional twist of gold thread but instead the very fabric backing of the weave. This makes it difficult to translate into other languages, and Beckett and Péron had their work cut out producing a French version which is even so only moderately successful. The works composed after his return to Paris in 1946 are written in a French that is as stark, bleak and syntactically spare as his Anglo-Irish is dense, allusive and syntactically opulent. To read his postwar prose immediately after a prewar passage is like turning from Bernini's 'Saint Teresa in Ecstasy' to a Henry Moore 'Reclining Figure'. For example:

It dawned on Neary that he was not where he thought. He rose.

'What is the finest tram in Europe,' he said, 'to a man consumed with sobriety?'

'But by Mooney's clock', said Wylie, 'the sad news is two-thirty-three.'

Neary leaned against the Pillar railings and cursed, first the day in which he was born, then – in a bold flashback – the night in which he was conceived.

(*Murphy*, p. 35)

Fortunately, Wylie 'knows no holy hour' and leads Neary to a café where throughout the day they serve coffee heavily laced with brandy. I wonder how many readers unfamiliar with Dublin topography and Irish licensing laws would make sense of this passage, which like all the best jokes relies on the complicity of shared experience. They would, however, have no difficulties with the following, written some twelve years later:

I am in my mother's room. It's I who live there now. I don't know how I got there. Perhaps in an ambulance, certainly a vehicle of some kind. I was helped. I'd never have got there alone. There's this man who comes every week. He gives me money and takes away the pages. So many pages, so much money. Yes, I work now, a little like I used to, except that I don't know how to work any more.

(*Molloy*, p. 7)

Even in English translation, this sounds completely different from the *Murphy* passage which preceded it. The sentences are short, uncomplex syntactically and lexically simple. Wit there is still, but no more in-jokes. By using French as his medium of expression Beckett pruned at a stroke the lushness of his prose, opting for the pollarded plane trees so characteristic of France in preference to the thickly-leaved beeches of his native land. After the war and his experiences during the occupation Beckett no longer felt able to indulge in the ironic brilliance of *Murphy* but wanted to turn away from the language in which he spontaneously expressed himself with tortuous elaboration, and adopt what amounted to another literary personality in a language in which he could make a fresh start and refashion, after an austerer mould, sharper tools for his trade. The naked, clipped first-person sentences in French thus replaced the oblique, intricate third-person periods in English.

Watt is especially significant in this regard as a work of transition, a novel written in farewell to the mother tongue and announcing already, through its at times curious near-*franglais*, the great works that Beckett was shortly to contribute, in another language, to another literature. As one might expect from a transitional creation, it is a not wholly satisfactory piece of work, oddly out-of-focus, almost self-alienated. Watt is a manservant who sets out from the city (clearly Dublin) to take up employment in the kind of rather grand suburban house in which Beckett himself grew up. Its owner is Mr Knott. The experience of working for Mr Knott is a devastating one for Watt, in that the anxious question 'what?' (Watt) meets the blank refusal 'not' (Knott). When he leaves the house two years later Watt is 'sicker, aloner' and, worse still, he is mentally deranged (the narrator Sam meets him in a lunatic asylum).

The nullity of Mr Knott's world has a profoundly debilitating effect on him: the novel is therefore a frightening account from the inside of mental breakdown. It is full of black comedy, such as the conversation overheard by Watt between his colleague Arthur and Mr Graves the gardener. Arthur tells Mr Graves about a patent medicine, an aphrodisiac (unfortunately for Mr Graves banned by the Irish authorities) that bears the apt French name of Bando. Another hilarious (and equally coarse) scene is set in Trinity, where an academic committee is convened to hear Ernest Louit account for the college funds advanced him to facilitate the pursuit of his investigations into the mathematical intuitions of the Visicelts. Needless to say Mr Louit has diverted them to unauthorised purposes, which explains why the investigating committee calls a halt to his research activities and he launches himself instead upon a new career as managing director of the house of Bando.

Beckett would have chuckled at these academic jokes as he sat during the long wartime evenings at his writing table in the village of Roussillon in the Vaucluse, and one can see just what he meant when he said that he wrote the book to take his mind off the unpleasant aspects of his enforced prolonged vacation in the south. At the same time, the Kafkaesque atmosphere which critics were quick to note in the story shows that its composition was accompanied by the ever-present fear of a man in trilby and trenchcoat knocking at his door, or even more terrifying, of a *feldwebel* tapping on it with the barrel of his machine pistol.

Echoes of that daily experience of terror – the sending of anonymous letters of denunciation to the occupying authorities was something of a national sport in France, so no fugitive could ever be certain of getting through the day unmolested – can be heard too in *Molloy*, the first major work written in French after the war. In the passage quoted earlier Molloy speaks of writing things which are collected regularly. He goes on to say that he does not know the identity of his visitor, only that he has no choice but to meet the deadlines the man sets. Similarly, in the second part of the novel, the narrator Moran is required to write a report:

A letter from Youdi, in the third person, asking for a report. He will get his report. One day I received a visit from Gaber. He wanted the report. I have spoken of a voice telling me things. I was getting to know it better now, to understand what it wanted. It told me to write the report. I went back into the house and wrote, It is midnight. The rain is beating on the windows. It was not midnight. It was not raining.

(*Molloy*, pp. 188–9)

It is not too fanciful to say that these enigmatic but highly charged closing sentences of Beckett's greatest novel come straight from a nightmare he must have had during the war, and for some time afterwards, featuring a compulsion to write which at first is imposed by an outside authority and afterwards is internalised (the order comes originally from Youdi the boss, then from Gaber the messenger, and finally from the voice). The obligation to perform some duty that is unclear, unspecific and/or difficult to carry out is a common anxiety dream which any person living a life of danger or threat is liable to experience. But the fact that Moran feels at the end of his story that he has understood the nature of the task which his inner voice has set him indicates that the psyche has come to terms with the problem which first gave rise to the anxiety dream. Once this problem-solving therapy is completed the psyche is able to dispense with the subterfuges it felt obliged to adopt at the outset, which is why Moran contradicts at the very end the statements he made – about the time, and the weather – at the beginning of his narrative.

No one disputes that *Molloy* with its two-part structure – in which Molloy's account and Moran's harmonise like orchestral parts in a musical score – is a psychological thriller of great force. I fully go along with this assessment; what I am arguing is that

Beckett could not have written such a novel, comparable in power and stature to *Moby Dick*, without the maturing and sobering effect the war had upon him. With hindsight it is astonishing how sound his instincts in his mid-twenties were. Had he stayed at Trinity, he would have become a professor as his father intended. But he chose to throw up a promising academic career for years of wandering, insecurity and exile. At the time, this seemed an act of the purest folly. This was no way to get a mortgage and save for a pension. And when war broke out, far from being able to spend it in the comfort and safety of neutral Dublin, he had to endure hardship and danger. He could easily have died as Léon and Péron did. Then there would have been no *Molloy*, no *Waiting for Godot*. But if he had spent the war in a set of rooms in Trinity, he would not have written those works at all, but continued in the manner of *Murphy*. That would have made him a kind of Flann O'Brien, that is, an Irish author of distinction; but not the international writer of genius which the war, and his sufferings during it, turned him into. That he was fully conscious of this was shown in his reply to an interviewer's question: 'I conceived *Molloy* and the rest the day I became aware of my stupidity. Then I sat down and wrote the things I feel'.[8]

What I have been describing are what might be called indirect or oblique references to the situation of a compromised man on the run that can be discerned in the works written between 1942 and 1949. There seems also to have been direct reminiscence. In 1943 the Vichy propaganda machine put out a poster attacking the black market and warning people of the penalties they risked incurring if they were tempted to indulge in it as buyers or sellers. Such posters were printed in large quantities and were widely distributed, with instructions to local authorities to ensure that they were prominently displayed; one can therefore be sure that anyone living in occupied France would have seen them on the walls of their village or town not once but many times. This particular poster shows two bowler-hatted figures standing side by side with their backs to the spectator. They are dressed in dark overcoats and one passes a banknote to the other, who in exchange holds out a *baguette* loaf. A yellow hangman's noose, the same colour as the bread, is shown poised between the two hatted heads. The caption 'Black Market: A Crime Against the Community' is explicit and menacing. The subtext is equally clear: the spectator is being told that hunger stalks the land, and that some people will sell their honour to get bread while others risk their lives for profit.

Anyone looking at this poster today cannot but be struck by parallels between it and the imagery Beckett deploys in *Waiting for Godot*, a play written in 1949 in which two bowler-hatted characters talk of hanging themselves. Indeed, were it not for the caption, the poster could serve perfectly well as a playbill for a production of *Waiting for Godot*. I am convinced Beckett remembered it, consciously or unconsciously, when composing the play. Images used in advertising are repeated so unremittingly that we internalise them and thereafter subconsciously recognise and respond to them. An example which most people of my generation will remember is the 'Bisto kids' poster, which showed hungry children sniffing the aroma of Bisto gravy coming from the kitchen, but there are innumerable other instances, such as the series which the London Underground commissioned in the 1930s to get people to use the tube to visit leafy parks, the zoo or sporting events, all invariably bathed in bright sunshine such as England usually enjoys for only a few days in any year.

Such posters soon become collectors' items and are widely imitated, adapted or pastiched in other advertising. The pastiche only works if the original is utterly familiar. This would have been the case with the posters issued by the Vichy regime, so long as they were designed by artists of real talent. It so happens that there was such an artist, employed by an agency which fulfilled a number of commissions from the Vichy authorities. The artist was Philippe Noyer; the agency was the Equipe Alain-Fournier. They deserve to be honoured, however sinister the purpose their high quality work was put to. Certainly Beckett would have been struck by the aesthetic quality of the poster: he had a sure eye in matters of art and design and was a connoisseur of no mean ability, with particularly acute discernment where avant-garde painting was concerned. This fine poster – and it is fine, whatever one thinks of its message – undoubtedly made an impression on him which six years later had still not faded.[9]

So I return to my starting point. Rightly or wrongly, the Irish Republic held aloof from the titanic struggle of 1939-45. Equally rightly or wrongly, 'Sam l'Irlandais', as Beckett was known in Resistance circles, did not. Whatever history's verdict about the former decision is, literary criticism can have no doubts about the second. World War II, quite simply, transformed Samuel Beckett from a distinguished Irish author into one of the world's greatest writers. Not unlike Joyce opting for exile and cunning, Beckett embraced personal danger and suffered the loss of close friends. The end result is that Ireland has produced yet another writer whose stature is out of all proportion to her size and importance. Whenever I visit Dublin, and tread the cobblestones in the quads where Sam might so easily have ended his days as professor emeritus, I ponder all this, and marvel at it, but above all I envy Trinity's knack of producing great men. Their statues are there to prove it. No doubt a bronze likeness will be raised one day to Samuel Beckett too, perhaps in front of the rooms he occupied at 39 TCD, horrified though he would have been by the very suggestion. But there is no hurry. His presence can still be felt in the precincts. When the memory begins to fade, that will be time enough to honour one of Ireland's greatest sons in the grounds of one of her most venerable institutions.

'WAR'S AWFUL ILLUMINATION': ELIZABETH BOWEN'S *THE HEAT OF THE DAY*

JOSETTE LERAY

The theme of war is an important one with Elizabeth Bowen. Two of her best-known novels largely deal with it: *The Last September* published in 1929 conjures up that period of Irish history significantly called the Troubles, using a socio-historical perspective to evoke the life led by the Anglo-Irish Ascendancy and the dangers that led to the destruction of many Big Houses. *The Heat of the Day* came out in 1949: the first five chapters had been written by 1944 but Elizabeth Bowen found that only well after the war was over could she get down to re-writing them and finishing the book. There too she required some distance in time to get a full view of what the war had meant.

Each time Elizabeth Bowen had the subject-matter at heart. As inheritor of her ancestral home, the Big House, Bowen's Court in County Cork, she was deeply concerned with the historical fate of her own class, the Anglo-Irish Ascendancy, and with tracing the reasons for its fall. This accounts for the predominant socio-historical perspective in *The Last September*. She also got a direct experience of the Second World War as she courageously chose to stay in London when she could have found a shelter in neutral Ireland. Her own flat was bombed twice, she did her duties as an air-raid warden and served in the Ministry of Information, travelling to Ireland and making reports about Irish attitudes towards England's part in the war. She felt the war to be a challenge, a test to her resilience and a stimulus; to that extent she had 'a good war', as she wrote to her friend William Plomer in 1945. Louis MacNeice who also stayed in London during the Blitz and the Battle of Britain shared that spirit, expressing it through a vivid analogy worth quoting:

There is plenty of degradation . . . but there is also an exaltation and, when I say that, I do not mean anything in the nature of Rupert Brooke heroics or last ditch bravado, I mean something much bleaker and, in one sense, humbler, something like the feeling you get on top of a mountain on a cold, grey day.[1]

Yet *The Heat of the Day* and her war-time short stories are no war-fiction. She makes this clear in her postscript to *The Demon Lover*, where the twelve stories she wrote during the war are collected:

These are all war-time, none of them war, stories . . . These are, more, studies of climate, war-climate, and of the strange growths it raised. I see war (or should I say feel war?) more as a territory than as a page of history.[2]

The difference in outlook between *The Last September* and *The Heat of the Day* or the war-years stories is manifest. From the representation of a specific social class at a specific moment of national history, she has shifted to the representation of the workings of the human mind in time of stress and general disorientation. So she now draws from her own day-to-day experience of the war but she needs the overall experience to come to a full grasp of the impact of the war on the psyche. The war is now seen as a catalyst; a character in the story 'Pink May' acknowledges the fact: 'Whatever you are these days, you are rather more so. That's one thing I've discovered in this war'.[3] We may here stress again the similarity between Elizabeth Bowen and Louis MacNeice who makes the same point:

This atmosphere of danger may coarsen you in some ways but it makes you more perceptive in other ways and it concentrates, rather than disperses, people's essential personality.[4]

The characters of *The Heat of the Day*, according to the critic Walter Allen, 'are caught in the glare of a searchlight'.[5] In the story 'Summer Night', we read these central lines: 'I say, this war's an awful illumination; it's destroyed our dark, we have to see where we are'.[6] Elizabeth Bowen is set on anatomizing the mental landscape of the human beings in the 'war-climate' because the war obviously creates new conditions of living and thinking which act as a challenge to established modes. At the same time it generates a basic common situation that gives the particular experience a general significance, as she asserts in the postscript to *The Demon Lover*: 'Through the particular, in war-time, I felt the high-voltage current of the general pass.'

In between the writing of *The Last September* and *The Heat of the Day*, Elizabeth Bowen took up this subject when just before the outbreak of the Second World War she started writing an account of her own family history called *Bowen's Court*, which came out in 1942. The Afterword that she wrote in 1963 makes clear the relevance of that genealogy to the time of war and establishes a link between the two novels:

War is not an accident: it is an outcome. One cannot look back too far to ask, of what?

...I have stressed as dominant in the Bowens factors I saw as dominant in the world I wrote in – for instance, subjection to fantasy and infatuation with the idea of power... Fantasy is toxic: the private cruelty and the world war both have their start in the heated brain.[7]

Whether through fiction or through family history, writing is for her a means to approach truth, to assess the stark reality of the war and try to account for it. The acuteness, the precision with which personal dramas are related to an historical state of civilization may give an impression of relentlessness. This is rather one of her qualities because it springs from depth of insight, honesty and, paradoxically, sensitivity. By publishing *Bowen's Court* less out of a narcissistic gratification than out of a wish to show the 'big analogies', as she says in the Afterword, between the times her ancestors lived in and her own war-time, she stresses the idea that the war is not an abstract notion but the historical outcome of human realities that she wants to trace back and point out. It is significant that *Bowen's Court* should have appeared in between her two war-time novels; it makes explicit what she is seeking when handling the theme of war. In *The Last September* and *The Heat of the Day* the novelist looks at war from different angles, but her purpose remains the same: she means to show that wars are brought on by men and do not merely happen.

* * *

The Heat of the Day[8] is a much more complex novel than *The Last September* because its scope is wider. The author points out that the general disorientation has been intensified by the war but was already there as a symptom of the more remote and hitherto hidden failures of a failing civilization. Most critics have noticed how well she succeeded in depicting the ills brought by the war and conjuring up the tensed atmosphere of the time. Viewing her as a female novelist whose work inevitably belongs to 'the novel of sensibility' – female sensibility versus male obduracy, I suppose

– they found her evocation of war-time most sensitive in its particulars. Anthony Burgess's judgement on the novel is quite representative: he praises it for 'the very feel and smell of London in the Nineteen Forties', but his praise is double-edged because it is for him a typically feminine approach, as female writers 'fall in love with the accident and miss the essence'.[9] Here Burgess misunderstands the novel as London and its accidents matter far less than the meaning of the war; individual dramas are constantly related to an ailing civilization and not merely to the influence of the war, which is seen as a symptom of the disease, not its agent. Harrison makes the point early in the novel: 'War, if you come to think of it, hasn't started anything that was not there already' (p. 33).

So the war is not seen in social or political terms. There is no ideology, the author never sharing the communist or fascist ideals of the thirties. The war is not set in a strictly historical perspective either because, though the reality of History is acknowledged, it is grasped only through the relative view the individual may get of it. Elizabeth Bowen is not concerned either with violence, which is always kept backstage because she is not interested in its dramatic or picturesque appeal and does not wish to write an action-packed war-novel. There is no stress either on the absurdity of war, no corrosive detachment emphasizing the grotesque and derisory aspect of war; though there are touches of comedy in the scenes with Louie, there is no series of comical incidents, no satire on war and on the army as we may find in Evelyn Waugh's *Put Out More Flags* or *The Sword of Honour* Trilogy. All these negatives point to the fact that Elizabeth Bowen focuses her investigation strictly on the psychological aspect of the war.

I. *THE HEAT OF THE DAY* AND THE SPY NOVEL

The Heat of the Day parodies the spy novel. We are presented with a spy, Robert, a counter-spy, Harrison, and many would-be spies as everyone is or ends in spying on the other. Because of Harrison's information on Robert, Stella cannot help watching her lover for some confirmation of Harrison's accusations and reproaches Harrison with having succeeded in making a spy of her (p. 138). Robert may be said to have inherited spying as his mother is shown as a caricatural family spy strategically positioned at the centre of her house (p. 108), and his father's insistence on getting truth by looking at his children 'straight in the eye' (pp. 119, 186) induces in the son a 'repugnance' for the

human eye (p. 227). Louie the factory girl does her share of
spying, first watching the reluctant Harrison out of sheer curiosity,
then keeping 'a look-out' for him in the park because '"You never
know, these days", she would say to anyone who would listen.
"You do have to watch"' (p. 144). Her friend Connie does her own
kind of spying, a more intellectual one:

Connie's reading of papers was for the most part suspicious; nothing
was to get by unobserved by her ... what she was doing was reading
between the lines ... and [she] was therefore a tiger for information.
(p. 153)

Places, too, foster spying. Holme Dene, Robert's home, with its
fake Gothick is signalled by 'a notice saying "Caution: Concealed
Drive"' (p. 105), which, in the general context of spying, has an
obvious symbolic import. The grill-bar where the counter-spy
Harrison takes Stella is fitted with such a garish lighting that
'there survived in here not one shadow: every one has been
ferreted out and killed' (p. 225). The loaded imagery is deliberate
of course.

Yet *The Heat of the Day* is no real spy novel: there is no apparent
action, the actual chasing of Robert the spy being kept behind the
scenes with his indeterminate end given in a mere fragment of a
sentence: 'Robert's fall or leap from the roof' (p. 291). Mainly, the
novel is not based on established moral values as a spy novel is
bound to be in order that the reader may know on which side of
the fence to stand and who are the good and the wicked. In *The
Heat of the Day* conversely the war makes everything and everyone shadowy, plunging them into a kind of opaque void so that
words and actions are felt as vague, equivocal and doubtful.
Indetermination is the keynote of the novel, for World War II has
blurred all clear-cut distinctions between good and bad, right and
wrong, and has led to a questioning of the absolutes which fed the
heroics of World War I. The novelist uses the parody of the spy
novel to emphasize the subversion of values that has taken place
and led to a war which in turn underlines that subversion. The
deliberately melodramatic starting-point of the novel – one main
character being accused of being a spy, shadowed by an enigmatic
counter-spy who also blackmails the spy's lover – arouses the
usual expectation of dramatic suspense but what transpires is a
moral and psychological investigation.

Elizabeth Bowen was the more concerned with spying – a
reality that the war brought to the fore – since she herself was
acting as an intelligence agent in Ireland for the Ministry of

Information in London. She was both loyal to Great Britain and sympathetic to Ireland's neutrality, which might be resented or despised in England at a time of tension between the two countries in 1940, when Churchill almost held Ireland responsible for the British losses at sea because of her refusal to give access to her ports.[10] She wrote in her report to the Ministry:

It may be felt in England that Eire is making a fetish of her neutrality. But this assertion of her neutrality is Eire's first free self-assertion, as such alone it would mean a great deal to her. Eire (and I think rightly) sees her neutrality as positive, not merely negative. She has invested her self-respect in it.[11]

Of course she did not consider herself as a spy but she experienced the impact on her own mind of carrying out secret activities. She transfers the experience to Stella in choosing to have the heroine 'employed, in an organization better called Y.X.D., in secret, exacting, not unimportant work . . .' (p. 26).

More generally, the secretiveness enforced by the war on people, which is turned into the literary metaphor of spying in the novel, is from the start integrated into the exploration of the inter-relation between cause and consequence and the awareness of how difficult it is to allot responsibility for moral negatives to either war or human nature. After stating Stella's work, Elizabeth Bowen significantly goes on thus:

The habit of guardedness was growing on her, as on many other people, reinforcing what was in her an existing bent: she never had asked much, from dislike of being in turn asked. Or, could that have been circumstance? – for by temperament she was communicative and fluctuating. (p. 26)

The refusal to ask questions does not spring from the fear of being told lies. When, much later in the book, the fairly limited Ernestine, Robert's sister, crudely asserts: 'In any case, ask no questions and you'll get told no lies. – Don't you, Mrs Rodney, find that to be a golden rule?' (p. 185), Stella does not agree: 'anything I did want to know I should ask, always' (p. 185). Her answer doesn't contradict what the author wrote earlier on, because the reluctance to ask questions is shown to be induced not by a fear of being told or having to tell lies, but by an unwillingness to face up to the truth as an unpleasant reality.

Asking the meaningful question becomes a symbolic act needing courage because it is the only way to fight the corrosion of uncertainty and the abdication of trust in moral values. It will take two months for Stella to summon up enough courage to put the crucial question to Robert as to whether he is a spy and thereby assert moral relevance against moral disintegration. It is noteworthy that after being evaded by Robert the question is put a second time behind the scenes as Elizabeth Bowen chooses to begin Chapter 15 with Robert's answer to it:

'And if I am?' he repeated. 'If that is what I am doing?'
Not a sign, not a sound, not a movement from where she at a distance from him lay, exhausted by having given birth to the question. (p. 267)

The stylistic figure of the ellipsis stresses the fact that the question hits the sore point. The connected metaphor of the exhausting birth shows that it means for Stella the painful delivery of a new commanding being, Moral Discrimination. Robert now cannot escape its requisition and is forced into an answer. His attempt at self-justification does not convince Stella and she is left unsettled and torn between her love for him, her need for moral recognition, and the confusion of the war as exemplified by her disquieting relationship with Harrison. Her perplexity is representative of the general state of bewilderment in wartime, when the subversion of values and disorientation are made manifest by war. Ironically enough, Stella, in spite of her Christian name, is no guiding star but this is no time for magi either – only for spies, even though both Robert and Harrison look to her for a sense of direction in their lives as she remains for them the traditional image of Woman, that is, Love and Stability, an image that the war proves wrong or at least obsolete.

II. THE SUBVERSION OF VALUES

1. Treason

The theme of treason runs through the novel to illustrate the point. Structurally it is intimately related to the form of the spy novel so that it seems to spring naturally from it. Treason can be read at many levels so that the meaning of treason is questioned and shown to be less clear-cut than might be expected. Political treason, as exemplified by Robert, substitutes one set of abstractions for another, 'order' for 'freedom' as Phyllis Lassner says, who perceptively adds:

He is imperilled . . . by his particular use of the language he inherits from his patriarchal forebears. He interprets the abstractions which serve as hallmarks of any cultural order as absolute ends in themselves, so that the language of broad philosophical flexibility becomes an absolute weapon of destruction.[12]

Robert for instance turns law into an absolute to be set against 'inorganic', chaotic freedom: 'We must have law – if necessary let it break us: to have been broken is to have been something' (p. 269). Yet the reader, in 1949 onwards, can translate these concepts into concrete historic events and shudder at the vision of what his Nazi rhetoric has come to mean in History. At the same time, Robert is representative of the disenchanted generation who between the wars felt the acute need to restore meaning to an apparently meaningless and restless civilization, and who were ready to embrace extreme ideologies – either communist or fascist ones. The death of ideals, the failure of democracy that Robert is denouncing, were already common topics in the Thirties.

Yet Elizabeth Bowen exposes the perils of looking for a legitimacy in any authoritarian ideology and believing in absolutes as a saving resort against disintegration. Furthermore she weakens Robert's position by hinting that his ideological and political quest for strength, authority and law is at bottom a quest for a father figure that his own wife-dominated father could not provide him with. She makes a psychically wounded man of Robert. The wound he got at Dunkirk is a symbol of the mental one, and Robert himself is fleetingly aware of the connection: 'I was born wounded; my father's son. Dunkirk was waiting there in us' (p. 272). The identification with a depreciated father image and the harmful influence of a castrating mother accounts for his destructive nihilism. Once more war and human nature combine to share responsibility for his attitude.

Elizabeth Bowen shows that the notion of treason is a complex, uncertain one. She reinforces the idea by engaging a minor character, Cousin Francis, the former Irish landlord, in secret war activities for the benefit of England. As Ireland insisted on remaining neutral, his activities may be considered politically subversive. So he is careful not to tell even his best friend, who is shocked when he hears of his hidden visits to London. This is the relevance of the little scene between Colonel Pole and Stella who informs him of Francis's appointment with Harrison in London (p. 80); as it is Colonel Pole's single brief appearance in the book, the author obviously created the character in order to stress that Francis, though acting for a good cause, dared not openly acknowledge his activities in Ireland for fear of the awkwardness it might lead to. Was it legitimate for him as an Irishman to take part in the war?

Besides the problem of legitimacy, Elizabeth Bowen raises the problem of collective responsibility. Is not the war our common responsibility? Haven't we all betrayed civilization by betraying the past and the moral values it stood for in spite of its imperfections? Is the Second World War the result of the betrayal of innocence and the consequent loss of faith in moral worth? Is the betrayal itself the result of the disillusionment brought about by the First World War? Can the First World War then be held responsible for the second one?

These fundamental questions are raised but prove difficult to answer. The complexity of the new age is contrasted with the simplicity of the old one. Passing references to the Great War – quite rare and very brief – are significant as they give it as the time of a dying order, 'simple' though in that it was still an order. Stella's brothers who died in Flanders as soldiers 'had been made heroes while things were simple' (p. 277). World War II testifies that a new order has not yet been found; the new war has sprung from the vacuum that was left after the death of the former order, which gave room to all sorts of distortions and betrayals.

At the personal level, people are guilty of minor or not-so-minor betrayals that reflect the general mood. Robert betrays Stella's trust in him, Harrison betrays Stella's expectations by ultimately rejecting her offer, Louie cannot remain faithful to Tom, Stella betrays her own inheritance and her own self by almost deliberately letting herself pass for 'a bad woman' twice.

2. Time and Place

The war has brought the past to an end, while barring the way to the future. Tradition is dead and places are diminished or destroyed. This gives rise to a feeling of disinheritance and disorientation. The life that is now lived is 'life in the moment and for the moment's sake' (p. 95). As the future bears no promise, nostalgia for order and fruitfulness is perversely projected onto its emptiness as a phantasmatic idle activity. Clock-time (there are numerous references to clocks in the novel) becomes a kind of parody of what time should be but no longer is, and the more intense moments are felt to be lived outside time.

The war seems to have arrested time because it has put men in-between – in-between life and death, past and future, real and unreal, language and silence. A character in the story 'Sunday Afternoon' asks: 'Where shall we be when nobody has a view of life?' The answer is, in-between, where nowhere is felt to be everywhere. Stella for instance 'saw the Kelways suspended in the middle of nothing' (p. 114). An existential anguish is shared by everyone in wartime because every one is kept waiting in-between, 'going into abeyance' as is said of Harrison (p. 141), in a state that is very close to that depicted by Samuel Beckett. As in Beckett's novels, people are waiting for things either to happen or not happen, hence the high frequency of the word 'happen' in *The Heat of the Day*. The war gives a specific status to the event and puts people in a new disturbing relationship to it: both people and things are hovering in-between, in the indefinite space of uncertainty. One is waiting without hope, yet faith is in the waiting as in Beckett's world. In a fit of Beckettian sensitivity, the girl Louie wonders 'In hopes of what, then, was one led on, led on? How long, looking back on it, it had lasted – that dogged, timid, unfaithfully-followed hope!' (p. 307). Beckett is more pessimistic in that he sees the predicament as one inherent in the human condition at all times.

People are also left waiting in-between, in a kind of limbo above the abyss, because things are never completed, always lacking definition and failing to connect. The last words of Stella are significant: 'I always have left things open' (p. 322). In such conditions History cannot be expected to bring much light because its meaning will remain shifting and elusive. This skepticism over History is conveyed in a comical mode by the exposure of the cliché used by the simple-minded Louie asking her friend: 'But isn't much to be learned from the lessons of History, Connie?' and being informed: '. . . one thing you don't learn from is anything anyway set up to be a lesson' (p. 155).

The subversion of time and place with its consequent indetermination converges in the representation of the Irish Big House, which becomes a symbolic focus of all the elements we have noted. At first sight *The Heat of the Day* appears to bring back the Big House as a symbol of order, permanence and continuity, the Irish Mount Morris being contrasted with the ever-for-sale English Holme Dene. Yet a close reading of the novel soon shows the ambiguity of the figure of Mount Morris, which proves double-edged, both a dangerous lure and yet a sustaining illusion. The war has made the Big House obsolete and irrelevant to the times. This is brought out through three leitmotifs that are metonymically connected to the Big House: the painted fan, the short-lived Persian rose, the sunk boat. Modern places have no more weight than the Big House and Stella, Robert and Harrison are wanderers drifting from one place to another, and acknowledging none as their own.

III. WAR AND FICTION

The destructiveness of the war sharpens the sense of vacuum already aroused by the loss of direction – deaths of people, bombings of houses create concrete metaphors for it; the war thus giving concrete expression to the vacuum conversely drains reality and de-realizes it: 'her bedroom window – which, glassless since two or three nights ago, ran up with a phantom absence of weight' (p. 93). This pervasive sense of unreality in wartime is stressed all along in the book. From the beginning 'the unreality of the room' (p. 54) in Stella's lodgings is explicitly stated and subtly defined. War deprives things of their substance, makes them feel strange and mute, dispossessed of 'the music of the familiar that is awaited' (p. 55). Reality is abstracted. The unreality that replaces it is fraught with a sense of death so that, during the black-out in the vault-like room, paradoxically the only living thing that is happening is death, symbolized by the fall of petals:

... the room, sealed up in its artificial light, remained exaggerated and cerebral.

In spite of this, something happened – petals detached themselves from a rose in the bowl ... Roderick watched them; she turned her head to see what he was looking at and watched also. (p. 56)

The themes of unreality, spying and 'happening' are conjoined.

The war de-realizes things by crystallizing their substance, hence the recurrence of the word 'glassy'; we read for instance: 'between the last of sunset and first note of the siren the darkening glassy tenseness of evening was drawn fine' (p. 90). Time also is arrested, so that people stay 'afloat on this tideless, hypnotic, futureless day-to-day' (p. 100). In such an atmosphere, precision itself becomes phantomatic: Stella 'saw Robert's face with a despairing hallucinatory clearness' (p. 93). The word 'ghostly' often recurs in the novel.

Wartime London feels like an empty stage and people see their lives in terms of parts being played. The metaphor of the theatre quite naturally comes to be associated with that of unreality. Settings and text have to be built up. The love affair between Stella and Robert is from the start a stage affair enacted on the scene of war where unreality carries the day. Having met during an air-raid, 'the extraordinary battle in the sky transfixed them; they might have stayed for ever on the eve of being in love' (p. 97). Later on, 'she felt herself going to a rendezvous inside the pages of a book. And was, indeed, Robert himself fictitious? ... everything came to be woven into the continuous narrative of love' (pp. 97, 99). The war, paradoxically, becomes a poetic space because in wartime reality is seen through imagination as imagination is the only way to come to terms with an otherwise unbearable reality.

The de-realization of both people and things achieved by the war must be counteracted by a compensating fiction which will enable the 'uncertain I' to play a part, whatever that be. Words like 'story', 'fiction' recur with a striking frequency. The war has speeded up the deconstruction of an identity which must now be reconstructed along new lines. All the characters are thus prone to conceive identity – theirs and that of the others – in terms of the stories they may read into the persons, and places themselves feel like settings for stories.

For Stella, her furnished flat is the setting where her 'narrative of love' mostly takes place. This is what Roderick senses, waiting in the front room of his mother's: 'This did not look like home; but it looked like something – possibly a story . . . Roderick admired the scene in which he could play no part' (p. 47).

Roderick's inheritance is for him the means to play a part. Mount Morris becomes the metaphor for his future self and simultaneously endows him with a structure. As a soldier, he is an anonymous social entity with no scope for self-expression; as 'the Master of the House', he is an acknowledged person, who may invent his own story.

Harrison, the elusive discontinuous and 'impossible' (p. 140) character depends on Stella to build a story that will establish his identity as a lover, providing him with the recognition and stability that his secret activities as a counter-spy cannot bring him. The spy world allows him a breathing space, one where he may calculate and act, but it does not supply a story in which he can find a place for himself. This is what he aims at and is looking for beyond the sexual gratification when he is blackmailing Stella into becoming his lover. His ultimate rejection of her when she is at last ready to accept him in order to save Robert is a further proof of his deep need: he doesn't so much want her to be his lover as wish himself to be her lover. This is indeed the wishful story that he builds for himself without really believing in it. To have Stella as a reluctant partner would be the end of the love story he imagines as a compensation for the dryness of his war activities. Stella is unconsciously aware of the danger of this story-making – imagination may be catching in the wartime void – and she refuses to listen to it: 'Coming out of that vacuum, the reiterated unrelated story of his desire could but be unmeaning'

(p. 141). Yet it is through the 'story of his desire' rather than through his actual blackmail that he acquires some substance as a person in her eyes.

Louie, the lower-middle class girl, acts out the fancy almost literally. Out of helplessness and in her desire for survival, she builds up her new identity from the various stories she reads in the newspapers:

Once Louie had taken to newspapers she found peace . . . Dark and rare were the days when she failed to find on the inside page of her paper an address to or else account of herself. Was she not a worker, a soldier's lonely wife, a war orphan, a pedestrian, a Londoner, a home and animal-lover, a thinking democrat, a movie-goer, a woman of Britain, a letter writer, a fuel-saver and a housewife? (pp. 151–2)

The long list of the clichés found in the wartime newspapers with which Louie identifies points to a pathetic fragmentation and uncertainty beyond the satirical effect.

Nettie's policy of near madness is a neat refusal to lend herself to any more storying, so to speak:

'I don't know who is alive. But what story *is* true? Such a pity, I sometimes think, that there should have to be any stories . . .'
'Something has got to become of everybody, I suppose, Cousin Nettie.'
'No, I don't see why. Nothing has become of me: here I am and you can't make any more stories out of that.' (p. 214)

Nettie is the only character in the novel to assert her identity in the most straightforward and bare terms ('here I am') challenging the need for story-building as a means to establish or acknowledge identity in wartime, but she is also the only one to stand outside war.

War activities themselves are seen as stories. Stella comes to think of the political activities of Harrison and Francis as part of the general fiction: 'that last London meeting between the two must have been a continuation of some actual story, however cock-and-bull' (p. 170). The war itself is viewed as 'the larger story' (p. 195), part of a still larger one, History. That History should be felt as the largest story of all is a sign of its ambiguity – or at least of the author's cautious attitude before it. What is History, ultimately? The question is left unanswered.

Why should the war foster such story-making in people? For Elizabeth Bowen, it does not merely spring from a need for compensation. Fascinated with the fiction-making power of the war, she goes deeper into her investigation. She perceives that because the war makes everything look unreal, it turns reality into fiction, a text to be read. But this text is written in a new language so that it must be deciphered in order to be re-interpreted. Reading becomes equivalent to naming so that the convolutions of the language witness to the general bewilderment. Each character painfully tries to find a decoding language to translate the text of war, which is the harder to decipher as it offers itself to the interpreter as a tattered one, its meaning lying in the blanks and the silences. Louie might also be a heroine of Beckett in her painful groping for language: 'It was the blanks in Louie's vocabulary which operated inwardly on her soul; most strongly she felt the undertow of what she could not name' (p. 306). This might be an excellent definition of what will be, a few years later, the predicament of Beckett's heroes. Before Beckett, Elizabeth Bowen felt it reflected the general dislocation of wartime; all her characters share that difficulty in expressing themselves and often speak in a dislocated stilted language that has sometimes put readers off the novel. The old language must be rejected as 'dead currency' (p. 268). 'War's awful illumination' has revealed that 'we no longer express ourselves ... our currency's worthless – our "ideas", so on, so on. We've got to mint a new one', as a character says in 'Summer Night'.[13] But all languages are exposed as being inadequate or misleading or impossible to construct.

In wartime, events must enter the realm of fiction in order to get meaning: 'By the rules of fiction with which life to be credible must comply, he was a character . . .' (p. 140). Confronted with the need to re-interpret life and lives according to the new war terms, the characters are led to build up stories and read them into reality. But the text the war writes is not the one that was expected. Either one cannot grasp it or what one may read is not what one was willing to read. Stella for instance will ultimately have 'to re-read' Robert 'backwards' (p. 270).

So in wartime, everything becomes a sign to be watched for. The metaphor of spying takes on its full value at this level. For the characters, the war, by turning everything into a story, simultane-ously turns everything into a question because events, in a story, don't merely happen, they necessarily have a meaning, however obscure. The characters who are most strongly bent on surviving – Louie, Roderick – are always asking questions. Yet the war, as Harrison well knows, shows that things may happen without having to be meaningful. They happen merely because they do. Then what does 'to happen' mean? Do we have to watch things happening, as Roderick and Stella watched the fall of petals in the room? How can we be sure things are happening or have

happened? Is their not happening a happening? We are taken back
to the attitudes of the spy and counter-spy, but at a much deeper
level, a philosophical one.

Yet even if stories cannot properly be deciphered because of the
ambiguous status of the event in wartime, the war ensures a kind
of syncretism that will allow various 'stories' to mix into one social
and psychological space. In that respect, Louie's story meets
anyone's; the war becomes the focal point whereto all the
characters converge. Hence the importance of the doubles in the
novel, Harrison and Robert, Roderick and Nettie, Stella and Louie.
The stories built up or read by the characters can be fused with the
stories made up by the novelist to compose the novel. *The Heat of
the Day* begins and ends with the story of Louie; the secondary
plot may be meant to frame the main plot, but it also challenges its
claim to priority. Elizabeth Bowen's aesthetic ordering of the plots
throughout the novel points to a kind of egalitarian space, all
stories being made even by the war. They are homogenized by
being all wartime stories. Turning reality into a story is the only
way for the characters to accommodate and for the novelist to
penetrate the chaos of the war.

*   *   *

What is striking in Elizabeth Bowen's anatomy of the war is her
lucidity and implacable honesty. Although she laments the loss of
the values of the past and the consequent impoverishment of our
civilization, she rejects nostalgia, romanticism and over-subjec-
tivity in her desire to face up to the situation. She wrote in 1951:

I should like to see a whole generation keep the power of taking
moments 'straight' – not half overcast by fantasy, not thinned down by
yearning.[14]

She showed that the Second World War has destroyed what was
already going to ruins and has made us see where we were. Her
ultimate message is positive: let the war be cathartic, the heat of
the war-days be truly a purifying fire leading man to 'break
through to a new form' as a character hopes in 'Summer Night':

'On the far side of the nothing – my new form'
'You feel this war may improve us?' said Robinson.[15]

The question is not answered but at least it is asked.

DENIS JOHNSTON: NEUTRALITY AND BUCHENWALD

TERRY BOYLE

Over half of Johnston's plays deal, either directly or indirectly, with the subject of war. He has written an autobiographical account of his experiences as a war correspondent in the Second World War, *Nine Rivers from Jordan*, which he later made into an opera with the same title. The necessity of war is, for Johnston, never brought under intellectual scrutiny (the 'whys') but rather how warfare is conducted by those actively engaged with fighting (the 'hows') is of the utmost importance. Johnston's first hand encounters with warfare, both in Ireland and internationally, tend to reaffirm his belief that: 'It is a game to be played according to certain fixed principles and assumptions.'[1]

This quotation typifies Johnston's attitude towards war which, significantly, did not change through his life. If war is to be an inevitability, and Johnston believed it was, then, he wrote, 'it is more important to keep it the good thing that it is, than to win or lose it' (*NRJ* p. 119). It is the intention of this essay to argue that Johnston approached the process of war with a romantic and sentimental view of human nature. He was philosophically opposed to any ideological understanding of humankind which, in his understanding, made us appear anything less than fundamentally 'sane' and civilized. And this aversion towards any pessimistic belief regarding humanity is largely based, it will be argued, on his inability to cope personally with the consequences of such views which, Johnston contested, would ultimately strip humanity of any reason to continue with its existence and consign it to a futile and meaningless future devoid of hope. This refusal to accept fully the capriciousness and cruelty of warfare dominates Johnston's portrayal of fighting in his works in which his men of war adhere to a common code of chivalry.

During the 1916 Rising Johnston and his family were held

hostage by the rebels. The behaviour of these men towards their prisoners was exemplary. Johnston later wrote:

Of the rebels, I principally remember their charm, their civility, their doubts, and their fantastic misinformation about everything that was going on. Of the men in khaki there remains an impression of many cups of tea, of conversations about everything except the business in hand, and of a military incompetence of surprising proportions.[2]

This incident made a deep impression on the young boy and, I would suggest, was the key event which led to his subsequent philosophical understanding of warfare. The good natured patriots are replicated by Johnston in his dramatic works, particularly in *The Scythe and the Sunset* (1957). His earlier plays, *The Moon in the Yellow River* (1931) and *A Bride for the Unicorn* (1934), are, to some degree, examples of this philosophical perspective in embryo. Set in the post-Civil War years in Ireland, *The Moon in the Yellow River* deals with the conflict between the free staters and the republicans. When Lanigan, a free stater, kills the unarmed Blake, a republican, the killing is justified by Johnston who suggests that although there appears to be no moral or legal justification for such a ruthless action, this ritual bloodletting was necessary if the newly established government was to survive. It is deemed expedient that one man should die in order to preserve the common good. 'This', wrote Johnston, 'was all very sobering and disgusting. Yet it is hard to see what other answer could have been made to a continuance of underground warfare, provided that we were to have any government at all.'[3]

The overriding feeling of this play is an innate sense of fair play. There is no judgment of Lanigan's pragmaticism. He is caught in a moral dilemma from which there is no easy escape and for which there is certainly no clear answer. War may lead to the enactment of some malicious and cruel deeds, Johnston at this point believes, but these are in the long term justifiable. There are no heroes or villains with Johnston who resists such stereotypes. Instead there is an underlying sympathy for all his characters. Even in Johnston's earlier play, *The Old Lady says, 'No!'* (1929), in which he depicts the man of war, in this case Robert Emmet, as a monomaniac, there is a romantic portrayal of the patriot. Emmet encapsulates both the terrible and the beautiful and as such retains some dignity. In *A Bride for the Unicorn* the main character, Jay, is forced into national service when an economic emergency is declared. The forces of money, politics and law combine together in an effort to cover up their financial mismanagement. The ordinary man, as represented by Jay, becomes embroiled in a battle for which he is necessary only as a pawn. Jay's first encounter with the enemy brings him into contact with an old friend, Barney. The good natured rapport between these men threatens to make them incapable of killing each other. They lose the instinct to kill when they discover the basis for the battle.

Johnston's idealism with regard to men at war is, in these early works, quite transparent. The decorum with which his main characters interact with each other is based on a mutual respect for the political, theological and social differences of others. Johnston's understanding of the fundamental goodness of mankind is never seriously called into question. It is not until he becomes involved in the Second World War in 1942 that Johnston is confronted with the stark cruel face of warfare; and when the actuality of war is thus directly revealed to him his response is, as will be suggested, evasive and unsatisfactory. In *Nine Rivers from Jordan*, more than any of his other writings, he shows a distinct capacity to avoid coming to terms with the real suffering and hardship of battle. This text will therefore provide the main focus for discussion in what follows.

Johnston, who had volunteered to act as a war correspondent for the BBC, was posted to Cairo in July 1942. On entering the war he is idealistically determined to 'describe soberly and sensibly ... the Truth, the Whole Truth, and nothing but the Truth, whether happy or unfavourable' (*NRJ* p. 8). From the outset Johnston sets himself up as the neutral and therefore the objective voice. He admits to his arrogance and sense of superiority later when it becomes apparent to him that neutrality affords no escape from the consequences of battle. Initially, however, Johnston is not in the direct line of fire and only hears of the fighting via military sources. Much of what is reported to him has been vetted by the war censors and as such becomes highly suspect. Johnston was sceptical of the censor's reportage which was highly propagandist. This subversion of the truth made it particularly difficult for him to believe anything which sought to dehumanize the enemy and which caricatured the German troops as barbarian. The deliberate suppression of stories in which the enemy showed itself capable of acts of altruism left Johnston wondering if any of the supposed acts of cruelty of the opposition were true, or if they were the result of the overactive imagination of the war censor. On top of this any attempt by Johnston to discover the 'facts' was frustrated by the multiplicity of viewpoints represented. He wrote:

There are Facts (and a 'common-sense' view of them) as seen by the soldier in the slit trench. There is usually quite a different view of both Fact and Common-sense in the Allied Embassies in Cairo. And there are various intermediate viewpoints at Corps, at Division, and at Army – all perfectly sincere, and all, in a sense, equally true. A crooked propagandist does not really have to invent a single lie, for there are sufficient Facts to prove or disprove almost any thesis, and the only problem is one of selection.

(NRJ p. 111)

Reports, therefore, of ethnic cleansing policies and news of major victories are treated by him with a certain amount of cynicism. Indeed his own experience during those initial months in the desert led him to believe that 'war, as these men play it, need not be some sordid squabble into which we are drawn weeping and with reluctant feet. It is a game to be played according to certain fixed principles and assumptions' (*NRJ* p. 119). To substantiate this idealistic view of the war Johnston cites a story he has heard in which those involved act with integrity. In the story he relates how two RAF men, captured by the Italians, were 'taken for internment to the island of Pantellaria. When they arrived there with their escort, it was discovered that there was nobody available on Calypso's island to make a fourth at Bridge, so the party set out again by air for Sicily, in search of another player. It was a very bumpy day, and before long the Escort began to feel airsick. When he was no longer interested in anything except the condition of his stomach, the prisoners gently relieved him of his gun, and went forward with it to talk to the Pilot' (*NRJ* pp. 117–118). The pilot agrees to fly the British to Malta on condition that the plane when it is delivered into Allied hands 'would not be used for operational purposes, but would ever afterwards be confined to the neutral and humanitarian task of spotting the airmen of both sides who were unlucky enough to fall in the drink' (*NRJ* p. 118). After a horrendous landing with the British on the ground shooting at the oncoming enemy plane the aircraft was dutifully taken over by the Malta air force who honoured the pledge. Stories such as this, which were originally suppressed by the censors, vindicated, to Johnston, his belief in the fundamental sanity of human behaviour. By failing to contextualize the episode or comment on it in relation to other aspects of human behaviour in war, he seems to trivialize and reduce warfare to a deadly game played by gentlemen.

With nothing in his experience to prove the case otherwise

Johnston concentrates on those things which make war not only tolerable but even in his view beneficial to those actively engaged in fighting. The 'virtue of violence' as Johnston terms it, calls forth in man qualities that distinguish him as 'sane' and sympathetic even when dealing with the enemy. In the midst of battle, Johnston believed, man is forced out of the normal mediocrity of daily living when the superficialities of everyday existence are stripped away and 'one lives more abundantly, and experiences a deeper sense of the meaning of life' (*NRJ* p. 119). Essentially this is what Johnston's play about the 1916 Rising, *The Scythe and the Sunset* (1957), exemplifies. Johnston concentrates on how the rebels carry out their plans for revolution. The emphasis is not on the violence and destruction brought about by war but on the intrinsic goodness it produces in those actively engaged in the battlefield. Unlike O'Casey's portrayal of the same event in his play, *The Plough and the Stars*, Johnston's dramatic re-enactment of this battle concentrates on how these men fight. Courage, loyalty and conviction, Johnston suggests, are amongst those heroic virtues which spring from the human heart in the throes of warfare. The true moral fibre of the patriots is finely expressed in Maginnis's 'unholy joy' when he bravely fights against the enemy but it is better shown in Tetley – Johnston's 'man with the idea', i.e. Pearse. Tetley's heroism finds its perfect counterpart in Palliser, the unionist. Both men treat each other with courtesy and respect without infringing on the other's freedom of choice while honourably remaining faithful to their political aspirations.

In some ways Johnston's perception lacks the necessary component of personal experience to authenticate such observation and as such his comments can appear facile. Johnston takes pride in his ability to stand apart as a neutral and observe. This stance may have certain advantages, in so far as it allows him to speculate on the larger existential questions concerning the Second World War, but it also distances him from the ordinary soldiers for whom this camaraderie may disguise their fear of death. As the war poet Arthur Graeme West puts it:

> How rare life is!
> On earth, the love and fellowship of men,
> Men sternly banded: banded for what end?
> Banded to maim and kill their fellow men –[4]

Johnston, unfortunately, makes the mistake of concocting a false sense of reality. There is nothing, in either his notebooks or *Nine Rivers from Jordan*, to suggest that he ever remotely anticipated the possibility that he might discover evidence to counter his ideas. Philosophically and intellectually he could not conceive of there being occasions when mankind fell into the kind of depravity that would not be known in the worst type of predator of the animal world. It is only as he begins to follow the Allied troops through Italy and into Germany that Johnston's idealistic view of human nature comes under attack. In Italy he begins to see signs of a 'grimmer kind of struggle'. He disguises his doubts, at this point in *Nine Rivers from Jordan*, in the form of allegories. It is important to note that whenever Johnston becomes affected personally by the war he tends to depersonalize the issues by the use of allegory. This technique not only creates a distance between the reader and the narrator but also illustrates Johnston's unwillingness to allow anything to destroy his own romanticized perception of mankind. In a deliberate parody of Bunyan's *Pilgrim's Progress* he cloaks his inner struggle in a debate between two fictional characters over whether war is the result of evil. The atheist, Doubtful, who represents Johnston, is not convinced that evil has any real existence. He refuses to accept the argument put forward by Holy Orders, a priest, that war is a 'curse that man brings down upon himself through Evil' (*NRJ* p. 140). The playful bantering between these characters once again illustrates, through its philosophical abstractness, Johnston's detachment from the realities of war. The levity with which he treats the war underscores the fact that he is a person who has had only a superficial encounter with the fighting. There are, however, signs that he is unable to keep at bay the possibility that war is essentially cruel and destructive. He is forced to think about the horror of war the closer he gets to the actual fighting. The scepticism with which Johnston has regarded the stories of German brutality comes under siege when he is shown evidence to support the claims of barbarity. He refuses to accept these accounts of torture as facts. Even when shown two concentration camps in France and told of their function Johnston is not convinced that this is not yet another attempt by the propagandist to discredit the enemy.

Johnston's inability to accept these reports of arbitrary killings lies in his refusal to believe that mankind is capable of such deeds. If man were guilty of such capriciousness then, for him, mankind is more or less reprobate. It is significant that when Johnston goes in search of Annelise Wendler, a German woman whose letters he found in a dead German soldier's trench coat, he accidentally stumbles upon the liberation of Buchenwald. The letters, for Johnston, humanize the German army and are a counterbalance to the rumours of their depravity. Gene Barnett, in his book *Denis Johnston*, defends Johnston against early reviewers of *Nine Rivers from Jordan* who interpreted the author's attitude as that of a 'benevolent neutral' 'who happened in on the holocaust not caring – at first – who won...'[5] Barnett argues that this criticism misjudges Johnston and he commends the author for taking the risk of not seeking to play down or omit his idealism. While I would agree with Barnett that Johnston, for the sake of authenticity, takes the unfavourable position of admitting to disbelieving the accounts of torture and indiscriminate killing within these institutions it is difficult, with the author's previous dismissal of these stories and his flippancy with regard to the issues being fought for by the opposing sides, to accept that this statement of naiveté is in fact a form of self-accusation. It is possible that Johnston, as an act of atonement, has deliberately or unconsciously concentrated on his obvious impertinence and arrogance as a form of self-reproach. In light of the subsequent experience of Buchenwald the early part of *Nine Rivers from Jordan* may be read as self-effacement. I am not convinced, however, that this honest attempt at self-recrimination means that Johnston allowed the horror of Buchenwald to radically affect his idealistic view of human nature. It is perhaps ironic that Johnston, who, as a playwright, had earned the reputation of a debunker of myths, should find himself guilty of self-delusion. His former idealized conception of mankind is shown to be inadequate and flawed. If we trace the experience, as he records it in *Nine Rivers from Jordan*, we can see how Johnston struggles to maintain his benevolent view of man despite the bombardment of evidence to the contrary.

Driving to the concentration camp he saw 'a continual stream ... of filthy, emaciated creatures...' (*NRJ* p. 392). A group of Displaced Persons made their way through the woods near the camp. On the main gate an inscription was placed which read: 'To Each what is coming to him'. To begin with Johnston is shown a lorry 'piled high with emaciated yellow naked corpses.' From here he is taken to the crematorium where there are more 'sub-human specimens . . . all in a state of indescribable filth'. The repugnance of these hideous sights, smells and sounds makes it impossible for him to retain his earlier scepticism with regard to the Nazi atrocities. In an attempt to regain some of his former idealism he asks one of the prisoners if this 'state of affairs' is 'normal'. His question leads him further into the moral abyss. The prisoner tells him that the inmates were kept working for sixteen hours a day, most of them suffering from malnutrition, until they were not fit for work and then 'what followed was quite deliberate.' On hearing that the Americans were gaining ground five hundred SS men were designated to kill all 70,000 prisoners, which they would have done if they had not been prevented by the early arrival of the liberators. During this macabre tour Johnston could hear the prisoners hunting out SS men in the woods. Confused and bewildered he was finally taken back to a 'block' inhabited by 'tier upon tier of what can only be described as shelves. And lying on these, packed tightly side by side, like knives and forks in a drawer, were living creatures . . . skeletons with the skin drawn tight over their bones, with heads bulging and misshapen from emaciation, with burning eyes and sagging jaws' (*NRJ* p. 395). There was no escaping the fact that this sadistic act of war was perpetrated not as a final chaotic act but as the result of a well worked-out, pragmatic programme. 'This', wrote Johnston, is 'deliberate . . . This is what logic divorced from conscience can bring men to. This is the wilful dehumanisation of the species, and an offence against man himself' (*NRJ* p. 396).

Johnston, in an attempt to exonerate mankind and salvage his belief in the fundamental goodness of human nature, begins to attribute this clinical, pragmatic whittling down of a race of people to the absence of any moral absolutes. He believes that modern atheism is to blame for this dehumanizing process. In an attempt to demythologise religion, Johnston suggests, atheism has created a moral vacuum and as such paved the way for this type of barbarity. In abandoning the tenets of traditional religion modern man has not, Johnston purports, replaced the social and ethical value of religious practice with anything to stop mankind from plunging itself into self-destruction. The philosophical theories of the behaviourist and the fatalist, he suggests, have reduced man to the level of animals. Without the aid of an objective frame of reference, such as the ten commandments, Johnston believed anarchy and genocide would ensue. It is only after his exposure to the human suffering at Buchenwald that Johnston takes seriously the subject of the moral function of religion. Up until this point he is quite indifferent about the role of religion in society. This changes when he realizes that without a moral framework, such as the ten commandments, society's view of human life may be formed by a secular philosophy that strips mankind of dignity and respect.

Suddenly, in the midst of an institution purposely designed to destroy human beings, neutrality, war and the existence of evil begin to have a new importance and meaning for Johnston. He can no longer adopt the detached role of the observer. This type of cruelty involved all mankind. There is no excusing such actions: 'we have been made fools of. Appeals to reason were just a cover-up for this! Our good will has been used as a means to betray us; and that is as great a crime as the degradation of humanity, for it means that good will is a mistake – that destruction is our only means of preservation' (*NRJ* pp. 396–7). The violation of all that Johnston formerly thought sacred to his understanding of mankind leads to him accepting a Luger as a souvenir. In direct contrast to his decision to remain neutral Johnston takes the weapon, which has now become a symbol of his despair. He writes in *The Brazen Horn*:

In the light of that fantastic expression of the dehumanisation of Man, it was shameful to pretend any longer that the issues at stake had nothing to do with me, whether or not there was still a lot that might be said against the motives and behaviour of both sides. The outward and visible sign of that change of heart was, I suppose, the taking of that Luger. The weapon itself was just another symbol. I was not proposing to go roaring through the streets of a prostrate Germany, loosing it off in all directions as an expression of a distaste of Hitler. It was no more than a tangible reminder that I was no longer a 'neutral', and that I was deeply embarrassed by the fact that I had ever been one.[6]

The despair which Johnston experiences appears to be short lived. This episode is not, however, I would suggest, as Harold Ferrar puts it in *Denis Johnston: A Retrospective*, an experience which Johnston 'digests' and 'transcends'[7] but one which he still continues to avoid. As he rationalizes the horrific sights of Buchenwald, Johnston cannot forsake his belief in human goodness. A lawyer by profession, he desperately looks for the loophole which will save mankind from the responsibility for such acts of depravity. He artfully evades the repercussions of this type of atrocity philosophically by refusing to appreciate fully the magnitude of the actual event. In *Nine Rivers from Jordan* the incident is followed by another allegory, (a mode, which, as I have already suggested, is used as a distancing technique) and in this allegory he begins his defence of mankind. His unwillingness to engage philosophically with the truth of Buchenwald exposes the depth of Johnston's romantic idealism. He is not prepared to make the necessary paradigm shift to accommodate the reality of such ruthless behaviour and instead retreats from the challenge by resurrecting his former beliefs concerning the nature of man. The resurgence of Johnston's idealism is not, as Ferrar puts it, evidence of 'realism' but, I would suggest, a lack of realism. Ferrar states:

Johnston is full of pity for suffering, but is not paralyzed by it. He says of his renewed and deepened faith – for it *is* faith . . . that the meaning of 'life is life itself.' It is possible to be a realist *and* a lover of divine principle. The man of faith and compassion is, in the final analysis, the true realist.[8]

There are no clear grounds for Ferrar's elevating Johnston's reaction to Buchenwald to the level of spiritual struggle; and in fact such a reading may obscure the fact that he was incapable of acknowledging the horrendous implications of such places. There is evidence to suggest, in both Johnston's diaries and works, that when it comes to facing up to emotional pain or personal crisis, he tends to withdraw and the trauma is sanitized through rationalism. Johnston's speculations over the nature of evil, in the Faust playlet which follows his account of Buchenwald and in the final section of *Nine Rivers from Jordan*, become a metaphysical argument which attempts to implicate God as the true source of evil. The judgment against mankind is tempered by Johnston with the inclusion of a transcendental being into the scheme of his argument. Mankind, as he sees it, is not solely responsible for its tendency towards destruction. If God exists, and Johnston believed that he did, then any discussion about the origins of evil must include this divine entity. In the first of these metaphysical debates the 'human race' is put on trial. The case against man, as Johnston sees it, lies with mankind's death wish: 'For a considerable time the prisoners at the bar have been seeking out a way in which to destroy themselves' (*NRJ* p. 416). In a moment of profound disillusionment Johnston is willing to admit that mankind may not be essentially good. The court deems the human race guilty and they are allowed to have their 'hearts' desire . . . Endwaffe' (self-annihilation) (*NRJ* p. 416). Initially, it seems, Johnston is ready to accept that his former conclusions about mankind are wrong, but this move away from a positive form of idealism is replaced by a negative form of exculpation. If mankind is not good then, he deduces, it must be bad; and hence in the second of these debates the case against mankind becomes the case against God, man's Creator.

Johnston's 'faith', therefore, as Ferrar describes it, could be interpreted as nothing more than pious escapism. In an effort to redeem mankind he introduces a concept of God that is designed simply to rescue man from the notion of total depravity. Johnston accepts and defends the need for an ultimate being, not because he believes that such a being exists but because the refusal to acknowledge the possibility of a supreme force would, in his opinion, make man solely culpable for his self-destructive actions. God, as a concept, is therefore necessary to explain the origin of evil. Religion, he believed, is also a necessary component in human existence insofar as it provides society with a mechanism to protect itself from devaluing human life and repeating the crimes of Buchenwald. The function of religion, in Johnston's terms, is to save man from a ruthless form of pragmatism that wantonly destroys life without conscience. Therefore, he is opposed to those like Nietzsche who held the opinion that religion is a 'war against life, against nature, against the will to live. . . .'[9] At a very basic level this view of the moral function of religion concurs with Locke's understanding of the need for religion. Locke believed that if atheism were true then 'it leads to our annihilation or everlasting insensibility . . . If theism is true, it brings eternal happiness, whereas falsity entails our annihilation.'[10] God and religion, as necessary facets of human existence, provide for Johnston a way in which he can legitimately argue for his conviction that man is essentially altruistic.

The spiritual debate between Johnston's representative for humanity, the Acolyte, and God is a frantic attempt by him to salvage his former idealism. God has created man 'to fight for his existence / And plagued him with a Pity for the things he has to kill' (*NRJ* p. 448). War, in Johnston's opinion, illustrates this divine discrepancy. Once again the assumption is that man feels pity for those he kills. There is no accounting for those who ruthlessly kill without any sense of remorse or indeed those for whom the deaths of certain sections of the human race are necessary. The issues raised by Buchenwald, regarding the savage and the morally indefensible killing of human beings by men who were without pity, are avoided. Johnston's representation of mankind is a romanticised ideal. A man wracked with self-doubt, the Acolyte is unable to reconcile the killing instinct with the desire to love. He is typical of a classic tragic hero whose fatal flaw is his natural empathy for those he destroys. Johnston's man of conscience exhibits those qualities idealized in his earlier plays and typifies the kind of character he would personify in the later works. The 'return to innocence' which Johnston advocates is necessary in order for mankind to survive and entails a resurrection of the belief that mankind is fundamentally sane and, despite evidence to the contrary, i.e. Buchenwald, that there is hope for humanity.

Even though Johnston tries to piece together his former optimism in relation to mankind there are, nevertheless, signs that this hope is conditional, and depends on man's desire to retain a moral and ethical framework which helps to curtail his innate tendency towards self-destruction. Through his discourse with God the Acolyte discovers that his 'maker' is not only capricious and cruel but that he too is a victim to that self same 'pity' with which he has endowed man. Both Creator and creation are reconciled by a mutual acknowledgment and acceptance of this failing. A recognition of this dualism is what saves Johnston from despairing over scenes like those of Buchenwald. Existential questions about the nature of good and evil are, it appears, resolved for Johnston when they are accepted as intrinsically part of life. The tragedy of Buchenwald, Johnston states, is that it epitomizes a society reared without the security of any moral absolutes and therefore whose conscience is inoperative. This loss of moral absolutes is, as he sees it, part of the ongoing acceptance by western man of philosophies that cause man to see himself as devoid of choice, i.e. behaviourism and fatalism, and which, if not stopped, will create more places like Buchenwald. If the concentration camps are the result of a generation taught that life is determined and meaningless then, Johnston states, we need to re-evaluate the whole basis of these deterministic and destructive ideologies. It is important to see that Johnston attributes the inhumanity of Buchenwald to the radical demythologizing of religion by secularists who, in their enthusiasm to rid society of the superstitious nature of faith, fail to replace the moral void they create with any meaningful reason to continue with existence. The proponents of fatalism and behaviourism have not considered, he suggests, what effect the loss of these absolutes might have on the survival of the human race. Buchenwald is the logical consequence of a society bereft of a moral and ethical framework. The absence of moral absolutes makes man's existence and freedom of choice, Johnston argues, seem illusory and this inevitably leads to chaos and anarchy.

Johnston in a discussion with Professor A.J. Ayer, a proponent of logical positivism, said:

... here are many things that it is necessary to believe, in spite of the fact that one knows them not to be true. There are several important topics that it is best to accept, if one wishes to avoid the alternative of suicide. Amongst these I would place an unpragmatic view of social behaviour, a dislike of Determinism, and an insistence that there is some point in being alive. There are strong arguments against all of these eccentricities that are difficult to answer, but had better be wrong.[11]

The conclusions of the behaviourists, Johnston warns, will always be to reduce human thoughts and choices to simply being the result of conditional reflexes. Such speculations, he feared, have a negative effect on society and lead to despair which in turn threatens the continuance of the human race. If, however, man is seen as more than the sum total of his background then, Johnston purports, this will enable him to make choices which will save him from the cycle of retribution and revenge.

Johnston's argument seems to be contradictory. If man is essentially humanitarian then why is it necessary for him to have absolutes? If his nature is a mixture of both good and evil and these traits are guided by reasoning, which is fundamentally altruistic, then why is it important that he should be advised against the possibility of mass destruction? Johnston's reluctance to endorse the findings of behaviourists may be regarded as another facet of his inability to face the possibility that his optimism with regard to humanity is not wholly justified. At Buchenwald Johnston's faith in human nature is shattered and in the aftermath of this event we see him unable to accept fully the horror of the situation and instead he retreats into the realms of philosophy and theology in an effort to redeem his former romantic view of humanity. Mankind is excused from total responsibility by his introduction of the notion of a flawed Creator who is ultimately accountable for the existence of evil. The devil, in this new creed of Johnston's, is the behaviourist who, as he sees it, tempts man to give in to his natural inclination to destroy himself. Mankind is, therefore, saved by fixing its attention on any creed that stops it from annihilation; even if this belief is untrue it will protect humanity from itself.

Johnston's post-Buchenwald works continue to portray warfare in a civilized and dignified manner. Indeed it could be argued that this desire of his to focus on man's innate goodness at times appears to be exaggerated. For instance in his play *The Scythe and the Sunset* both Palliser and Tetley begin to regard each other with such respect that it is, at times, difficult to take their opposition seriously. At the climax of the play they discuss everything from the virtue of good manners, through to war, theology and poetry. The larger issues of death and destruction are sidelined by these almost glib after dinner-type conversations. It is only when Johnston comes to write *The Brazen Horn* that we see the real impact that Buchenwald has had on him. His defensive attitude towards those who would attempt to debunk man's innate sense of goodness, his fear of nuclear annihilation and his desperate search for a religious and scientific basis for believing that man has free will are all indicative of a man who is unable to face the reality of what Yeats terms the 'blood-dimmed tide' ('The Second Coming'). At Buchenwald Johnston witnesses the antithesis of all he believed about man. He is forced to reckon with the horrible truth that man can and does act in ways that are abhorrent and unpalatable to his idealistic view of humanity. In the play *The Moon in the Yellow River* Dobelle, Johnston's cynic, tells Tausch, the optimist, 'in the mists that creep down from the mountains you will meet monsters that glare back at you with your own face.'[12] At Buchenwald Johnston was not expecting to find himself a victim of self-delusion. The monster he encountered there had a human face and could have potentially destroyed all that he held to be sacred. Rather than face the horrendous implications of attributing to mankind the full responsibility of the concentration camps Johnston evades the issue. He redesigns his philosophical perspective on humanity, incorporating into it a religious dimension which appears to deal with the situation but which, in fact, is an act of postponement. The frightening prospect that man was capable of devising and constructing a means of destroying the whole human species with no regard for the sanctity of life was for Johnston too terrible to contemplate.

READING PROTESTANT WRITING: REPRESENTATIONS OF THE TROUBLES IN THE POETRY OF DEREK MAHON AND GLENN PATTERSON'S *BURNING YOUR OWN*

JOHN GOODBY

INTRODUCTION: NOVELISTS, POETS, CRITICS, TROUBLES

The tensions which were to explode in the Troubles dominated Northern Irish literature from the inception of the state. Both explicitly and as its 'unsaid' (in the Machereyan sense) the sectarian basis of society shapes work by authors as different as Sam Hanna Bell, John Boyd and W.R. Rodgers. But while these writers might criticise the abuse of power, major challenges to the structure of the state by the minority had to occur before the cultural implications of sectarianism could be thoroughly understood (the example of John Hewitt and the 1940s Regionalists, who queried these constraints, illustrates the impossibility of overcoming them in a purely cultural sense). Change took a dual form: first, over a relatively lengthy period, through the socio-economic effects of the Welfare State; second, through the political challenge to the status quo posed successively by a restive Protestant working class, O'Neillite reform, the Civil Rights movement and revived nationalism. These accelerated cultural change during the 1960s when Catholic-background writers emerged as part of a progressivist postwar generation which included Seamus Heaney, Stewart Parker, Michael Longley and Derek Mahon. The *zeitgeist* permitted a reshaping of an earlier, rather inflexible, opposition-as-Dissidence (with a socialist spine in Hewitt's case) or of old-style republicanism (elements of which can be discerned in John Montague's *The Rough Field*, for example).

Novelists coped less well with this period of reshaping, and consequently with the Troubles themselves, than the poets. Precisely because of the stronger tradition of fiction writing in the province, they either failed to adapt or did so in predictable ways.[1] More enmeshed with, and subject to, market-driven demands for the staple clichés of 'Irishness', they were perhaps too easily confined to a mixture of subjective lyricism and undemanding realism. 'Serious' fiction's traditional thematic paradigm, a blend of religious and cultural identity, family domination and sexual repression, was pressured and fractured by the events of the early 1970s, such that even the best new writers of the time – Eve Patten instances Jennifer Johnston and Bernard McLaverty – succumbed to 'the compulsive . . . stereotype . . . of the Irish writer defiantly extracting the lyrical moment from tragic inevitability [rather] than . . . engaging with a multi-textured and abstruse society'.[2] The ironic inverse of this failure was a complementary flourishing of what J. Bowyer-Bell has called 'The Troubles as Trash' in the sensationalist genres of Troubles romance, thriller, crime and faction.[3] The division of fictional labour resulted from the difficulty involved in visualising the Troubles in new ways: that is, as anything but an abnormal eruption cutting across 'normal life' (imagined as love or family). The complementary aspect of this can be seen in the way that, unable to present characters as interacting dynamically with the social roots of violence, novelists like Benedict Kiely (in *Nothing Happens at Carmincross* or *Proxopera*), Bernard McLaverty (in *Cal*) and Brian Moore (in *Lies of Silence*) rely on the mechanisms and structures of the thriller in order to achieve conventional fictional closure. As Eamon Hughes has argued, the crucial assumption underlying both types of fiction is that Northern Ireland is 'a fated place of always-unfinished business, static and unresolved . . . The failing of the novel in regard to Northern Ireland is that, by accepting the image of the North as fated, it has not allowed for the interplay of characters, form and circumstances'.[4] Similarly, the stylistic grip of a limited realism was confirmed, along with the general tendency to offer 'a consensual (and usually apolitical) liberal humanist comment on the [Northern Irish] predicament.'[5] It is perhaps worth noting that acceptance of this 'static', 'fated' quality also affects the only full length study of the Northern Irish novel to date, John Wilson Foster's *Forces and Themes in Ulster Fiction*.

Like many liberal humanist stances, those which governed the novel were full of undeclared assumptions – about race/ethnic identities, creed, gender and class. Unwilling to concede the extent to which Northern Irish identity was founded on *difference*, and of the dynamic, evolving relationships this implied, older novelists accepted the division between public and private spheres and hence of what could be deemed 'private' or 'political' in the first place. For those mesmerised by the concept of 'community' – whose conceptual validity was accepted even as its atavistic forms were deplored – these areas were strictly delimited in advance. It was in poetry and drama, and particularly with the emergence of a second 'wave' of Northern Irish poets in the late 1970s, that alternatives began to develop, alternatives also adopted by young novelists in the mid- to late-1980s. With Robert MacLiam Wilson, Glenn Patterson, Danny Morrison and Frances Molloy Troubles fiction emerged which began to address the pervasive violence with the non-moralizing subtlety suitable to a complex modern (and in some respects postmodern) society.

If novelistic representations of the Troubles were initially limited, Northern Irish poetry was distinguished by its potentially flexible and self-critical qualities almost from the outset. During the early and mid-1960s Northern Irish poetry was unusually open to an unusually heterogeneous mixture of influences; English Movement and Group poetics, elements of Ulster Regionalism, the formalism of Frost and Yeats, European aestheticism, a lyrical tradition centred on Trinity College Dublin, UK regionalist populism and others. Certain individuals – Philip Hobsbaum most famously – acted as catalysts, linking Belfast with London and the regional energies of other British cities. The new poetry was conservative to begin with (strong conservative strains remain to this day). But the overdetermined variousness of the blend and the talents of the better poets involved soon enabled the exploration of a new set of literary possibilities within a singularly unexploited 'cultural ecology', to use Terence Brown's phrase. This was a dual process; the 'cultural ecology,' as it were, also began to explore the well-made lyric. The eventual result of this was a radical mutation of the conservative inheritance in the work of the generation which included Tom Paulin, Paul Muldoon, Medbh McGuckian and Ciaran Carson.[6] With these poets the Northern Irish situation is seen from a markedly anti-insular point of view, identity is revealed as based on difference and fixed positions are eschewed in favour of a metamorphic pluralist approach.

The feeling that, as Heaney put it, Northern Irish writers 'lived / In important places,'[7] led to widespread critical interest in their work. Predictably, most of the criticism has centred on the poetry; even more than in most western literary cultures, Irish poetry carries the burden of being a distillation of significant utterance and poets may be attributed a vatic or divinatory role which would seem incongruous, even ludicrous, in many other societies. Like the effects of a Northern Irish 'cultural ecology' on poetic form, this has been a two-way process; certain kinds of critical reading have had an effect on the work of younger poets in particular. Thus while most criticism has explored the extent to which poets had a public duty to represent the experience of their communities and the ways in which it clashed with essential human and/or other political and aesthetic values, poetic reactions to such assumptions have changed massively between generations. Although the origins of the Belfast Group did not coincide chronologically with those of the Troubles, the 1960s generation of poets accepted a complexly mediated link between both phenomena and postwar change. This takes on the force of an historical and moral imperative in their work, all the more powerful when (as often) it is negatively expressed. But such a commitment to representation, either in a political-moral or aesthetic sense, was by no means allowed by those who followed them. Criticism (like poetry itself) may be defined according to this dual issue of representation, and be seen to assume three main forms. The first might be dubbed the 'radical conservative'; it emerged with the poetry, and up to a point is its own self-consciousness and self-advocacy (the house journal was, and to some extent still is, *The Honest Ulsterman* magazine). With a New Critical eye for close reading and a Leavisite moral passion, this criticism championed the empirical, discursive and 'well-made' against the abstract and experimental, viewing the business of poetry as a struggle for essential human values in embattled times. As with Leavis himself a social dimension was allowed, but in a subordinate capacity; unlike Leavis (whose problems with Modernism were in any case legion) Modernist aestheticism was dismissed – art's autonomy was best preserved by being packed in the 'ancient salt' of formal metrics. At its blandest this stance takes the form of Frank Ormsby's Preface to *A Rage for Order: Poetry of the Northern Ireland Troubles* (1992), which advocates 'the affirmative thrust' of a poetry which is 'sturdily and enhancingly alive' – sentiments difficult to reconcile with the apocalyptic meditations of Mahon, let alone Muldoon. (The growing disparity between a complacent criticism and an increasingly disturbed poetry can be seen in the brickbats Heaney's *North* attracted, as well as in the attempts to label Muldoon 'heartless' or to recuperate his work for bourgeois humanism.) The strength of this tradition lies in its insistence on close attention to the text as well as its unrivalled insider knowledge. Yet although it gives a powerful sense of the way poets work within a given tradition its commitments to pluralism and tolerance are belied by a consistently intolerant tone and unpluralist failure to examine its own philosophical and political presuppositions.[8]

Balancing criticism which often slides into a neo-loyalist position (the 'apolitical' argument inevitably acts as an apology at some level for the Northern Irish *status quo*) is that which might be labelled, with some inevitable simplifications, as its neo-nationalist mirror image. More theoretically aware than its opponent, it has broken with Leavisite/New Criticism and the valorization of the well-made lyric. In particular, it has insisted on reading Northern Irish writing in the context of the history of the state and its formation. Despite its taste for theory however, Marxist (or class-based) and feminist models are noticeable by their absence. Seamus Deane, representative in this as in much else, is the author of at least one revealing anti-socialist outburst, as well as the more notorious and public exclusion of women's writing from the *Field Day Anthology*. Both blindnesses demonstrate neo-nationalism's inability to escape its petit-bourgeois ideology, with its touchstones of an undifferentiated 'Irish people' and national unity as the end of politics. Deane and Declan Kiberd exemplify the backward-looking paradigm in their criticism of Northern poetry for failing to rise to the demands of the Troubles conceived in terms of 1916–1923 (in this schema Mahon and Paulin become Fanon's 'colonizers who refuse,' while Michael Longley and other 'second wave' poets are marginalized or misconstrued).[9] Thus, while such criticism uses recent theory, the strains of adapting its most radical variants to a traditionalist template of national and individual autonomy is often all too evident.

Finally, a strain of criticism has emerged over the last decade which would seem to be better equipped to deploy theory by virtue of its outsider detachment and greater expertise. Certainly a book such as *The Chosen Ground* (1992) marks an advance on traditionalist efforts and shows how the grip of categories drawn from a sectarian sociology may be weakened. While there are certain limits to its radicalism – there is no use of the work of Northern Irish Marxist historians Paul Bew and Henry Patterson, for instance – *The Chosen Ground* clearly shows the benefits of an awareness of poststructuralism and gender politics. If there are problems with these approaches they are related to the lack of a class and political awareness hinted at, a lack which may lead to a guiltily post-imperial, uncritical identification with nationalist or republican positions, or a conflation of these with a radical politics. In addition, there are a number of neo-Stalinist, cultural materialist or Gramscian Marxist readings of poetry. These run from Stan Smith's *Inviolable Voice* (1982), with its dismissal of Longley and Mahon as 'shell-shocked Georgians,' via David Cairns's and Shaun Richards's conflation of class and national categories in the otherwise excellent *Writing Ireland* (1988), to David Lloyd's *Anomalous States* (1993) in which Heaney is damned as 'minor' and 'bourgeois' – a judgement whose moralist lack of sophistication hardly needs to be laboured.[10] Yet despite the simplifications (and often downright wrongness) of this third group, it has at least revealed the extent to which the first two share assumptions about the inviolability of the poem-as-artefact and 'authenticity', and critically naive positions on organic form and a unitary speaking voice. In doing so they have made it possible to raise questions of religion, class and gender difference which did not figure in the older critical scheme of things, albeit in the wake of writers who have long been in the business of deconstruction.

PROTESTANT HISTORY, PROTESTANT TROUBLES

To explore the question of intra-communal, class and gender differences raised here I want to focus on two Protestant-background writers; the 1960s-generation poet Derek Mahon (b. 1941) and the novelist Glenn Patterson (b. 1962), whose first novel appeared in 1988. There are four main reasons for this choice. The first is the intensity of the repression of these elements in Protestant writing, and the problems of self-representation faced by Protestants (the lack of women writers from this background, for example, is symptomatic of more than one kind of repression).[11] The second, related to this, is the relative weakness of the identification of the majority of Protestant writers not only with their 'community', but increasingly with the notion of community as such (another way of putting this is to say that Protestant writers did not feel under the same obligation to express a long-suppressed ethnic identity as did writers from Catholic backgrounds, a tendency connected with what W.J.

McCormack has described as the Anglo-Irish literary view of its tradition as a kind of betrayal).[12] Third is the simple lack of critical accounts of the development of writing by Protestants in Northern Ireland, or of attempts to relate this to the development of the Troubles. The fourth relates to the way in which Protestant writing has been a hidden influence on other, more widely discussed authors (I will argue that it is precisely the difficulties facing Protestant writers – self-censorship and relative invisibility – which have led some of them to explore new ways of writing about the Troubles).

The characteristic features of Ulster Protestantism have, of course, been listed many times. They include a 'frontier society' mentality (and accompanying ambivalent regard for the rule of law), hyper-patriotism, a unity which ferociously represses dissidence or channels it into sectarian forms, and a general insecurity (the result of a sense of being multiply besieged). As John Wilson Foster points out, the cost of communal and state integrity is often, paradoxically, a profound 'lack of wholeness' for individuals, 'an uneasy acceptance of our usurpation' and the essentialization of the Catholic, who must be made 'inescapably Other'.[13] The lack of a self-critical Northern Irish Protestant response to the crisis of the state – in sociology, history, politics – put the onus for self-understanding on literature. The absence is linked to an ingrained, purist image of the chosen people backed both by Protestantism and by the exclusive Whig idea of liberty as a radical phenomenon. Despite radical pretensions this liberty has historically operated only within the presbytery, not beyond it: as Terence Brown argues, the myth of Protestant unity is 'disabling in the political sphere since all political possibilities are subordinated to the basic determination to maintain the historically authenticated resistance.'[14] Unity is only apparent, of course, as the class dynamics of Protestant politics since 1968 shows. In both Paisleyism and paramilitary Loyalism a working-class animus against grandee Unionism is apparent, but deflected from political positions which would threaten existing structures of wealth and power. Both can be read, somewhat mechanically, as sublimated (but ineffectual) forms of class protest sup-plementing the potentially treacherous ruling class and British-reliant state. One effect of the reactionary cast of Protestant politics (particularly working-class politics) has been to recommend alternative sources of critical and subversive energies to younger writers, particularly those of gender and sexual transgression.

DEREK MAHON: STATES OF SIEGE

(a) The Protestant Poet: Self-Editing and Censorship

Michael Longley has said that it wasn't until he met Seamus Heaney that he 'realised there was an invisible apartheid in our community' – a sentence in which one can see words like 'our' and 'community' straining to resist the narrower definitions implicit in Heaney's famous quest for symbols adequate to 'our' predicament. To Mahon's and Longley's liberal Protestant generation, the intransigence of Unionism and the Loyalist backlash came as a negative enlightenment (a political realization which, as Longley's comment indicates, took place in an appropriately *literary* context). Mahon's alienation from his background is, from the first, more marked than Longley's, while his distance from the Hobsbaum Group is a matter of record.[15] Indeed, in his work the failure of Unionism becomes, for a time, the pretext for questioning the postwar Western social consensus as such. The typical Mahon poem hovers between MacNeice's unquiet tourist's vision and that of Beckett's minimalist existentialism, and the contradictory responses to Modernism these allegiances suggest are of the essence of his work. In Freudian terms the struggle is between a sublimation of repression by identifying with an artistic community distinguished by purity and excess – Van Gogh, Villon, De Quincey, De Nerval – and the unreasonable, purgative self-hatred of the speaker of a poem such as 'Ecclesiastes'. One way of examining the double response is by aligning Mahon's work with contemporary cultural and social developments and the terms of Freud's essay on 'Negation':

[T]he content of a repressed image or idea can make its way into consciousness, on condition that it is *negated*. Negation is a way of taking cognizance of what is repressed; indeed it is already a lifting of the repression, though not, of course, an acceptance of what is repressed. We can see in this how the intellectual function is separated from the affective process. With the help of negation only one consequence of the process of repression is undone – the fact, namely, of the ideational content of what is being repressed not reaching consciousness. The outcome of this is a kind of intellectual acceptance of the repressed, while at the same time what is essential to the repression persists.[16]

In the early 1970s, as the equilibrium between repression and negated expression was disturbed by the slide towards civil war, Mahon began to take the Troubles more overtly as his theme. If, for Heaney, violence was that which would ('ineffably' and abjectly) be suffered, for Mahon it was inescapably that something which had been carried out in his name and which, at one level, he had inflicted – even if (as in 'Last of the Fire Kings') he would rather fall on his sword than turn it on another. Internalised violence became the 'desperate ironies' of 'Rage for Order', in which the speaker is 'far from his people ... tearing down / to build up with a desperate love'. The process finds its most blackly parodic expression in 'Matthew V. 29–30'. The poem's speaker begins with his text – 'Lord, mine eye offended, so I plucked it out' – but is compelled to progress, according to the logic of the Biblical injunction, to destroy his entire body, records of existence, the minds of those in whom he is remembered, those to whom they are connected, and eventually the entire universe. Only with the entire material universe erased does the voice conclude that he is 'fit for human society.' The savage, monomaniac inventiveness of the attack derives from a sublimation of repressed divisions within the community of the chosen (although it would be unwise to overlook the comedy of the procedure, self-punishment is the point).

A poem such as 'Matthew V. 29–30' may be taken to signal a rejection of the flesh, stigmatised as female, subversive and sinful by patriarchy. There are few women in Mahon's early poetry; 'A Mythological Figure', an exception to the rule, offers a female figure as a symbol of a peculiar kind of repression. This figure is condemned to sing whenever she tries to speak. Purely 'natural', like a bird, she is simultaneously made fluent 'as a mountain stream' and excluded from the discursive realm defined by patriarchy, since 'her songs were without words, / Or the words without meaning – / Like the cries of love or the cries of mourning.' Little needs to be said about linkages between sex, death and female inarticulacy; Mahon's own 'The Death of Marilyn Monroe' hymns the quintessential modern example, even if the figure is a type for the marginalized poet. What is interesting is the way this points towards the role gender plays in Mahon's self-censorship and the way it is connected to his representations of violence.

But repression operates at a formal as well as at a thematic level in Mahon's poetry. His commitment to traditionalist verse forms (one of the 'conditions' of Freudian negation which permits expression of the content of the 'repressed image or idea' in the first place) enforces a continual, repressive self-revision. It is a critical commonplace that poems are never finished, merely abandoned; even so, Mahon is a notorious reviser of his work.

Many of his poems have appeared in several finished versions, suggesting parallels between textual struggle and the thematics of self-punishment; I want to look at two such poems with the question of gender in mind.

The first of these is 'Afterlives' from *The Snow Party* (1975). The revision is of the fourth stanza, and involves an attack on liberal Protestant identity in which the repressed charges of gender (and class) are realized only to be denied:

> What middle-class cunts we are
> To imagine for one second
> That our privileged ideals
> Are divine wisdom, and the dim
> Forms that kneel at noon
> In the city not ourselves.[17]

The effect of this crudeness is complex. Mahon's shock tactic covers several concerns – class betrayal; the aesthete figured as (ultimate male insult) the female genitalia; bitterness at the idealism of those naive meliorists among whom the poet numbers himself. The inter-involvement of the unsaid, repressed areas of gender and, to a lesser extent, class – their confusion with, and hidden disruption of, mythic unity – is revealed fleetingly here. Repression is 'lifted' through the insult, but only in a form (aggressively proletarian) which ensures its non-'acceptance' by the poetry-reading 'middle-class' reader. In its ugly, sexist self-hatred this moment is true to the motives of the homecoming speaker, his addressee (James Simmons) and the Troubles in their most vicious phase. Yet in the *Selected Poems* of 1991 'cunts' has become 'twits'. The effect is to conceal the self-loathing produced by a politics of suppressed difference which the original version revealed even as it colluded with them. What was genuinely provocative has been rendered bathetic, almost silly.

In one sense the failure of the revision points to the self-defeating nature of all revisions. In this it resembles the more drastic 'revisions' carried out in 'Matthew V. 29-30'; the more the poet attempts to finalise meaning the more he destabilises it. What is the poem's definitive version? The irony is that continual revision makes textual authority weaker, not stronger. More importantly, Mahon's procedures reveal a violent instability inherent in the text which mimics the violence from which, as aesthetic object, the poem claimed detachment even as it recognized the Troubles.

(b) Cleanliness is Next to Godliness: 'Courtyards in Delft'

To further develop these points I want to look at another, more elaborate, example of Mahon's revisions. 'Courtyards in Delft' appeared as the title poem of a 1980 pamphlet. It was incorporated into *The Hunt by Night* in 1982 and subsequently reappeared nine years later in *Selected Poems*. Between 1982 and 1991 it was also printed in Paul Muldoon's *The Faber Book of Contemporary Irish Poetry* (1986) and the *Penguin Book of Contemporary Irish Poetry* (1990), co-edited by Mahon himself with Peter Fallon. In these eleven years the piece has enjoyed a chequered history. The earliest version concluded:

> I lived there as a boy and know the coal
> Glittering in its shed, late-afternoon
> Lambency informing the deal table,
> The ceiling cradled in a radiant spoon.
> I must be lying low in a room there,
> A strange child with a taste for verse,
> While my hard-nosed companions dream of war
> On parched veldt and fields of rain-swept gorse.

For publication in *The Hunt by Night*, however, an additional verse was provided:

> For the pale light of that provincial town
> Will spread itself, like ink or oil,
> Over the not yet accurate linen
> Map of the world which occupies one wall
> And punish nature in the name of God.
> If only, now, the Maenads, as of right,
> Came smashing crockery, with fire and sword,
> We could sleep easier in our beds at night.[18]

The new verse was kept for the Faber and Penguin anthologies, but dropped from the 1991 *Selected Poems*. In that volume the once-again-last, fourth verse was changed to include something of the lost fifth verse; its final lines now read 'While my hard-nosed companions dream of fire / And sword upon parched veldt and fields of rain-swept gorse' ('fire and sword' presumably keep the specific imperial locations suggested by 'veldt' and 'rain-swept gorse' and retain something of the apocalyptic flavour of the deleted verse).

So why the changes of mind? The rest of the poem hints at conflicts which might be responsible. The title of 'Courtyards in

Delft' comes from the Dutch genre painter Pieter de Hooch's series
of courtyard paintings. Yet the location of the poem is not fixed: it
moves, after the opening verse, to works by other Dutch painters;
traces of Vermeer, Metsu and Steen can be discerned. The effect is
of a meditation on a representative, composite Golden Age
painting which Mahon has assembled to suit his critical purposes.
The scene the first verse establishes, the backyard of a Dutch
middle class house, is straight from one of De Hooch's pictures.
The second verse tells us what the painting is not (either an
allegorical or low-life interior; the domestic space is defined by its
position between these extremes).[19] Its last line insists that 'We
miss the dirty dog, the fiery gin', hinting at 'excluded lust, chaos
and ruin' and at the pressures to rebel which bourgeois existence
may engender.[20] The third verse, like Keats' 'Ode on a Grecian
Urn', meditates on the relative timelessness of the art object
through the figure of the girl who will wait in the corridor for 'her
man to come home for his tea' until the paint disintegrates, at
which stage the Netherlands themselves will be destroyed as
'ruined dykes admit the esurient sea.' 'Yet this is life too', the
verse insists – that 'yet' a reference back to the 'trite' surroundings
being depicted, but also, albeit grudgingly, to a manner of
representation. The painting's details, like those of Mahon's poem,
'are life too', made up – tautologously, as reflections are – of
'verifiable facts'.

The scene is set for the fourth verse in which the speaker enters
the painting through memories of his childhood, and generalizes
his bohemian disdain to anti-imperialist critique. Here the violent
obverse of Protestant cleanliness and work ethics is drawn by
aligning England/Ireland and The Netherlands/South Africa. The
connections between the apparently inoffensive qualities of
cleanliness and sobriety and colonial violence are teased out.[21] If
the 'glittering' coal and 'late-afternoon / Lambency' show that the
ironic 'oblique light' of the opening cannot completely dissolve
the aura of childhood memory, the ambiguity of that light clearly
also provides the cue for the supplementary verse in which it is
threatening, destructive. Here the suggestive indictment is
widened to include all post-Enlightenment culture; the 'map of the
world' is a tool of imperial expansion, of utilitarian measurement,
as well as a wall decoration. Like Protestant hegemony in Ulster it
is backed by 'linen'; its 'pale light' will spread over the globe 'like
ink or oil', the twin liquids which fuel indirect and direct
domination over 'nature' (which is also the colonizers' own
human nature) while the 'natural' natives are 'punished . . . in the

name of God'.[22] The ambiguous representation of the 'facts' of the painting suggests a complex awareness of the double nature of progress. Edna Longley identifies something of this in her claim that 'the [fourth] stanza's proto-poet signifies how this way of life, this way of art might incubate its opposite: a Munch, a Mahon.'[23] But this is true only in the limited, artist-as-rebel sense; what the poem also hints at is the more difficult truth that the poetry of 'a Mahon' and the wars waged by his society are not separate but a division of labour within (Protestant) capitalist societies, one stemming from their class nature. Those who 'dream of war' are, in one sense, 'my companions'. Mahon thus aligns the poet with the specialists of Weber's *The Protestant Ethic and the Spirit of Capitalism*. However, if he allows this rather deterministic reading of events, the poem's dialectical awareness also recalls Adorno and Horkheimer's *Dialectic of Enlightenment* since (as its form shows) it attacks 'instrumental reason' rather than rationality as such.

The origins of the supplementary final verse, then, lie in the light/Enlightenment imagery of the previous four verses and their studied restraint. The verse makes explicit and self-punishing what was guiltily suggestive, and in this sense it recalls 'Matthew V. 29–30' and 'Afterlives'. Paradoxically it is the addition rather than the subtraction of material which is intended to purify the poem in this case, clarifying the link between culture and violence, and critiquing the aesthetic even as the poem as a whole embodies it in typically shapely form. But in achieving this aim Mahon changes and perhaps compromises the poem's relationship to its subject, invoking an excess which mimics the violence it ostensibly opposes. The additional verse might be said to fruitfully complicate things by allowing the reader a choice of symbolic and allegorical interpretations, as in 'A Disused Shed in Co. Wicklow'. But there are also difficulties. These are apparent if we consider a passage from Mahon's article 'Poetry in Northern Ireland', published in 1970:

The poets themselves have taken no part in political events, but they have contributed to that possible life, or to the possibility of the possible life; for the act of writing is itself political in the fullest sense. A good poem is a paradigm of good politics – of people talking to each other, with honest subtlety, at a profound level.[24]

The passage has been cited by Edna Longley as approving the doctrine that 'Poetry and politics, like church and state, should be separated': that art, in other words, gestures towards an aesthetic

paradigm of the 'possible life' beyond present division. I have
already suggested the ways in which this conflict-resolving
interpretation echoes the belief of critics that art has a communal
function – echoing 'people talking to each other' – and it is of a
piece with Longley's attempts elsewhere to invoke the 'therapeutic,
aesthetic realm' a little too readily to overcome Mahon's historical
unease. Certainly the use of Mahon's work to illustrate the
political inviolability of poetry finds its complement in Seamus
Deane's attempt to bracket the Mahon of *The Snow Party* with
Montague and Heaney in *Celtic Revivals*. Deane rightly detects the
way in which Mahon's work has been misread – taken as a whole
it clearly does not conform to liberal humanist formulae.[25] The
problem is that this insight, as in Longley, is used as the occasion
for suppressing the differences which so obviously haunt the
poetry. In a passage as remarkable for its animus to the idea of
class, even its self-loathing, as for the light it sheds on Mahon,
Deane claims:

A recognition of the depths from which violence springs often leads to
feelings of dismay at the apparent shallowness of the liberal or rational
mentality. Mahon's contempt for the modern socialist, the professional
tourist who visits and measures everything and knows nothing, the
expert locked in his own force-field, is inexhaustible. Such a creature is
indeed one of the products of secular civility. Emotionally gelded, he
cannot know the lust for history or the grief of utter loss which the
instinctual life knows.[26]

Nevertheless the general rejection of liberalism points to the way
in which revisions such as those to 'Courtyards in Delft' register
an oscillation between the desire for consensus and a more radical
late-Modernist aesthetic which helps explain the self-accusations
of the poetry. To some extent, then, 'Courtyards' enacts the critical
differences I have sketched out; but it also attempts, through its
supplement, to find ground beyond it in a radically anti-humanist
gesture – the eruption of the mythic and poet-dismembering
Maenads into the rationally reflective space of the poem. The
Maenads are a pagan rebuke to what has been done in 'the name
of God', transmogrified versions of the 'wives / Of artisans' of the
first verse, and they represent the return of the repressed in both a
political and aesthetic sense. But they are, crucially, *female* figures
of retribution (poetic precursors include Rimbaud's 'Bacchantes
des banlieus' and Shelley's fierce Maenads); and so, as in
'Afterlives' – although in a figural way – a crisis in representation
brings about violence gendered as female.[27]

Significantly *The Hunt by Night* as a collection represents a move
to include female figures in the previously male-dominated world
and repressions of Mahon's poetry.[28] Yet if the female Maenads
owe something to this shift, their function accords far more with
an older masculine urge to self-punishment. The over-explicitness
of the verse, which mimics the violence the poem has already
condemned, may therefore be behind its later disappearance.
Similarly, it could also be argued that the verse is suspect because
it aestheticises its violence by investing the poet with the kind of
mythical afflatus Mahon usually debunks, most notably in 'Lives'.
In terms of the politics of representations, the sudden switch to a
non-realistic order – while it marks a rupture with the hypocrisies
of the surface, of keeping up bourgeois appearances – might not
seem wholly convincing. (In an art historical sense the leap at this
point is from Dutch realism – and reliance on the visible – to the
Italian Mannerism and neoclassicism which were its contemporary antithesis.)[29] There is, moreover, something more than
faintly risible about figures of classical mythology 'smashing
crockery, with fire and sword'; hints of plates being smashed at
the end of a meal in a Greek restaurant, perhaps. And while
mocking his hubristic desire for punishment may have been part
of Mahon's intention, it may also have seemed to have run counter
to the gravity deemed appropriate for the poem's critique of
western power and culture.

The fate of the last verse is thus related to Mahon's career and
the transitional nature of the cultural dominant within which the
poem was written. Like the early poetry of McGuckian and
Muldoon, 'Courtyards in Delft' falls between a Modernist vision
of history as alienation and an incipient, never-quite-realised
postmodern one in which history is not 'the great / Adventure we
suppose', but instead 'some elaborate / Spectacle put on for fun /
And not for food'. To return to Freud, the irony of Mahon's work
up to the late 1970s is the form of negation in which only one kind
of consequence of the process of repression is undone. In order to
ironically preserve a negatively-defined identity the 'ideational
content' of what is being repressed is allowed to reach
consciousness in a poem like 'Afterlives', while its affective roots –
in gender, sexuality, class – tend to be revealed only occasionally
and tortuously (and it is precisely this effort to 'unsay' in his work
which critical labour ought to strive to reveal). 'Courtyards in
Delft' admits some of these disruptive elements, although at the
risk of dissolving the exclusory drive for authentication in
playfulness. In its supplemented version the poem hovers

discontentedly at the edge of redefining the relationship between *gemeinschaft* and *gesellschaft*, the private and the political. Older allegiances led Mahon to eventually confirm a suggestive, (neo)Modernist-symbolist ending, but the extra verse hints at that combination of symbolic and allegoric modes mentioned earlier which has been his peculiar contribution to a kind of postmodernism – adapted to Irish circumstances – used by successor poets.

GLENN PATTERSON – DUMPS AND CARNIVALS: *BURNING YOUR OWN*

If class and gender are sublimated in Derek Mahon's poetry, the threat they pose becomes in Glenn Patterson's work an alternative to both communal stereotypes and to the ideals of purity and perfection on which neomodernism is built – ideals of the sort ironised, but relatively undeconstructed in Mahon's poetry. Significantly, Patterson has written of 'the often sterile and unimaginative fictional representations of my own country', glimpsing positive possibilities in the urban Troubles experience.[30] He acknowledges Ciaran Carson as an influence; both are Belfast writers who share a vision of the city as *process*, rather than as static site of exile, poisoned land, or divided territory. For both the city embodies change, its checkpoints and strictly defined zones contrasting with its mongrel blendings of memories, desires, identities and narratives. Although sharing Mahon's interest in ironic displacement, Patterson, as Eve Patten points out, 'purposefully transcends it in order to address issues of identity through a restorative fictional anthropology'.[31]

Burning Your Own deals with the growing pains of a ten year-old Protestant boy, Mal Martin, in the summer of 1969. It ends on August 15th, with British troops arriving on the streets of Belfast. Mal lives in the mainly Protestant working class estate of Larkview on the edge of the city, and the novel interweaves the crumbling of Unionist hegemony with lesser breakdowns – of parental authority, Mal's parents' marriage, and Mal's relationship with his ethnic peer group. The alternative to these is embodied in Francy Hagan, a fourteen-year-old Catholic whose friendship Mal seeks, and with whom he finally identifies. The narrative revolves around the 'burning' of the novel's title, one which hints at Mahonesque self-punishment. But Patterson details the inwardly-directed violence without neomodernist detachment or a striving for transcendent resolution. Significantly, I feel, considering the importance of class to the book, Patterson has given the composition of *Burning Your Own* an English as well as an Irish context, explaining how it was written in England at the time of the 1984–5 miners' strike.

An awareness of class and his urban realism places Patterson in the Protestant urban novel tradition. But although limitedly realist in style *Burning Your Own* is very different from the work of other city novelists, from the 'progressive bookmen' to Brian Moore and after. Belfast is seen in this novel neither as the locus of depravity and poverty, nor as the passive background against which individual destinies are pursued; most importantly, unlike earlier Troubles fictions, this one does not attempt to make the Troubles articulate some universal human condition. This is clear in the way its central character – a child – refuses to be read as symbolic of innocence in the face of bigotry and violence. The riven and contradictory nature of Protestant self and society is encoded in Mal; an uncertain newcomer to the estate, his chief desire at the start of the novel is to be accepted by the Larkview gang. He accepts the petty bullying which passes for initiation into the gang, a microcosm of a society and family summed up in the catch-phrase 'you'll be sorry'.[32] But his very name catches at a marginal and uncertain status; 'Mal' is an abbreviation of Malachy, a name which Mr Martin had insisted should appear in its shortened form on the birth certificate because, as Mrs Martin says, he is 'Terrified people will think he's Catholic when if you had an ounce of education you'd know the name's Hebrew'.[33]

'Mal', then, stands for Malachy but has been shortened so that it suggests 'Malcolm', a more orthodox Protestant name. (The importance of misinterpreted names can be gauged by the fact that the possession of a 'Catholic' name, and subsequent bullying at school, has been cited as a reason for the psychopathic anti-Catholicism of Lenny Murphy, the leader of the Shankill Butchers).[34] The ability of the name to signal more than intended is further elaborated in the other, unofficial initiation Mal goes through with Francy: 'Malarkey, Malakos, Malcontent... Malentendu, Malevolent, Malfeasance, Malformation, Malfunction ... Malice, Malign, Malignant... Malingering, Malison, Malleable, Malemaroking Martin – hereinafter, Mal du Siècle, Malkin the Ill, The Great Malacophilous...'.[35] 'Mal', in other words, is 'bad' in refusing the identity of 'his' community for identification with Francy. The process of going over isn't a seamless one; Mal betrays Francy when he sides with Andy against two Catholic boys who want to join in a football game, and by coining the epithet 'Derrybeggars'. But unwilling though he is, Mal embodies the possibility of rejecting – as well as the need to be included within – imposed communal identities.

Mal's instability runs through his family and the estate as a whole. Mr Martin is an ineffectual father; unemployed, given to embroidering his past and to blaming others for his problems. The culmination of his weakening authority occurs, appropriately enough, near the Eleventh Night bonfire. As it collapses Mr Martin drunkenly mocks the fifteen-year-old Mucker's previous boasts about the size of the fire. Mucker knocks him down, adding, 'Don't talk to me about failure, mister, for you're the biggest failure ever drew breath as sure as I'm standing here.'[36] After lugging her husband home, Mrs Martin leaves him, taking Mal off to her brother's house. The fact that this happens immediately after Big Bobby's injunction to 'have no fighting among ourselves' underscores the point about communal division. But the point is not a simple one. Mucker's action, which at this stage can be read as part of a general Protestant shift from the Unionist grandees to a younger plebeian, hardline Loyalist leadership, acquires a different content when we discover later that he has been secretly associating with Francy and has been rejected by 'the Lodge'. Complex interaction and interdependency is the rule rather than the exception; thus Mal's (Protestant) Uncle Simon is in charge of the extension of the Catholic area of Derrybeg towards Larkview, and after he is given a job on the site by his brother-in-law Mr Martin comes under local pressure to allow the work to be sabotaged. Mucker, in turn, is framed for the sabotage. The sequence illustrates the way in which, as violence intensifies, dissent and difference become more difficult to maintain. Identity is now defined absolutely by exclusion. Mal comes to see the idea that sectarianism can be bypassed as a middle-class delusion; after Mucker is framed he realises that 'what he hadn't seen was how easy it was to think such things up there at his aunt and uncle's house, with its patio and breakfast bar and long, long garden . . . Whatever didn't fit in got excluded; that's what it boiled down to'.[37] Armed with this insight he breaks with family and communal loyalties.

If a togetherness based on ignoring difference is no real togetherness, Patterson also shows histories are made rather than essential. 'Surfaces', as Mal notes, 'could fool you'.[38] The novel foregrounds contradictions (some of which may escape Mal himself) in order to reveal threats to even the most secure identities. On the one hand we are reminded of the contradictory history which preceded the Troubles; the chapel supposedly destroyed by King Billy is revealed by Francy to be less than a hundred years old.[39] The incident is typical of the way in which origins are demythicised in Patterson's work. On the other hand, particular stylistic and fictional tactics unknown to the older forms of realism are used to weave excluded histories and elements of the fantastic together with more humdrum material to provide a multiple vision of Northern Irish society. In this way we are reminded of the (albeit) slim chances for advance provided by Belfast's optimistic expansion in a speech given by Francy as he casually makes a 'ratcharm' from a dead rat.[40] The construction and limited ethnic mix of Larkview stand for aspects of the wider postwar growth and social consensus in Britain, of which Northern Ireland was only part: passages with a deliberate epic and all-inclusive sweep detail the massive labour of building the estate and list the areas the new tenants came from:

They came from everywhere: from Newtonards Road, Beersbridge Road and Ballymacarrett in the east; from Ardoyne, the Oldpark, Legoniel, in the north; from Ormeau, Annadale, Sandy Row, the Village, in the south; and in the west from Shankill, Springfield, Woodvale – aye, and even a few from the Falls and Whiterock Road.[41]

The symbolic weight carried by Patterson's incremental, realist technique here alerts us to the way the novel also includes symbolic elements which exceed realistic requirements. Patterson has written that the 'single most important factor' in setting the novel in Northern Ireland was *Midnight's Children*'s treatment of countries as collective fictions.[42] The terminology, which recalls that of Benedict Anderson's *Imaginary Communities*, should remind us that while Rushdie's influence is not too obvious, trace elements of magic realism do feature in *Burning Your Own*. The dump and Francy himself are the best examples. Francy's dump – once the estate's omphalos, but also 'its arse-end' – is between Larkview and encroaching Derrybeg. It is described realistically, but also in a way which suggests its status as the estate's alter ego or repressed, a zone of temporary ambivalence, even possibility, between polarised opposites. On his first visit to the dump Mal is intrigued by the way his view of the estate has been changed. Its seeming order now appears chaotic: 'He lived here, but he did not recognize this place, could not reconcile the jumble with the neatly hedged rows he walked through day to day'.[43] The actual instability of Larkview is made visible within the other order of the world of the dump, a fact which Francy, its ruler, has long understood. Later Mal too comes to see that the chaotic vision of the estate is the true one. The dump operates differently to the outside world. '"Lesson number ... whatever: their rules" – [Francy] jerked a thumb vaguely over his shoulder – "stop at the fence. When they dumped that, it ceased to mean anything other than what I wanted it to mean."'[44] The dump, then, has the occult power of disorientating those unused to it; known landmarks disappear, and Mal gets lost on his second visit. Its sheer weirdness may partly be a function of Mal's youth (the dump has one antecedent in the children's classic *Stig of the Dump*), but we become progressively less sure: 'Who'd have believed it was real? ... "there you are," Francy said cryptically. "The real secret's believing. Most people find nothing, because nothing's what they expect to find."'[45] At the end of the novel the dump cannot preserve itself as 'a collective fiction' against external forces. As Francy himself insists in his final despair: 'It's all lies – the hut, the dump, everything'.[46]

With Mal as his protagonist Patterson can hint at the fantastic while remaining faithful to an undemonstrative 'Protestant' realism. Like one of Foucault's heterotopias (as distinct from a utopia), the dump is a space which is 'absolutely different' from the society it speaks about, but which is nevertheless inseparably linked to it. (According to Foucault societies maintain themselves by *incorporating* these 'other spaces' within which their ideologies may be contested, travestied and inverted.)[47] Heterotopias are of two types: those which create real spaces, imbued with order, intended to offset the chaotic nature of reality, and those which create an illusory space for the purposes of critique. Francy's dump, as we have seen, certainly inverts Mal's notions of order *vis à vis* the estate. But in doing so – and given the imminence of the Troubles – it is clearly also a critical space which frames the novel, the site of Francy's opening appearance and of his final spectacular immolation. As the originating site for Larkview the dump symbolises Ulster Protestantism's attempt to ignore its own raw ideological origins, and the way in which the work of repression falters under the pressure of fresh sectarian violence. Stuck between Larkview and Derrybeg it can only function briefly as a meeting point for Catholic and Protestant, and only for disaffected, marginalized representatives at that. The end of the novel makes it clear that any positive moment accompanying the breakdown of old certainties has passed. Alluding to the ancestor worship which underlies sectarian identity, the gloating epitaph for Francy refers the reader back to Big Bobby's father's urn, the 'spiturn' into which Francy gobs, and which he brandishes at the close of his mock(ing) auction.[48] Finally, the disintegration of society is symbolised in the literal dismemberment of Francy and the epitaph he receives; breakdown is now wholly malign: 'Even in the light of early morning the letters were burning white against the creosoted wood. Two feet high and still dripping. "FRANCY HAGAN", they read. "REST IN PIECES."'[49]

The contesting of sectarian spaces and identities is also pursued in gender terms. *Burning Your Own* has an Oedipal subtext, but is about a crisis of maleness in a larger sense. Allon White and Peter Stallybrass have argued that the process of self-fashioning, in which sexual identity plays such a large part, is one in which 'what is socially peripheral is often symbolically central'.[50] Mal's unformed male sexuality allows social proprieties to be explored and rebellion to find a form. Sexual symbolism underlies the narrative; the burning of the phallic centrepole of the bonfire by Mucker, in cahoots with Francy, is one example. Mal's own growing sexual awareness is linked to his revolt, taking taboo forms as it shifts from a girl from school, to his cousins and – in a milder form of Saleem Sinai's progress in *Midnight's Children* – to his aunt. Burgeoning dissent is associated with what patriarchy has labelled as sexually deviant. The contradictions which result are illustrated in Andy's description of Mucker as both impotent and 'a fucking fruit' at the point when he is declared to be politically unsound.[51] For Mal, such desirable wrongness centres on Francy. At his last meeting with him, '. . . Mal threw his arms about him and parting his lips kissed his open mouth', finding his 'roughsmooth face' to be 'reminiscent of the coarse feel' of his cousin Alex's arm. In this moment Mal literally becomes the 'Fenian lover' he will be cast as later on.[52] The novel constantly worries at rigid sexual identities, associating them with dysfunction and unhappiness; but it also provides an example of the link made by Stallybrass and White between the instability generated by the threat of the marginal and taboo and the need of the dominant centre to incorporate them. Mal's revolt is an individual act, but it illustrates a structural point: 'the fundamental rule . . . that what is excluded at the overt level of identity-formation is productive of new objects of desire'.[53] As Larkview's borders are defined by graffiti and red, white and blue kerbstones, so attempts are made to delimit the body and its economy of desire. And, just as inevitably, the 'taboo-laden overlap' between desire and revulsion proves impossible to eliminate.

Protestant Larkview, then, associates Catholics with impurity which is always, in some sense, sexual. Francy and the dump embody the threat of dirt, nub-ends, spittle, deviance, a dangerous fertility ('they breed like rats') which must be purged. The result, predictably, is an increase rather than a dimunition of anxiety, a discipline so excessive that its very negativity concedes the power of 'precisely those groups, practices and activities which it . . . [seeks] to marginalise and destroy'.[54] The exposure of this 'inner complicity of disgust and desire [which] fuels [a society's] crisis of values', and the spectacle of a repressed minority suddenly refusing any longer to 'join in', triggers violent reaction.[55] The conjunction of dirt and purity, centre and margin, recalls Mahon. However Mal's limited, child's perspective permits the balancing of individual rebellion with 'a sympathy for the defensive strategies and contrived political solidarity of the wider [Protestant] community'.[56] The main symbolic act of defence is the Eleventh Night bonfire, a fit emblem of cleansing. The fire and the ritual surrounding it might be viewed in terms of what Bakhtin calls the carnivalesque. 'Carnival' for Bakhtin is a celebration of the low over the high, of base and impure bodily appetite and sensuality over the spirit and intellect, and it has become a critical happy hunting ground for utopian leitmotifs. Nevertheless its relevance to *Burning Your Own* is clear: on Eleventh Night solidarity is reaffirmed in a populist event which signifies a continuity of shared values between adults and the children and youths whose responsibility it is to build the fire.

Yet unlike some forms of carnival the purpose of these celebrations is not to mock authority. Although it could be argued that all carnival is to some extent complicit with the authority it ostensibly subverts, the events surrounding the Twelfth confirm the cross-class alliance of Ulster Protestantism. Not all carnival is liberatory; the discharge of potentially threatening social energies can take the form of reinforcing hierarchy, sublimating undischarged tensions by scapegoating society's others. Referring to the problems of the politics of carnival, Stallybrass and White remind us of 'its nostalgia; its uncritical populism (carnival often violently demonises *weaker*, not stronger social groups – women, ethnic and religious minorities . . . – in a process of *displaced abjection*); its failure to do away with the official dominant values, its licensed complicity'.[57] This short-circuiting and repression of class and other difference to generate *ressentissment* and violence is clearly seen in the novel; the 'burning' of the title consumes those who do the burning as well as those they burn.

POSTMODERN PROTESTANTISM?

In the twenty years or so from Mahon to Patterson I have attempted to trace the development of the ways in which a specifically Protestant scepticism towards a metaphysics of identity and identitarian politics has tried to deal with the Troubles. In Mahon's poetry the aesthetic and exilic distances of Modernism are offset by guilty, often anguished attachments figured in conservative form and local particulars. Challenging the cyclical, mythic history of a Heaney, the poet is also deprived of the alternative Whig or progressivist myth; balancing between the losses represented by the impossibility of these positions, his poise is threatened by the specific exclusions and repressions which originate in the Ulster Protestant experience (in this essay I have instanced gender and class), a threat embodied and resisted in anti-humanist or chiliastic postures. But although Mahon shares the late Romantic/Modernist desire for symbolically resolving social contradiction, his work is characteristically Protestant (or Anglo-Irish, to use an obsolete term) in its mixing of this mode with allegory. Allegory is what disturbs the plenitude of symbol, in Benjamin's terms; it signals a political unconscious in Irish Protestant writing which gives a priority of meaning over experience, and stems from a feeling that meaning is always already prescribed by an inherited mythology, that (postcolonial) experience is narrow, starved and unrepresentative.[58] This modal uncertainty gives the poetry its critical vitality, and to the extent that Mahon succeeds in generating it, Stan Smith is misguided when he writes of Mahon's as 'a consumer's view' of the Real of history 'refused in the name of ordinariness'.[59]

In *Burning Your Own* we recognize a similar Protestant set of concerns, as well as a blend of modes which recalls Mahon's. But it is also possible to discern ways in which the conventional, separate if problematized realms of Mahon's poetry – text, state and self – are imbricated with, rather than being simply threatened by, the Troubles. For Mal, violence is part of a developmental process, not just an external imposition; in line with this, the novel 'deconstructs' itself at the end, blowing up Francy literally, and Mal psychically, rather than offering a worked-out closure. Patterson also insists on a view of the Protestant community riven by petty class distinctions; as he comments, 'the characters in the book, working people, will blame themselves, becoming self-destructive, or blame other working people, creating social unrest, rather than accept that the [sectarian] assumptions themselves are at fault'.[60] And, although this is an overwhelmingly male world, the novel subtly blurs the boundaries which generally delimit gender role and desire. Static images of community and self are destabilised.

It is by grasping not just the Northern Irish, but also the Protestant context of Patterson's and Mahon's work, that we may gauge the extent to which a term like 'postmodern' can be applied to Troubles writing. Most critics, rightly, have challenged the idea that Northern Irish writing can simply be annexed by changes in the cultural 'dominant' which have occurred in the USA, or elsewhere in the UK. Nevertheless, one of the main faults in assessments of Troubles literature in the past (as of the Troubles in sociological, historical and political terms) has been Irish criticism's own conviction of Irish uniqueness, and of the irrelevance to it of developments in the outside world. Despite this the group of poets which followed and built on the achievements of the 1960s generation (as well as recent novelists), recall elements of the Modernism/postmodernism distinction made by Frederic Jameson; chief among these is the historical hypothesis of postmodernism that 'concepts such as anxiety and alienation ... are no longer appropriate' to it.[61] Jameson adds that the 'shift in the dynamics of cultural pathology [is characterizable] as one in which the alienation of the subject is displaced by the latter's fragmentation'.[62] Alienation, that is, assumed a belief in authenticity which postmodernism regards as untenable, replacing it with the kind of fragmented subject which, as we have seen, is literalized at the end of Patterson's novel (as it is, frequently, in the poetry of Muldoon).

But this does not mean that the strategies of Mahon were somehow 'superseded' in a simple, developmental way. On the contrary it was from Mahon's poetry (and also from Michael Longley's and Louis MacNeice's) that the postmodern-influenced later writers learned most. Edna Longley has made the point that Muldoon writes against the grain of his Catholic background (ie: that he deconstructs the early Heaney), but the same could also be said of McGuckian and Carson. Protestant writers' automatic 'outsider' status, their turning of repression and exclusion against themselves (as if in a sort of jiu jitsu), their scepticism and refusal to endorse boundaries, incubated the forms and strategies adopted by later writers. To some extent the similarities bear out the comments made by Eamon Hughes that '... borders recognised as arbitrary are a condition of what we have come to call the postmodern world. Northern Ireland exists as both a ghetto and a postmodern entity'.[63] Any final assessment of these ideas of cultural change would, I think, have to lay particular emphasis on two points. First, the need to situate all of these developments against the turning point of the mid- to late-1970s when containment and 'Ulsterization' strategies were set in place, and when a sea-change was engineered in British politics (these events were not entirely unconnected).[64] For Catholics, this was the time when the possibility of major structural reform was discarded in favour of gradual social advance and the British State moved to a 'security problem' approach. For Protestants, it was the beginning of the process which led to the Anglo-Irish Agreement, the implications of which (in the form of the renewed ceasefire of 1997) are still being worked out. Second, following on from this, is the crucial 'unspoken' role of differences such as those of class and gender in shaping literary responses to the Troubles. The material fractures these open up again and again within notions like 'community' make it possible to observe the extent to which the supposedly discrete and fixed entities like 'self', and 'poem' are in fact fluid, strategies and interventions rather than achieved forms. As Glenn Patterson has written:

I had grown up in a society characterised . . . as morbidly immutable; yet there was another, equally valid reading which said that, quite the reverse, change was in fact the society's only constant . . . While there can be no ignoring the destabilising effects . . . of all this (I choose the words deliberately) deconstruction and revision, it nevertheless contains within it a certain liberating potential.[65]

A NECESSARY DISTANCE? – MYTHOPOEIA AND VIOLENCE IN FRIEL, PARKER AND VINCENT WOODS'S *AT THE BLACK PIG'S DYKE*

ALAN J. PEACOCK – KATHLEEN DEVINE

Recently, in the Irish theatre, two plays have been remarkable for the things which they have in common, Brian Friel's *Dancing at Lughnasa* and Vincent Woods's *At the Black Pig's Dyke*. They both make use of complicated ellipses of time in a way that makes demands on the audience; they both make crucial use of narrative as a theatrical device; they use dance, not in an incidental way but to provide central scenes of powerfully involving theatrical spectacle; and, most importantly, they use myth and ritual to provide a rich substratum to the more explicit story-line and thematic content. They show an allusive play, in this area of reference, which involves animal sacrifice (in the case of *Lughnasa*), and rituals of death and renewal. Episodes of extreme and disturbing violence (in the case of *At the Black Pig's Dyke*) and primitive rites involving fire and animals (in the case of *Dancing at Lughnasa*) take place within small Irish communities in a way which seems to go on quite independently of any system of 'civilized' civic structures. Violence seems to have a cyclical life of its own. Old, dark myths and pagan beliefs seem to be authenticated by the social and historical experience of our own century. The perspective therefore in both plays is if anything 'anthropological' rather than political; and both make use of stage-properties drawn from pagan tribal ritual (shields, ritual head-dress, dancing-sticks etc.) within a depiction of twentieth-century Christian communities in Ireland.

In utilizing such theatrical and thematic resources as a means of approaching a particular moment of twentieth-century Irish historical experience, *Dancing at Lughnasa* paves the way for the similarly rich and ambitious dramaturgy of Woods's play. Friel's play is not of course about the recent political Troubles in Ireland (though violence of a ritual kind and the political backdrop of the Spanish Civil War are important in the play), but it is an obvious enabling precedent for Woods's play which, if not directly and explicitly 'about' the Troubles, constitutes through its mythic framework and startling revisions of customary perspectives (both geographical and political) a spine-chillingly immediate evocation of the human impulses involved. It is Woods's achievement in this connection which will be examined in the latter part of this chapter. In approaching *At the Black Pig's Dyke* however it is proposed to argue how, exemplified in plays by Friel and Stewart Parker, there is a developing tendency within Irish theatre towards obliquity of treatment of the Troubles which involves a decisive movement away from a narrowly documentary realism. Woods's play is, arguably, the apogee of this trend which of course requires a broadened sense of what a 'Troubles' play may be.

The tendency is away from a political or historical treatment of contemporary violence, and towards mythopoeia. A given historical event within the recent Troubles does, as will be seen, figure by suggestion in *At the Black Pig's Dyke*, but the play's major statement is achieved by its framing myth of the 'Strange Knight', a narrative predicated on archetypal myths of death and renewal. There is no graphically realistic violence, and yet the symbolic representations of sectarian murder, blood-lust and vendetta are powerful and disturbing. The recourse to myth, that is, is in no sense an evasion, but rather a necessary distancing, a positive way of achieving a perspective on events which allows for something beyond mere documentary accuracy, political analysis or one-for-one fidelity to historical events. Friel's work in particular and his recorded thinking about the Troubles as a subject for drama demonstrate the value, and perhaps necessity, of this evolving strain within the otherwise predominantly naturalistic tradition of plays about the Troubles. The issue was crystallized for him by the 'Bloody Sunday' events of 1972 in his home city and, as will be seen, resolved in theatrical terms which insist on other than political dimensions. The obliquely assimilative processes of the creative artist do not necessarily directly echo the strict tempo of events and involve a complex mix of ethical and aesthetic imperatives.

* * *

Friel's *oeuvre* has been deeply and humanely conditioned by the process of historical events in Northern Ireland since the outbreak of the Troubles in 1968. Obliquity however (and, often, complex temporal perspective) has been an insistent emphasis. In 1971 for instance, Friel voiced a disinclination in the foreseeable future to write a play about the Northern Irish situation because he was 'too much involved emotionally to view it with any calm': he felt that he had 'no objectivity in this situation'.[1] *The Freedom of the City* of course marked a revision of this view in 1973. Prior to this, though, in less directly historical and political terms, Friel's mind was obviously working at some level on the broad question of violence and division in human and communal relations. *The Gentle Island*, which appeared in 1971, as the Troubles were building to their 1972 peak, was not indeed focused on the North (in accordance with Friel's instincts just noted), but it provided a revisionistic (or reversionary if one thinks of Synge) version of Western Ireland seen in terms of extreme communal violence, hideously cruel treatment of animals and the human ability to distort myth, history and fact to give spurious sanction to, for example, possessive patriarchy, territorial possessiveness and murderous sexual jealousy. The vision is as stark and visceral as that in *At the Black Pig's Dyke*, and similar play is made with ideas of patriarchy and male possession, fertility and sterility.

Violence is a pervasive, disturbing 'given' and complicated, as in *At the Black Pig's Dyke*, by its relation to sexual instincts; and in these broad terms (tending again in fact towards the anthropological in tenor rather than the political) Friel was clearly, consciously or unconsciously, developing an attitude to violence where individual acts are seen as the precipitate of received communal codes, histories and fates which are deeply imprinted. In contradistinction to its immediate predecessor *The Mundy Scheme*, the play eschews political topicality.

The topical, the immediately politically relevant, was seen as problematic by Friel. In February, 1970 in an *Irish Times* article he declared himself 'too much involved' in a transitional situation to take up the theme of Northern politics, and indeed envisaged an interval of 'ten or fifteen years'[2] before such a play might be written. His view of the artist's role in such circumstances is recorded by D.E.S. Maxwell: the writer

must maintain a perspective as a writer, and – equally important – he will write about the situation in terms that may not relate even remotely to the squalor of here and now.[3]

The problem, that is, is not so much the avoidance or otherwise of political themes as such, but the avoidance of 'a confusion of the artist's and the journalist's function' and art as agitprop. To find his orientation *qua* artist, as opposed to concerned citizen, required perspective in temporal (as he saw it) and formal terms. The events of Bloody Sunday in January, 1972 and the controversial findings of the subsequent Widgery Tribunal clearly telescoped Friel's idea of a necessary temporal perspective. The aesthetic and ethical question however remained; and although Friel's decision to write a play in response to Bloody Sunday and Widgery inevitably gave rise to hostile responses in critical and other terms (the London run of the play was disturbed by bomb-scares), what is immediately notable about *The Freedom of the City* is the distance that Friel puts between the play and the events of 1972. It is set, for instance, in 1970 and the events it covers are located in the Derry Guildhall rather than the Bogside. Thematically it only broadly echoes historical events and, in political terms, it avoids narrowly conceived partisanship. If the judiciary and the British army are seen, in the central thrust of the play, as benighted and biased, so are other sources of opinion and comment (sociology, the Irish media, the clergy, Republican balladry) seen in various degrees as sectional, unreliable, imperfect. In these ways, Friel avoids the danger of producing the kind of topical propaganda-piece that was expected of him in some quarters and that some responses to the play perceived or assumed. Most crucial though, in theatrical terms, is the formal conception of the play which is an aesthetic response to the kind of misgivings that, as an artist, Friel had been voicing with respect to Northern political subject-matter. The use of different linguistic registers and jargons, for instance, to represent conflicting sectional perspectives on events immediately avoids the univocal modes of propaganda.

Crucially though, as in *At the Black Pig's Dyke*, the action of the play is sandwiched between non-naturalistic framing-sections which hold it within a particular formal and temporal perspective. The three protagonists, who have blundered into the Mayor's parlour of the Derry Guildhall in the midst of disturbances following a civil rights demonstration in Guildhall Square, are seen immediately and proleptically in the initial tableau lying dead on stage, and, finally, frozen where they stand at the moment of their mortal fate (Frank McGuinness was of course to use similar transfiguring techniques with his First World War, Orange protagonists in *Observe the Sons of Ulster Marching Towards the Somme*). The ordinary human is thus transmuted into the realm of the mythic, the iconic, as they meet the fate predetermined in the opening tableau. Moreover, as they walk from the Mayor's parlour in the Guildhall to their fate,

They begin to move very slowly downstage in ritualistic procession. The moment Skinner closes the door, the auditorium is filled with thundering, triumphant organ music on open diapason.[4]

Thus, before the freeze-frame tableau of their gunning down (preceded by a flash-forward Telefis Eireann report on their funeral, and the reading of the subsequent tribunal report) they are already, by visual and aural suggestion, imbued with a simultaneous aura of victimage and triumph.

Nor is this a merely socio-political mythicising. We have already, within the non-naturalistic, non-chronological patterning of the play, been in receipt of the victims' *post-mortem* response to the moment of death – in Lily's case, for instance, epiphanic, full of access of insight and with something of the haunting cadence to be found at the close of *Faith Healer* and *Dancing at Lughnasa*:

The moment we stepped outside the front door I knew I was going to die … And in the silence before my body disintegrated in a purple convulsion, I thought I glimpsed a tiny truth: that life had eluded me because never once in my forty-three years had an experience, an event, even a small unimportant happening been isolated, and assessed, and articulated. And the fact that this, my last experience, was defined by this perception, this was the culmination of sorrow. In a way I died of grief.[5]

Critics who are troubled by the sudden change in Lily's idiom need perhaps to make more allowance for the fact that Friel in this play is concerned with issues beyond mere sociological verisimilitude or political comment, and is experimenting with theatrical techniques of flash-back and montage in a humane exploration of the problem of human self-definition in the face of extreme circumstances. Using technically complex time-schemes and narrative techniques, Friel 'maintains' what he views as a necessary 'perspective as a writer'; and if, under pressure of events, he has modified his notion that the writer 'will write about the situation in terms that may not relate even remotely to the squalor of here and now' his treatment of specific topical issues nevertheless strains centrifugally towards larger, more generalizing perspectives – and, as a corollary, more elaborate formal structures. In this sense *The Freedom of the City* gives a glimpse of the kind of thing which Friel was to achieve in *Dancing at Lughnasa* and, over and above the O'Casey-like naturalistic dialogue, an indication of what might be possible in drama of the Troubles beyond the limitations of realism.

* * *

Stewart Parker, in the 1980s, instinctively turned to dramatic techniques that reached away from realism in dealing with the current Troubles, deploying song and music as part of his theatrical resources and, like Woods later, harnessing the potential of myth to suggest the recurring nature of the psychic and other forces that lead to division and violence. In his (1987) television series, *Lost Belongings*, the myth of Deirdre and the sons of Usna is given a modern setting, its ethos of possession and jealousy repeated through the figures of the girl's young Catholic lover and Protestant uncle whose incestuous desire finds expression in contemporary sectarian violence. Deirdre embodies Parker's vision of the tragedy of the current conflict, imaged in the 'botched birth' of *Northern Star* or the abandoned, dead or miscarried infants of *Pentecost*. For him no beauty, 'terrible' or otherwise, will be born of violence and the Deirdre figure, pregnant in her modern manifestation, miscarries. Her blood flows down the steps of a church building while middle-class Belfast society sits at a celebration of foreign culture in the form of a classical concert, oblivious to the cultural heritage of its own dark myths that are here seen potently to re-enact themselves on its streets. The inter-penetration here between contemporary violence and remote pagan myth echoes, within the format of a six-part television series, simultaneous developments in Parker's stage-drama, culminating in his last play, *Pentecost*, which has recourse to non-realistic techniques and mythic elements in its exploration of contemporary violence and division.

In the Introduction to *Three Plays for Ireland*[6] (*Northern Star* (1984), *Heavenly Bodies* (1986) and *Pentecost* (1987)) Parker raises the related questions of identity, history and myth as they affect the current Ulster situation. 'Ancestral voices prophesy and bicker, and the ghosts of your own time and birthplace wrestle and dance, in any play you choose to write'[7] he says before outlining the situation in terms that have the elemental starkness of myth (and that anticipate Vincent Woods's invented myth of the Strange Knight): 'two men fighting over a field'. Here he echoes McCracken in *Northern Star* as he similarly reduces the elements of the Ulster situation to mythic simplicity: 'A field, with two men fighting over it. Cain and Abel. The bitterest fight in the history of man on this earth'[8] – the urge to possession that is at the heart of every nationalistic conflict.

In *Northern Star* Parker probes the dangers inherent in the attaching of myth unthinkingly to one's own situation and the play's historical setting is used to give the necessary distance from which, by implication, the current Troubles (and factional self-mythologizing) can be viewed with some objectivity. 'What did it mean to be Irish?' McCracken asks the peasant mother of his bastard child, thus raising in the play's first scene the whole question of identity and tradition that has become the entrenched channel of bitterness and division. Patterns of recurrence dominate and, like him, his fellow-rebels are consciously playing the roles their idea of their place in Irish history requires of them (though without his ironic self-awareness). Parker uses McCracken's ancestry – French Huguenot, Scottish Covenanter, to suggest (as Woods will do in images of inherited physical attributes) the 'mongrel' origins of the land's inhabitants and hence the absurdity of any one claim to exclusive possession. And in the context of the play's action, in which historical figures, ghosts and even 'future ghosts' interact as though time were a permeable membrane, priority of arrival is seen as a less than valid claim to possession. Parker's use of a self-parodying 'hero' of '98, of humorous pastiche and cliché ghosts, signals his rejection of realism as an adequate mode for exploring the Province's cyclical Troubles.

Radicalism of technique and obliquity of perspective on themes of violence, possession and identity are also a feature of Parker's second play in his triptych, *Heavenly Bodies*, where not just divisions in time but also those between the living and the dead are playfully dissolved in this farcical treatment of Boucicault (dead but refusing to acknowledge it in his colloquy with his defunct 'friend' Patterson). As he reviews his life and career Boucicault is the paradigm of the Irish refusal to face squarely questions of identity and origin, obfuscated as they are by traditional stances that lead to stereotypical self-images. Boucicault is a shape-changer as befits his insecure cultural identity. A perfect example of Parker's 'mongrel crew', he invents an 'authentic' Irish patrimony as the legitimate offspring of a respectable Dublin wine merchant, frantically rejecting his true origin as the bastard son of Lardner, 'the Protestant goat'. His claims to Irishness on the world stage are equally invalid as he spawns his stage Irishmen that perpetuate one of the myths of Irishness, in his Miles-na-Coppaleen and the Shaughraun. His life enacts McCracken's point about role and player in *Northern Star*.

The parasitism and self-serving nature of his role-playing are graphically imaged when, as Alan Raby in his play *Vampire*, he sinks his teeth in the neck of Anne Guiot, thus renewing himself with her life-blood. In just such a manner has he 'bled' Ireland for his stage success, draining the Irish character of real life and integrity to offer a mock-up that will please commercial English taste. The name Anne Guiot, of course, is a reminder that his mother's name is also Anne, and so, in a symbolic moment typical of the lively but pointed element of playfulness in Parker's work, we have a reversal of the 'old sow that eats her own farrow'.

Fintan O'Toole, reviewing Lynne Parker's revival of *Northern Star*, observed 'how ... normal *Northern Star* seems' within the present theatrical context in Ireland, with its anti-naturalistic premises and postmodernist assumptions. In the same place, he notes, with reference to the range of plays in the 1996 Dublin Theatre Festival, the emphatic defunctness of the 'well-made play' and observes how 'The striking thing about the first week, indeed, was how little social realism it contained, how little it seems to be concerned with simple reflections of contemporary life. Even in Irish work of the 1980s and 1990s, the classical world was more in evidence than the modern world ...'[9] He notes specifically Paul Mercier's *Kitchensink* with its 'very strong element of ritual ...' The citation of Stewart Parker as a precursor of these developments in a process where 'we are reminded that, in the theatre, the difference between the past and the present fades to nothing, and that people don't have to be alive to be our contemporaries' is apposite and echoes Parker's stage directions which describe the setting of the play as 'Ireland, the continuous past'.

Pentecost provides a further bold and imaginative example of this clearly discernible instinct towards complexly allusive distancing techniques calculated to allow a conspectus going beyond the limits of 'yesterday's outrage' or drama as reportage, and beyond the limitations of any actual (or perceived!) political or ideological affiliation – a process symbolized in formal terms in the move through the play away from realism. As the title indicates, though the play is set historically during the period of the 1974 UWC strike which brought about the demise of the then power-sharing executive, its scope expands to an ambitious projection of a parallelism between day-by-day events in one house in an embattled area and large concepts of community, humanity and possible redemption, for which biblical ideas of a 'holy family' or the pentecostal descent of the Holy Spirit, provide objective correlatives.

These larger symbolic structures however develop on from a first act characterised by a strong comedic element, where Parker's invention and sharp ear for dialogue provide a very successful recuperation of the resources of the Irish tragi-comic tradition as action and tone flip unpredictably between the two constituent elements. Social and historical reality (sectarian division, social and familial violence, the impending strike and then its intimidating actuality) is registered in swift, laconic repartee. Piquantly, however, within this quick-fire, post-Sixties 'street-wise' development of O'Casey's similarly localised but broadly resonating version of Dublin tenement society at momentous historical junctures, the house's resident ghost, Lily Matthews, is given a speaking part as a personification of Parker's version of the Protestant psyche. This initially startling, postmodernist disturbance of the otherwise realistic conventions of the first act with a character out of a seemingly quite different dramatic dispensation prepares for the play's first major epiphanic moment when Marian, the Catholic intruder into Lily Matthews' domain, finds a basis of empathy and fellow-feeling in the discovery of the chequered private history behind Lily's prim and carefully preserved Nonconformist public persona.

Parker's dramaturgy however, in Act II, moves to a much more ambitious freighting of characters and situation with symbolic implication. The dialogic interplay gives way to a new dispensation whereby, by turns, the characters (ghost and all) deliver confessional speeches where the angst beneath the social front is manifested, and where a heavy-duty didactic/mythopoeic structure is set up as the group of characters discusses itself explicitly in terms of a parody of the Holy Family. Ultimately, some spirit of communion settles on them (hence the play's title), but although passages from the Bible are recited at this juncture, what transpires is not a conventional religious epiphany, and the process has to be attended to carefully if the crucial signals are not to be missed or simplistically registered. For, as with *The Freedom of the City*, the final moments of the play gesture towards ideas for which realism is ultimately inadequate.

Moments before, Lenny has recounted his experience, after playing his trombone all night in a pub, where on an idyllic beach his 'lady vocalist' friend, high on drugs, 'starts crooning . . ."Just a closer walk with thee . . ."' as 'she begins to peel her clothes off', while a group of nuns strip off their outer clothes and frolic in the sea:

...and it doesn't take a lot to see that the nuns are experiencing their sex and the vocalist her spirit. And for a crazy few seconds I all but sprinted down to the nuns to churn my body into theirs, in the surf foam, and then bring them all back to the lady vocalist, for a session of great spirituals...and maybe that's how it was...what it was like here. Before Christianity. Is what I'm saying.[10]

This epiphanic vision of wholeness (immediately rejected by Ruth in a conditioned-reflex outburst – 'You don't even know Christianity' – which leads to initially competitive, divisive Bible quoting with Peter) leads to a key episode where Marian finds a sudden access of individual insight in the experience of the death of her child. She repudiates institutionalized religious redemptive agencies – 'Forget the church. Forget the priests and pastors' – in favour of 'the christ' within:

The christ in him absorbed into the christ in me. We have got to love that in ourselves. In ourselves first and then in them. That's the only future there is.[11]

The shift to a lower-case 'christ' in the published text pinpoints Marian's fellow-feeling with Lenny's secular vision of redemption – an amalgam of the polarities of human experience. She now repudiates recrimination and the demonizing of 'them' in favour of an inclusive ethic based on individual agency within an aspiration towards 'the fullest life' where kindred dead are not, as so routinely in Ulster, the justification of murder but, in Parker's attempt to short-circuit endemic, cyclical patterns of violence, those to whom we owe it to live 'the fullest life for which they could ever have hoped'. Barriers and antagonisms are dissolving and, at this point even Ruth, taking her cue from Marian's words, knits in and recontextualizes a passage from the Acts of the Apostles which, like Lenny's vision, combines the spiritual and physical: 'Therefore did my heart rejoice, and my tongue was glad; moreover also my flesh shall rest in hope...'[12] Deployed in this defamiliarized way, the familiar cadences of the Bible merge with the sound of Lenny's trombone solo – played now in the open air and listened to through an opened window by the others – to supply a final scene of redemptive harmony. The mould-breaking fusing of secular and religious values, the destabilizing of routine shibboleths and boundaries, is aptly symbolized in the fact that the piece which Lenny plays on his trombone, 'Just a Closer Walk with Thee', is the same hymn sung by the naked, drugged 'female vocalist'.

The resolution of the play is a network of such subtly tuned congruences – in fact the effect is perhaps too subtle. Some of the intricate distinctions of register may not be easily communicated in theatrical performance. In the printed text, for instance, the use of the lower case 'christ' in Marian's speech emphatically signals that we have now moved into a metaphorical application of Christian terminology – a sign-posting obviously denied the performed text (after the preceding 'straight' citations from scripture); and the shift is crucial. The *Sunday Tribune* review of the 1995 Rough Magic production notes how: 'this is a marvellously crafted piece which while polemical and over-evangelical in its final fling compels us to stay with the writer and characters as they grope for faith and redemption'.[13] If, as this response might suggest, in the crucial final moments of his play Parker perhaps is not entirely successful in making the shift from the 'heightened realism'[14] (Parker's own term) which has been the staple mode so far to a mythopoeic register fully consonant with the concluding vision of wholeness and involving a radically defamiliarized application of Christian terminology, the full complexity of his enterprise (as with *The Freedom of the City*) is nevertheless a pointer towards the potential scope of non-realistic dramatic modes in approaching issues and ideas arising from the Troubles. Vincent Woods's *At the Black Pig's Dyke* is, as will be seen, more successful in this line of development in that its ultimate import is predicated on a mythic structure which is incrementally deployed through the play to frame a text which is itself at one postmodernist remove from 'heightened realism'.

* * *

As was suggested earlier, Woods's *At the Black Pig's Dyke* is in many ways comparable with Friel's *Dancing at Lughnasa* in, for instance, the central use of narrative, dance and elements of folk-lore and ritual to provide unusual and disturbing perspectives on communal experience in twentieth-century Ireland. At every level, in a way underlined by the inventive sets and imaginative direction of their initial productions, these plays seemed to mark a new maturity and technical boldness in their approaches to themes of communal trauma and dysfunction. In a very interesting way, however, both plays elude any charges of parochialism of outlook or limited purview by means of a richly allusive frame of reference. *Lughnasa* makes reference to the Spanish Civil War, to African tribal custom and ritual – and its geographical reference also includes Wales and Sweden. Similarly,

At the Black Pig's Dyke, in the songs which are used, in the costumes of the initial production, and in its ethnographic and other sources, goes quite beyond its primary Irish setting and frame of reference in small-town County Leitrim.

In *Dancing at Lughnasa*, a child's kite becomes, in the final tableau, a tribal shield – echoing the conversion to African tribal practices and beliefs of the priest, Father Jack. In *At the Black Pig's Dyke*, even more radically, the social and historical reality of the mummers, who are central to the play's dramatic design, is given a special, suggestive edge by their conflation with, for instance, the Wren Boys, and, in visual terms, by the Viking look of some head-dresses in the initial production, together with the unmistakable Ku Klux Klan look of others. There was a multi-ply anthropological suggestiveness in the presentation of these ominous dancing figures, just as the songs and textual sources utilized in the play are drawn from disparate spheres: the Barbara Allen song; the repeated quotation from the beginning of Dickens's *A Tale of Two Cities*; the Leitrim folk-lore concerning the Black Pig etc.

This kind of verbal and visual imagery is integral to the particular vision which the plays, with different emphases, present of Irish psychic and social reality in relation to an emphasized pagan substratum of historical experience. Lugh, for instance, is commonly represented as a harvest god, associated with positive ideas of renewal. In Friel's play, however, a darker side is emphasized in the violent and mysterious rituals taking place in the 'back hills'. Similarly, in Woods's play, the mummers can be seen as capering representatives of a colourful knock-about tradition of folk-lore and custom. Woods however evinces a more sinister view of their masked dancing and cryptic doggerel in their traditional play of death and renewal. Behind the frightening masks lurk men of violence. The anonymity of the mummers is equated with the anonymity of political and sectarian violence. However, with a dark irony, it is the 'doctor' figure in the mummers who is the murderer in the play. This kind of reversibility and metamorphosis, this obverse and reverse view of Irish life, myth and culture, is central to the concept of the play.

The specific social focus of the play is sectarian tension and conflict between Protestant and Catholic elements in post-Independence Ireland. A cycle of violence and vendetta is disclosed in which Frank Beirne is responsible for the murder of Jack Boles and his wife, Lizzie. She is slaughtered essentially for her exogamous marriage to a Protestant by Frank, her Catholic nationalist 'suitor'; and it is the deep-structure pathology of such acts within and between communities that the play examines rather than politics or specific historical circumstance. The play therefore concerns the danger of fixed, tribal loyalties and enmities, fuelled by possessive jealousy in territorial or sexual terms. Ultimately too, it is about redemption and renewal – but, as will be seen, in optative rather than practical or analytical terms.

Lizzie's opening soliloquy immediately introduces the play's characteristic use of riddling, disorientating, contradictory and shifting linguistic formulations to express themes of threat and disorder:

It was a long time ago, Elizabeth and it was not a long time ago . . . It was a time when to go east was to go west, when to go south was to go north, when people sang songs at a wake and cried when a child was born. It was in a land where the sun never rose and the sun never set, where the dead prepared shrouds for the livin' and straw people walked the roads.[15]

She is holding a 'half-made straw wren' (the wren being of course the object of cruel scape-goating each St. Stephen's day in Irish rural tradition). Within this context, the seasonal knock of the local mummers at the door and their call for admittance are also strangely threatening. The language and the action of the play retain this folk-loric, richly suggestive dimension throughout, and mythic structures prevail over realism. Lizzie, for instance, who will in short order be discovered by the mummers murdered together with her daughter Sarah, is, inevitably at one level, a female personification of Ireland (in the age-old tradition of Kathleen ni Houlihan etc.). First, however, to further elaborate the mythic texture of the play, her grand-daughter Elizabeth, seen as a baby in the opening scene, manifests rear-stage, fully grown, in 'ghostly, unreal' lighting and delivers the first instalment of the framing-myth of the play, continued as prologue and epilogue to the second act. She delivers a mythic digest of the play's internal narrative, in her tale of the rapacious and murderous progress through a land of a Strange Knight. Though expressed in terms of universal fairy-tale-like archetypes it is anchored to the Irish focus of the play by its location 'in a land where the black pig had furrowed an endless tunnel under the earth and where it ran still, trapped and frantic beneath the ground.'

By its incremental deployment, the import of this framing-myth is diffused throughout the play and progressively generates an atmosphere in which the action is worked out against a backdrop of archetypal myths and symbols, with ideas of sacrifice and ultimately regeneration to the fore. It is a fully coherent narrative with its own logic. The Knight progresses, in Elizabeth's initial speech, from his first murder of an old woman whose riddle he refuses to answer in the required form to his next adventure where he judges between two claimants to a piece of land. In a black parody of the judgement of Solomon he resolves the claim in favour of the man whose love for the land makes him refuse to sell it, before shooting both claimants and taking the land for himself. The prologue to the play's second act carries the tale of the Strange Knight forward to his third adventure where his guile is now used against a community that has slain its king. He persuades them to elect him as their leader and then turns them against one another in a fight to the death so that 'there was no one left alive but the Strange Knight. And he was happy then'. In the final part of the tale, which closes the play, Elizabeth recites his fate as possession turns sour: 'the land around him grew rancid from the decay of bodies in the ground' and his human needs – for communal life, festivity and rejoicing, even for procreation – cannot be satisfied because his overweening urge to possess has destroyed all his fellow humans and his solitude becomes unbearable to him. He is forced to retrace his steps and to beg forgiveness at the grave of the first victim of his violence. This final adventure brings about 'the beginning of happiness' when his remorseful tears fall 'like rain on the soil'. The redemptive act of contrition, in Woods's own version of the corn-god myth here, results in a 'blood-red poppy' springing from the dead woman's grave. When the Knight plucks it, it sheds its petals from each of which spring a dozen women armed with 'hooks and seeds and implements to sow and harvest'. Remorse is only the beginning, however: the Knight cannot escape the consequences of his guilt. He is 'yoked to the ground' by the women and forced to take his part in the regeneration of the land he has laid waste: 'and so began the endless task of restoring the land to life and the beginning of happiness.'

To point a more immediate, contemporary symbolism, Elizabeth is wearing a poppy, and has a 'clutch' of them in her hand; and these details, plus the fact that Lizzie was first disclosed humming 'The Enniskillen Dragoons', inevitably calls to mind the 'Poppy Day' events in Enniskillen on Remembrance Sunday, 1987, when Marie Wilson died – to become an icon for subsequent peace initiatives. The obliquity of this reference characterizes the way in which the play engages with issues of contemporary violence in

Ulster. Direct reference is largely avoided, and sheer topicality is not the aim. Rather the elements of the framing-myth typify the play's characteristic perspective on violence, which is via folk-myth, legend and atavistically transmitted stories and attitudes.

As with Heaney's 1990 reworking of Sophocles' *Philoctetes, The Cure at Troy*, the difficult objective that the play sets itself finally is to offer a myth of renewal potent enough to counter the myths and stereotypes which fuel violence. Here too, the orientation is unexpected. The setting of the play is (largely) Leitrim rather than the North and this, together with the temporal recessiveness of the cycles of violence which it presents, helps to reinforce the fact that although the play is 'about' the Ulster Troubles, it is not directly, politically, about them – hence the demarcation of the border by reference to the legendary Black Pig's Dyke. Hence too the identification between the mummers and the characters in the main plot (played by the same actors), whereby, within a telling strain of irony in the play, Lizzie's brutal murderer, Frank, doubles as the 'Doctor' character in the mummers; and it is Tom Fool and Miss Funny who, like a comic chorus, draw the stark conclusions from depicted events –

> Miss Funny: That's a fine start to a play.
> Two dead; Men made of hay
> Or straw – what does it matter?
> Better keep back, Mind your place,
> Better watch the face beside you –
> You never know, in the latter end
> What's what, who's who, what will happen –

and make the link with the contemporary violence of the Troubles:

> Tom Fool: Better to talk about a bomb
> In a creamery can, a van in a ditch,
> The two dead: swingin' the lead
> Is no idle occupation around here.

Bombs in creamery cans are, for a present-day audience, inevitably evocative of the Northern situation. But the reference is generalised. Moreover, the violence within the play is pointedly sourced in the political South, and even this, as has been said, has been further contextualized within the domain of myth. Only when audience-response has been conditioned by the darkly riddling language of the framing-myth of the Knight, the plangent contradictions of Lizzie's opening narrative, the minatory badinage of the chorus of fools, and the visual impact of the mummers, 'an exotic spectacle of straw, elaborate masks and colourful costumes' does the main action proceed. It comprises in fact the sequence of events, layered in time, which lead to the murder of Lizzie and her daughter Sarah.

In what becomes a post-mortem flash-back technique therefore, reminiscent of *The Freedom of the City* and *Northern Star*, the young Lizzie and her suitor Jack Boles materialize on stage and fantasize about an idyllic boat trip 'to the new world' under the flag of 'the white hand of nowhere'. Coming from opposite sides of the sectarian divide, they are happy to fly 'orange' or 'green' and (as it turns out within the unexpected perspective of the play) to adopt Ulster as their 'new world' in their flight from sectarianism. Their Edenic notion is however shadowed as, in a further temporal recession, young Lizzie recalls the drowning accident where Lord Leitrim's nephew, William Clements, and his retainer Jack Brolly died in circumstances which provide a powerful image of social division and perverted possessiveness:

> Young Lizzie: Clements drowned Brolly because he couldn't swim himself and he couldn't bear to see his servant survive. His boast was there wasn't enough water in the lough to drown him . . .
> . . . The old people used to say there was some – matter of honour, some promise broken. I know Brolly had a sister Mae – and I think maybe she had a child – Clements' child . . . I'm not certain.

These events form the background for Lizzie and Jack's ill-fated marriage as they plan to make a new life across the border ('Is Fermanagh new world enough?'). In a way which reverses familiar representations of the 'Ulster Troubles', the North is consistently seen in the play as the territory into which violence generated further south bleeds, and Protestants, within this Southern context, are presented as the aggrieved minority. Moreover, Jack has vowed, notwithstanding the sectarian murder of his brother and father, 'that I'd never use a gun or shoot any livin' thing so long as I lived.' The hope is that Frank Beirne (the Beirne family are the putative killers of Jack's family) will not pursue Lizzie further after the marriage. However, as Tom Fool has already said:

> A border never stopped a shot
> That set its target years before.

In these ways the exegesis of violence is always pushed back away from immediate political determinants, and directed towards the points where history intersects with myth or folk-lore.

As the play unfolds the full history of the multi-generational tragedy – the marriage of Lizzie and Jack in Enniskillen, the murder of Jack in their own fields by Frank and his associates, and then the final murder of Lizzie and her daughter – it sets these acts of violence strategically against a back-drop of a post-Independence Ireland pictured as devoid of ideology, pacifically embracing civic values and based on neighbourly commerce and religious integration. Jack's stock are, in Lizzie's words, 'shop-keepers and decent people'; and her father, Michael Flynn, has served in the British army and (though a Catholic) is loyal to his connection with England on practical experiential grounds (when he needed work to feed his family, England provided it). Though Lizzie enthusiastically sings of de Valera's 'Coronation', she happily works for the Boles family. Yeats's reductive image of an Ireland of the 'greasy till' is thus systematically turned on its head; and, counter to the aisling tradition, representatives of female Ireland are threatened by native rather than foreign male figures. This latter re-working of sanctified myths, done with a postmodernist élan and according to drastically revisionist determinants, is typical of Woods's radical and unpredictable play of ideas.

Frank, for instance, is consistently presented as mouthing an ideology tainted, if not determined, by perverted self-interest. If Lizzie rejects him as a suitor, it must (in his terms) be because she is the latest manifestation of the paradigm provided by Leitrim's nephew's seigneurial misuse of Mae Brolly; and hence Jack is the representative of 'them as owns half the place and goes north for the Twelfth' and 'that'd glawn our women and have their pick of the best of them . . .' Similarly, when Frank's father and brother murdered Jack's father in his shop, 'They stole the ledgers so there'd be no trace of the money they owed – and all the credit the Boles's gave them that kept food in their mouths.' Frank's anthem is 'Barbara Allen', a song 'of love and jealousy', a 'love' however articulated by him in terms of crude male possession:

> For betwixt this and Easter
> I'll have Lizzie Flynn on a halter,
> The altar'll be the next stop.

It is this kind of imagery which indicates the true focus of the play: it is the local, the intimate operations of violence which are anatomised. The external events of the political world are a background, distilled via folk-history and oral tradition into the alliances and hatreds of community lives. Folk-tales and ballads are the cited authority for the characters' allegiances (as they are also source-materials for the play-wright), and this involves condensation and simplification with an almost melodramatic distinction between 'good' and 'bad' characters – except that this is melodrama with the cutting edge of nightmare. The play works on our deepest fears through powerful verbal and visual imagery. By the same token, the action of the play is able to mesh with the mythic, allegorical import of the framing-story of the knight with its strong overtones of sacrifice and renewal. When Jack is murdered, he is surrounded by Strawmen who 'fold the straw wall around Jack so that it looks like a sheaf' and he is associated, by his child Sarah's song, with the sacrificial wren. Moreover when, late in the play, Lizzie recalls the events the same elements are stressed. It is August, 'the big meadow is still down' and the redcurrants which she has picked for Sarah become associated with Jack's spilled blood. In the same way, when in Act 2 the fate of Sarah's husband, Hugh Brolly, is enacted (on the northern side now of the Dyke), there is an insistent stress on the imagery of the wren, variant versions of whose victimage are offered by Captain Mummer and Tom Fool. Hugh, a semi-reluctant conscript to violent activity since the murder of his brother Sean, is ritually killed for informing and subverting what he discovers to be his part in a lethal mission against his neighbours. Here events are approaching present-day Northern political circumstances, but they remain essentially mythicised. It is still not the political border but the Dyke that Hugh crosses to collect the bomb, and Lizzie refers to his activities as 'risin' the black pig'. There is a sense of cyclical forces at work, of fate being worked out at a pre-political level of consciousness. When Lizzie learns of Hugh's involvement she speaks in the following terms:

Revenge is the longest road. Revenge doesn't know where to stop . . . And there's some doesn't want it ever to stop. There's some men and they're only happy if there's a smell of blood on the wind . . .

Hugh is slaughtered under Frank's chilling direction; and Frank showers red confetti on the corpse in a parody of a wedding, still singing 'Barbara Allen'. The resulting tableau is according to the stage direction 'timeless and ancient'.

If this chilling scene is the end of the action, it is not of course the end of the play's import. For it is precisely here that, in the way described earlier, the final instalment of the myth of the

Strange Knight is deployed with its sequence where remorse and severe reparations precede the final vision of 'the beginning of happiness'. Woods, in his more integrated and sustained use of mythic and non-realistic elements through the play, has avoided the difficulties which, as was suggested, attach to the full theatrical realization of the closing implications of Stewart Parker's *Pentecost*. His wholesale incorporation of mythic and folk-loric elements within a free-wheeling postmodern eclecticism frees the drama, in the avoidance of naturalism, from the constraints of a resolution within the strict frame of political plausibility.

* * *

At the Black Pig's Dyke, through its mythopoeia, its black comedy and its use of folk-lore, popular song and ballad, eschews therefore a specific topicality in its oblique approach to contemporary political and sectarian violence. Its didactic focus in this respect is in fact established through the symbolism of the framing-myth and what is offered ultimately is a newly-minted myth of regeneration. Stereotypes are reversed and, by the drastic method of the formulation of an ersatz myth, hope is wrested from a seemingly ineluctable cycle of violence and revenge; and waste and sterility, personified as masculine, are supplanted by re-birth through feminine agency. If in these ways however the play is distanced from immediate one-for-one topicality and contemporary reference, the immediacy of its impact is, paradoxically, intensified. Through the simultaneously bizarre and yet affectively familiar rituals of folk-custom in the shape of the mummers, by the 'strange potency' (to echo Noel Coward) of popular song or ballad, and by the insistent imagery of victimage, death and renewal, it finds a viscerally effective way of touching on the deepest fears of the audience: the knock on the door, the malevolent threat, the confrontation with faceless men. By the avoidance of overt political reference in this way, by using the ambiguous, pantomimic, disturbing presence of the mummers as an insistent visual metaphor for contemporary political violence, the play sets up the possibility of a similarly figurative countervailing force in the framing-myth and its final vision, sternly prefaced by ideas of retribution and reparation, of 'the beginning of happiness'. The vision is as stark as it is hopeful.

NOTES

INTRODUCTION

Kathleen Devine

1 Papers from Terence Brown, John Goodby, A.N. Jeffares, Keith Jeffery, Jacqueline Genet, Declan Kiberd and Josette Leray were commissioned for the Symposium. Other essays were later commissioned for this book.
2 *The Listener*, 23 October, 1941.
3 *The Listener*, 10 October, 1963.
4 Violet McGuire, 'The Departure', in *They Go – The Irish*, ed. Leslie Daiken (London, Nicholson & Watson, 1944), p. 83.
5 Quoted in A.T. Tolley, *The Poetry of the Forties* (Manchester, Manchester University Press, 1985), p. 207.

IRISH PROSE WRITERS OF THE FIRST WORLD WAR

Keith Jeffery

1 For example, Katharine Tynan, *The Years of the Shadow* (London, Constable, 1919); Monk Gibbon, *Inglorious Soldier* (London, Hutchinson, 1968). Unless otherwise stated, quotations are taken from the first edition.
2 Enid Starkie, *A Lady's Child* (London, Faber & Faber, 1941); C.S. Lewis, *Surprised by Joy* (London, Geoffrey Bles, 1955); E.R. Dodds, *Missing Persons: an Autobiography* (Oxford, Clarendon Press, 1977).
3 William Orpen, *An Onlooker in France, 1917–1919* (London, Williams & Norgate, 1921; rev. edn 1924); John Lavery, *The Life of a Painter* (London, Constable, 1940).
4 Nora Robertson, *Crowned Harp* (Dublin, Allen Figgis, 1960); Denis Ireland, *From the Jungle of Belfast* (Belfast, Blackstaff, 1973).
5 Michael MacDonagh, *The Irish at the Front* (London, Hodder & Stoughton, 1916); idem, *The Irish on the Somme* (London, Hodder & Stoughton, 1917); Bryan Cooper, *The Tenth (Irish) Division in Gallipoli* (London, Herbert Jenkins, 1918); Felix Lavery (ed.), *Great Irishmen in*

War and Politics (London, Andrew Melrose, 1920).

6 W. Allison Phillips, *The Revolution in Ireland, 1906–1923* (London, Longmans, 1923); P.S. O'Hegarty, *The Victory of Sinn Fein* (Dublin, Talbot Press, 1924).

7 These are too numerous to list here. The bibliography by the Ulsterman, Cyril Falls, *War Books: a Critical Guide* (London, Peter Davies, 1930), remains a particularly useful guide to unit histories.

8 Robert Graves, *Goodbye to All That* (Harmondsworth, Penguin Books, 1960), pp. 30, 229.

9 Alfred Perceval Graves, *To Return to All That* (Dublin, Talbot Press, 1930). In chapter xix, pp. 318–34, Graves took the opportunity to correct errors in his son's book.

10 *Everything is Thunder* (London, Bodley Head, 1935). The main character of the book, Hugh McGrath, is 'a lieutenant of Irish infantry'.

11 Cary wrote two autobiographical short stories 'Bush River' and 'The Raft', which drew on his service during the Cameroons campaign, but evidently considered them minor works as he refused to publish them during his lifetime (Malcolm Foster, *Joyce Cary: a Biography* (London, Michael Joseph, 1969), pp. 102–3).

12 *A Padre in France* (London, Hodder & Stoughton, n.d. [1918]).

13 There is a short passage of reminiscence about the Western Front in Margaret Barrington, *My Cousin Justin* (London, Cape, 1939), pp. 260–4. Barrington was married to Liam O'Flaherty from 1926 to 1932.

14 Garry O'Connor, *Sean O'Casey: a Life* (New York, Atheneum, 1988), p. 247.

15 *The Novels of World War I: an Annotated Bibliography* (New York & London, Garland, 1981) .

16 Figures taken from David Fitzpatrick, 'Militarism in Ireland, 1900–1922', in Thomas Bartlett & Keith Jeffery (eds), *A Military History of Ireland* (Cambridge, Cambridge University Press, 1996), pp. 388, 390.

17 These points are discussed in my essays 'The Great War in modern Irish memory', in T.G. Fraser & Keith Jeffery (eds), *Men, Women and War* (Dublin, Lilliput Press, 1993), pp. 136–57; and 'Irish culture and the Great War', *Bullán: An Irish Studies Journal*, vol. 1 no. 2 (Autumn 1994), pp. 87–96.

18 Rev. Frederick Simpson, in Great St Mary's Church, Cambridge, 2 Nov. 1932, quoted in Ronald Hyam, *Britain's Imperial Century* (London, Batsford, 1970), pp. 378–9.

19 Dublin, Hodges Figgis, 1927.

20 London, Heath Cranton, 1929.

21 MacLysaght, however, was no political innocent. He was, for example, the only republican sympathiser in the ill-fated Irish Convention of 1917–18.

22 London, Andrew Melrose, n.d. (1936).

23 This is despite the fact that on 1 July 1916 alone 23 men from the Bushmills area were killed in France. See Robert Thompson, *Bushmills Heroes, 1914–1918* (Coleraine, privately published, n.d. [*c.* 1994]).

24 Jacques Darras, 'A man from across the Channel: poet with a view', p. 17, in Maurna Crozier (ed.), *Cultural Traditions in Northern Ireland* (Belfast, Institute of Irish Studies, 1991), pp. 8–20. For a careful investigation of the resonances of the war in *Ulysses*, see Robert E. Spoo, '"Nestor" and the nightmare: the presence of the Great War in *Ulysses*', *20th Century Literature*, xxxii (1986), pp. 137–54.

25 In the House of Commons, 3 Aug. 1914 (*Hansard*, 5 ser., lxv, col. 1829).

26 London, Methuen, 1915.

27 For Hannay's war service see *A Padre in France*; and idem., *Pleasant Places* (London & Toronto, William Heinemann, 1934). See also Hilda Anne O'Donnell, 'A literary survey of the novels of Canon James Owen Hannay (George A. Birmingham)' (unpublished M.A. thesis, Queen's University Belfast, 1959); and Andrew Gailey, 'An Irishman's world', *Irish Review*, no. 13 (Winter 1992/93), pp. 31–9.

28 London, Methuen, 1919.

29 London, Methuen, 1912; facsimile edition, with an introduction by R.D.B. French, Shannon, Irish University Press, 1972.

30 Dublin, Talbot Press, n.d. [1916].

31 In the Royal Irish Academy library catalogue.

32 Newry, privately published, 1917. This is a 31-page pamphlet. There is a copy in the National Library of Ireland.

33 Dublin, Maunsell, 1917. The quotations below are taken from the Macmillan edn, New York, 1920.

34 Some of the scenes in the novel are confirmed from other sources. See, for example, Maurice Headlam (who recalls meeting Ervine in Dublin during the Rising), *Irish Reminiscences* (London, Robert Hale, 1947), pp. 49, 166–7.

35 Norman Vance, *Irish Literature: a Social History: Tradition, Identity and Difference* (Oxford, Basil Blackwell, 1990), p. 186. Brooke appears in the novel as Gerald Luke, who is killed in France.

36 Dodds, *Missing Persons*, pp. 38, 43. The tensions arising both from conflicting British and Irish loyalties, and that between parents and children, are explored in a short story by Daniel Corkery, 'Cowards?' (in *The Hounds of Banba* (Dublin, 1921)), where an Anglo-Irish landlord who forced his nationalist-inclined son into the army only for him to be executed for cowardice encounters the funeral of a hunger-striker whom he had accused of cowardice for refusing to join up. I am most grateful to Dr Patrick Maume for this reference.

37 Dodds, *Missing Persons*, p. 67.

38 As n. 13 above.

39 Dublin, Martin Lester, n.d. [1919].

40 Robert Hogan, *Eimar O'Duffy* (Cranbury N.J., Associated Uni-

versities Press, 1972), p. 14; W.J. Feeny, 'Eimar O'Duffy's "A Military Causerie"', *Journal of Irish Literature*, Vol. x, no. 3 (Sept. 1981), p. 92.

41 London, Heinemann, 1936. Quotations from first U.S. edition (New York, Doubleday, 1936). For biographical details, see Adele M. Dalsimer, *Kate O'Brien: a Critical Study* (Dublin, Gill & Macmillan, 1990).

42 Tynan, *Years of the Shadow*, p. 186. See also Marilyn Gaddis Rose, *Katharine Tynan* (London, Associated Universities Press, 1974).

43 London, Eveleigh, Nash & Grayson, 1924.

44 London, Collins, 1922.

45 Patrick MacGill, *The Amateur Army* (London, Herbert Jenkins, 1915), p. 7.

46 Idem, *The Red Horizon* (London, Herbert Jenkins, 1916), p. 199.

47 With the exception of *The Dough-Boys* (see below, n. 50), all MacGill's books were first published by Herbert Jenkins in London.

48 Owen Dudley Edwards, 'Patrick MacGill and the making of a historical source: with a handlist of his works', *The Innes Review* (Scottish Catholic Historical Association), xxxvii, part 2 (1986), pp. 73–99, is an indispensable source for MacGill.

49 For example in Anne M. Brady & Brian Cleeve, *A Biographical Dictionary of Irish Writers* (Dublin, Lilliput Press, 1985), p. 147.

50 New York, George H. Doran, 1918; London, Herbert Jenkins, 1919.

51 See Patrick O'Sullivan, 'Patrick MacGill: the making of a writer', in Seán Hutton & Paul Stewart (eds), *Ireland's Histories: Aspects of State, Society and Ideology* (London & New York, Routledge, 1991), pp. 203–22.

52 Esher to his son, Oliver Brett, 25 Oct. 1915, quoted in Dudley Edwards, 'Patrick MacGill', p. 96 n. 6.

53 *Ibid.*, p. 75.

54 Sales figure taken from an advertisement in a 1918 printing of *The Brown Brethren*.

55 MacGill, *Soldier Songs*, p. 8.

56 Although couched in the third person, the unsigned introduction, 'What this story is about', may well have been written by MacGill himself.

57 John Onions, *English Fiction and Drama of the Great War, 1918–39* (London, Macmillan, 1990), p. 52.

58 Noted in the fourth printing (n.d.) copy in Belfast Central Library.

59 London, Mandrake Press, 1929.

60 Patrick F. Sheeran, *The Novels of Liam O'Flaherty* (Dublin, Wolfhound Press, 1976), p. 67.

61 Onions, *English Fiction*, p. 54.

62 Hugh Cecil, 'The literary legacy of the war: the post-war novel – a select bibliography', p. 220, in Peter Liddle (ed.), *Home Fires and Foreign Fields: British Social and Military Experience in the First World War* (London, Brasseys, 1985), pp. 205–30.

63 *T.L.S.*, 21 Nov. 1929, p. 938.
64 First published in O'Flaherty's collection, *The Mountain Tavern* (London, Cape, 1929), pp. 163–74. John Zneimer erroneously remarks that *Return of the Brute* is O'Flaherty's 'only use of his wartime experiences in fiction' (Zneimer, *The Literary Vision of Liam O'Flaherty* (Syracuse, Syracuse University Press, 1970), p. 111).
65 This is the theme of Samuel Hynes' important *A War Imagined: the First World War and English Culture* (London, Bodley Head, 1990).
66 London, Gollancz, 1932. Quotations taken from the Penguin edition (Harmondsworth, 1946) .
67 There is a clear echo of the impact of Great War casualty lists in Annie M.P. Smithson's *The Marriage of Nurse Harding* (Dublin, Talbot Press, 1935), which describes predominantly from the women's perspective the history of an Ascendancy family from the turn of the century to the 1930s. In 1916 Aileen Hewdon, like Annie Smithson, a strong republican sympathiser yet a Protestant, reacts to the fifteen executions of Easter Rising leaders over a period of ten days in much the same spirit as Hinkson's character: 'Aileen, reading those terrible lists in the newspapers – the superb Roll of Honour which will be enshrined forever on Irish hearts – was glad when at last the tears came, and she could weep' (p. 104).
68 *My Cousin Justin*, p. 123. Although recruitment fell off very markedly after the first few months of the war, from 1 Aug. 1915 to 11 Nov. 1918 65,118 Irishmen still enlisted, 46 per cent of the total number who joined throughout the conflict (Patrick Callan, 'Recruiting for the British Army in Ireland during the First World War', *Irish Sword*, xvii no. 66 (Summer 1987), p. 42).
69 Ervine, *Changing Winds*, p. 436.
70 *My Cousin Justin*, p. 122.
71 *The Red Horizon*, p. 40.
72 Lennox Robinson, *Bryan Cooper* (London, Constable, 1931), p. 83. This is also the theme of Robinson's play *The Big House*, first produced at the Abbey Theatre in Sept. 1926.
73 Ulster's response is, however, quite well served in non-fiction. See, for example, the accounts in Cyril Falls, *The History of the 36th (Ulster) Division* (Belfast, McCaw, Stevenson & Orr, 1922); Sir Frank Fox, *The Royal Inniskilling Fusiliers in the Great War* (London, Constable, 1928); and St. John Ervine, *Craigavon, Ulsterman* (London, George Allen & Unwin, 1949).
74 Starkie, *A Lady's Child*, p. 206.
75 A point made with a political edge by St. John Ervine. In Great Britain 'stringency had come. We were tightening our belts. But not in Southern Ireland, where belts were loosened' (*Craigavon*, p. 326).
76 I would particularly like to thank Terence Brown, Kathleen Devine, Lindsay Duguid, Samuel Hynes, Alvin Jackson, Jane Leonard, Patrick Maume, Eunan O'Halpin, Martin Staunton, Christopher Woods and the participants of the September 1992 Symposium

on Modern Irish Writers and the Wars for their help and encouragement with this paper.

1916: THE IDEA AND THE ACTION

Declan Kiberd

1 Quoted in William Irwin Thompson, *The Imagination of an Insurrection* (New York, Oxford University Press, 1967), p. 20.
2 Quoted by Yeats, *Autobiographies* (London, Macmillan, 1955), p. 424.
3 W.B. Yeats, *Collected Poems* (London, Macmillan, 1950), p. 393.
4 George Russell, *The Living Torch*, ed. Monk Gibbon (London, Macmillan, 1937), pp. 135–44.
5 Yeats, *Collected Poems*, p. 375.
6 V.I. Lenin, *On Ireland* (Moscow, Progress Publishers, 1949), pp. 32–3.
7 Conor Cruise O'Brien, 'The Embers of Easter', *1916 The Easter Rising*, ed. Owen Dudley Edwards and Fergus Pyle (London, Macgibbon and Kee, 1968), p. 227.
8 On this phenomenon in other revolutionary situations see Crane Brinton, *The Anatomy of Revolution* (New York, Alfred Knopf and Random House, 1965), pp. 34, 42, 53, 68 ff.
9 Russell, *Thoughts for a Convention* (Dublin and London, Maunsel and Co., 1917), p. 7.
10 Yeats, *Plays and Controversies* (London, Macmillan, 1923), p. 24. There are *some* anti-English outbursts in the writings of Pearse, but even Fr Francis Shaw – no admirer of Pearse – comments that 'nowhere does Pearse teach as explicitly as Tone the duty of hate', 'The Canon of Irish History: A Challenge', *Studies*, Summer 1972, LXI, p. 126.
11 Shaw, *The Matter with Ireland*, ed. David H. Greene and Dan H. Lawrence (London, Rupert Hart-Davis, 1962), p. 112.
12 Yeats, *Collected Poems*, p. 205.
13 Thomas MacDonagh, 'Language and Literature in Ireland', *The Irish Review*, IV, March-April 1914, pp. 176–82.
14 P.H. Pearse, *Plays, Stories, Poems* (Dublin, Phoenix, 1924), p. 336.
15 *The Collected Letters of W.B. Yeats*, ed. Allan Wade (London, Rupert Hart-Davis, 1954), p. 295.
16 Quoted by Conor Cruise O'Brien, *Ancestral Voices* (Dublin, Poolbeg, 1994), p. 68.
17 Pearse, *Plays, Stories, Poems*, p. 44.
18 Joseph Mary Plunkett. *Poems* (Dublin, The Talbot Press, 1916), pp. 59–60.
19 Yeats, *Collected Plays* (London, Macmillan, 1952), p. 591.
20 Richard Sennett, *The Fall of Public Man* (New York, Vintage Books, 1978), pp. 184, 186.
21 *Ibid.*, p. 192.
22 Yeats, *Plays and Controversies*, p. 161.

23 *Ibid.*, pp. 157–8.
24 J.P. Sartre, *Life/Situations* (New York, Pantheon Books, 1977), p. 167.
25 *Beltaine*, No. 3, April, 1900.
26 Yeats, *Collected Poems*, p. 373.
27 Jose Ortega Y Gasset, *España Invertebrada* (Madrid, 1922), pp. 3, 146–50.
28 Yeats, *Collected Plays*, pp. 431–46.
29 Harold Rosenberg, 'The Resurrected Romans', *The Tradition of the New* (Chicago, University of Chicago Press, 1982), pp. 155 ff.
30 Brinton, p. 203.
31 Maire nic Shiubhlaigh, *The Splendid Years* (Dublin, J. Duffy, 1955), p. 87.
32 Quoted by Tim Pat Coogan, *Michael Collins* (London, Hutchinson, 1990), pp. 53–4.
33 On this see Robert Wohl, *The Generation of 1914* (Cambridge, Mass., Harvard University Press, 1979).
34 Pearse, *Plays, Stories, Poems*, p. 323.
35 Yeats, *Collected Poems*, p. 206.
36 Desmond FitzGerald, *Memoirs, 1913–16* (London, Routledge & Kegan Paul, 1968), pp. 142–3.
37 Pearse, *Plays, Stories, Poems*, p. 324.
38 Max Weber, *The Protestant Ethic and the Spirit of Capitalism* (London, Unwin Books, 1985), pp. 104 ff.
39 Quoted by Bruce Mazlish, *The Revolutionary Ascetic* (New York, Basic Books, 1976), p. 85.
40 J.J. Horgan, *From Parnell to Pearse* (Dublin, Browne & Nolan, 1948), p. 285.
41 Shaw, *Studies*, Summer 1972, p. 123.
42 'The Coming Revolution', November, 1913 in *Political Writings and Speeches* (Dublin & London, Maunsel & Roberts, 1922), pp. 91–2.
43 See Eric Hobsbawm, 'Mass-Producing Traditions: Europe 1870–1914', *The Invention of Tradition*, ed. Eric Hobsbawm and Terence Ranger (Cambridge, Cambridge University Press, 1983), p. 271.
44 Ronald Paulson, *Representations of Revolution 1789–1820* (New Haven, London, Yale University Press, 1983), p. 14.
45 Tom Paine, *The Rights of Man* (Harmondsworth, Penguin, 1969), pp. 71, 73.
46 Bernard MacLaverty, *Cal* (Belfast, Blackstaff, 1983), p. 73.

YEATS AND WAR

Jacqueline Genet

1 'Easter 1916', *Variorum Edition of the Poems of W.B. Yeats*, ed. P. Alt and R.K. Alspach (New York, Macmillan, 1940), p. 392. All quotations from the poems are from this edition.

2   W.B. Yeats, *Essays and Introductions* (London, Macmillan, 1961), p. 499.
3   *The Collected Letters of W.B. Yeats*, ed. Allan Wade (London, Rupert Hart-Davis, 1954), pp. 599–600. Henceforth *Letters*.
4   *The Gonne–Yeats Letters 1893–1938: Always Your Friend*, ed. Anna MacBride White and A. Norman Jeffares (London, Hutchinson, 1992), p. 347.
5   *Letters*, p. 682.
6   *Ibid.*, p. 693.
7   *Variorum*, p. 836.
8   *Letters*, pp. 811–12.
9   *Variorum*, p. 837.
10 *Letters*, pp. 850–1.
11 *Ibid.*
12 W.B. Yeats, *Autobiographies* (London, Macmillan, 1955), p. 559.
13 W.B. Yeats, *Letters on Poetry to Dorothy Wellesley* (London, Oxford University Press, 1940), p. 195.
14 *Essays and Introductions*, p. 519.
15 *Letters on Poetry to Dorothy Wellesley*, p. 122.
16 *Letters*, pp. 612–13.
17 *Ibid.*, p. 614.
18 *Ibid.*
19 W.B. Yeats, *Collected Plays* (London, Macmillan, 1952), p. 442.
20 *Letters*, p. 649.
21 *Ibid.*, p. 680.
22 *Ibid.*, p. 668.
23 'My last symbol, Robert Artisson, was an evil spirit much run after in Kilkenny at the start of the fourteenth century', Yeats explains (*Variorum*, p. 433).
24 *The Senate Speeches of W.B. Yeats*, ed. Donald R. Pearce (London, Faber & Faber, 1961), p. 87.
25 *Letters*, p. 696.
26 *Ibid.*, pp. 698–99.
27 Quoted by G. Freyer in *W.B. Yeats and the Anti-Democratic Tradition* (Dublin, Gill & Macmillan, 1981), p. 67.
28 W.B. Yeats, *A Vision* (London, Macmillan, 1962), p. 268.
29 W.B. Yeats, *Mythologies* (London, Macmillan, 1959), p. 276.
30 *Variorum*, p. 827.
31 W.B. Yeats, *On the Boiler* (Dublin, Cuala Press, 1938), p. 20.
32 *A Vision*, p. 268.
33 Stan Smith, *W.B. Yeats: A Critical Introduction* (Dublin, Gill & Macmillan, 1990), p. 117.
34 *On the Boiler*, p. 29.
35 *Ibid.*, p. 30.
36 *Essays and Introductions*, p. 526.
37 *Ibid.*, p. 502.
38 *On the Boiler*, p. 20.

39 *Variorum*, p. 580.
40 *Letters on Poetry to Dorothy Wellesley*, p. 196.
41 *On the Boiler*, p. 22.
42 *Autobiographies*, p. 195.
43 *Essays and Introductions*, p. 210.
44 *Autobiographies*, pp. 194–5.

MAUD GONNE: ROMANTIC REPUBLICAN

A. Norman Jeffares

1 *The Gonne-Yeats Letters 1893–1938: Always Your Friend*, edited by Anna
   MacBride White and A. Norman Jeffares (London, Hutchinson, 1992,
   New York, Norton, 1992). Henceforth cited as *L* in the text.
2 Maud Gonne MacBride, *A Servant of the Queen: Reminiscences*
   (London, Victor Gollancz Ltd., 1938; 1974). A new revised edition,
   edited by Anna MacBride White and A. Norman Jeffares, was
   published by Colin Smythe Ltd, Gerrards Cross, 1994. See also her
   'Yeats and Ireland', in *Scattering Branches: Tributes to the Memory of
   W.B. Yeats*, ed. Stephen Gwynn (London, Macmillan, 1940).
3 These include Samuel Levenson, *Maud Gonne* (London, Cassell,
   1976); Nancy Cardozo, *Maud Gonne, Lucky Eyes and a High Heart*
   (London, Victor Gollancz, 1979); Margery Brady, *The Love Story of
   Yeats and Maud Gonne* (Cork, The Mercier Press, 1990); Margaret
   Ward, *Maud Gonne: Ireland's Joan of Arc* (London, Pandora Press,
   1990). See also Geoffrey Elborn, *Francis Stuart: A Life* (Dublin, Raven
   Arts Press, 1990) and Conrad A. Balliett, 'Micheál MacLiammóir
   Recalls Maud Gonne MacBride' in *The Journal of Irish Literature* Vol.
   VI, 2, 1977 and 'The Lives – and Lies – of Maud Gonne' in *Eire-
   Ireland* Vol. 14, 3, Autumn 1979 and Beth McKillen, 'Irish Feminism
   and Nationalist Separatism 1914–1923' in *Eire-Ireland*, Vol. 17, nos 3
   and 4, Autumn and Winter 1982.
4 See Tania Alexander, *A Little of All These: An Estonian Childhood*
   (1967; 1992) and 'Irish Micky in Estonian Exile' in *The Guardian*, 22
   Nov. 1988. Mrs Wilson had earlier had a son by her legal husband
   who was described as having been killed in an Irish uprising; this
   child was looked after in a home. She was fortunate in becoming
   part of the Zakrevsky family, who greatly respected her and were
   very kind to her. Eventually she died in Estonia, having earlier
   smuggled three of the Zakrevskys out of St. Petersburg in 1917, and
   helped the family to settle into a small dower house and run a
   smallholding after their estate was confiscated.
5 See Conrad A. Balliett, 'The Lives – and Lies – of Maud Gonne',
   Eire-Ireland, Vol. 14, 3, Autumn 1979, who argues that Maud had
   met Millevoye in her nineteenth year, before her father's death. See

also his 'Micheál MacLiammóir Recalls Maud Gonne MacBride', The *Journal of Irish Literature*, Vol VI, no 2, May 1977.

6   See footnote 7. below.

7   There is an ironic account of this in James Joyce, *A Portrait of the Artist as a Young Man* (Paladin edn., London, Paladin, 1988), p. 187: 'In the roadway at the head of the street [Grafton Street] a slab was set to the memory of Wolfe Tone and he remembered having been present with his father at its laying. He remembered with bitterness that scene of tawdry tribute. There were four French delegates in a brake and one, a plump smiling young man, held wedged on a stick, a card on which were printed the words: Vive L' Irelande!'

8   Yeats's anxiety was exacerbated by Maud and Connolly having drafted a leaflet entitled 'The Rights of Life and the Rights of Property' which began with quotations from Pope Clement I, Pope Gregory the Great and Cardinal Manning. Some of the text is given in Maud Gonne MacBride, *A Servant of the Queen* (London, Gollancz, 1938) chapter XVII, pp. 226–228. Maud gave Connolly £25 from the money she had collected on her American lecture tour to pay for the printing of the leaflet and a journey to Kerry. The extracts given in *A Servant of the Queen* do not specifically urge the tenants to kill the landlords; whether Yeats read the leaflet or not is not known; he spoke to Lady Gregory of Maud's *plans* to incite the tenants. See Diary entry of 14 February 1898, cited by John Kelly, 'Friendship is the Only House I Have', *Lady Gregory, Fifty Years After* (Gerrards Cross, Colin Smythe Ltd., 1987), p. 200.

9   MacBride told his brother that he was in Algeciras on the day the King was in Gibraltar.

10 It is possible to trace this in various letters of hers to him: 'Why don't you write' (Feb. 1909); 'What a long time it is since you wrote to me' (August 1909); 'What ages it is since I heard from you! Where are you? Are you in love? I think there must be something very interesting which keeps you from writing to me for so long. I hope you are not going to get married!' (8 Feb. 1911); 'I was surprised to hear you were in Paris . . . How strange it seems to think of you in Paris just the time I am away!' (May 1911, written in Italy); 'I heard you were in town last Friday and wondered why you didn't write' (Wed [?] 1911); 'I was sorry to see so little of you in Dublin' (Friday [?] 1911); 'What has happened? I am getting weary at getting no news from you – I hope it only means that you have been very busy . . .' (29 Aug. 1912); 'This is too disappointing missing you everywhere' (17 Nov. 1912); 'It was very disappointing missing you in Dublin and in London' (28 Nov. 1912); 'It was a great disappointment to me and to Iseult to hear that you had changed your plans and would not have time to come to Paris' (April 1913); 'I was anxious at your silence' (? June 1913); 'It was sad not seeing you on your way through London' (Nov. 1913); 'It is a great disappointment you not being able to spend Xmas with us in Paris'

(Dec. 1913); 'I am very disappointed, I would so have liked to have seen you before you start for America' (Jan. 1914); ' How I wish you were here with us' [in the Pyrenees] (25 July 1914). Yeats during this time was involved in a predominantly physical relationship with Mabel Dickinson (which began in 1908 and ended stormily in 1913). In 1911 he met Georgie Hyde Lees, whom he married in 1917. He was in the USA in 1911 on his lecture tour and somewhat less involved with the Abbey Theatre after Lenox Robinson had become manager in 1910; his friendship with Ezra Pound had begun in 1909. It was a period when he visited many country houses in England, spent his summers in Coole, and was somewhat less interested in Irish affairs, except for the Lane controversy.

O'CASEY AT WAR

Christopher Murray

1 All dates of plays in this essay are of first production, unless otherwise stated.
2 Sean O'Casey, 'A Terrible Beauty is Borneo', *Inishfallen, Fare Thee Well*, in *Autobiographies* (2 vols., London, Macmillan, 1981), 2, p. 138.
3 C. Desmond Greaves, *Sean O'Casey: Politics and Art* (London, Laurence and Wishart, 1979), p. 79.
4 Sean O'Casey, 'Under the Plough and the Stars', *Drums under the Windows*, in *Autobiographies*, 1, p. 608. Cf. *The Story of the Citizen Army*, in *Feathers from the Green Crow*, ed. Robert Hogan (Columbia, University of Missouri Press, 1962; London, Macmillan, 1963), p. 193.
5 Roger McHugh, '"Always Complainin": The Politics of Young Sean', *Irish University Review*, 10.1 (1980), p. 93.
6 *The Story of the Irish Citizen Army*, in *Feathers from the Green Crow*, p. 236.
7 Mrs Hanna Sheehy-Skeffington, in a letter to the *Irish Independent*, 23 February 1926, taking issue with O'Casey's treatment of 1916. See *The Letters of Sean O'Casey 1910–1941, Volume I*, ed. David Krause (London, Cassell, 1975), p. 172.
8 *The Plough and the Stars*, in Sean O'Casey, *Collected Plays* (4 vols., London, Macmillan, 1949–51), I, p. 193 and I, pp. 202–3. Subsequent quotations from O'Casey's plays refer to this collected edition, hereafter *CP*.
9 Sean O'Casey, *Autobiographies*, 2, p. 138.
10 *The Collected Plays of W.B. Yeats* (London, Macmillan, 1953). p. 57.
11 David Krause, *Sean O'Casey: The Man and his Work*. An Enlarged Edition (New York, Macmillan; London, Collier, Macmillan, 1975), p. 35.
12 Gabriel Fallon, *Sean O'Casey: The Man I Knew* (London, Routledge and Kegan Paul; Boston, Little, Brown, 1965), p. 17.
13 *Ibid.*, pp. 24–5.

14 Sean O'Casey, 'Comrades', *Inishfallen, Fare Thee Well*, in *Auto-biographies*, 2, p. 91.
15 Sean O'Casey, 'The Silver Tassie', *Rose and Crown*, in *Auto-biographies*, 2, pp. 270–71.
16 R.F. Foster, *Modern Ireland 1600–1972* (London, Allen Lane/Penguin Press, 1988), p. 472. Italics in original.
17 *The Letters of W.B. Yeats*, ed. Allan Wade (London, Hart-Davis, 1954), p. 743. Italics added.
18 *The Letters of Sean O'Casey, Volume I*, p. 166. Later, in a letter dated 21 March 1958, O'Casey wrote: 'The fact is, I believe, that Yeats for one reason or another, wanted to be my boss; to dictate to me the way I should go, but I wasnt [*sic*] having [any] of that now!' See *Letters, Volume III*, ed. David Krause (Washington, D.C., Catholic University of America Press, 1989), p. 571.
19 Letter dated 24 March 1960, *The Letters of Sean O'Casey, Volume IV*, ed. David Krause (Washington, D.C., Catholic University of America Press, 1992), p. 129.
20 See Gabriel Fallon, *Sean O'Casey: The Man I Knew*, pp. 46–8. See also Brenna Katz Clarke and Harold Ferrar, *The Dublin Drama League 1918–1941* (Dublin, Dolmen; Atlantic Highlands, Humanities Press, 1979).
21 August Strindberg, *Plays: Two: The Dance of Death, A Dream Play, The Stronger*, trans. Michael Meyer (London, Methuen, 1982), p. 175.
22 *The Letters of Sean O'Casey*, IV, p. 130.
23 *The Letters of Sean O'Casey*, I, pp. 118–9.
24 *The Letters of W.B. Yeats*, ed. Allan Wade, p. 741.
25 *Lady Gregory's Journals: Volume Two: Books Thirty to Forty-Four: 21 February 1925–9 May 1932*, ed. Daniel J. Murphy (Gerrards Cross, Colin Smythe, 1987), p. 307.
26 *Sean O'Casey: The Man and his Work*, p. 109.
27 *The Letters of Sean O'Casey*, 1, p. 822. Cf. 'Black Oxen Passing By', *Rose and Crown*, in *Autobiographies*, 2, p. 335.
28 *The Poems of Wilfred Owen*, ed. Edmund Blunden (London, Chatto & Windus, 1931), p. 75.
29 Carol Kleiman, *Sean O'Casey's Bridge of Vision: Four Essays on Structure and Perspective* (Toronto, University of Toronto Press, 1982), p. 28.
30 Jack Mitchell, *The Essential O'Casey: A Study of the Twelve Major Plays of Sean O'Casey* (Berlin, Seven Seas Publishers, 1980), p. 112.
31 Heinz Kosok, *O'Casey the Dramatist*, trans. Kosok and Joseph T. Swann (Gerrards Cross, Colin Smythe; Totowa, N.J., Barnes and Noble, 1985), p. 136.
32 Gabriel Fallon, *Sean O'Casey: The Man I Knew*, p. 47.
33 Sean O'Casey, 'A Long Ashwednesday', *Rose and Crown*, in *Autobiographies*, 2, p. 352.
34 Sean O'Casey, 'From Within the Gates', in *Blasts and Benedictions: Articles and Stories*, ed. Ronald Ayling (London, Macmillan; New York, St. Martin's Press, 1967), pp. 111–7 (esp. 114–5).

35 Garry O'Connor, *Sean O'Casey: A Life* (London, Hodder and Stoughton, 1988), p. 304.

36 C. Desmond Greaves, *Sean O'Casey: Politics and Art*, p. 142.

37 Jack Mitchell, *The Essential O'Casey*, p. 155.

38 *The Sting and the Twinkle: Conversations with Sean O'Casey*, ed. E.H. Mikhail and John O'Riordan (London, Macmillan, 1974), p. 120.

39 *The Letters of Sean O'Casey*, I, p. 849. Agate had dismissed *Within the Gates* as 'pretentious rubbish' and had drawn down O'Casey's wrath, expressed in his book of essays *The Flying Wasp* (London, Macmillan, 1937).

40 *The Harvest Festival: A Play in Three Acts by Sean O'Casey*. With a Foreword by Eileen O'Casey and Introduction by John O'Riordan (Gerrards Cross, Colin Smythe, 1980).

41 See Hugh Hunt, *Sean O'Casey* (Dublin, Gill and Macmillan, 1980), p. 108.

42 *The Letters of W.B. Yeats*, ed. Allan Wade, p. 741.

43 *The Letters of Sean O'Casey*, III, p. 303 (letter dated 11 September, 1956).

44 *The Letters of Sean O'Casey*, IV, p. 70 (letter dated 2 October 1959).

FRANK O'CONNOR'S 'WAR BOOK': *GUESTS OF THE NATION*

Elmer Andrews

1 Frank O'Connor, *An Only Child* (London, Macmillan, 1961), p. 210. Hereafter, *An Only Child* will be abbreviated to *OC* and page references will be incorporated into the text.

2 James Matthews, *Voices: A Life of Frank O'Connor* (Dublin, Gill and Macmillan, 1983), p. 26.

3 Frank O'Connor, in *Writers at Work: The 'Paris Review' Interviews*, ed. Malcolm Cowley (Harmondsworth, Penguin, 1958), p. 166.

4 James Matthews, *Frank O'Connor* (New Jersey, Associated University Presses, 1976), p. 20.

5 Frank O'Connor, *'The Big Fellow' A Life of Michael Collins* (London, Nelson, 1937).

6 'The mirror in the roadway' is a phrase O'Connor borrowed from Stendhal for the title of his study of the modern novel, *The Mirror in the Roadway* (London, Hamish Hamilton, 1957). Stendhal attributes the phrase to the historian Saint-Real.

7 In *The Mirror in the Roadway*, 'The flight from fancy' is the subtitle O'Connor uses for his chapter on Jane Austen, pp. 17–42; 'The flight from reality' the subtitle for his chapter on Stendhal, pp. 42–61. Hereafter, *The Mirror in the Roadway* will be abbreviated to *MR* and page references will be incorporated into the text.

8   Frank O'Connor to Nancy McCarthy, 1 January 1931. Quoted in Matthews, *Voices*, p. 76.
9   Frank O'Connor, *The Lonely Voice: A Study of the Short Story* (London, Macmillan, 1963), p. 19. Hereafter, *The Lonely Voice* will be abbreviated to *LV* and page references will be incorporated into the text.
10 Quoted in Matthews, *Voices*, p. 65.
11 See Matthews, *Voices*, p. 68.
12 Frank O'Connor, *Writers at Work: The 'Paris Review' Interviews*, p. 167.
13 Lionel Trilling, 'Introduction', *Isaac Babel: Collected Stories* (Harmondsworth, Penguin, 1961), p. 10. Quotations are taken from this edition.
14 Trilling, 'Introduction', *Isaac Babel: Collected Stories* p. 20.
15 Gerard Genette, *Narrative Discourse*, trans. by Jane E. Lewin (Oxford, Blackwell, 1986), p. 235.
16 Bakhtin makes a fundamental distinction between 'centripetal' and 'centrifugal' forces. The 'centripetal' is the tendency towards a unified and centralised textual and ideological world. The 'centrifugal' forces are those which parody, criticise and generally undermine the pretensions of the ambitions towards a unitary language and culture. See M.M. Bakhtin, *The Dialogic Imagination: Four Essays*, trans. by Caryl Emerson and Michael Holquist (Austin, University of Texas Press, 1981).
17 'Few writers have had so clear a vision of what the short story could do', wrote O'Connor of Sherwood Anderson in *The Lonely Voice*, p. 35.

SEAN O'FAOLAIN'S *MIDSUMMER NIGHT MADNESS AND OTHER STORIES*: CONTEXTS FOR REVISIONISM

Patrick Walsh

1   Maurice Harmon, *Sean O'Faolain* (London, Constable, 1994), p. 263.
2   *Ibid.*, p. 262.
3   *Ibid.*, p. 89.
4   Sean O'Faolain, *Midsummer Night Madness and Other Stories* (USA, Viking, 1932), p. vii.
5   Harmon, *op. cit.*, pp. 88–89.
6   Patrick Maume, *'Life that is Exile' Daniel Corkery and the Search for Irish Ireland* (Belfast, Belfast Institute of Irish Studies, 1993), p. 138.
7   Ciaran Brady (ed.), *Interpreting Irish History: the debate on historical revisionism* (Dublin, Irish Academic Press, 1994), See Brady's Introduction.
8   Sean O'Faolain, 'Daniel Corkery' *Dublin Magazine* 11, (Apr.–June 1936), p. 60.
9   *Ibid.*, p. 59.

10 L.M. Cullen, 'The Hidden Ireland: Reassessment of a Concept' *Studia Hibernica*, Vol. ix, (1969), p. 47.
11 Sean O'Faolain, *The Collected Stories of Sean O'Faolain Volume 1*, (London, Constable, 1980), p. 145.
12 *Ibid.*, p. 148.
13 *Ibid.*, p. 128.
14 Maume, *op. cit.*, pp. 127–8.
15 Sean O'Faolain, *The Collected Stories, Volume 1*, p. 146.
16 *Ibid.*, p. 161.
17 *Ibid.*, p. 162.
18 *Ibid.*, p. 63.
19 Harmon, *op. cit.*, p. 52.
20 Sean O'Faolain, *The Collected Stories, Volume 1*, p. 66.
21 *Ibid.*, p. 68.
22 *Ibid.*, p. 73.
23 *Ibid.*, pp. 81–82.
24 *Ibid.*, p. 101.
25 *Ibid.*, p. 10.
26 *Ibid.*, p. 10.
27 *Ibid.*, p. 18.
28 *Ibid.*, p. 43.
29 Sean O'Faolain, *Vive Moi! An Autobiography*, (London, Rupert Hart-Davis, 1965), p. 275.
30 *Ibid.*, p. 116.
31 The same conception can be traced in his editorials for 'Ulster Issues' of *The Bell* of July 1941 and July 1942: e.g., 'The important thing is that so long as the gantries go on producing writers like them in this and the next issue the victory is not with the brutality of nineteenth century industrialism, non-conformity, the kirk, the lodges, the bosses but with the fine and intelligent humanity of the natural, wide-awake Ulsterman.' From *The Bell* Vol. 4 no. 4, July 1942, p. 231.
32 Sean O'Faolain, *An Irish Journey*, (London, Readers' Union with Longmans, Green, 1941), p. 220.
33 Sean O'Faolain, *Foreign Affairs and Other Stories*, (London, Constable, 1976). Quoted in the publisher's introductory note.
34 The reference is of course to Benedict Anderson's *Imagined Communities*, (London, Verso, 1983). His meditation on how post-imperial nations still carry the geography and conceptual frameworks of the imperial power seems particularly apt here.

ROADS TO SPAIN: IRISH WRITERS AND THE SPANISH CIVIL WAR

Kathleen Devine

1 Reported in *The Irish Times*, 9 March, 1937. In the North, of course, dangers were perceived on both sides of the Spanish question and in

his autobiography, *Even Without Irene*, Robert Greacen notes: 'that Franco was supported by the Roman Catholic Church did not seem a good omen to Protestant Ulstermen' (Belfast, Lagan Press, 1995, p. 70).

2   Thomas O'Brien who was involved with the New Theatre Group in Dublin also went to Spain. His writings, of no great literary interest in themselves, show the attitudes to the Spanish war that typified English socialist response but these give way later to pacifism. His work is collected in *Strong Words Brave Deeds*, ed. by H. Gustav Klaus (Dublin, The O'Brien Press, 1994). On the right, Eoin O'Duffy's *Crusade in Spain* (Dublin, Browne & Nolan, 1938) gave an account of his efforts on Franco's behalf.

3   Quoted in K. Hoskins, *Today the Struggle: Literature and Politics in England During the Spanish Civil War* (Austin, University of Texas Press, 1969), p. 20.

4   To Ethel Mannin he writes of his concern about the effects of increased Catholic bigotry on 'my "pagan" institutions the Theatre, the Academy' if General O'Duffy returns a hero and in one letter he says 'we constantly discuss the war in Spain'. *The Collected Letters of W.B. Yeats*, ed. Allan Wade (London, Rupert Hart-Davis, 1954), pp. 873, 881, 885.

5   It has been suggested that the girl in the poem is Cora Hughes with whom the young poet, Charles Donnelly, was in love and that the orators are Peadar O'Donnell and George Gilmore. Cora Hughes sold copies of the Republican Congress paper while other members of the organization spoke. For this and other information about George Gilmore and his relation with Charles Donnelly I am indebted to Dr Anthony Coughlan who has been unfailingly generous in sharing his knowledge of 1930s socialist Dublin.

6   Quoted in G. O'Connor, *Sean O'Casey: A Life* (London, Hodder & Stoughton, 1988), p. 312.

7   Louis MacNeice, *Collected Poems* (London, Faber & Faber, 1966), pp. 110–12. All quotations from MacNeice's poems are taken from this volume.

8   Louis MacNeice, *The Strings are False* (London, Faber & Faber, 1965), pp. 158–63.

9   *Ibid.*, p. 196.

10 *Salud! An Irishman in Spain* (London, Methuen, 1937), p. 8. Subsequent quotations are from this edition and indicated thus in the text: *S*.

11 O'Donnell's enthusiasm for expelling mass ignorance is evident in his suggestion for universal education via a university of the air with the invention of television. Recounting a conversation with some Anarchists he says: 'We shot ahead of our day when I urged that as soon as television achieved a technique to permit of it they should pioneer the idea of widening the whole conception of the university by bringing the lecture-room within sight and sound of the youth of the whole nation' (*Salud*, p. 42).

12 Foreword to *Drums Without End*, (Portree, Aquila, 1985). All quotations from the prose are taken from this collection.
13 As in the case of John Cornford, there is some uncertainty about the actual date of Donnelly's death. That usually given, 27 February, 1937, is challenged by Peter O'Connor who helped carry his body back from the front for burial. He gives the date as 23 February.
14 'The Death Song', *Comhthrom Féinne*, December, 1931.
15 'Philistia: An Essay in Allegory', *Comhthrom Féinne*, March, 1932.
16 Joseph Donnelly quotes Milne's memory of Donnelly saying: '... you don't think I'm going out to Spain like a lot of those romantic fools, do you, Milne? ... I'm going to study the military position and what has happened to military strategy in Spain . . .' in *Charlie Donnelly: the Life and Poems* (Dublin, Dedalus, 1987), p. 45. For the anecdote about the matchsticks I am indebted to Dr and Mrs Flann Campbell.
17 *Charlie Donnelly: The Life and Poems*, p. 78. Subsequent quotations are from this edition.
18 'Greater Love', *The Poems of Wilfred Owen*, ed. Jon Stallworthy (London, Hogarth Press, 1985), p. 143.
19 'Into Battle' in *Men Who March Away: Poems of the First World War*, ed. I.M. Parsons (London, Chatto & Windus, 1965), pp. 38–9.
20 *Alamein to Zem Zem*, ed. Desmond Graham (Oxford, New York, Oxford University Press, 1979), p. 16.
21 Keith Douglas, *Complete Poems*, ed. Desmond Graham (Oxford, Oxford University Press, 1978), 'Dead Men' and 'Landscape with Figures 2', pp. 96, 103.

LOUIS MacNEICE AND THE SECOND WORLD WAR

Terence Brown

1 Louis MacNeice, *The Strings Are False* (London, Faber and Faber, 1965), p. 212.
2 Quoted in Peter McDonald, *Louis MacNeice: the Poet in his Contexts* (Oxford, Clarendon Press, 1991), p. 97.
3 E.R. Dodds, *Missing Persons* (Oxford, Clarendon Press, 1977), p. 39.
4 *Ibid.*, p. 67.
5 *Ibid.*
6 Louis MacNeice, 'The Way We Live Now', *Selected Prose of Louis MacNeice*, ed. A. Heuser (Oxford, Clarendon Press, 1990), p. 82.
7 McDonald, *op. cit.*, p. 98.
8 *Ibid.*, p. 99.
9 *Ibid.*
10 Louis MacNeice, *Collected Poems* (London, Faber and Faber, 1966), p. 165. Henceforth given as *C.P.* in the text.

11   Louis MacNeice, *The Last Ditch* (Dublin, Cuala Press, 1940), p. 7.

12   *Ibid.*, p. 10.

13   *Ibid.*, p. 11.

14   *Ibid.*, p. 5.

15   Heuser, p. 116.

16. MacNeice, *The Strings Are False*, p. 21.

17   *Ibid.*

18   *The Strings Are False* it must be admitted is a document over whose publication the author had no control. It has been produced from the textual remains of a work in progress by E.R. Dodds, who adjudicated between two drafts. It is not certain, though I believe it probable, that the first three chapters would have remained at the beginning of the work, if MacNeice himself had completed it for publication. Dodds reports: 'Louis's final intention may have been to transfer the substance of chapters i and ii (which were still in rough draft) from the beginning of the book to their chronological place at the end, either omitting chapter iii or perhaps using part of it as an introduction. But that plan would have involved considerable rewriting, which was never done. I have accordingly left chapters i to iii where they stand in B [one of the drafts]. They introduce Louis at a pause in his life, isolated in a temporary limbo between two worlds, looking back over his past and forward to a future which for him as for all British subjects was in 1940 dark and uncertain'. (*The Strings Are False*, p. 12.) Dodds derived the title for the book from a typscript of chapter xxxii of the work 'evidently designed for separate publication in some journal, which bears the superscription "A Visit to Spain: Easter 1936 (excerpted from a book, now in preparation, entitled *The Strings Are False*"'. *Ibid.*, p. 11. In my view the title suggests, with its reference to the eve of battle, that Dodds did right to structure the work as he did. That impression would have been significantly lessened had he or MacNeice moved the first two chapters to the close of the work.

19   MacNeice, *The Strings Are False*, p. 21.

20   *Ibid.*, p. 35.

21   Quoted in William T. McKinnon, *Apollo's Blended Dream* (London, Oxford University Press, 1971), p. 32.

22   Louis MacNeice, 'Traveller's Return' in Heuser *op. cit.*, p. 83.

23   Louis MacNeice, *The Poetry of W.B. Yeats* (London, Oxford University Press, 1941), p. 1.

24   *Ibid.*, pp. 1–2.

25   Louis MacNeice, 'The Morning After the Blitz' in Heuser *op. cit.*, p. 117.

26   *Ibid.*, p. 118.

27   Louis MacNeice, 'London Letter [5]: Reflections from the Dome of St Paul's' in Heuser *op. cit.*, pp. 133–34.

28   *Ibid.*, pp. 135–36.

29   Louis MacNeice, *The Poetry of W.B. Yeats*, pp. VII–VIII.

30   *Ibid.*, p. 9.

31 *Ibid.*, p. 10.
32 'Broken Windows or Thinking Aloud' in Heuser, *op. cit.*, p. 142.

BECKETT AND WORLD WAR II: *IN MEMORIAM SAMUEL BECKETT, 1906–1989*

John Fletcher

1 Cf. 'L'Histoire d'Yvonne Picard' by Bianca Lamblin, *Esprit*, May 1992, pp. 88–99.
2 See 'Che Sciagura' by 'D. E. S. C.' [Samuel Beckett], *T. C. D., A College Miscellany*, 14 November 1929, p. 42.
3 This is made clear by – *inter alia* – a reference to the Easter Rising, which took place when Beckett was an impressionable ten-year-old: the narrator of 'Text for Nothing III', whose opinions are 'republican', remembers 'potting at the [British] invader from behind a barrel of Guinness'; see *No's Knife* (London, Calder & Boyars, 1967), pp. 83—84.
4 Reprinted in *Collected Poems 1930-1978* by Samuel Beckett (London, John Calder, 1984), p. 56, hereafter referred to as *Poems*. Passages (abridged where necessary) from *Murphy* and *Molloy* by Samuel Beckett are taken from the Calder editions also, dated 1963 and 1966 respectively. Quotations from *Waiting for Godot* and *Endgame* are taken from the editions published in London by Faber & Faber, dated 1965 and 1958 respectively.
5 See *Samuel Beckett: His Works and His Critics* by Raymond Federman and John Fletcher (Berkeley and Los Angeles, University of California Press, 1970), p. 107, hereafter referred to as F & F.
6 Details about Georges Pelorson's wartime career are taken from *Vichy et les Français*, ed. Jean-Pierre Azéma and François Bédarida (Paris, Fayard, 1992), pp. 417–418, and from *La Propagande sous Vichy*, ed. Laurent Gervereau and Denis Peschanski (Paris, BDIC, 1990), pp. 45, 47–48, 57; the latter is hereafter referred to as BDIC.
7 See F & F, nos. 1308, 1379, 1581.
8 Quoted in *The Novels of Samuel Beckett* by John Fletcher (London, Chatto & Windus, 1964), p. 176.
9 For a colour reproduction of the poster see BDIC, p. 237.

'WAR'S AWFUL ILLUMINATION': ELIZABETH BOWEN'S *THE HEAT OF THE DAY*

Josette Leray

1 *Selected Prose of Louis MacNeice*, ed. Alan Heuser, (Oxford, Clarendon Press, 1990), p. 135.

2   *The Demon Lover and Other Stories* (Harmondsworth, Penguin, 1966), p. 197.
3   *The Collected Stories of Elizabeth Bowen* (New York, Knopf, 1981), p. 73.
4   Louis MacNeice, *op. cit.*, p. 135.
5   Walter Allen, *Tradition and Dream* (Harmondsworth, Penguin), p. 216.
6   *The Collected Stories of Elizabeth Bowen*, p. 590.
7   *Bowen's Court & Seven Winters* (London, Virago, 1984), pp. 454–55.
8   *The Heat of the Day* (Harmondsworth, Penguin, 1962). Quotations are from this edition and indicated by page reference in the text.
9   Quoted by Hermione Lee in *Elizabeth Bowen, An Estimation* (London and Totowa, New Jersey, Vision & Barnes & Noble, 1981), p. 231.
10 For further information on the part played by Elizabeth Bowen during the war and its impact on *The Heat of the Day*, see Dominique Gauthier, 'Guerre, Espionnage et Ideologie dans *The Heat of the Day* d'Elizabeth Bowen' in *Guerre et littérature dans le monde anglophone*, Université du Maine, Colloque Le Mans, 1988.
11 Public Record Office (Kew) F.O. 8000000/310, Bowen to Dominions Office, 9–11–1940. Quoted by Dominique Gauthier, *ibid.*
12 Phyllis Lassner, *Elizabeth Bowen* (London and Basingstoke, Macmillan, 1990), p. 129.
13 *Collected Stories*, p. 590.
14 'The Cult of Nostalgia', *The Listener* XLVI (9 August, 1951), p. 225.
15 *Collected Stories*, p. 591.

DENIS JOHNSTON: NEUTRALITY AND BUCHENWALD

Terry Boyle

1   *Nine Rivers from Jordan* (London, Derek Verschoyle Ltd., 1953), p. 119. (Hereafter abbreviated to *NRJ*).
2   Denis Johnston, *Selected Plays*, ed. Joseph Ronsley (Gerrards Cross, Colin Smythe Ltd., 1992), p. 327.
3   *Ibid.*, p. 94.
4   *War and the Creative Arts*, ed. John Ferguson (London, Macmillan, 1972), pp. 231–232.
5   Gene A. Barnett, *Denis Johnston* (Boston, Twayne Publishers, 1978), p. 110.
6   Denis Johnston, *The Brazen Horn* (Dublin, Dolmen Editions, 1976), p. 159.
7   *Denis Johnston: A Retrospective*, ed. Joseph Ronsley (Gerrards Cross, Colin Smythe Ltd., 1981), p. 200.
8   *Ibid.*
9   James Collins, *God in Modern Philosophy* (London, Routledge & Kegan Paul, 1960), p. 265.

10 *Ibid.*, p. 102.
11 Denis Johnston, *The Brazen Horn*, pp. 40–41.
12 Denis Johnston, *Selected Plays*, p. 121.

READING PROTESTANT WRITING: REPRESENTATIONS
OF THE TROUBLES IN THE POETRY OF DEREK MAHON
AND GLENN PATTERSON'S *BURNING YOUR OWN*

John Goodby

1 Eve Patten, 'Fiction in Conflict: Northern Ireland's Prodigal
   Novelists', from Ian A. Bell (ed.), *Peripheral Visions: Images of
   Nationhood in Contemporary British Fiction* (Bridgend, Seren Books,
   1996), p. 129. I am grateful to Eve Patten for allowing me to see this
   essay before publication, to Ian A. Bell for allowing me to read
   Glenn Patterson's piece, and to Glenn Patterson himself for a
   discussion about his work when he was Writer in Residence at
   University College Cork in 1992–3. The novelists Patten refers to are
   Michael McLaverty, Sam Hanna Bell, Janet McNeill, Brian Moore
   and Maurice Leitch.
2 Eve Patten, *Ibid.*, p. 2.
3 See Elizabeth Bouché, 'No Big Thrill', *Fortnight*, December 1992, p. 46:
   'There are many novels on the "Troubles" – the basic genre being a
   thriller, usually set in the "terrorist" heartlands of Belfast. About 250
   have their own corner in the Linen Hall Library political collection,
   gathered in a kind of freak show by the librarian Robert Bell.'
4 Eamon Hughes (ed.), *Culture and Politics in Northern Ireland*,
   'Introduction: Northern Ireland – border country', (Buckingham,
   Open University Press, 1991), p. 5.
5 Eve Patten, Ian A. Bell, *op. cit.*, p. 6.
6 Terence Brown, 'A Northern Renaissance: Poets from the North of
   Ireland, 1965–1980', *Ireland's Literature: Selected Essays* (Mullingar,
   The Lilliput Press, 1988), p. 209.
7 Seamus Heaney, *North* (London, Faber and Faber, 1975), p. 63.
8 For an example of the best of this criticism, see Edna Longley, *The
   Living Stream* (Newcastle-upon-Tyne, Bloodaxe, 1994).
9 See, for example, Kiberd's comments on Northern poetry in the
   section on Contemporary Irish Poetry in the *Field Day Anthology*,
   Vol. III (Derry, Field Day Publications, 1990), pp. 1315–1316: 'in only
   a few poems has even Heaney managed to capture the appalling
   intensity of the conflict . . . The poets, though brave enough to
   accuse themselves of evading the deepest issues . . . nevertheless opt
   always for a mode of even-handedness'.
10 Stan Smith, *Inviolable Voice: History and Twentieth Century Poetry*
   (Dublin, Gill and Macmillan, 1982). I discuss Smith's criticism in my
   conclusion, but it may be summed up here in his comment that in

Derek Mahon's work 'Literariness becomes a recurrent technique for putting a distance between the middle-class self and its panic.' This is an extraordinary and very *English* lapse, it seems to me, and stems from reading Mahon as though he writes from an English context and subjecthood. David Lloyd's attack on Heaney appears in *Anomalous States: Irish Writing and the Post-Colonial Moment* (Dublin, Lilliput Press, 1993). For Lloyd the urge to aestheticize is political insofar as it attempts to transcend difference; Heaney aestheticizes violence 'in the name of a freedom expressed in terms of national or racial integration' and in locating it beyond even sectarian division he 'renders it symbolic of a fundamental identity of the Irish race, as "authentic."' While I find much of this suggestive, 'bourgeois' seems inexact; and in a pseudo-radical way, Lloyd links Marxism, via cultural materialism's dematerialized Gramsci, to a 'militant nationalism' which Marx, at least, is on record as abhorring. W.J. McCormack has pointed out that 'The notable aspect of Heaney's poetry is that "bourgeois subject" remains still a highly charged and historically problematical category in the social conjuncture from which he writes.' (*The Battle of the Books*, Gigginstown: Lilliput Press, 1986, p. 38). Lack of clarity on these points leaves Lloyd open to the charge that the root of his gripe with Heaney is that he has not sufficiently endorsed 'the continuing anti-colonial struggle in Northern Ireland' (Lloyd, p. 3).

11   The differences between Catholic and Protestant inflections of patriarchy need to be borne in mind; the former offers a major female figure of veneration (albeit as an impossible ideal) and the troping of Ireland as female. Both have proved exploitable by Catholic-background women writers. On the other hand 'The patriarchal nature of Protestantism leaves out the imagery of women and in turn women become invisible,' according to Monica McWilliams, 'Women in Northern Ireland: an overview', in Hughes, *op. cit.*, p. 86.

12   See W.J. McCormack, 'Introduction', *From Burke to Beckett: Ascendancy, Tradition and Betrayal in Literary History* (Cork, Cork University Press, 1994), pp. 17–23. McCormack has noted that the emancipatory moment of post-Yeatsian Anglo-Irish writing tends generally to be at odds with any stable sense of the self and that in its sense of belonging the act of writing raises questions concerning the validity of the aesthetic realm towards which it strains. As he has also pointed out, however, the difficulties involved in dismantling an identity politics from within Unionism nevertheless remain substantial.

13   See John Wilson Foster, *Colonial Consequences* (Dublin, Lilliput Press, 1991), pp. 263–77. Foster's analysis has limits, limits indicated by the following; 'Very little of what I have said can be explained away by class. The integrity of Protestant Ulster has transcended class to the despair of those socialists who have not acknowledged . . . the

repressed or frustrated nationalism of that community.'
14 Brown, *op. cit.*, p. 237.
15 For another alternative – that of fatuousness posing as insouciance see James Simmons's breezy dismissal of the Troubles in his Introduction to *Ten Irish Poets* (Manchester, Carcanet, 1974), p. 9. 'There is no unjust monster to be endured or resisted; but the uncomfortable knowledge that we and our immediate ancestors have burnt our collective backside, and we must sit on the blister.'
16 Sigmund Freud, 'Negation', in Richards, A. (ed.), Pelican Freud Library 11, *On Metapsychology* (tr. J. Strachey) (Harmondsworth, Penguin, 1984), p. 438.
17 Derek Mahon, *Poems 1962–1978* (Oxford, OUP, 1986), p. 57.
18 Derek Mahon, *The Hunt by Night* (Oxford, OUP, 1986), p. 10.
19 See Svetlana Alpers, *The Art of Describing* (Harmondsworth, Penguin, 1989). By moving indoors the poem has recourse to a different pictorial language; as Mahon's second verse suggests, there are elements in Dutch Golden Age interiors of an 'emblematic' iconography of narrative moralities seemingly at odds with the empiricism of 'verifiable fact.' Nevertheless such interiors are still primarily concerned with representation and stem from a 'visual culture', Alpers argues, as opposed to Italianate High Renaissance and Baroque humanist culture which focusses on the nude and relies on text and narrative. Mahon's poem predates Alpers's study (which first appeared in 1983), and at one level rehearses the dispute between emblematic and representational viewpoints which occurs in criticism of Dutch painting.
20 See Edna Longley's brief but suggestive discussion of this poem in 'No More Paintings About Poems?', *The Living Stream: Literature and Revisionism in Ireland* (Newcastle upon Tyne, Bloodaxe, 1994), pp. 243–4.
21 One of the best accounts of the significance of rituals of cleanliness in the seventeenth century Netherlands is to be found in Simon Schama's *The Embarrassment of Riches: An Interpretation of Dutch Culture in the Golden Age*, which devotes a whole chapter to the subject. Of the connection between cleanliness and imperialism, Schama notes, for example; 'Nor was it accidental that Admiral Maarten Tromp tacked a broom to the bowsprit of his flagship. Tromp was a fervent Calvinist, devoted to "sweeping the seas" of tyrants, papists ... To be clean, militantly, was an affirmation of separateness ... Dirt made things general and undifferentiated; cleansing exposed distinctness,' pp. 379–80. This emphasis on cleanliness was bound up with religious sectarianism; 'In colloquial Dutch, the rag mop was also known as either the Pope's or the Turk's head,' p. 382.
22 The most famous representation of a map (although of the Netherlands only) is in Vermeer's *The Art of Painting*, in which the artist associates mapping and painting by signing the map 'I-Ver-

Meer'. Svetlana Alpers's book devotes a chapter to 'The Mapping Impulse in Dutch Art', *op. cit.*, pp. 119–168.

23 Edna Longley, *The Living Stream, op. cit.*, p. 244.

24 Derek Mahon, 'Poetry and Politics in Northern Ireland', *Twentieth Century Studies*, 4, 1970, cited in Clair Wills, *Improprieties: Politics and Sexuality in Northern Irish Poetry* (Oxford, Clarendon Press, 1993), p. 30.

25 This occurs in various guises – ironic disdain for consumerism, intimations of apocalypse (millenarianism with a post-nuclear or Green inflection), attacks on anthropomorphism, or 'the knacker's yard / Of humanistic self-regard' in 'Beyond Howth Head', Mahon, *Poems 1962–1978, op. cit.*, p. 53.

26 Seamus Deane, *Celtic Revivals* (London, Faber, 1985), p. 161. Deane, it should be noted, places a question mark over his claims: 'It would be extravagant to say that Mahon now begins to elaborate some kind of confrontation with history, but he certainly dismisses it with less assurance'.

27 Arthur Rimbaud 'Villes', *Les Illuminations* in Wallace Fowlie (ed. and transl.), *Rimbaud: Complete Works, Selected Letters* (Chicago, University of Chicago Press, 1975), p. 240. Mahon has of course translated Rimbaud's 'Le Bateau Ivre'.

28 Examples are 'An Old Lady', 'At the Pool', 'Girls on the Bridge', 'The Globe in North Carolina', as well as the poems with a domestic theme (and female adressee) – 'The Woods' and 'Another Sunday Morning'.

29 Dutch Golden Age painting carefully avoids transcendence for almost super-realistic representation of the visible. This has important consequences for the representation of written texts in paintings. Alpers devotes a chapter to the subject and uses 'The Courtyard in Delft', a 1658 canvas from de Hooch's series, to illustrate some of her points. In the painting de Hooch represents an inscription over the entrance to the passage through the house in which the maid waits. The tablet reads: 'This is Saint Jerome's Vale. Enter if you wish to repair to patience and meekness. For we must first descend if we wish to be raised'. Alpers claims that 'continuity is demonstrated between rendering the visible world and reading words', contrary to artistic practice before this, which was to invoke texts but not to represent them. In other words, texts are made level with appearances and take their place 'among other objects represented in the pictorial world and like them are to be seen as [a] representation rather than as [an] object for interpretation', Alpers, *op. cit.*, p. 207.

30 Glenn Patterson, 'I am a Northern Irish Novelist', in Ian A. Bell, *op. cit.*, p. 150.

31 Patten, *op. cit.*, p. 4.

32 Glenn Patterson, *Burning Your Own* (London, Sphere Books, 1989), p. 8.

33 *Ibid.*, p. 69.

34 The suggestion is made in Martin Dillon, *The Shankill Butchers: A Case Study of Mass Murder* (London, Pan, 1989). For a dismissal of this as 'just wild guessing', see Steve Bruce, *The Red Hand: Protestant Paramilitaries in Northern Ireland* (Oxford, OUP, 1992), pp. 181–189.

35 Glenn Patterson, *Burning Your Own, op. cit.,* p. 63.

36 *Ibid.,* p. 93.

37 *Ibid.,* p. 201.

38 *Ibid.,* p. 203.

39 *Ibid.,* p. 216.

40 Patterson, Ian A. Bell, *op. cit.,* p. 151.

41 Glenn Patterson, *Burning Your Own, op. cit.,* p. 17.

42 Ian A. Bell, *op. cit.,* p. 151.

43 *Burning Your Own,* p. 14

44 *Ibid.,* p. 61.

45 *Ibid.,* pp. 213–14. The novel manipulates us in other ways, too; narratives and time schemes are compressed and distorted, for example. Thus, while the Troubles occur in verifiable historical sequence, Mal seems to mature far more rapidly than he might have done in 'real' time. But although there is room for orthodox historical irony (the outbreak of atavistic violence takes place at the time of that supreme technological human achievement, the Apollo moon landing), this does not mean that 'real' history is some kind of stable background against which other events play.

46 *Ibid.,* p. 230.

47 Michel Foucault, 'Of Other Spaces', *Diacritics* 16, 1987, pp. 22–27.

48 An aura of the uncanny clearly surrounds Francy too. His phenomenal powers and startling appearance ally him with the shaman, or trickster figure. Francy plays a complex role in the novel, functioning at times as historical chorus, communal memory, scourge, substitute father, scapegoat and sacrificial victim. As the demonised Other of all that Protestant Larkview stands for, he is hated – as Mal crucially realises – not because he can't belong, but *'because* he wouldn't join in' (*Burning Your Own, op. cit.,* p. 113). This is a crucial insight into the way in which the violence of exclusion works, its roots in a unionist need to monopolise the right to reject. The minority must always display their desire to be included. Francy's refusal to do this is a rejection of the Protestant power of rejection, the negation of a negative definition of identity. While the novel shows that to some extent Mal idealizes Francy (and his evicted family), it also clearly endorses his breaking of the boundaries of his ethnic group: 'It was as if, in refusing to be cowed any longer by the dire warnings of his elders, he had broken through some invisible barrier, across which he now faced them', *ibid.,* p. 211.

49 *Ibid.,* p. 249.

50 Peter Stallybrass and Allon White, *The Politics and Poetics of Transgression* (London, Methuen, 1986), p. 20.

51 Glenn Patterson, *op. cit.*, p. 177.
52 *Ibid.*, p. 231.
53 Peter Stallybrass and Allon White, *op. cit.*, p. 21.
54 *Ibid.*, p. 21.
55 *Ibid.*, p. 20.
56 Eve Patten, Ian A. Bell, *op. cit.*, p. 139.
57 Peter Stallybrass and Allon White, *op. cit.*, p. 19.
58 The most famous example of this in Mahon's poetry are of course the mushrooms of 'A Disused Shed in Co. Wexford'.
59 Smith's criticisms of Mahon, mentioned earlier, generally focus on the weaker poems to 'prove' that they uphold 'A division of history between everyday life and apocalyptic fantasy' which 'perpetuates that larger separation of the privileged poetic self from the violation of actual historical change': Smith, *Inviolable Voice: History and Twentieth-Century Poetry* (Dublin, Gill and Macmillan, 1982), p. 192.
60 Glenn Patterson, Ian A. Bell, *op. cit.*, p. 150.
61 Interestingly, in making this argument Jameson takes as Modernist exemplars two of Mahon's subjects – Munch's The Scream and Van Gogh.
62 Frederic Jameson, *Postmodernism, or, The Cultural Logic of Late Capitalism* (London and New York, Verso, 1991), p. 14.
63 Eamon Hughes, *op. cit.*, p. 3.
64 I refer here to both the political situation in Europe and worldwide of a revolutionary upsurge in the early to mid-1970s; and to the specific response to a perceived revolutionary threat by the British state as evidenced in the MI5 plot against Harold Wilson's Labour Government, and which originated in Northern Ireland; see Paul Foot, *Who Framed Colin Wallace?* (London, Macmillan, 1989).
65 Glenn Patterson, Ian A. Bell, *op. cit.*, p. 151.

A NECESSARY DISTANCE? – MYTHOPOEIA AND VIOLENCE
IN FRIEL, PARKER AND VINCENT WOODS'S *AT THE
BLACK PIG'S DYKE*

Alan J. Peacock and Kathleen Devine

1 Quoted by Des Hickey and Gus Smith, *A Paler Shade of Green* (London, Leslie Frewin, 1972), p. 222.
2 'The Future of Irish Drama', *The Irish Times*, 12 February, 1970.
3 D.E.S. Maxwell, *Brian Friel* (Lewisburg, Bucknell University Press, 1973), p. 29.
4 Brian Friel, *Selected Plays* (London, Faber and Faber, 1984), p. 167.
5 *Ibid.*, p. 150.
6 Stewart Parker, *Three Plays for Ireland* (London, Oberon Books, 1989).
7 *Ibid.*, p. 9.

8   *Ibid.*, p. 57.
9   Fintan O'Toole, 'Social Realism Bites the Dust', *The Irish Times*, 12 October, 1996.
10 *Three Plays for Ireland*, pp. 203–4.
11 *Ibid.*, p. 207.
12 *Ibid.*, p. 208.
13 *The Sunday Tribune*, 15 October, 1995.
14 *Three Plays for Ireland*, p. 10.
15 We are grateful to Vincent Woods for letting us see the play-script for the 1992 Druid Theatre Company production of *At the Black Pig's Dyke*. Quotations are from this script.

NOTES ON CONTRIBUTORS

ELMER ANDREWS is Senior Lecturer in English at the University of Ulster at Coleraine. He is the author of *The Poetry of Seamus Heaney: All the Realms of Whisper* and *The Art of Brian Friel*, and he has edited *Seamus Heaney: A Collection of Critical Essays, Contemporary Irish Poetry: A Collection of Critical Essays* and the Icon Critical Guide to Secondary Sources relating to *The Poetry of Seamus Heaney*.

TERRY BOYLE is a graduate of the University of Ulster where he completed his D. Phil. on the life and work of Denis Johnston.

TERENCE BROWN is Professor of Anglo-Irish Literature at Trinity College, Dublin where he is a Fellow of the College. He is also a member of the Royal Irish Academy and of the Academia Europaia. He has published and lectured widely on the subject of Anglo-Irish Literature. He is currently working on a critical biography of W.B. Yeats.

KATHLEEN DEVINE is Lecturer in English at the University of Ulster at Coleraine. She has written a number of articles on the literature of the World Wars and is co-editor of *Louis MacNeice and his Influence* (1998).

JOHN FLETCHER is Professor of European Literature at the University of East Anglia in Norwich. He is well-known for his contributions to Beckett studies, ranging from bibliography to editions of Beckett's plays.

JACQUELINE GENET is Honorary President of the French Society of University Professors of English and is Emeritus Professor at the University of Caen. She is the author of *W.B. Yeats: les fondements et l'evolution de la création poétique* (1976); *La Poétique de W.B. Yeats* (1990); *Le Théâtre de W.B. Yeats* (1995); *Littérature irlandaise* (with Claude Fierobe, 1997). She has edited and participated in the *Cahier de l'Herne* on Yeats; *The Big House in Ireland: Reality and Representation; Studies* on *Yeats, Joyce, Heaney,*

The Irish Contemporary Theatre; and *Rural Ireland, Real Ireland?* She co-edited *Perspectives of Irish Drama and the Theatre,* and *Irish Writers and their Creative Process.* She has translated many of Yeats's prose works and some of his plays into French and several volumes of Irish short stories. She has received the Honorary Degree of D. Litt. from the National University of Ireland and the University of Würzburg.

JOHN GOODBY is Lecturer in English at the University College of Wales at Swansea and is co-editor of *A Vanishing Border: Feminist Remappings of Modern Anglo-Irish Literature* and *From Stillness into History: Irish Poetry 1950–1995* (both forthcoming 1998), as well as numerous articles on twentieth century Irish, Welsh and British poetry. A selection of his own poetry was included in *Poetry Introduction 8* (Faber and Faber, 1993).

A. NORMAN (Derry) JEFFARES has lectured (in Classics) at Trinity College, Dublin, (in English Literature) at the Universities of Groningen and Edinburgh, and held Chairs in Adelaide, Leeds and Stirling. He has written on and edited the work of many Irish writers, including Swift, Farquhar, Goldsmith, Maria Edgeworth, George Moore, Yeats and Joyce. Recent work includes *Images of Invention, The Yeats-Gonne Letters* (co-edited with Anna McBride White), *Victorian Love Poems, A Pocket History of Irish Literature,* and *Irish Love Poems.* Third revised editions of *Yeats: Man and Poet* (1949) and *Yeats's Poems* (1989) were published in 1996; and an edition of Gogarty's *Poems and Plays* is in preparation as well as an illustrated book on Irish writers for the National Portrait Gallery, London.

KEITH JEFFERY is Professor of Modern History at the University of Ulster at Jordanstown. He has edited *A Military History of Ireland* (1996); *An Irish Empire? Aspects of Ireland and the British Empire* (1996); and is co-author of *Northern Ireland Since 1968* (second edition, 1996).

DECLAN KIBERD is Professor of Anglo-Irish Literature and Drama at University College, Dublin. He is author of *Synge and the Irish Language* (1979, 2nd ed. 1993), *Men and Feminism in Modern Literature* (1985), *Anglo-Irish Attitudes* (1985), *Idir Dhá Chultúr* (1993). He has also edited sections of the *Field Day Anthology of Irish Writing,* edited and annotated the Penguin Twentieth Century Classics *Ulysses* (1992), co-edited (with Gabriel Fitzmaurice) *An Crann faoi Bláth: the Flowering Tree* (1989). His most recent book *Inventing Ireland: The Literature of the Modern*

Nation (1995) won the Irish Times Prize for Non-Fiction, the Oscar Wilde Award for Literary Achievement and the Michael Durkan Prize of the American Committee of Irish Studies for literary and cultural criticism.

JOSETTE LERAY is Professor of English at the University of Caen. She has published various essays in French on Elizabeth Bowen, Ivy Compton-Burnett, Mervyn Peake and William Golding. She has written on Elizabeth Bowen's *A World of Love* in *The Big House in Ireland: Reality and Representation*, on William Golding's *Darkness Visible* and Patrick White's *The Aunt's Story* in *Fingering Netsukes* (ed. F. Regard, University of Saint Etienne in association with Faber and Faber, 1995).

CHRISTOPHER MURRAY is Associate Professor at University College Dublin where he has taught in the Department of Modern English and American Literature since 1970. In 1990 he helped found the UCD Drama Centre and was its first director (1990–95). From 1987–97 he was editor of *Irish University Review*, having guest edited a special issue on O'Casey in 1980. He has published extensively on Irish drama, and is author of *Twentieth-Century Irish Drama: Mirror up to Nation* (1997). He is working on a biography of O'Casey for Gill and Macmillan.

ALAN J. PEACOCK has lectured at Magee University College and the University of Ulster. He has written a range of articles on English poetry from the seventeenth to the twentieth century and has published on modern Irish writers such as Kavanagh, MacNeice, Longley and Heaney. He has edited *The Achievement of Brian Friel* (1993) and co-edited *Louis MacNeice and His Influence* (1998).

PATRICK WALSH is an English lecturer in the Graduate School of Education at Queen's University, Belfast and has lectured part-time at the University of Ulster. He is author of the pamphlet, *Strangers: Reflections on a Correspondence between Daniel Corkery and John Hewitt*, and is a contributor to the *Oxford Companion to Irish Literature*. He is at present working on a comparative study of the work and influence of Daniel Corkery and John Hewitt.

INDEX